Palgrave Texts in Counselling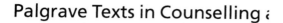

Series Editors
Arlene Vetere
Family Therapy and Systemic Practice
VID Specialized University
Oslo, Norway

Rudi Dallos
Clinical Psychology
Plymouth University
Plymouth, UK

To Jane and Richard
Love from
Harry

This series introduces readers to the theory and practice of counselling and psychotherapy across a wide range of topical issues. Ideal for both trainees and practitioners, the books will appeal to anyone wishing to use counselling and psychotherapeutic skills and will be particularly relevant to workers in health, education, social work and related settings. The books in this series emphasise an integrative orientation weaving together a variety of models including, psychodynamic, attachment, trauma, narrative and systemic ideas. The books are written in an accessible and readable style with a focus on practice. Each text offers theoretical background and guidance for practice, with creative use of clinical examples.

Arlene Vetere, Professor of Family Therapy and Systemic Practice at VID Specialized University, Oslo, Norway.

Rudi Dallos, Emeritus Professor, Dept. of Clinical Psychology, University of Plymouth, UK.

More information about this series at
http://www.palgrave.com/gp/series/16540

Harry Procter · David A. Winter

Personal and Relational Construct Psychotherapy

palgrave
macmillan

Harry Procter
Department of Psychology
University of Hertfordshire
Hatfield, UK

David A. Winter
Department of Psychology
University of Hertfordshire
Hatfield, UK

ISSN 2662-9127   ISSN 2662-9135   (electronic)
Palgrave Texts in Counselling and Psychotherapy
ISBN 978-3-030-52176-9   ISBN 978-3-030-52177-6   (eBook)
https://doi.org/10.1007/978-3-030-52177-6

Cover credit: Sergey Ryumin/gettyimages

This Palgrave Macmillan imprint is published by the registered company Springer Nature Switzerland AG
The registered company address is: Gewerbestrasse 11, 6330 Cham, Switzerland

To my wife Jane Procter and our sons David and John Procter.
Jane was enormously helpful in the preparation of this manuscript.
—Harry Procter

To my parents and ow awen Gernewek meurgerys.
—David A. Winter

Preface

The roots of this book go back at least to the late 1960s, when we both began our university studies of psychology. The sixties were heady, exciting times, but for each of us one of the most exciting moments was when, at our separate universities, we independently stumbled upon George Kelly's psychology of personal constructs (PCP). We were struck not just by the rich, holistic, and optimistic model of the person that this provided, but also by its respectful way of working with people that took seriously their views of the world. Coincidentally, in each case this initial encounter with PCP was through learning about the research of the British personal construct psychologist Don Bannister on clients diagnosed as 'thought disordered schizophrenics', whose patterns of thinking were not dismissed as bizarre or as symptoms of an illness but were seen as the individuals' ways of trying to make sense of a confusing world.

This stimulated both of us, in our first ventures in the use of personal construct psychology, to carry out repertory grid research on clients diagnosed as schizophrenic and their families. Indeed, we first met when one of us (DW) gave a talk on his research in this area. HP had completed his Ph.D. at Bristol University looking at families through the lens of

PCP, developing the idea of family construct systems and looking at the social origins of construing, which initiated the relational extension of personal construct psychology. DW, initially during his Ph.D. research at the University of Durham, went on to apply repertory grid technique in other areas, particularly in the evaluation of psychological therapies, including approaches that he developed from personal construct models of particular problems. More recently, we have continued to take somewhat different directions in our explorations with personal and relational construct psychology: the philosophical background to PCP and qualitative constructivist assessment methods in HP's case, and the understanding of people at the edge of human experience (e.g., those who harm or kill themselves or others; survivors of civil war; and people who have been radicalised) in DW's.

We each started work as clinical psychologists in the English National Health Service (NHS) in the early 1970s. This was a time when clinical psychology had become much more open to the provision of a range of theoretical and therapeutic approaches than it is now, and we were both able to base our clinical practice on personal construct psychology and to ensure that this was a major component of the clinical services which we eventually managed. The 1970s also saw the beginning of international congresses on personal construct psychology, at which (and eventually at European conferences in the intervening years) we met up every two years, including each being involved in their organisation, DW and HP for the 21st International Congress of Personal Construct Psychology, which was held at the University of Hertfordshire in 2015, and HP for the 14th European Conference of the European Personal Construct Association, at the University of Edinburgh in 2019.

We also each played an increasing role in the training of clinical psychologists, which for one of us (DW) culminated in becoming Programme Director of the Doctorate in Clinical Psychology at the University of Hertfordshire. This course adopted a constructivist and constructionist philosophy, and HP was a major contributor to it in terms of teaching and research supervision as well as developing a comprehensive family therapy service in child and adult mental health in the County of Somerset, training many colleagues from the different professions. DW is continuing a training role by directing (and, predictably enough, incorporating constructivist ideas into) a new M.Sc. in Clinical and Counselling Psychology in Sri Lanka. We have also contributed to the teaching and training programmes and enjoyed productive collaborations with the staff of various other universities and institutes outside the UK.

Somewhat surprisingly, given the parallel courses of our professional lives and interests, our first collaborative writing venture, a chapter on formulation from a personal and relational construct perspective, was fairly recent (Winter & Procter, 2014). Since this was not just a painless, but also a thoroughly enjoyable, experience, we were very pleased to be given the opportunity to co-author this book. Again, the process has been a remarkably smooth one, in which we each prepared first drafts of roughly half of the chapters before agreeing on their final form. We have each brought to the book nearly half a century of experience in clinical practice and research, but more importantly also the child-like excitement at exploring, applying, elaborating, and extending Kelly's ideas that has not wavered since we first discovered his work. If we can convey to you something of this enthusiasm and perhaps a glimpse of renewed optimism as you struggle to survive in increasingly constrained and constraining clinical services, our efforts will have been worthwhile.

Hatfield, UK   Harry Procter
March 2020   David A. Winter

Reference

Winter, D., & Procter, H. G. (2014). Formulation in personal and relational construct psychology: Seeing the world through clients' eyes. In L. Johnstone & R. Dallos (Eds.), *Formulation in Psychology and Psychotherapy* (2nd ed., pp. 145–172). London: Routledge.

Acknowledgements

We are deeply grateful to all those people who have courageously, whether as clients or research participants, shared their stories with us over the years, and who have had a major influence on the development of the approach that we describe in this book. We are also indebted to the many colleagues and students with whom we have worked, debating with them and elaborating our ideas. This process of debate and elaboration has continued with the invaluable input of the two editors during the writing of the book. However, perhaps our largest debt of gratitude is to George Kelly, whose vision helped make us open to fresh possibilities many years ago when we ourselves were students, and has provided us with opportunities for adventures of which we could not previously have dreamed, including contributing to the development and application of his ideas in five continents.

Praise for *Personal and Relational Construct Psychotherapy*

"In this *magnum opus*, Procter and Winter generously offer us the distilled wisdom and encyclopedic knowledge of not one but two professional lifetimes spent in the creative extension of personal construct psychology and its application to psychotherapy. Delving into the cornucopia of clinical cases, the fresh rendering of classical Kellian concepts, and their substantial elaboration by subsequent generations of construct theorists, I discovered a book as readable as it was comprehensive, and as practically relevant to my weekly work with clients as it was theoretically coherent. For any helping professional who has ever wondered, *"Whatever became of personal construct theory?"* I recommend this book as the definitive, accessible, and eye-opening answer. Or perhaps it is more than an answer–it is an invitation to deep and fruitful dialogue with a living tradition that has much to tell us and teach us half a century after the death of its founder."

—Professor Robert A. Neimeyer, author of *Constructivist Psychotherapy* and Co-Editor of the *Journal of Constructivist Psychology*

"A fascinating presentation of the Personal Construct Psychotherapy perspective and its developments through a relational key, expressing the growing convergences between systemic psychotherapies and Kelly's clinical perspective. Richly researched and elegantly written, this remarkable book is destined to become a point of reference not only in the PCP world but also in the larger field of clinical psychology and psychotherapy."

—Professor Valeria Ugazio, *University of Bergamo and Scientific Director, European Institute of Systemic-relational Therapies, Milan, Italy*

"A well written, succint and updated primer for contemporary constructivist therapy based on both the Kellyan and systemic traditions, this book deserves to be read by psychotherapists of all orientations who are striving for fresh intellectual air. Indeed, the approach presented as *Personal and Relational Construct Psychotherapy* is a highly integrative endeavour offering ways of understanding human suffering in a relational context, with a strong focus on meanings (both shared and individual) rather than labels or personality types. Readers will find here the voice of two writers who have a lifelong experience as psychotherapists but with a strong grounding in the philosophical, theoretical, and scientific bases of their approach. The book is full of practical guidance and clinical tips, including a series of very specific questions to be used with clients or patients."

—Professor Guillem Feixas, *University of Barcelona*

"Constructivism consists of the idea that humans construct the psychological meanings that they live by. To genuinely understand someone, it is necessary to appreciate how they experience the world on their terms. Understanding others—and thus the process of psychotherapy—requires that we take a credulous approach to the other. We must begin with the idea that, no matter how foreign the other's pattern of thinking, feeling and action appears to us, they make sense to the other—or at least are the result of the other's authentic quest to make sense of their world. If there was ever a book that reveals how practitioners, theorists and researchers alike can engage the meanings that mediate the mentalities of the other, it is this one.

Building upon and extending Kelly's (1955) personal construct psychology, Procter and Winter's *Personal and Relational Construct Psychotherapy* illuminates the social origins of personal meaning and the ways in which practitioners can collaborate with their clients in order to effect genuine transformation in their personal meaning systems. They bring the reader through an engaging, accessible and thorough discussion of the nature of the conceptual and philosophical foundations of personal and relational construct psychotherapy; the process of constructivist clinical interviewing, assessment and case formulation; and the process of engaging in psychotherapy with individuals, couples, families and other groups. Documenting empirical evidence that supports the effectiveness of constructivist psychotherapy, they explain the importance of reflexivity in clinical practice and identify relations between constructivist and other forms of psychotherapy. In short, no stone is left unturned. Procter and Winter have written a volume that is both comprehensive and succinct; practical and theoretically grounded; and readable without compromising conceptual rigor. It will be useful to practitioners, practitioners in training, graduate students, theorists, researchers, and anyone else who wishes to learn how to foster constructive transformation through deep interpersonal engagement."

—Professor Michael Mascolo, *Merrimack College, Massachusetts*

"This text consolidates many years' experience in this field by the two authors. They present a robust defence for the continued relevance of his work whilst also taking Kelly's words literally—that psychological theories should be considered 'ultimately expendable'—and significantly developing the social and relational aspects of the original model. The result is an approach to clinical work that builds on personal construct psychotherapy in a logical and sympathetic way.

Kelly's work was extraordinarily thoughtful, and the authors don't shy away from covering this depth, providing insight into the underlying philosophy of the approach, and giving a flavour of the context in which the ideas were formed. They also convey a real sense of how therapy based on these ideas works, with clear accounts of clinical strategies, and approaches to measurement and formulation. Above all, they capture the creativity which is perhaps a key feature of the therapy. For those whose only knowledge of personal construct psychotherapy is that it was a major influence on the development of cognitive psychotherapies, it may come as a surprise to read about the contemporary flavour of so much in this book, such as the approach to diagnoses and formulation, and the significant political dimension to the ideas. Case material brings the approach to life, and again may surprise some in the range of problems treated, with useful chapters on working with families and couples, groups, and supervision and reflective practice. Alongside a critique of many of the aspects of current evidence-based practice, the final chapter summarises the evidence for personal and relational construct psychotherapy and offers a way in which research consistent with the approach might be conducted, satisfying the needs of both practitioners and managers."

—Dr. Gary Latchford, *University of Leeds clinical psychology training programme*

"This book is a guide for therapists helping people bring about change in their lives. Based on Personal Construct Therapy, it advocates collaborative ways of assisting people solve problematic situations, by focusing on future possibilities, rather than over-emphasising the past, and by treating relationships less as a hindrance, and more as a resource to be placed at the heart of therapy. The approach is thus both more optimistic and egalitarian than many mainstream practices currently in use. It is equally suitable for work with individuals and families.

The authors provide detailed research in relation to a variety of therapies, research that should inspire therapists who are struggling with restrictive policies in their own agencies. Throughout, the text is accompanied by accessible case scenarios from the authors' own wide-ranging clinical practice. For readers not already familiar with PCT, links with more familiar and conventional theories are helpfully spelled out, allowing for a rich integration of existing and novel ways of thinking and practising.

Family therapists/systemic practitioners will find much that is already familiar to them, but then suddenly discover that a new angle reveals itself, offering a fresh set of ideas for thinking and practice—truly the difference that can make a difference: not too much, not too little! Indeed difference, whether in the form of polarities, opposites or contrasts, lies at the centre of an approach that can enrich any therapist, whatever their orientation.

The book provides a sympathetic critique of the systemic field, and makes a useful contribution to bridging the old gap between the first- and second-order approaches (the one based on behaviours, the other on meanings) that troubled the family therapy field for so many years."

—Sigurd Reimers, *Family Therapist, West of England*

Contents

About the Authors

David A. Winter and Harry Procter

Harry Procter, Consultant Clinical Psychologist and Visiting Professor, University of Hertfordshire, worked for many years in mental health settings in the National Health Service in Somerset, UK. His research in the 1970s at Bristol University involved combining Kelly's psychology with family systems theory, thus initiating the development of Personal and Relational Construct Psychotherapy. He has taught in a number of countries and has published over 60 papers and chapters covering a variety of topics including working with children and families, psychosis, autistic spectrum disorders, using qualitative grids in therapy and in making sense of literature, and the implications of personal construct theory for society and culture. He is currently engaged in researching the philosophical background of personal construct psychology.

David A. Winter is Professor Emeritus of Clinical Psychology at the University of Hertfordshire (where he was Programme Director of its Doctorate in Clinical Psychology) and Director of Postgraduate Programmes at Colombo Institute of Research and Psychology. Most of his career was spent in the UK National Health Service, including as Head of Clinical Psychology Services for Barnet, and he has held visiting positions at universities in various countries and worked in mental health settings in Sierra Leone. He is a past Chair of the Psychotherapy Section of the British Psychological Society. He has around 200 publications, including *Personal Construct Psychology in Clinical Practice: Theory, Research and Applications* (Routledge, 1992), *The Wiley Handbook of Personal Construct Psychology* (edited with N. Reed; Wiley-Blackwell, 2016), and *Trauma, Survival and Resilience in War Zones: The Psychological Impact of War in Sierra Leone and Beyond* (with R. Brown, S. Goins, & C. Mason; Routledge, 2016).

List of Figures

List of Tables

1

Brian's Story

Brian, aged 30, was referred by his Consultant Psychiatrist for a general assessment of his personality and symptoms. The referral stated that he had been diagnosed as suffering from paranoid schizophrenia and was being treated with anti-psychotic medication. He was said to be very suspicious and to express thoughts of violence and revenge against people he thought were against him. He had spent much of the past six years as an inpatient with compulsory admissions after many years of heavy drinking, and had attended court on two occasions for being involved in fights and carrying a knife. He was first admitted, compulsorily, to psychiatric hospital after attacking two strangers, who he claimed had been following him in a car. He had not been offered any psychological therapy apart from ward groups. He was very opposed to these and never spoke in them.

He was seen by HP for an initial assessment. From this I recommended psychotherapy and we went on to work together for the next 18 months. All this happened many years ago whilst I was still in training as a clinical psychologist, and before many of the developments described in this book, but it was an important formative experience for me. The case illustrates many of the values and approaches to psychotherapy

© The Author(s) 2020
H. Procter and D. A. Winter, *Personal and Relational Construct Psychotherapy*,
Palgrave Texts in Counselling and Psychotherapy,
https://doi.org/10.1007/978-3-030-52177-6_1

as originally advocated by George Kelly, which we shall describe and develop in the coming chapters.

Brian was shy and at first quite formal, avoiding eye-contact, but he soon began to talk freely about his experiences and ideas and we got on well throughout the time that I was working with him. I think he accepted me because I focussed with genuine interest on the way he saw things and avoided any talk deriving from medical discourse. Indeed, in the spirit of the personal construct approach, I never thought of his experiences in terms of 'illness', 'symptoms' or 'schizophrenia'[1] throughout the months that we worked together, but rather regarded him as a fellow human being struggling with the difficulties of life.

His father's family were middle class, having owned a cider-making company, but this had been subject to a hostile takeover with the factory being asset-stripped. The money the family gained from the sale all went to his father's sisters as his father himself had been seen as a 'dropout'. There seems therefore to have been a significant downward step in social mobility for Brian's parents. Brian was the fourth of five siblings and he had lost his younger brother in a road accident five years previously. Brian was married with two children of 12 and 10, and lived in a small terraced house in a run-down area of town. I wonder now whether the family's loss of status and standard of living had contributed to his general sense of resentment of and antipathy towards other people.

Brian was clearly bright and articulate and had enjoyed school from an academic point of view, but he was bullied a lot and he saw everyone as false and hypocritical. He chose not to join the 'grammar stream'[2] because he hated the people in it so much. Although he was strong at maths, science and English, he left hoping for a better social life but was bitterly disappointed in this. He worked as a steel erector, and as a taxi and lorry driver but became very frightened when he began to think people were against him. He avoided claiming any benefits because he was frightened of the other claimants there. He was therefore financially dependent on his wife. He felt bad about not being able to support his family. His wife was getting very fed up with him, threatening to leave him. He said he would kill her if she left him and she believed him. He was very jealous, even of his wife's previous boyfriends. If anyone in his family had any trouble with anyone, he would threaten to go and beat them up.

Brian's Construing and Relationships

A central idea in Kelly's approach is the *personal construct system* (PCS). It refers to the way an individual's unique construing of the world and their ways of approaching things shape experiences. The PCS governs our anticipations and how we act, how we make choices and judgements. Therapeutic change and progress involve revising and altering it, developing new ways of seeing things. Kelly advocated many ways of finding how people *construe* the world. This word 'construe' is a deliberately broad term designed to cover how we see things, feel about them, how we act and relate to people (see Fig. 2.2 and Chapters 2 and 3). The main way of establishing a person's construing is by listening carefully to them. In addition to talking with Brian, I gave him Kelly's *role construct repertory test*. This 'Rep Test' is an early form of the *repertory grid* (see Chapter 6 for this and other assessment methods). The names of important people in his life were written on cards. He was invited to spread these out on the table and to talk about how the people were alike or different and to tell stories of his encounters with them. I also used two other tools that, although not devised by him, Kelly advocated: the Thematic Apperception Test (TAT),[3] a series of evocative pictures about which the person is invited to tell a story, and the Rotter Incomplete Sentences Blank, in which one has to complete sentences from a series of words or phrases. Later, I got Brian to write a *self-characterisation sketch* (see Chapter 6). Brian also shared poems and a journal that he kept. They all proved to elicit a rich picture of how Brian construed his life, himself, and others.

Brian felt resentment of and hostility towards other people, as we have noted, seeing them as *false* and *hypocritical*. He felt *frightened* of others and felt they were *against him*. Other words he used commonly were that people are *insincere* and that they *ridicule* him. When he was quite young, he saw a Santa Claus beard fall off, which proved to him the *falseness* of people. In his self-characterisation, written in the third person, from the point of view of a 'sympathetic friend', as Kelly recommended, Brian wrote:

> As a child he suffered a great deal from other children. He often found himself the centre of ridicule and was bullied to quite a degree. He used to give the bullies his toys and money in the hope that they would leave him alone. They didn't. In the end he stayed away from school and ever since if anything threatens him, he stays away. He does not take these episodes at school lightly; he burns with a sullen anger and indulges in daydreams of revenge.

A word he used a lot to describe his feelings was '*embarrassment*'. He was embarrassed by sports, dancing, and woodwork. From an early age he felt *different* to other people. From a PCP point of view, all these descriptions, or 'constructs', clustered together in a 'tight' constellation (see Chapter 3) which distinguished '*Me*' from '*Them*'. He even saw his wife as 'one of them'. At one stage, early on, we went for a walk together whilst he described how suspicious he felt about people in the streets, particularly men. The fear that he felt led him to be very vigilant and on the lookout. He felt that he was *stared* at a lot by people with their '*imposing* eyes'. Sometimes he would even feel that people on television were referring to him. One card in the TAT is completely blank. He said, 'can see the sea, waves coming in, just medium sized waves and on each wave is a face'. His response to others' threatening attention was to turn away or to put his head down whilst still looking straight ahead with his eyes. Of course, this furtive behaviour would be likely to attract attention and make him appear different, their reactions validating his construing that people were noticing and staring at him. This kind of interactional loop can be usefully drawn up in a diagram known as the 'bow-tie' (see Chapter 4). His approach to people could also be seen as involving *hostility* as defined by Kelly—extorting evidence to prove one's construction (see Chapter 3).

Perhaps as a response to all these threats, Brian had retreated into a world in which he was obsessively fascinated by death, corpses, cemeteries, and the lurid writings of Edgar Allen Poe. His self-characterisation again:

Death is his favourite subject, the idea he is most obsessed with. No other person I know has dwelt so constantly on it, and delved into it so deeply...these feelings make him want to be on his own and he finds it impossible to lead an ordinary existence.

He wrote a poem including the lines, 'My coffin – oh polished wooden womb...and six feet south isn't far to roam, for where I lie – I lie alone. In this place I can't love the less, so lovely is the loneliness!' Kelly (1955, p. 15) wrote optimistically, 'no one need paint himself into a corner; no one needs to be completely hemmed in by circumstances, no one needs to be the victim of his biography'. However, unfortunately for Brian, he had apparently painted himself into a corner and was living an increasingly alienated life in the 'career' of a psychiatric patient.

One of the things Kelly insisted was that constructs are 'bipolar', they always have two ends or 'poles', providing a person with avenues of movement and choices between alternatives (Chapter 3). It is notable that all the words and descriptions Brian uses—false, insincere, against me, frightening—cluster at one end of a construct dimension. We never hear of what lies at the other end—could that be 'sincere, trustworthy, genuine, kind'? We don't know, and we should never assume that we know, what people's contrast poles are. Fransella pointed out (Chapters 3 and 7) that if we have an elaborate set of ideas at one end of a dimension and almost none at the other end (e.g., being 'fluent' for the stutterer), we find it hard not to slip back into the familiar end where we have learnt to deal with things in spite of them being problematic. Brian instead saw himself in his self-characterisation as having two 'selves', 'one the quiet family man interested in films and books, the other frightened, being obsessed with death, fear and predestined and inescapable doom'. These two aspects of himself were apparently dissociated from each other—two fragmented construct subsystems in PCP language (see Chapter 3). He seemed to be caught in an 'implicative dilemma' (see Chapter 6), preferring solitude and resenting interruptions and invasions of his privacy and yet, at the same time, craving for relationships.

Therapy

I felt, soon after meeting Brian, that Kelly's 'Fixed-Role Therapy' (FRT) would be a very appropriate and useful procedure for him to engage in. Kelly used enactment and role-playing frequently in both individual and group therapy (see Chapters 8 and 10), and it typifies the playfulness and experimental spirit that characterises his approach.[4] FRT is a particular form of enactment for which he became well-known and respected. It involves playing the part of a prescribed role continuously for a limited period of time, usually two weeks. The role is carefully worked out by the therapist in accordance with Kelly's prescription that it is based on a construct which is 'orthogonal' or 'at right angles' to the main construct governing the client's current situation. Thus, the role should not be too different—exhorting somebody to do or be the opposite of their current constructions of self is actually merely to go to the other end of the same (two-ended) construct. It is usually not helpful asking a depressed person to 'cheer up' or a worried person to 'calm down'—they are already trying to do that and failing. Instead, a sketch is written which introduces a new construct or overall theme which overlaps with or covers the same ground—in this case Brian's preoccupation with other people being *for* or *against him* is replaced by a character who finds other people *fascinating and interesting* versus *dull and boring*. The following role-sketch for him to enact was worked out:

JOHN ULVERSTON: FIXED-ROLE SKETCH

John Ulverston is a rather quiet individual most of the time but when he gets involved in a discussion that interests him, he becomes quite talkative and his eyes light up with enthusiasm. He treats his fellow human beings very much as equals and doesn't like the idea of one person telling others what to do. This arises from his philosophy which he likes to think of as a "scientific" analysis of human behaviour. This is not to say he likes everyone; in fact, he is rather fussy about who his friends are.

John extends this "scientific" way of looking at things to all his areas of interest. He is interested in reading horror stories and science fiction because he likes to theorise about how authors dream up such weird fantasies. However, he doesn't see this sort of thing as being important in everyday life.

His point of view has the advantage that it gives him the strength to let people have their own way. He is more interested in observing people and seeing how situations make them behave in certain ways. If someone boils over with rage he sits back and wonders how long it'll be before they calm down. The trouble with this is that people tend to get a bit fed up with him and think he is a bit cold and clinical at times, but he takes this in his stride as well.

The sketch is written without prescribing too many behaviours or reactions, leaving it sufficiently vague for creativity and spontaneity to operate, but under the new orthogonal theme of observing people for interest rather than checking for their hostility. The name helps to provide an 'anchor', to remind the person to maintain playing the role and to reinforce the make-believe nature of the exercise. The idea is not to 'replace' his character with a model, but to have him playfully engage in a relevant learning experience. He was intrigued by the task. Rehearsing the idea with Brian, we discussed how he, in the role of this character 'John Ulverston', would deal with different situations that he might encounter as he pretended to be John, enacting examples in the session, including swapping roles briefly. He was encouraged to read the sketch through several times a day and 'become' the person for two weeks. He was given an engaging science fiction novel to read over this period to accompany John's interest in 'scientifically' observing the behaviour of other people.

We met five times over the fortnight period of the fixed role to check on how it was going and refine the experiment. Brian returned to these sessions saying it was a powerful experience and he was very enthusiastic. To his surprise, he (John!) had been able to enter various situations without fear. He had spoken to a neighbour, he went to the corner shop and chatted to the shopkeeper, travelled on a bus, and went to the cinema—things he had not done for a very long time. In the cinema, he had been pleased that he had avoided a confrontation with some noisy kids, when he felt that normally he would have become aggressive. Of the neighbours, he said, 'I see their view now – I haven't spoken to them for nine years!' This is particularly significant as it involved what Kelly described as *sociality*—the ability to put himself in the shoes of his neighbours and see their point of view, rather than being totally absorbed in his own fears and suspicions about them. We will see how essential sociality is in our approach in the coming chapters.

A central process in the method is probably that a slightly different demeanour in the role-player leads others to respond to him in subtly different ways, modifying the usual interactional 'loop' that had been operating. This opens the door to different mutual construing between the participants. Of course, this is not a 'magic cure'; Kelly argued that the aim of FRT is to set ongoing processes in motion rather than creating a new state. It provided new material to work with in the sessions subsequent to the experiment: John Ulverston often came up in the conversations we had in the following months.

Progress and Recovery

I continued to see Brian in regular sessions for the following 16 months, after which we had to stop because I was moving to a new job. During this time, two significant turning points occurred. The first, after a further eight months, was paradoxical. I received a letter from him saying he had decided not to come for therapy anymore and that 'he realised he was unalterable'. I visited him at home and reassured him that I still wished to help him and urged him to continue. He agreed to persevere.

In the next session, he asked if he was still making progress, indicating a new reflection on how 'alterable' he might be. He appeared to have 'hit bottom', and in some profound way had ceased to strive for change. And yet, after this, all the issues of death, which had occupied much of our conversations, simply vanished from his concerns. I had raised the issues of goals and the fact that therapy would one day end. Some kind of spontaneous change in his construing seemed to have occurred, seemingly involving a reappraisal of his life. His interest in death was replaced by a new project involving a similar attention to detail—to take up learning to play ragtime guitar.

This is interesting in the light of what he had said in response to the first TAT card during the assessment. This depicts a boy sitting staring at a violin.[5] Brian had already written on the Rotter test, completing a sentence beginning with the prompt *Boys*, 'Boys are mirror images of their fathers'. He had also said of his 'dropout' father (an excellent violin player) that 'he had got all the bad qualities of his father and none of the good'. About the TAT card, he said:

> 'Well, it looks to me as though, assuming by the look on his face that that was his Dad's violin. I think his Dad, well it appears from the way he's looking at it, that he's dead. Um, he's just wishing that his Dad was here to play it. Um, wishes he could play it like his Dad did. That's all....' (is that all?). 'He may be deciding that he'd learn to play it....' (how did it turn out?) 'He eventually learned to play the tunes that he knew his Dad liked'.

The transitions and elaborations of meaning through these sentences are notable, moving from missing his father (third sentence) to wishing he could do something as well as his Dad. He then describes a state of deciding to learn to play, with an outcome of having achieved approval from his father.

I suggested that he bring his guitar to our sessions and for a series of Thursday mornings, I also brought my guitar to the Psychology Department! We worked together for part of the hour, studying the finger-picking arrangements of the guitarist Stefan Grossman.[6] I believe that the following months consolidated a trust and companionship between us that he had not experienced with anyone before. The music provided a vehicle for the meetings, during which he could reflect on his ongoing life and experiences without the embarrassment that a direct focus on them might have involved.

About four months after this, a second turning point occurred. He wrote a letter to me saying, 'It's about time I got off my backside and got myself a job like everyone else...I have been out of hospital for 15 months now which is the longest I've ever managed'. A very significant session occurred after this in which he talked a lot about his family and how his wife demanded more of him than he felt he could give. He still felt periods of paranoia from time to time but got a job driving buses, the very situation that had been so threatening to him. Terminating the therapy was difficult, but after I left, he kept in touch with me by letter and telephone for a further three years. During this time, he told me that he had been taken off his medication.

Review and Reflection

This case illustrates how the central focus of concern in personal construct psychotherapy is the construing of the client. We seek to understand the client's understanding of the world in a non-judgemental way, what Kelly called 'the credulous approach'. Everyone has a unique set of constructs, both in terms of the *content* (e.g. Brian's seeing others as *false, hypocritical, frightening, against him*) and structure (how these constructs cluster together, for example in a tightly interrelated way— see Chapter 3 for a discussion of Kelly's 'professional construct' of *tight* versus *loose* construing). Brian had approached the social world using a single major dimension of *for me* versus *against me*, a situation that has been described as *monolithic construing*. It was this that led the therapist to consider fixed-role therapy, revising and loosening this tight structure by temporarily encouraging him to consider people according to an *orthogonal construct* as we have described.

Another central principle of our approach is that we tend not to use normative construing such as the constructs of psychiatric diagnosis as laid out in the DSM-V. A critique of this categorical, 'nosological' approach to diagnosis will be found in Chapter 7 on formulation, where we replace the 'pigeon-hole' approach with a dimensional approach, emphasising a person's potential avenues of movement. It is not that we reject this way of construing entirely. We apply the credulous approach to our medical colleagues too. Psychiatric diagnosis may be useful in deciding on what physical treatments might be most appropriate and helpful. R. Neimeyer (2009) reports that 15–20% of his clients are taking psychotropic medication, which they generally report as being helpful. He writes:

In my view, nothing in this practice is incompatible with a constructivist therapy. What is inimical is considering pharmacotherapy as a substitute for self-understanding, reflexivity, self-change, resistance against oppressive circumstances and problem resolution at more psychological levels. (R. Neimeyer, 2009, p. 103)

It is ironic that the term 'schizophrenia' includes under the same umbrella people who have very tight construct systems such as Brian and at the other end of the scale very *loose* systems, where the person's constructs are vague and varying, a situation which has been reliably shown to characterise 'schizophrenic thought disorder' (see Chapter 7). If Brian's construct system had been loose, fixed-role therapy would certainly not be indicated as it would probably have contributed to further loosening and chaotic experience for the client.

The therapy for Brian was helpful, and this underlines that psychological therapy such as personal and relational construct psychotherapy can be very effective and indeed is essential in people who have serious psychopathological diagnoses. It was possible to help him make profound changes and from a cost-effectiveness point of view, weekly expenditure of one-hour sessions of therapy prevented further admissions to inpatient treatment, which he had endured for six years. It enabled him to return to work. The psychiatrist reported after 11 months of treatment that he found him 'much more communicative and friendly than on previous occasions. His relations with his wife appear to have improved'. The Hostility and Direction of Hostility Questionnaire (Caine, Foulds, & Hope, 1967), administered at the beginning and end of the therapy, indicated a significant reduction in various measures of hostility, although he remained quite critical of himself.

Probably, an important therapeutic factor was allowing him to experience a supportive relationship in which the therapist listened carefully to him, stuck by him through difficult phases, and provided a warm alliance with him that he appears not to have experienced before in his life. The fixed-role therapy was very helpful in kick-starting him back into an involvement with others, but I believe that the long period of subsequent therapy was essential in consolidating these changes. The two 'turning points' were indications of profound change in his construing of self, beginning to appreciate his own potential, and putting his interest in death matters behind him. The music therapy[7] allowed him to find an area where he could develop new skills and ways of expressing himself. Also, learning to play the guitar seems to have allowed him to identify himself with a positive aspect of his father—his violin playing—and not just 'all the bad qualities'. His comments indicate that his construing of his father was central to his identity. By learning to play the guitar, he may have found that he could at last share a love of music with the memory of his father, the shift in this crucial relationship enabling him to reconstrue himself more positively. This was likely to have had implications for his own current role as a father. Unfortunately, he is no longer with us—it would have been good to reflect with him on this.

This case was conducted before the therapist had become experienced in applying Kellian principles to working with families (see Chapter 9). If I were to tackle this case again, I am fairly sure that I would have placed family intervention more centrally, allowing us to address his marital issues and also problems with his daughter, who had started refusing school. However, Brian's preference for tackling things by himself and his embarrassment about his state may well indicate that one-to-one individual therapy over an extended period would still be the treatment of choice.

Notes

1. The personal construct theorist Don Bannister (1968) had described schizophrenia as too diffuse and incoherent a term to be used in scientific research.
2. The higher level, where pupils would go on to further education.
3. The Thematic Apperception Test (Morgan & Murray, 1935) was recommended by Kelly (1955) as a good way of eliciting constructs. It consists of a series of pictures of situations in which the client is invited to tell a story about what is going on.
4. The work of Tom Ravenette with children is a particularly good example of the spirit of playfulness in PCP (see Chapter 5).
5. This can be seen by searching 'TAT Violin' on the internet.

6. 30 years later, in 2008, I was lucky enough to meet Stefan Grossman at one of his gigs. I told him how important his guitar books had been in helping Brian make a recovery from serious mental health problems.

7. The music in therapy as well as the use of tools such as the Rotter test and the TAT illustrate how the construct approach is willing to use methods from any source, not just those developed within the tradition. In this way it can be seen as an integrative 'meta-theory' as well as a therapeutic approach in its own right (Procter, 2009).

References

Bannister, D. (1968). The logical requirements of research into schizophrenia. *British Journal of Psychiatry, 114*(507), 181–188.

Caine, T. M., Foulds, G. A., & Hope, D. (1967). *Manual of the Hostility and Direction of Hostility Questionnaire*. London: University of London Press.

Kelly, G. A. (1955). *The Psychology of Personal Constructs. Vol. I, II*. New York: Norton (2nd printing: 1991, London and New York: Routledge).

Morgan, C. D., & Murray, H. A. (1935). A method for investigating fantasies: The thematic apperception test. *Archives of Neurology & Psychiatry, 34*, 289–306.

Neimeyer, R. A. (2009). *Constructivist Psychotherapy*. London: Routledge.

Procter, H. G. (2009). Reflexivity and reflective practice in personal and relational construct psychology. In J. Stedmon & R. Dallos (Eds.), *Reflective Practice in Psychotherapy and Counselling* (pp. 93–114). Milton Keynes, UK: Open University Press.

2

The Philosophical Background

The approach to psychotherapy and counselling introduced in this book was originally inspired by George Kelly's Personal Construct Psychology (PCP). The essence of Kelly's approach is that each of us in our life develops a unique understanding and view of the world. People are deeply influenced by the traditions and beliefs of the culture/s in which they are brought up, but each person develops within these a unique take on reality which is carved out in a unique developmental path with all its experiences and challenges. This is nicely illustrated in how siblings from the same family, with such similar genetics and environment, are just *so different*, as Dunn and Plomin (1991) explore.[1] Kelly develops a rich set of theoretical concepts and practical methods for helping us to discover how the world is seen from the person's point of view, to 'get inside their shoes' and to understand the unique meanings that words and experiences have for them. These remain as fresh and applicable today as they were when he first developed them. However, in our own work over many years, we have supplemented Kelly's original vision with a recognition that people are not isolated entities, but live in a web of relationships and interactions, in which each person's positions and understandings are

© The Author(s) 2020

H. Procter and D. A. Winter, *Personal and Relational Construct Psychotherapy*,
Palgrave Texts in Counselling and Psychotherapy,
https://doi.org/10.1007/978-3-030-52177-6_2

dynamically interconnected as they struggle to make sense of and thrive in the ongoing relational situations that face them.

This profound and radical development of PCP has led us to re-title our approach *Personal and Relational Construct Psychotherapy* (PRCP). We preserve within this Kelly's original brilliant theoretical and practical contributions but add to it a whole new series of ways of thinking about human life which have profound implications for how we proceed in helping people in their situations. We devote Chapter 3 to describing Kelly's original approach and Chapter 4 to describing these relational extensions and developments before turning, in later chapters, to the practical application of our approach. But before doing any of that, we shall look at the philosophical background and assumptions that underlie both Kelly's and our own thinking and practice.

The Philosophical Background and Assumptions of PRCP

George Alexander Kelly, who originated our approach, is normally classified as a psychologist. Indeed, he was an important figure in developing the profession of clinical psychology. However, his vision is really much broader than the discipline of psychology. He had a varied background in his formative years, including, in addition to psychology, an expertise in mathematics and physics, degrees in sociology and education, research in reading and speech difficulties and labour relations, experience in aviation training in the navy during the Second World War, and so on (Chiari, 2017a; Fransella, 1995). During the 1930s he made a detailed study of philosophy. We believe that he can rightly be considered as a *philosopher* in his own right (Procter, 2014a). Intrinsic to his approach is a philosophy, and, as we shall see, an implicit ethics, which should be recognised as much as his contributions to psychology and psychotherapy, for which he is well-known. We believe that this broader framework, together with our own further developments designed to take account of relational and sociological factors in human life, makes it comprehensive and powerful enough to respond to the complexities and challenges faced by psychotherapists and counsellors dealing with all the varied difficulties in life that people bring to us.

At the beginning of *The Psychology of Personal Constructs*, Kelly (1955, pp. 6–7) outlines seven basic assumptions in asking 'what kind of universe?'. These can be found in Table 2.1. We will briefly discuss each of these in turn.

1. *All Thinking Is Based, in Part, on Prior Convictions*

This first statement captures the essence of Kelly's views—that we never know anything directly; there are no independent 'givens' or bare facts. We always see and know things through our *construing* of them. This is the core of what is called both *constructivism* and *social constructionism* or what Kelly would call *constructive alternativism*. There are always other ways of making sense of what confronts us, we are never hemmed into only one definitive understanding of any situation. This may be contrasted with the view that we know reality *directly*, that our senses copy what we see like a camera. We always use a set of values, we always look and experience from a *position*. We are not particularly aware of this. In therapy, we do our best to reflect on both the clients' preconceptions and, importantly as therapists, our own. We can never fully 'escape' from them, but identifying our construing is vital in

Table 2.1   Kelly: what kind of universe?[a]

1.	All thinking is based, in part, on prior convictions
2.	The universe is really existing...it is a real world that we shall be talking about, not a world composed solely of the flitting shadows of people's thoughts
3.	Man is gradually coming to understand it
4.	Thoughts also really exist
5.	Correspondence between thoughts and the world is a continually changing one
6.	The universe is integral...in the long run all events are interlocked
7.	The universe is continually changing with respect to itself...something is always going on

[a]This table is drawn from Procter (2014a), where each of the assumptions is compared with similar proposals given by the founder of pragmatist philosophy, Charles S. Peirce

tackling our own prejudices and very freeing, allowing us to consider situations from a new and fresh perspective which can lead to new pathways forward. Because each person and situation are unique, we must particularly beware of using standardised formulations based on doctrine or normative research. When Kelly inserts 'in part' into his statement, it underlines that as human beings, we are *creative*: we can *invent* a new hypothesis, new ways of looking at things.

2. *The universe is really existing…it is a real world that we shall be talking about, not a world composed solely of the flitting shadows of people's thoughts.*

There is a core of assumptions about which we cannot doubt such as 'I am here', 'I have a body', and 'the earth exists and is round' (Procter, 2016a; Wittgenstein, 1969). It is absurd to doubt them. They usually remain in the 'background' of our daily lives. They are profoundly *action based* and must be assumed in order for our practices to be comprehensible and able to be carried out (Misak, 2011). When I walk across the room, I am making the silent assumption that the floor will withstand my weight and hold me up. As we shall see later, they are part of what Kelly calls *core* or *superordinate constructs* (see Chapter 3).

We could say that the world and I are real, but what does this word *real* mean? Charles Peirce (1998b), who founded the tradition of pragmatism within which Kelly developed his approach, says, 'There must be such a thing, for we find our opinions constrained; there is something, therefore, which influences our thoughts, and is not created by them' (p. 57), something we are all too aware of when we encounter an extra step that we were not expecting at the bottom of a staircase!

In talking of the 'flitting shadows of people's thoughts', Kelly is dissociating himself from *idealism*, that the world and all our experience is just a dream. But he also says, 'I am not a realist…and do not believe a client or therapist has to lie down and let facts crawl all over him' (Kelly, 1969b, p. 225). As Kelly's first statement above says, everything we are aware of is *construed*. He brilliantly took an intermediate position here, stating that there is a reality but that we only experience the reality that we have constituted. This may seem like a contradiction but is a profound resolution of the centuries-old standoff in philosophy between idealism and realism, positions which continue to be held because they each have some validity and something vital to contribute. Separating the *objective* from the *subjective* is something humans do to try and make sense of things, but actually they are inseparable and always form a *unity*. As William James said, we can think of paint in a paint-shop objectively as a 'saleable commodity' or on a canvas as a subjective artistic expression: 'We have every right to speak of it as subjective and objective both at once' (James, 2003, p. 9). The reality proposed by the most 'objective' of sciences is still subjectively construed by the scientists of the day. Kelly (1955, p. 208) said that PCP is '*more objective* because it is *more projective*', because it starts with how people actually experience and apprehend situations. This places Kelly nicely within the tradition of *phenomenology*, a designation which has been claimed by several writers.[2]

However certain we may be about things, because what we know is always construed, we may always turn out to be wrong. There was a time, of course, when people were certain that the earth was not round but flat. This is a principle that Peirce called *fallibilism*, that any current beliefs might be mistaken. Kelly (1955) applies this to his own framework, to PCP itself, in saying that a psychological theory should be considered 'ultimately expendable' (p. 44). This translates into a position of humility and a continual questioning of our conclusions that should inform all of our dealings in psychotherapy.

3. Man is gradually coming to understand it.

Kelly likes to use the metaphor that people are a bit like scientists in confronting the situations of their lives, making hypotheses and being involved in a process of *inquiry*. This is quite a good model for what clients and therapists are doing as they struggle together to makes sense of things and find new paths forward. Kelly, in this grand third statement, reflects the prevailing optimism of the period in which he was writing, shortly after the Second World War. As we consider the state of play in the world in the twenty-first century, it would be easy to take a more jaundiced view. The idea that the whole of humanity is converging towards a better understanding is contentious. But the belief that we can get a better handle on things in more local, specific areas of life is a fruitful stance to be bringing into the therapy room. That changes can be made, a belief intrinsic to PRCP, is a vital factor in countering the inevitable despair and loss of hope that clients experience, trapped as they are in repeating patterns of unsatisfactory emotion and interactions. As Rorty (1999, pp. 232, 277) writes, 'Loss of hope is an inability to construe a plausible narrative of progress – a gesture of despair…Utopian social hope is still the noblest imaginative creation we have on record'.

4. *Thoughts also really exist.*

It is hard for us now to remember that Kelly was at the vanguard of opposing the prevailing ideology in psychology at the time—behaviourism—with its attempt to deny experience and consciousness. Back in 1874, Brentano (1995, p. 20) had said, 'our mental phenomena are the things which are most our own, they are true and real in themselves'. He said that they can be grasped immediately, with absolute certainty, and because of this we can make real discoveries about them (Moran, 2000). The reality of our experience is particularly shown when we struggle against our own thoughts and emotions, for example in fighting off feelings of jealousy or downplaying and minimising signs of illness. This also applies, of course, to our struggles with the reality of *other people's* thoughts and feelings, even though we can never experience these directly. For Kelly, this assumption lies at the basis of his whole attitude of taking human experience and construing seriously. When he says here '*thoughts*', he means not just cognition but the whole range of human subjective experience—feelings, emotions, perceptions, attitudes, judgements, intentions, and so on. For Kelly, it is wrong to split experience up into these compartments. This will become clearer as we proceed.

5. *Correspondence between thoughts and the world is a continually changing one.*

When Kelly talks of 'correspondence', this raises the question of the relationship between our thoughts and the world. We have already said that we do not copy reality like a camera. To say that our thoughts are like a mirror, a true image or representation is problematic. Stam (1998) asks, if representations are the source of knowledge, how do we have access to that which corresponds to its representation? 'To know what it is that is being represented, a system must already have some knowledge of the object represented. But this is precisely what the representation is supposed to provide in the first place' (p. 188). Representation suggests that there is a 'correct' view of the world, which runs against our emphasis on personal uniqueness and constructive alternativism, that there are many useable ways of construing the world. It is an approach that cognitive psychology is fond of using, embodied in the word 'schema' (see Chapter 12). A useful distinction here is offered by Von Glasersfeld (1984, p. 3), who compares the ideas of 'match' and 'fit'. A key can *fit* a lock and unlock it even though a key is quite different to a lock. The key a burglar uses to get into our house may look very different from the key we are used to using. We will see later that Kelly's approach finds a third way that does justice to both ideas embodied in this metaphor.

To describe how our thoughts relate to the world, another idea is 'reference' or 'standing for'. When we indicate something or use a word to refer to it, what we mean can vary according to the context, what point we are trying to get across, and how we anticipate what sense the hearer will make of it. This view does better justice to cultural diversity and to the uniqueness of the webs of meaning that each of us holds, which, as we will cover in the next chapter, Kelly calls our personal construct systems. We will see there how Kelly approaches the issue, with meanings based on similarities and differences.

When we are discussing something, we never really know whether the other person is thinking about the object referred to in the same way, even if they use the same words that we do. Deep and extensive conversation and mutual acquaintance is necessary here to reach better understanding, to clarify our similarities and differences, to negotiate our agreements and disagreements. The words and meanings we use tend to vary each time we speak, according to what sense we anticipate a hearer will make of them and according to how the sense we make of things in general is always changing and growing as we move through life's path.

6. *The universe is integral...in the long run all events are interlocked.*

If we stand back and look more broadly, the patterns of relationships between events and the interconnected parts of the world become observable.[3] Kelly says this of the whole universe. At a more local level, it applies to interpretations and judgements, which do not stand alone but are always part of an interconnected web of meanings. It also applies to individuals, who do not struggle alone to make sense of the world, but are part of systems of relationships such as families, organisations, subcultures, nations, schools of thought, and so on. Just as persons have unique views, we can talk of groups as taking positions on things and holding systems of beliefs or 'mission statements'. For example, families have a 'family construct system' which consists of the interconnected positions that the members take up, with all the alliances, disagreements, complementarities, and power relationships that comprise their ongoing politics and interactions. As therapists, the more aware we are of these processes within which our clients are living, the better. Whether we are working with individuals or with several members of a group, we are always intervening in an ongoing system of relationships. Our concern and understanding should be for all the individuals in the network, however much we may personally approve or disapprove of their positions and actions.

7. *The universe is continually changing with respect to itself...something is always going on.*

Again, what applies to the universe applies to everything in it including ourselves and our social reality. Kelly (1955) is at pains to emphasise that as individuals, we are active, always changing, we are 'a form of motion'[4] (p. 48). He opposes the view that we are static and require being pushed or pulled into action by the likes of 'energy', 'stimuli', 'reinforcements', or 'drives'. For Kelly, we are always on the move, involved in discovery, inquiry, and creativity. If we appear unmotivated at times, this is not stasis but more like moving round in circles, trapped in repetitiousness.

We know this from what James called our stream of consciousness, in which we are aware of a continuous flow of thoughts, ideas, and feelings. Actually, this is much more than just a surface phenomenon. Peirce (1998a, p. 99) wrote, 'Each former thought suggests something to the thought which follows it…But, in addition to the principal element of thought at any moment, there are a hundred things in our mind to which but a small fraction of attention or consciousness is conceded'. We know this because, often, an idea or fresh perspective will 'pop into our minds' or be present when we awaken, indicating that we have been working over the solution to a problem without being aware of doing so. We are continually anticipating events and other people's reactions, and our stance alters according to whether these anticipations are validated or invalidated.

This process is in our view fundamentally *dialogical*. New ideas are born out of dialogue and conversation. If this happens in our own minds, we see this as still dialogical, because, as Mair (2015a) emphasised, we are a *community of selves*: we have internalised and made our own an array of different 'voices', some being those of influential figures in our network or 'reference group', together with a range of possible positions and opinions on things. For example, in making a decision we may call on 'my risky self', my 'sensible self', 'what my mother and my friend (whose opinions we can imagine) would say about this', and so on. Each subself, or position that we can take up, can, as it were, converse and debate with other selves or positions in deciding what to do. We see this above in Peirce's 'thought suggesting something to the thought that follows it'. He said, 'All thinking is dialogical in form. Your self of one instant appeals to your future self that is just coming into life in the flow of time' (Peirce, 1998d, p. 262). It is in this way that our webs of meaning or 'construct systems' grow, elaborate, and extend, allowing us to develop new perspectives and new courses of action to address situations.

Dualities

When we look at the deep assumptions that underlie our understanding of the world, we frequently encounter paired alternative views about how to make sense of things. We have already touched on *real* versus *ideal*, *objective* versus *subjective*, *representation* versus *reference*, and *static* versus *moving*. These alternatives, or *dualities*, tend to define themselves against their opposites: 'No, it isn't like that, it's like this!' In fact, as we mentioned above, each of these positions is *useful* for dealing with aspects of our rich and complex reality and continues to survive in Darwinian fashion because of this. Typically, Kelly found a middle way between these extremes and managed to create an elegant framework of assumptions that synthesised or integrated them. Other dualities on which he found a middle path are *personal/social*, *free/determined*, and *past/future*.

Personal and Social

We use the same principle in our development of PCP to address a central and ubiquitous duality that exercises therapists and scholars in this field: are our meanings and constructions fundamentally more *personal* (as in 'constructivism') or *social* (as in 'constructionism')? In discussing these terms, we could talk about the 'v word' or the 'n word'! Social constructionism, the n word approach, minimises the emphasis on the personal, prioritises interaction and relationship from the very start in a baby's life, and sees meanings as fundamentally shared and social, reflecting the language, discourses, and practices of the culture in which we grow up.[5] As we see in Fig. 2.1, we can construct a scale from an individual, biological emphasis through to a social and sociological emphasis. At the left-hand end, the radical constructivists, such as Maturana, stress the individual as being like a biological cell, with a membrane that strictly controls and shapes what can come in from the outside. Von Glasersfeld (1995, p. 1) writes, 'Knowledge, no matter how it is defined, is in the heads of persons, and the thinking subject has no alternative but to construct what he or she knows on the basis of his or

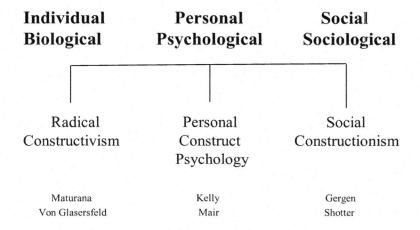

Personal and Relational Construct Psychology

Fig. 2.1 The integrative position of our approach: PRCP incorporates aspects of the approaches across the spectrum

her own experience. What we make of experience constitutes the only world we consciously live in'.

On the right-hand end of the scale we include theorists such as John Shotter and Kenneth Gergen. To quote Gergen (1994), 'Constructivists posit a mental world and then theorize its relation to an external world…In contrast, the chief focus of interest for the constructionist is microsocial process…the site of explanation for human action moves to the relational sphere' (pp. 68–9). As we shall see in Chapter 4, a key notion here is the concept of 'joint action' or 'intersubjectivity' (Schütz, 1971; Shotter, 2011; Trevarthen, 1979).

Kelly can be seen as taking a median position on this scale. As the title of his approach suggests, he emphasises the *personal.* He sees our development as like scientists, struggling to make sense of the world and gradually building up hypotheses, evidence, and understandings to account for all the events that confront us. Science is, of course, a deeply social affair. No scientist has ever developed in isolation from a community of scientists and a scientific tradition. And Kelly leaves plenty of room in his model to examine and understand relationships and the social context, as we shall see later.

We have developed and elaborated the social and relational aspect of Kelly's approach further, to such an extent that we have re-titled our approach as Personal and Relational Construct Psychology and its clinical application Personal and Relational Construct Psychotherapy. In the debate depicted in Fig. 2.1, we see our approach as *incorporating aspects* of the whole dimension. We see no reason why we cannot accept many of the claims in both the extremes and combine them into a single framework (see also Radley, 1979). The contributions of each tradition come together in a vision of 'microsocial process' or 'joint action' (Shotter, 2011) between individual 'personal scientists' each construing self, other, the context, and the relationship between them in a continuing dance of anticipation and moment-by-moment decision making. The overall patterns of interaction shape the individual contributions, and vice versa in an ongoing and continuous dynamic.[6] As Schütz (1971, p. 218) points out, this relational context is and has always been present from the beginning of our lives: 'The world of daily life into which we are born is from the outset an intersubjective world'.

Free and Determined: Ethics

Kelly's view fundamentally unites the ideas that people have free will, that we can choose between alternatives freely and with responsibility, and that we are also determined or governed by the structure of meanings and construed options that we currently use to make choices and to make sense of the world and of situations. This web of meanings, or what Kelly calls our *construct system* (see Chapter 3), governs our actions, feelings, and interpretations but we also have the potential to elaborate and revise it as time goes on. For Kelly (1955, p. 21), 'determinism and freedom are two sides of the same coin – two aspects of the same relationship'. He says, 'like good and evil, hope and despair, north and south – without one, the other would make no sense' (Kelly, 1959, p. 8; see also Hobart, 1934). When we make a choice between alternatives, we are then committed to the implications and circumstances that it involves. He reflexively applies this to the very two alternatives being considered here: we can look at things as if we are either *free* or *determined*! 'When we compare two or more courses of action, we are thinking freely. When we choose a point of departure and set off in pursuit of its consequences, we are accepting determinism' (Kelly, 1959, p. 9). Each of these ways of looking at things has its uses and its appropriate sphere of application.

Kelly's treatment of this old issue, unusual in contemporary psychology, which usually privileges determinism, allows us properly to consider *ethics*. By underlining the aspect of *free choice*, we recognize that people have *responsibility, obligations, duties*, and *rights*—all these being the stuff of ethics, or how we *ought* to act. But, the aspect in which people are also *determined* allows us to maintain a compassion towards people who are 'lumbered' with a set of views and circumstances, who 'can't help the way they are', but with an optimism that there is always a way forward through looking at things in new ways.

It is a central understanding of our approach that people develop their own unique personal ethical systems that inform and govern their moral conduct (Raskin & Debany, 2018; Stojnov, 1996). Whilst informed by cultural discourses and traditions, we select and actively carve out our own versions of the meanings of what is *right* and *wrong*, what is *good* and *bad* in order to make sense of the experiences and events in our biography. Table 2.2 shows how different members of one family take up very different positions about what is good and bad—emphasising *knowledge, religious faith*, and *good interpersonal relationships* respectively.

As 'personal scientists', we develop different positions on things. But Kelly (1959) criticised the idea that science can ever be value-free. He insisted that values and knowledge or belief 'belong to the same system of

Table 2.2 Three versions of the meaning of good and bad in one family[a]

Good	Bad
Thirst for knowledge is good	Being tame and yielding is bad
Loving God and being resigned and forgiving is good	Lacking faith in God is sinful
Mutual love between family members is good	Splitting loved ones apart is bad

[a]Kelly (1969a) discusses ethics in the light of the Garden of Eden story in his paper 'Sin and Psychotherapy'. Table 2.2 is drawn from a version of this story as depicted in Byron's brilliant play 'Cain – A Mystery' (Procter & Procter, 2008)

discourse. The distinction…is another one of those unfortunate dualisms that has become so concretized that it prevents one gaining perspective' (p. 7). Whilst we should not confuse the *is* and the *ought*, in practice people develop systems of belief in which these two are thoroughly intertwined and integrated. It is of central importance in psychotherapy that we establish and understand clients' values and beliefs and how these are shown in their actual spontaneous decisions and conduct.

PCP is designed to establish people's views of the world in as faithful a way as possible, while minimising the imposition of our own values and biases. But, in line with what Kelly says about science having values, he said, 'I do think of Personal Construct Theory as an implicit ethical system; just imagine a world in which we understood one another as people!' (quoted in Hinkle, 1970, p. 107). He advised that we should take a venturesome, risk-taking, and experimental stance, challenging accepted truths (Walker, 1992). He recommended taking an 'invitational' attitude, advising people to try looking at things from new and fresh perspectives. Above all, we should do our best to establish and comprehend other people's outlooks, which in Stojnov's (1996) view usually requires engaging in a moral dialogue of respect and acceptance. Butt (2000) said,

> We should make the effort to stand in the other's shoes… Our best hope of changing ourselves comes when we reconstrue and take on the perspectives of others. We act morally then, when we seek to understand human action, either our own or others', and understanding it means contextualizing it. (p. 94)

Contrasted with this approach to others is being judgemental: in the words of Kelly's (1959) admonishment, 'One should never make black and white judgments about people' (p. 3). We need to keep a constant eye on our own prejudices and biases. We shall have more to say about this in Chapter 11 on reflective practice.

The ethical implications of our approach broaden further as we extend Kelly's PCP in the direction of the relational and to social construction in general. If we look again at the family depicted in Table 2.2, the top two positions taken by the members are strongly opposed to each other.

Scientific versus religious positions here underlie serious disagreement and argument between the son and the rest of his family. A young man rejects his parents' and brother's faith. His wife tries to be the peace-keeper because, for her, harmony in the family is extremely important. This third position governs the wife's attempt to mediate between the first two and prevent escalation and estrangement.[7] Working with any of these individuals in therapy requires an understanding of the overall pattern and context, with an obligation on the therapist to understand the construing of all the members, not just the client/s being seen.[8] This applies whether we are working with all the members in conjoint sessions (as we shall discuss in Chapter 8) or not. Blame and criticism of the positions of other people in a client's network, only backing one's own client in conflicts and tensions, can lead to a serious escalation and destabilisation of situations. It interferes with the client's feeling of loyalty, which can be held even in the face of strong disagreement with the other's position.

Kelly acknowledges the pragmatist philosopher John Dewey as a major influence. Dewey wrote that ethics in the modern world needs to be concerned with how society is organised, not just with personal decisions of the individual (Anderson, 2014; Dewey, 1932). This takes us into the realm of politics with both a big and a small p. If we are concerned with promoting relational systems and social structures which permit constructive alternativism and diversity and endorse individual freedoms, then we should take a position which opposes forces that work against individuals being able to thrive without discrimination, prejudice, and subjugation (see Stojnov, Miletić, & Džinović [2017] for an integration of PCP with Foucault's discussion of power). In therapy this may involve taking a position on issues which transcend psychotherapy itself, for example when we need to confront and involve others in cases of, for example, child protection, domestic abuse, or slave labour.

Future and Past

For Kelly, *anticipation* is a key term in his approach as we shall see in the next chapters. It connects directly with his insistence that we have free choice. He says, 'All human movement is based on anticipations, the choice of an alternative through which we move is itself a matter of what one anticipates' (Kelly, 1955, p. 66). When we choose, there is an 'in-order-to' component. This applies to short term, immediate decisions as well as to long term goals that we aspire to. 'It is the future which tantalizes man, not the past. Always he reaches out to the future through the window of the present'[9] (Kelly, 1955, p. 49).

This reflects Kelly's development within the tradition of pragmatism. The emphasis on the future was genuinely new and revolutionary in philosophy.[10] Charles Peirce (1998c, p. 146), the founder of the movement, argued that the meaning of a conception is based on the 'practical bearings' or consequences that *would follow* in enacting it. We are able to conduct 'mental experiments' and explore the different consequences of making imagined changes and variations in a situation.[11] We settle on a course of action in the light of a hypothesis: 'In circumstance C, if I were to do A, then I would experience E'.[12] This all usually happens rapidly and without deliberation. When I say something in a conversation, I anticipate that the hearer will understand me and that s/he will likely interpret what I say in a certain way. My anticipation may not work out. Then I may re-construe the other's position and respond in the light of this new understanding. We will soon see that one's ability to construe another person's understanding and position on things is fundamental in human relating.

Kelly was impatient with explanatory models of human difficulties such as psychoanalysis or behavioural conditioning that saw problems as 'caused by past events'. The past affects us to the extent that it has shaped current construing and attitudes: exploration of the past is useful in understanding and getting inside a person's construct system but is not in itself necessarily central to the processes of therapeutic change and problem resolution. This was a radical departure in the practice of psychotherapy in the mid-twentieth century, which is still as relevant and compelling today as it was when first introduced.

From Dualities to Constructs

We have now completed this brief survey of the philosophical background of our approach. We have looked at Kelly's basic assumptions, each of which raises important philosophical issues and debates. A constant theme that is evident is the idea of *dualities*—pairs of alternative *positions* on things, each of which critiques the other but requires it in order to make full sense. We will see that these are what Kelly calls 'constructs', or in this case, *philosophical constructs*. Problems arise when distinctions are used as if they are part of an eternal reality that we are stuck with: when *dualisms* such as *body* versus *mind* or *yin* and *yang* are seen as objectively separate, rather than distinctions which we human beings draw in order to make sense of and deal with the world.

The idea that the mind divides up the world into *binary oppositions*, a view that can be found in the structuralism of disciplines like linguistics (de Saussure, 1959) and anthropology (Levi-Strauss, 1962), has been strongly critiqued in the post-modern movement (Polkinghorne, 1995). It is seen as the basis of prejudice where 'us versus them' discriminations are set up between a group which is privileged in comparison to a rejected or demeaned other, for example in relation to gender (Cixous, 2000). If some of these distinctions are used in discriminatory thinking, in which one pole is valorised at the expense of the other, that is not the fault of constructs themselves, but of the way people make use of particular distinctions and judgments based on them. To reject the idea of bipolar discrimination itself is to throw the baby out with the bathwater. Constructs are, rather, vital tools that we cannot avoid using. It is in the nature of human functioning that we form a 'cleavage line' across complex continuities in order to make sense of things, to act and to make decisions in order to survive in the world at all (Kelly, 1955, p. 57). Indeed, Kelly's methods, used in investigating extremism, show that PCP itself is a radical, critical approach which exposes and seeks to understand prejudicial thinking, for example in studies of radicalisation (Naffi & Davidson, 2017; Winter & Muhanna-Matar, 2020) and of Nazi war criminals (Reed et al., 2014) where the constructs that guide and justify the subjects' actions are carefully identified and analysed.

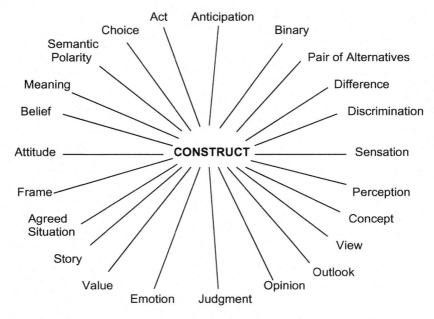

Fig. 2.2 Meaning and scope of the word 'construct' (Procter, 2009a)

Figure 2.2 illustrates how Kelly's brilliant conception of the construct brings together a wide range of aspects of human experience including attitudes, perception, sensation, discrimination, belief, opinion, values, motivation, emotion, action, and choice. It transcends the disciplinary domains of biology, psychology, sociology, and anthropology. As Procter (2009a) writes:

The Construct 'unifies a surprising range of apparently unrelated psychological concepts or aspects of human experience. This could be misconstrued, as if all these aspects could be reduced to a basic idea of the construct as simply a difference or discrimination. But the vision here is precisely the reverse of reductionist. Rather than seeing human experience as consisting of a lot of unrelated aspects, as taught in traditional psychology, the construct embodies the holistic nature of experience. It is all of the things on the outside of the circle. By linking them all and drawing them into itself, it becomes something that can reflect the extraordinary nature of human functioning. So rather than reducing anything, this conception elevates our psychology to do justice to what we are'. (pp. 22–23)

We will now turn, in Chapter 3, to an examination of how Kelly lays out his approach in detail.

Notes

1. Full siblings (except for identical twins) share 50% on average of their genetics. Because of their unique position in the family structure, siblings actually experience a *non-shared environment* (see Dunn & Plomin, 1991).
2. 'Phenomenology as a method of inquiry is well exemplified in personal construct psychology' (Warren, 1985, pp. 261–262); '(PCP) is a phenomenological approach – one that is primarily interested in the way in which the world appears to people' (Butt, 2004, p. 22); see Armezzani and Chiari (2014) for a detailed discussion of this connection.
3. A similar vision is expressed by Bateson (1972a) and the idea of the *ecology of mind*: 'nothing is separate from anything else' (Shotter, 2015, p. 8).
4. Daniel Stern 'sets the dynamic experience of movement as the original source of psychological life' (Español, Martínez, Bordoni, Camarasa, & Carretero, 2014). The infant, for Stern, is fundamentally drawn to 'forms of vitality', these being crucial in interpersonal encounters and later, the basis of our attraction to dynamic art forms such as dance, drama, and cinema (Stern, 2010).
5. We shall see later, in Chapter 3, how *construing* for Kelly is not necessarily *cognitive* or in *language*. The baby can already distinguish hunger, cold, or pain from satisfaction, warmth, and comfort. Construing embraces *feelings, emotions*, and *actions* as well as *thoughts*. Words and other symbols are attached to these (Kelly, 1955).
6. The origin of this vision came from combining Kellian theory with insights derived from the family systems approach of people like Bateson, Haley, and Watzlawick (see Procter, 1981, 1985a, and Chapter 4).
7. This pattern of three positions in which one mediates the conflict between another two will be seen later to form the basis of Ugazio's model of Semantic Polarities (Procter & Ugazio, 2017; Ugazio, 2013).

8. This is what Boszormenyi-Nagy (1987) calls 'multilateral partiality', a more active stance than mere 'neutrality'.
9. Kelly uses the terms 'man' and 'he', etc. consistently with his generation. The overall egalitarian spirit of PCP with its emphasis on respect for the 'person' is already part of the thrust to overcome sexism and other forms of discrimination.
10. It can also be found later in Husserl's phenomenology: 'If I pick up an apple, I have the expectation that I can bite into it…Each act of perception takes place within a horizon of anticipations. I know I will be able to see the other sides of a table if I walk around it' (Moran, 2000, p. 162).
11. This also connects with Husserl, who in his phenomenology stressed how important this process is in our apprehension of the world in what he called 'boundless free variation'—see Dougherty (1980).
12. Hookway (2012, p. 172). This emphasis on the role of hypotheses about future events has its origin in Peirce's extension of logic to include 'abduction' or 'retroduction'. More can be found on this in Procter (2016a).

References

Anderson, E. (2014). Dewey's moral philosophy. In E. N. Zalta (Ed.), *The Stanford Encyclopedia of Philosophy* (Spring 2014 ed.). https://plato.stanford.edu/archives/spr2014/entries/dewey-moral. Accessed 25 January 2018.

Armezzani, M., & Chiari, G. (2014). Ideas for a phenomenological interpretation and elaboration of personal construct theory: Part 2. Husserl and Kelly: A case of commonality. *Costruttivismi, 1,* 168–185.

Bateson, G. (1972a). *Steps to an Ecology of Mind.* Chicago: University of Chicago Press.

Boszormenyi-Nagy, I. (1987). *Foundations of Contextual Therapy: Collected Papers of Ivan Boszormenyi-Nagy, M.D.* New York: Brunner/Mazel.

Brentano, F. (1995). *Psychology from an Empirical Standpoint.* London: Routledge.

Butt, T. (2000). Pragmatism, constructivism and ethics. *Journal of Constructivist Psychology, 13,* 85–101.

Butt, T. (2004). Understanding, explanation, and personal constructs. *Personal Construct Theory and Practice, 1,* 21–27.

Chiari, G. (2017a). *George A. Kelly and His Personal Construct Theory.* https://drive.google.com/file/d/0BwZ5ZCZCN9j-MGZ3bFlpT1hDQVU/view. Accessed 25 January 2018.

Cixous, H. (2000). Sorties. In D. Lodge & N. Wood (Eds.), *Modern Criticism and Theory: A Reader* (3rd ed., pp. 358–365). London: Longman.

De Saussure, F. (1959). *Course in General Linguistics.* New York: The Philosophical Library.

Dewey, J. (1932). *Ethics. The Later Works, 1925–1953* (Vol. 7). Carbondale: Southern Illinois University Press.

Dougherty, C. J. (1980). The common root of Husserl's and Peirce's phenomenologies. *The New Scholasticism, 54,* 305–325.

Dunn, J., & Plomin, R. (1991). Why are siblings so different? The significance of differences in sibling experiences within the family. *Family Process, 30*(3), 271–283.

Español, S., Martínez, M., Bordoni, M., Camarasa, R., & Carretero, S. (2014). Forms of vitality play in infancy. *Integrative Psychological and Behavioral Science, 48,* 479–502.

Fransella, F. (1995). *George Kelly.* London: Sage.

Gergen, K. (1994). *Realities and Relationships: Soundings in Social Construction.* Cambridge: Harvard University Press.

Hinkle, D. N. (1970). The game of personal constructs. In D. Bannister (Ed.), *Perspectives in Personal Construct Theory* (pp. 91–110). London: Academic Press.

Hobart, R. E. (1934). Free will as involving determination and inconceivable without it. *Mind, 43*(169), 1–27.

Hookway, C. (2012). *The Pragmatic Maxim: Essays on Peirce and Pragmatism.* Oxford, UK: Oxford University Press.

James, W. (2003). Does consciousness exist? Reprinted in *Essays in Radical Empiricism* (pp. 1–20). New York: Dover.

Kelly, G. A. (1955). *The Psychology of Personal Constructs. Vol. I, II.* New York: Norton (2nd printing: 1991, London and New York: Routledge).

Kelly, G. A. (1959). *Values, knowledge and social control.* Centre for PCP document, Fransella/Mair Collection, University of Hertfordshire.

Kelly, G. A. (1969a). Sin and psychotherapy. In B. Maher (Ed.), *Clinical Psychology and Personality: The Selected Papers of George Kelly* (pp. 165–188). New York: Wiley.

Kelly, G. A. (1969b). Personal construct theory and the psychotherapeutic interview. In B. Maher (Ed.), *Clinical Psychology and Personality: The Selected Papers of George Kelly* (pp. 224–264). New York: Wiley.

Levi-Strauss, C. (1962). *Totemism.* Harmondsworth, UK: Penguin.

Mair, J. M. M. (2015a). The community of self. In D. A. Winter & N. Reed (Eds.), *Toward a Radical Re-definition of Psychology: The Selected Works of Miller Mair* (pp. 102–112). London: Routledge.

Misak, C. (2011). Presidential address: American pragmatism and indispensability arguments. *Transactions of the Charles S. Peirce Society, 47,* 261–273.

Moran, D. (2000). *Introduction to Phenomenology.* London: Routledge.

Naffi, N., & Davidson, A.-L. (2017). Engaging host society youth in exploring how they construe the influence of social media on the resettlement of Syrian refugees. *Personal Construct Theory and Practice, 14,* 116–128.

Peirce, C. S. (1998a). Some consequences of four incapacities. In E. C. Moore (Ed.), *Charles S. Peirce: The Essential Writings* (pp. 85–118). New York: Prometheus Books.

Peirce, C. S. (1998b). Review of the works of George Berkeley. In E. C. Moore (Ed.), *Charles S. Peirce: The Essential Writings* (pp. 51–63). New York: Prometheus Books.

Peirce, C. S. (1998c). How to make your ideas clear. In E. C. Moore (Ed.), *Charles S. Peirce: The Essential Writings* (pp. 137–157). New York: Prometheus Books.

Peirce, C. S. (1998d). What pragmatism is. In E. C. Moore (Ed.), *Charles S. Peirce: The Essential Writings* (pp. 262–280). New York: Prometheus Books.

Polkinghorne, D. E. (1995). Piaget's and Derrida's contributions to a constructivist psychotherapy. *Journal of Constructivist Psychology, 8,* 269–282.

Procter, H. G. (1981). Family construct psychology: An approach to understanding and treating families. In S. Walrond-Skinner (Ed.), *Developments in Family Therapy: Theories and Applications Since 1948* (pp. 350–366). London: Routledge and Kegan Paul.

Procter, H. G. (1985a). A construct approach to family therapy and systems intervention. In E. Button (Ed.), *Personal Construct Theory and Mental Health* (pp. 327–350). Beckenham, UK: Croom Helm.

Procter, H. G. (2009a). The construct. In R. J. Butler (Ed.), *Reflections in Personal Construct Theory* (pp. 21–40). Chichester, UK: Wiley-Blackwell.

Procter, H. G. (2014a). Peirce's contributions to constructivism and personal construct psychology: I. Philosophical aspects. *Personal Construct Theory & Practice, 11,* 6–33.

Procter, H. G. (2016a). Peirce's contributions to constructivism and personal construct psychology: II. Science, logic and inquiry. *Personal Construct Theory & Practice, 13,* 210–265.

Procter, H. G. (2016b). PCP, culture and society. In D. A. Winter & N. Reed (Eds.), *The Wiley Handbook of Personal Construct Psychology* (pp. 139–153). Chichester, UK: Wiley-Blackwell.

Procter, H. G. (2016c). Useful questions in interviewing families and children. *Rivista Italiana di Costrutivismo, 4,* 124–134.

Procter, H. G., & Procter, M. J. (2008). The use of qualitative grids to examine the development of the construct of good and evil in Byron's play 'Cain: A mystery'. *Journal of Constructivist Psychology, 21,* 343–354.

Procter, H. G., & Ugazio, V. (2017). Family constructs and semantic polarities: A convergent perspective? In D. A. Winter, P. Cummins, H. G. Procter, & N. Reed (Eds.), *Personal Construct Psychology at 60: Papers from the 21st International Congress* (pp. 68–89). Newcastle upon Tyne, UK: Cambridge Scholars Publishing.

Radley, A. (1979). Construing as praxis. In P. Stringer & D. Bannister (Eds.), *Constructs of Sociality and Individuality* (pp. 73–90). London: Academic Press.

Raskin, J. D., & Debany, A. E. (2018). The inescapability of ethics and the impossibility of 'anything goes': A constructivist model of ethical meaning making. *Journal of Constructivist Psychology, 31,* 343–360.

Reed, N., Winter, D., Schulz, J., Aslan, E., Soldevilla, J. M., & Kuzu, D. (2014). An exemplary life? A personal construct analysis of the autobiography of Rudolf Hoess, commandant of Auschwitz. *Journal of Constructivist Psychology, 27,* 274–288.

Rorty, R. (1999). *Philosophy and Social Hope.* London: Penguin Books.

Schütz, A. (1971). *Collected Papers Vol I: The Problem of Social Reality.* The Hague: Martinus Nijhoff.

Shotter, J. (2011, March 5–9). *Language, joint action, and the ethical domain: The importance of the relations between our living bodies and their surroundings.* Paper presented at IIIrd Congreso de Psicologia y Responsabilidad Social. Bogota, Colombia.

Shotter, J. (2015). On being dialogical: An ethics of 'attunement'. *Context, 137,* 8–11.

Stam, H. J. (1998). Personal construct theory and social constructionism: Difference and dialogue. *Journal of Constructivist Psychology, 11,* 187–203.

Stern, D. (2010). *Forms of Vitality: Exploring Dynamic Experience in Psychology, the Arts, Psychotherapy, and Development*. Oxford, UK: Oxford University Press.

Stojnov, D. (1996). Kelly's theory of ethics: Hidden, mislaid or misleading? *Journal of Constructivist Psychology, 9*, 185–199.

Stojnov, D., Miletić, V., & Džinović, V. (2017). Subjectivity: Kelly's discourse and Foucault's constructs. *Personal Construct Theory & Practice, 14*, 146–157.

Trevarthen, C. B. (1979). Communication and cooperation in early infancy: A description of primary intersubjectivity. In B. Bullowa (Ed.), *Before Speech*. Cambridge, UK: Cambridge University Press.

Ugazio, V. (2013). *Semantic Polarities and Psychopathologies in the Family: Permitted and Forbidden Stories*. New York: Routledge.

Von Glasersfeld, E. (1984). An Introduction to radical constructivism. In P. Watzlawick (Ed.), *The Invented Reality* (pp. 17–40). New York: Norton.

Von Glasersfeld, E. (1995). *Radical Constructivism: A Way of Knowing and Learning*. London: Falmer Press.

Walker, B. M. (1992). Values and Kelly's theory: Becoming a good scientist. *International Journal of Personal Construct Psychology, 5*, 259–269.

Warren, W. G. (1985). Personal construct psychology and contemporary philosophy: Examination of alignments. In D. Bannister (Ed.), *Issues and Approaches in Personal Construct Theory* (pp. 253–262). London: Academic Press.

Winter, D. A., & Muhanna-Matar, A. (2020). Cycles of construing in radicalization and deradicalization: A study of Salafist Muslims. *Journal of Constructivist Psychology, 33*, 58–88.

Wittgenstein, L. (1969). *On Certainty*. New York: Harper and Row.

3

Personal Construct Theory

The Originator of the Theory

George Alexander Kelly was born in 1905 on his parents' farm in Perth, Kansas, USA to a father who had been trained as a Presbyterian church minister and a mother who was the daughter of a sea captain. He was an only child, who was initially schooled at home, and there has been speculation about how the isolation of his birthplace and loneliness of his childhood might have contributed to his concern with imagining alternative worlds (Bannister, 1979, personal communication in Neimeyer, 1985; Cromwell, 2016; Fransella, 1995).

The diversity of Kelly's later educational background has been mentioned in Chapter 2, but when he eventually took up his first job, it was to teach psychology at Fort Hays Kansas State College. It was there that he ventured into clinical psychology, setting up a clinical service for school-aged children and adults and a travelling clinic for children. Returning from being commissioned as a naval aviation psychologist during the Second World War, and following a brief spell at the University of Maryland, he moved to Ohio State University, where he took over from Carl Rogers and eventually became Professor and Director of

© The Author(s) 2020
H. Procter and D. A. Winter, *Personal and Relational Construct Psychotherapy*,
Palgrave Texts in Counselling and Psychotherapy,
https://doi.org/10.1007/978-3-030-52177-6_3

Clinical Psychology. After 20 years at Ohio State University, he became Distinguished Professorial Chair in Theoretical Psychology at Brandeis University, where he worked for two years before his death in 1967.

While at Fort Hays Kansas State College, Kelly began writing a *Handbook of Clinical Practice* for his clinical students. In this handbook can be traced the origins of *The Psychology of Personal Constructs*, published in 1955, the two-volume magnum opus that was no less than an exposition of an entire new psychology. This psychology was intended as a radical alternative to the dominant psychologies of Kelly's day, with their mechanistic (treating people like machines), reductionist (reducing whole people to fragmented components), and primarily deterministic (seeing people's lives as determined by, for example, their biological make-up or their histories) assumptions. Since Kelly had published very little prior to this, his book must have come as a great surprise to much of the psychological and psychotherapeutic community—but not to those who, as students, had attended his regular Thursday night discussion groups about his developing manuscript.

Kelly's book had a mixed reception, but his theory and its associated methods became increasingly popular over the years, particularly in the United Kingdom, where they were publicised in particular by the clinical psychologist Don Bannister, subsequently in collaboration with Fay Fransella (Bannister & Fransella, 1986) and Miller Mair (Bannister & Mair, 1968). Although developed within the clinical sphere, the theory and its methods have had an extraordinarily wide range of application in fields as diverse as education, business, organisational consultancy, the arts, and politics (Walker & Winter, 2007; Winter & Reed, 2016). Personal construct theory has been seen as the forerunner of many subsequent developments in psychology and psychotherapy (including some for which Kelly may not necessarily have considered this a compliment!), but arguably is still radical today, just as when it first appeared on the psychological scene (Winter, 2012).

The Theory

Kelly's theory is highly unusual in being set out in a very formal way, as a 'Fundamental Postulate' and 11 corollaries to this postulate, with each word in these carefully chosen and precisely defined. Occasionally it uses new terms created by Kelly, partly so as not to borrow terms from other theories, which would each have come with a set of underlying assumptions not necessarily compatible with those of personal construct theory. Also, when familiar terms are used, Kelly sometimes defines these in a rather unusual way. These aspects of the theory do not make Kelly's two volumes the easiest of reads, but our intention in what follows is to provide a clear and relatively simple explanation of the theory and its terminology, and more importantly of the guiding principles of its use in therapeutic practice in a way that does not feel constrained by too much weighty jargon.

The Underlying Philosophical Assumption

As indicated in Chapter 2, the basic philosophical assumption of personal construct theory is *constructive alternativism*, which asserts that 'all of our present interpretations of the universe are subject to revision or replacement' (Kelly, 1955, p. 15). This is the principal, and optimistic, message that the personal construct psychotherapist attempts to convey to his or her clients, namely that they not only construct their worlds but can reconstruct them. Notwithstanding that some people's circumstances give much greater freedom for this than those of others, no matter how dire one's situation may appear to be, it can always be viewed differently.

The Fundamental Postulate

As also mentioned in Chapter 2, anticipation of events was key to Kelly's theory, as reflected in his Fundamental Postulate that 'A person's processes are psychologically channelized by the ways in which he anticipates events' (Kelly, 1955, p. 47). Here Kelly is saying that people are primarily concerned with predicting their worlds rather than, for example, with seeking pleasure. As we shall see, it is important to bear this in mind when trying to understand the seemingly incomprehensible actions of a client.

The Corollaries

Construction Corollary

The first corollary to the Fundamental Postulate goes on to elaborate on the process of anticipation, stating that 'A person anticipates events by construing their replications' (Kelly, 1955, p. 50). This essentially means that the person seeks and interprets repeated themes, and similarities and contrasts, in his or her experiences.

Individuality Corollary

The personal nature of construing is highlighted in this corollary: 'Persons differ from each other in their constructions of events' (Kelly, 1955, p. 55). It provides an important reminder to therapists or counsellors that it is all too easy to assume that clients see the world, including their presenting problems, in the same way that they do. While, as we shall see, some aspects of the client's, or some other person's, view of the world may be similar to one's own, no two people will ever construe an event in exactly the same way.

Organisation Corollary

Kelly (1955) states in this corollary that 'Each person characteristically evolves, for his convenience in anticipating events, a construction system embracing ordinal relationships between constructs' (p. 56). These constructs, 'transparent patterns or templets which' the person 'creates and then attempts to fit over the realities of which the world is composed' (Kelly, 1955, pp. 8–9), are organised in a hierarchical system in which some, termed *superordinate*, subsume, or embrace, others, termed *subordinate* (i.e., their relationships are 'ordinal'). The implication that some constructs are more important to an individual than others is one that the therapist or counsellor would be well advised to take into account in planning his or her interventions, not least because of Hinkle's (1965) demonstration of the resistance to change of superordinate constructs.

Dichotomy Corollary

Kelly's emphasis on dualities in people's views of the world has been noted in Chapter 2, and is expressed in this corollary in the statement that 'A person's construction system is composed of a finite number of dichotomous constructs' (Kelly, 1955, p. 59). Since constructs are thus viewed as bipolar, the personal construct psychotherapist or counsellor will focus on, and attempt to elicit, contrasts in the client's view of the world, including how the client would view himself or herself without their presenting symptom. Since the particular contrasts that people make are as individual as any other aspect of their construing, such exploration may yield some surprising insights into the client's predicament. For example, if we find that a depressed client's contrast to being depressed is to be arrogant rather than our own contrast between being depressed and being happy, this may help us to understand the client's apparent resistance to the loss of their symptoms.

Choice Corollary

It follows from the bipolarity of constructs that each construct provides the individual with a choice concerning which pole of it is applied to a particular aspect of the world. In the Choice Corollary, Kelly (1955) explains the basis of this choice, namely that 'A person chooses for himself that alternative in a dichotomized construct through which he anticipates the greater possibility for extension and definition of his system' (p. 64). Put more simply, the individual makes the choice (often not at a high level of awareness) that appears to allow the greater possibility for anticipating the world. Viewed in this way, even the most apparently self-destructive choices can seem comprehensible. For example, a classic study by Fransella (1972) demonstrated that for people who stutter, stuttering carries more implications and therefore possibilities for anticipating the world, offering them a more predictable and structured 'way of life', than does fluency. Stuttering will be unlikely to be relinquished by such individuals until fluency carries at least as many implications as does stuttering. The same argument can be applied to any other presenting symptom (Fransella, 1970).

Range Corollary

For Kelly (1955), 'A construct is convenient for the anticipation of a finite range of events only' (p. 68). Every construct has a *focus of convenience*, the aspects of the world, or *elements* (the term which Kelly applied to anything which may be construed), to which it is maximally applicable, and a *range of convenience*, including other elements to which it can be applied but not so well, but beyond which are elements to which it cannot be applied at all. For example, a person may readily apply the construct 'impressionist – expressionist' to paintings, these being in the construct's focus of convenience, and may, although less easily, apply the construct to other works of art, which are therefore within its range of convenience, but it may be difficult to apply the construct to different breeds of dogs. In psychology and psychiatry, approaches that view and treat humans as if they were, for example, machines or computers might be considered to involve the use of constructs in areas which are at the very limits of, if not beyond, their ranges of convenience.

Experience Corollary

As we have seen in Chapter 2, Kelly viewed people as operating rather like scientists in that they form hypotheses about the world, test these out, and if necessary, revise them. This is the process that is described in the Experience Corollary: 'A person's construction system varies as he successively construes the replications of events' (Kelly, 1955, p. 72). It is a cyclical process, as set out by Kelly (1970a) in the *Experience*

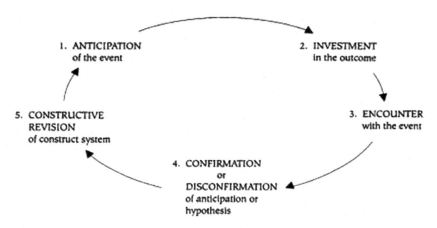

Fig. 3.1 The experience cycle (from Oades & Viney, 2012)

Cycle (see Fig. 3.1), in which a person anticipates an event, invests in this anticipation, encounters the event, finds the anticipation to be confirmed or disconfirmed (or, in other words, validated or invalidated), revises his or her construing if invalidated, and then repeats the process with a new anticipation. As Landfield (1980) has indicated, certain significant others (e.g., family members) may become the principal 'validating agents' for an individual's constructions, and this is a role that a psychotherapist or counsellor may come to be expected to fulfil.

Modulation Corollary

This corollary introduces the notion of permeability, the degree to which a construct can be applied to new elements of a person's world. It states that 'The variation in a person's construction system is limited by the permeability of the constructs within whose range of convenience the variants lie' (Kelly, 1955, p. 77). If a person is to adapt to new experiences, it is beneficial for his or her constructs, particularly superordinate constructs, to be relatively permeable.

Fragmentation Corollary

A construct system will generally consist of a number of subsystems. For example, many people have separate subsystems of constructs concerning issues in their personal and in their professional lives, and in each of these areas of life there may also be separate subsystems of constructs (e.g., in their personal lives, concerning parenthood, romantic relationships, cooking, and football teams), as illustrated in Fig. 3.2. These subsystems may not be entirely consistent: as stated in the Fragmentation Corollary, 'A person may successively employ a variety of construction subsystems which are inferentially incompatible with each other' (Kelly, 1955, p. 83). One of the advantages of permeable superordinate constructs is that they may be able to *subsume*, and provide a resolution of inconsistencies in, different subsystems. Consider, for example, the person who construes himself or herself as sometimes behaving kindly, and sometimes cruelly, towards his or her child but is able to encompass both of these behaviours within a superordinate construction of good parenthood, involving sometimes having to be cruel in order to be kind.

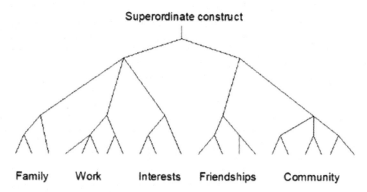

Fig. 3.2   The construct system as a hierarchical tree

Commonality Corollary

The first of Kelly's corollaries to be explicitly concerned with interpersonal relationships states that 'To the extent that one person employs a construction of experience which is similar to that employed by another, his psychological processes are similar to those of the other person' (Kelly, 1955, p. 90). Although each person's view of the world is individual, this does not preclude there being areas of construing that are similar to those of at least some other people. As we shall consider in more detail in the next chapter, such similarities may be particularly apparent in people within a particular social group, for example a family or a cultural group.

Sociality Corollary

For Kelly, the basis of all significant interpersonal relationships, including that between therapist and client, is the viewing of the world through the other's eyes. As stated in the Sociality Corollary, 'To the extent that one person construes the construction processes of another, he may play a role in a social process involving the other person' (Kelly, 1955, p. 95). The roles that we play in our relationships are based on our understanding of how the other people in these relationships view the world.

Diagnostic Constructs

The clinician's construing of the construction processes of the client is facilitated by the use of a set of 'professional', or diagnostic, constructs provided by Kelly (1955) that may be applied to these processes.

Covert Construing

Some of the diagnostic constructs concern construing that is covert, or at a low level of cognitive awareness. One such diagnostic construct is the notion that some constructs are *preverbal* in that they have no consistent verbal symbols (instead perhaps being experienced as feelings or bodily sensations that cannot be put into words), possibly because they were developed before the individual began using language. Since they are likely to have been developed in infancy, these constructs are often concerned with dependency relationships with people who were particularly significant at the time. For other constructs, while one pole is at a high level of awareness, the other is not, being termed as *submerged*. This may, for example, involve viewing other people in a uniformly positive light, with little apparent awareness of negatively evaluated contrast poles of the constructs concerned. As we shall see later, a rosy view of the world such as this is highly vulnerable to invalidation, which may sometimes lead to tragic consequences (Howells, 1983), but the attempted avoidance of which may also manifest itself in psychological problems (Winter & Gournay, 1987). A further type of covert construing is that an element of the person's experience or part of their structure of constructs may be *suspended* from awareness if it is incompatible with the remainder of the individual's personal construct system or its implications are intolerable.

Structure of Construing

We have already mentioned one diagnostic construct related to the structure of construing, namely that some constructs occupy a *superordinate* position in the individual's system while others are *subordinate*. A further, and related, distinction that the therapist would do well to make is that between a client's *core* and *peripheral* constructs. Since the former are central to one's 'identity and existence', it would not be wise for the therapist to launch without due care into challenges to the client's core constructs.

Strategies of Construing

Some of Kelly's diagnostic constructs may be considered to concern strategies that individuals use in an attempt to avoid invalidation of construing. One such pair of strategies contrasts *constriction* with *dilation*. In the former, the person who is faced with incompatibilities in their construing may draw in the outer boundaries of their perceptual field in order to minimise these. Many psychological problems can be viewed in terms of clients constricting their perceptual fields to a very limited area of attention, for example food for the person with an eating disorder, and excluding more potentially invalidating areas such as interpersonal relationships. Dilation, by contrast, involves the person extending the perceptual field, throwing himself or herself into new experiences, in order to try to deal with incompatibilities in construing by reorganising the construct system at a more comprehensive level. This strategy is also not without its potential problems, however, in that 'the person's exploration' may 'outrun his organization' (Kelly, 1955, p. 846).

A further pair of contrasting strategies is *tight* and *loose* construing. The former involves the individual making very precise predictions based upon a system in which constructs are strongly interrelated. In an unpredictable world, such a system is very vulnerable to structural collapse following invalidation. This is not the case in loose construing, where predictions are so vague that it is very difficult to invalidate them, but with the disadvantage that the person's construing provides little basis for their actions and may lead to them being very difficult for other people to understand. Loosening of construing is necessary for the creative generation of new ideas, but for these ideas to be developed into testable predictions, and into creative output, the construct system must be retightened, completing what Kelly (1955) termed a Creativity Cycle. When the two strategies are not used cyclically, but rather one is employed exclusively or persistently, this may, as we shall see in Chapter 7, manifest in psychological problems, just as in the case of the excessive use of either constriction or dilation.

Control

Another cyclical process of construing, which is involved in decision-making, was described by Kelly (1955), in one of his more cumbersome pieces of jargon, as the *Circumspection-Preemption-Control Cycle* (or *C-P-C Cycle*). An understanding of this cycle requires consideration of another distinction that Kelly made between different types of constructs, namely that between *preemptive*, *constellatory*, and *propositional* constructs. Preemptive constructs are those that do not allow any other constructs to be applied to a particular element, as when a person is viewed as a paedophile and nothing but a paedophile. Constellatory constructs do allow other constructs to be applied to an element, but essentially prescribe which constructs and how they are applied. Such construing may be observed in stereotypes, as when a person who is construed as a paedophile is also seen as necessarily being evil, callous, and dishonest. Propositional constructs do not determine the other constructs that may be applied to an element, so that, for example, someone who is regarded to be a paedophile may also be viewed as generous, caring, artistic, and religious, as well as in any number of other ways.

To return to the C-P-C Cycle, it is propositional construing that characterises the Circumspection phase of this cycle, in which the person uses a number of constructs to consider all of the issues involved in a decision. For example, in deciding upon whether someone is a suitable life partner, I may consider whether he or she shares my political beliefs, would be acceptable to my family, whether I love him or her, and whether he or she supports Queens Park Rangers Football Club. In the Preemption phase, the person selects the fundamental issue, or superordinate construct, in the decision. In the example, I may decide that all that matters is whether he or she supports Queens Park Rangers. Finally, in the Control phase, one pole of this construct is chosen as the basis for action. He or she supports Chelsea—therefore we have no future! As with other cycles of construing, an excessive focus on, or conversely dispensing altogether with, a particular phase of the cycle may lead to psychological problems. For example, a person may fail to engage in circumspection and consequently act impulsively; or may fail to leave the Circumspection phase and consequently be trapped in rumination.

Constructs of Transition

Kelly viewed people holistically rather than making the traditional distinctions between cognition, emotion, and motivation. Although he did use conventional emotional terms, he regarded all emotions as being associated with transitions in construing, and provided corresponding definitions of different emotions. For example, he defined *threat* as '*the awareness of imminent comprehensive change in one's core structures*' (Kelly, 1955, p. 489, italics in original). It is a foundation-shaking experience, and its elicitation may be regarded as a fundamental aim of terrorists, as by '9/11' profoundly invalidating Americans' belief in their inviolability in their homeland. However, it is also a common hazard in the therapy room, and, as we have seen, the psychotherapist or counsellor should tread carefully around the client's core constructs. If the anticipated change in core structures is incidental, rather than comprehensive, the resulting experience, in Kelly's view, will be *fear* rather than threat. For Kelly (1955), *anxiety* is '*the recognition that the events with which one is confronted lie outside the range of convenience of one's construct system*' (p. 495, italics in original). Essentially, it is the experience of finding events unconstruable, as with the client who is faced in therapy with having to explore their internal world when previously their approach to problems has been a purely practical one. A further 'emotion' that is very relevant to psychotherapy is *guilt*, the '*perception of one's apparent dislodgment from his core role structure*' (Kelly, 1955, p. 502, italics in original). This definition is a further reflection of the personal emphasis of Kelly's theory in that it indicates that guilt does not necessarily involve transgressing a society's moral code since the person who transgresses such a code will only experience guilt if following this code is part of their core role, their characteristic self-construction in relation to others. The hardened criminal will therefore be unlikely to experience guilt at committing some further offence but instead may feel guilty if construed as being 'soft' towards one of his or her victims. In the therapy room, pushing the client too quickly into some new role that the therapist considers desirable, for example assertiveness for the unassertive client, may do no more than provoke intolerable guilt.

Kelly's (1955) definitions of *aggressiveness* and *hostility* were also rather unusual, as compared to the lay meanings of these terms. For him, aggressiveness was '*the active elaboration of one's perceptual field*' (p. 508, italics in original). It therefore does not have the usual negative connotations of the term, although an aggressive person's constant experimentation may not be entirely comfortable, and may even be threatening, for those around him or her. Hostility, in Kelly's (1955) view, is very different in that it is '*the continued effort to extort valida-tional evidence in favor of a type of social prediction which has already proved itself a failure*' (p. 510, italics in original). The hostile person, rather than reconstruing in the face of invalidation, tries to 'cook the books' by making the social world fit with his or her constructions. Consider, for example, the client who views himself or herself as unfairly rejected by others, but finds this construction being invalidated by a rela-tionship with a therapist who is construed as accepting. The client may then manifest hostility by behaving in such a way, for example repeatedly missing appointments, that is likely to make damn sure that the therapist will reject him or her as well. It is all too easy to respond to hostility by hostility of one's own, and such destructive cycles of hostility have been observed not only in abusive intimate relationships (Doster, 1985) but also in client-professional (Aldridge, 1998) and international (Winter, 2020; Winter & Muhanna-Matar, 2020) relations.

Kelly's view of emotions was extended by McCoy (1981) with her distinction between 'negative emotions', such as threat, fear, anxiety, and guilt, which 'follow unsuccessful construing'; 'positive emotions', which 'follow validation of construing'; and 'behaviours associated with emotion', such as aggression and hostility. It has been suggested that the failures to anticipate which lead to 'negative' emotions are accompa-nied by a high level of physiological arousal (Mancuso, 1976; Mancuso & Adams-Webber, 1982; Mascolo & Mancuso, 1990). While the value judgements implied by construing some emotions as negative and others as positive can be challenged (Winter, 1992), some of McCoy's defini-tions of emotions that were not explicitly considered by Kelly may be useful in understanding a client's experience. For example, the view of anger as involving awareness of invalidation of construing may be valu-able in working with clients with problems involving anger (Cummins, 2005), while the experience of shame (and the fact that this experience is not necessarily accompanied by guilt) may be elucidated by viewing it as dislodgement from others' construing of one's core role (McCoy, 1981). A further elaboration of Kelly's view of 'emotion' is Leitner's (1985a) description of the 'terror', a conglomeration of threat, anxiety, and guilt, that is involved in significant interpersonal relationships, including that between therapist and client, since these involve the potential for core role invalidation.

From Theory Towards Clinical Practice

The reader should now have at least a flavour of personal construct theory and of some of its principal constructs. In Chapter 7, we shall see in more detail how these constructs can be used in understanding the problems presented by our clients, while later chapters, particularly Chapter 8, will further elaborate how Kelly's theory provides the basis for a particular approach to psychotherapy and counselling. First, though, in Chapter 4, we shall present an extension of this theory into the relational sphere.

References

Aldridge, D. (1998). *Suicide: The Tragedy of Hopelessness*. London: Jessica Kingsley.

Bannister, D., & Fransella, F. (1986). *Inquiring Man*. London: Routledge (first published by Penguin (1971)).

Bannister, D., & Mair, J. M. M. (1968). *The Evaluation of Personal Constructs*. London: Academic Press.

Cromwell, R. (2016). Foreword. In D. A. Winter & R. Reed (Eds.), *The Wiley Handbook of Personal Construct Psychology* (pp. xx–xxvii). Chichester, UK: Wiley.

Cummins, P. (2005). The experience of anger. In D. A. Winter & L. L. Viney (Eds.), *Personal Construct Psychotherapy: Advances in Theory, Practice and Research* (pp. 239–255). London: Whurr.

Doster, J. A. (1985). A personal construct assessment of marital violence. In F. Epting & A. W. Landfield (Eds.), *Anticipating Personal Construct Psychology* (pp. 225–232). Lincoln: University of Nebraska Press.

Fransella, F. (1970). Stuttering: Not a symptom but a way of life. *British Journal of Communication Disorders, 5*, 22–29.

Fransella, F. (1972). *Personal Change and Reconstruction: Research on a Treatment of Stuttering*. London: Academic Press.

Fransella, F. (1995). *George Kelly*. London: Sage.

Hinkle, D. N. (1965). *The change of personal constructs from the viewpoint of a theory of construct implications*. Unpublished PhD thesis, Ohio State University.

Howells, K. (1983). Social construing and violent behaviour in mentally abnormal offenders. In J. W. Hinton (Ed.), *Dangerousness: Problems of Assessment and Prediction* (pp. 114–129). London: Allen and Unwin.

Kelly, G. A. (1955). *The Psychology of Personal Constructs. Vol. I, II*. New York: Norton (2nd printing: 1991, London and New York: Routledge).

Kelly, G. A. (1970a). A brief introduction to personal construct theory. In D. Bannister (Ed.), *Perspectives in Personal Construct Theory* (pp. 3–20). London: Academic Press.

Landfield, A. W. (1980). Personal construct psychotherapy: A personal construction. In A. W. Landfield & L. M. Leitner (Eds.), *Personal Construct Psychology: Psychotherapy and Personality* (pp. 122–140). New York: Wiley.

Leitner, L. M. (1985a). The terrors of cognition: On the experiential validity of personal construct theory. In D. Bannister (Ed.), *Issues and Approaches in Personal Construct Theory* (pp. 83–103). London: Academic Press.

Mancuso, J. C. (1976). Current motivational models in the elaboration of personal construct theory. *Nebraska Symposium on Motivation, 24*, 43–97.

Mancuso, J. C., & Adams-Webber, J. R. (1982). Anticipation as a constructive process: The fundamental postulate. In J. C. Mancuso & J. R. Adams-Webber (Eds.), *The Construing Person* (pp. 8–32). New York: Praeger.

Mascolo, M. F., & Mancuso, J. C. (1990). Functioning of epigenetically involved emotion systems: A constructive analysis. *International Journal of Personal Construct Psychology, 3*, 205–222.

McCoy, M. M. (1981). Positive and negative emotion: A personal construct theory interpretation. In H. Bonarius, R. Holland, & S. Rosenberg (Eds.), *Personal Construct Psychology: Recent Advances in Theory and Practice* (pp. 95–104). London: MacMillan.

Neimeyer, R. A. (1985). *The Development of Personal Construct Psychology*. Lincoln: University of Nebraska Press.

Oades, L. G., & Viney, L. L. (2012). Experience cycle methodology: Understanding the construct revision pathway. In P. Caputi, L. L. Viney, B. M. Walker, & N. Crittenden (Eds.), *Personal Construct Methodology* (pp. 129–146). Chichester, UK: Wiley-Blackwell.

Walker, B. M., & Winter, D. A. (2007). The elaboration of personal construct psychology. *Annual Review of Psychology, 58*, 453–477.

Winter, D. A. (1992). *Personal Construct Psychology in Clinical Practice: Theory, Research and Applications*. London: Routledge.

Winter, D. (2012). Still radical after all these years: George Kelly's 'The psychology of personal constructs'. *Clinical Child Psychology and Psychiatry, 18*, 276–283.

Winter, D. A. (2020/in press). Sociality and hostility: A pernicious mix. *Journal of Constructivist Psychology*. Published online, 11 Aug, 2020, from: https://doi.org/10.1080/10720537.2020.1805062.

Winter, D., & Gournay, K. (1987). Constriction and construction in agoraphobia. *British Journal of Medical Psychology, 60*, 233–244.

Winter, D. A., & Muhanna-Matar, A. (2020). Cycles of construing in radicalization and deradicalization: A study of Salafist Muslims. *Journal of Constructivist Psychology, 33*, 58–88.

Winter, D. A., & Reed, N. (Eds.). (2016). *The Wiley Handbook of Personal Construct Psychology*. Chichester, UK: Wiley-Blackwell.

4

From the Personal to the Relational

The Primacy of Intersubjectivity

The essence of personal construct psychology is that a person uses bipolar constructs to make sense of the world and to anticipate events. As we said earlier, we wish to preserve Kelly's brilliant and original formulation but to place it within a wider framework, introducing the term 'relational'. Why? Writers from a number of diverse traditions including phenomenology, family systems theory, social constructionism, and developmental psychology have argued that social interaction or 'intersubjectivity' has primacy over the development of persons as individual entities. This has often led to a critique of PCP as being guilty of individualism and of ignoring the vital role of social and relational processes in our experience and development.[1] But in his framework, Kelly had already contributed significantly to an understanding of human relationships, in particular with his Commonality and Sociality Corollaries. By elaborating his contribution and placing it into a wider relational framework, we shall show how his vision throws much light on those approaches which emphasise the social, sometimes at the expense of the individual and personal.

© The Author(s) 2020
H. Procter and D. A. Winter, *Personal and Relational Construct Psychotherapy*,
Palgrave Texts in Counselling and Psychotherapy,
https://doi.org/10.1007/978-3-030-52177-6_4

The beginning of these developments occurred in research on the families of people diagnosed with schizophrenia, using the theory and methods of PCP as a framework of inquiry (Procter, 1978). An outcome of this work was the development of an approach which combined the insights of PCP with family systems theory, which emphasised the presence of 'patterns of interaction' which had a life of their own, regardless of the situation in which family members found themselves or what issue they might be negotiating. This work had been inspired by cybernetic theory, which described systems which self-regulate through corrective feedback and which utilised concepts such as 'escalation', 'homeostasis', 'distance regulation', and 'hierarchy' and saw a certain maintenance of the structures of relationships in families and other organisations. In his anthropological work in the 1930's, Bateson (1972a) described two modes of dyadic interaction: symmetrical escalation and complementary escalation. In the former, the contribution of one person is met with a *similar* reaction from the other person. This characterises conflicts and competition between people and indeed arms races between nations. This pattern could escalate but can also be met with 'regulation' in which a complementary configuration could take over. Complementary interaction characterises relations where two participants bring *different* contributions that 'fit together' such as in speaking/listening, dominance/submission, or where one person is depressed and feeling misunderstood and met with an injunction to 'cheer up' from the other. The core of this approach is the concept of 'circular causality', which regarded interaction as a *continuous process*. Watzlawick, Beavin, and Jackson (1968) wrote:

> Although an interactional sequence may be *punctuated* by the participants or the observer into a pattern of one-way causality, such a sequence is in fact circular, and the apparent 'response' must also be a stimulus for the next event in this interdependent chain. (p. 126, our italics)

The participants themselves, when interacting, tend to 'punctuate' it into segments, for example in saying, 'that makes me feel really sad', or 'it's your fault I am getting angry'. The relational view emphasises that the way we feel, think, and act is a product of a continuous co-creation, or of 'joint action', as we will see below. The moral of this view was that we should never look at a piece of human action, emotion, or thinking without looking at the immediate relational context in which it is occurring. This is to 'think systemically' as opposed, for example, to a process of psychiatric diagnosis or psychoanalytic interpretation, in which a 'symptom' is abstracted or 'punctuated' out of its context without regard to what the person is being confronted with and experiencing at the time, in the relational 'politics' of the situation.

A second source of claims for the primacy of the relational or inter-subjectivity can be found in various traditions in twentieth century philosophy. As early as 1904, the pragmatist Josiah Royce wrote that we are 'individuals only in social relations with others…The social is so primordial that even our conceptions of nature, as well as of the individual self are not initiatory but socially grounded' (cited in Sherover, 1987, p. 150). Mead (1962) argued that 'the self is not something that exists first and then enters into relationship with others; rather it is better characterized as an eddy in the social current' (p. 182). The phenomenologist Schütz (1971) said, 'the world of daily life into which we are born is from the outset an intersubjective world' (p. 218). Merleau-Ponty wrote that self and other are 'no longer those of head-on collisions between two consciousnesses, but the *dovetailing* into one another of two experiences which, without ever coinciding, stem from one and the same world' (cited in Spiegelberg, 1976, p. 521, our italics).

Developmental psychologists have also emphasised this 'relational primacy' over the contributions of individuals. Vygotsky (1978) argued in the 1920s that the child's thinking and all 'higher mental functions' are the result of internalising conversations and interactions originally occurring *between* people. Contemporary research in developmental psychology uses video to examine the interactions between infants and their caretakers. This indicates a process, for Trevarthen (1979), of 'primary intersubjectivity' already evident in interactions with the newly born child. Trevarthen and Delafield-Butt (2017) describe how alert infants were ready immediately after birth to imitate a wide range of movements of another person's head, eyes, mouth, vocal sounds, and hand gestures and to participate in a game of imitating tongue protrusion. Trevarthen and Aitken (2001, p. 4) write that 'the infant has an innate motive for companionship and is born with an awareness especially receptive to subjective states in other persons'. This implies a greater richness in what Kelly (1955, p. 459) called *preverbal construing* than we had ever been aware of before. Trevarthen and Aitken describe an active self-and-other awareness in infancy, an inherent and purposeful intersubjectivity, and claim that 'infants have intersubjective capacities as part of their natural intelligence' (p. 19). They argue that, 'it is a logical category error[2] to infer that interaction between subjects can be explained by decomposing their behaviours and perceptual discriminations into cognitive components' (p. 4), and that these should be viewed as the *outcomes* of an intersubjective process. This involves participants *sharing control*, requiring that the infant can predict what the other will do (Trevarthen, 1979).

This process of sharing control has been called 'joint action', a term introduced by Blumer (1966, p. 540) as a 'collective form of action that is constituted by the fitting together of the lines of behaviour of the separate participants'. Shotter (2011, p. 2) writes, 'instead of one person first acting individually and independently of another, and then the second replying, by acting individually and independently of the first, we act jointly, as a collective-we. We do this bodily, in a "living" way, spontaneously, without us having first "to work out" how to respond to each other'. Merleau-Ponty (1962) even claimed a merging of perspectives:

> In the experience of dialogue, there is constituted between the other person and myself a common ground; my thought and his (sic) are interwoven into a single fabric, my words and those of my interlocutor are called forth by *the state of the discussion*, and they are inserted into a shared operation of which neither of us is the creator. We are collaborators for each other in consummate reciprocity. Our perspectives merge into each other, and we co-exist through a common world. (p. 413)

Esterson (1970) draws a similar view from Sartre using the terms 'praxis' and 'process': 'Process refers to the events or pattern of events of which no doer or agent is the author. Thus, praxis expresses the intentions of a person or group, while process does not' (p. 2).

How does all this square with Kelly's claim in the Choice Corollary that as individuals we are continuously making choices between courses of action governed by bipolar personal constructs, and indeed that we are *persons* with unique constructions of the world?

Intersubjectivity and PCP

The first point to be made in answering this question concerns *anticipation*. It is interesting for us that Trevarthen (1979) claims that this capacity for prediction or *anticipation* is present in the infant at such an early stage. A close observation of the timing of interactions in videos indicates that the infant is already active and capable of *anticipating* the carer's response in interchanges by an interval of time undetectable in ordinary observation. Even a blind girl of five months was anticipating the rhythm of her mother's singing with her left hand by a third of a second, just like a professional musical conductor (Malloch & Trevarthen, 2018). This supports Kelly's (1955) view of the centrality of anticipation in his Fundamental Postulate, and that 'our lives are wholly oriented toward the anticipation of events' (p. 157). That this is already evident so early in the child's life is deeply validating of Kelly's vision. The infant in this sense is already functioning as a *person* in Kelly's terms. Anticipation clearly plays a key role in all processes of intersubjectivity and joint action. In a tennis game, it is vital that each player anticipates not only the speed, direction and spin of the oncoming ball, but the intentions of the other player in terms of the micro-moves they may make and the strategies that the opponent is planning.

Individuals engaging in joint action are faced with a 'process', a 'single fabric', a 'pattern of events', a 'state of discussion', and a coordination of activities, which 'cannot be traced back to the plans or intentions of participating individuals' (Chiari, 2017b, p. 64). However, this cannot mean that we have become passive entities propelled exclusively by social forces. We clearly act 'spontaneously' and do not have to 'work out' how to respond to each other (Shotter, 2011) but still, we are making our own unique sense of the situation and acting accordingly. If we pause at any moment a video of a conversation, the participants can report on what their thoughts, feelings, and reasons were at each instant. We are constrained by the game in which we are collaborating, in which rules of grammar and moral decorum apparently govern each person's conduct, but we are still making choices for which we are rightly deemed responsible. Kelly, in his Choice Corollary, states that choices are made in anticipating the greater possibility for extension and definition of the person's individual construct system. But the reality of joint action in relationships suggests the need for a broadening of the corollary here to a recognition that each actor is choosing to extend, define, or challenge a *joint construct system*. Persons are involved in co-creating, in the social situation, a way of construing the world for all the participants involved. We could call this *joint choice*. The participants are choosing, in an ongoing manner, to participate, cooperate, and to beg to differ. If they are reluctant and choose not to, this is still part of the joint action: as Watzlawick et al. (1968) insist, 'one cannot not communicate' (p. 49).

By asserting that participants in social interaction are continuously making choices in their joint actions, we are inherently critiquing the idea of 'circular causality' with its implication of mechanical cause-effect links between the actions of one person and another. But it is possible to preserve the vision of the early family therapists by seeing that the 'loops' or 'circularities' that they describe, with no clear beginning and end points, respect that the participants involved are always *construing* the actions of the others rather than simply reacting to them in a causal manner. Building on the work of Watzlawick et al., this led to the introduction of the 'bow-tie diagram' (Procter, 1985a, see Chapter 5), named from its shape, as depicted in Figs. 4.1 and 4.2. In this situation, a man at the beginning of a first session with a new therapist is crying and upset about his situation (action level), but feels uncomfortable disclosing such emotion to the therapist (construing level). Eron and Lund (1993) later called these levels 'viewing' and 'doing'.

The pattern could have continued, but shortly after, the therapist realises the client's discomfort and acknowledges that it is embarrassing for him (Fig. 4.2). In turn, he reconstrues the therapist as understanding him, allowing the therapeutic relationship to be established as something he finds helpful. The downward arrows represent Kelly's view that

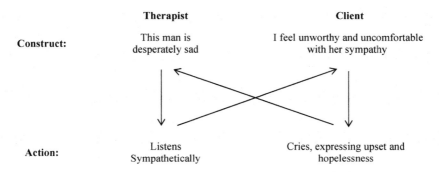

Fig. 4.1 Bow-tie of a man, early in therapy, not yet feeling comfortable with the therapist

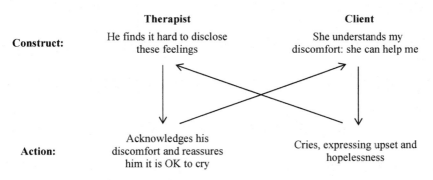

Fig. 4.2 He recognises the therapist as understanding and accepts the relationship as helpful

our actions are governed by the way we construe situations. The diagonal arrows represent the evidence that validates and justifies the way that each person construes the other. Even though there may be turn-taking in their conversation, the bow-tie captures that each is involved in a continuous process of action and appraisal.

In 1913, Scheler (2009, p. 260) wrote, 'We certainly believe ourselves to be directly acquainted with another person's joy in his laughter, with his sorrow and pain in tears, with his shame in blushing, with his entreaty in his outstretched hands…and with the tenor of his thoughts in the sound of his words'. Scheler was arguing against Husserl, who suggested that we know another person *by analogy* to ourselves: The body of the other over there 'receives analogically from mine the sense of another 'world' analogous to my primordial world' (Husserl, 1929, p. 118). Scheler is arguing rather for 'direct acquaintance' or perception of another's subjectivity. But does this mean that constructs are not involved? Of course they are, we affirm. It is clear that even young infants can discriminate different emotions in the face and voice of their caretakers. For PCP, they are already using constructs, just as they are already able to distinguish *warm* vs. *cold*, *hungry* vs. *satisfied*, or *pain* vs. *comfort*. This clarifies constructs as 'transparent templets' or spectacles through which we look at the world (Kelly, 1955, p. 7) rather than internal models or schemata. Wittgenstein agrees with Scheler here: 'Look into someone else's face, and see the consciousness in it, and a particular shade of consciousness. You see on it, in it, joy, indifference, interest, excitement, torpor, and so on… Do you look into yourself in order to recognize the fury in his face?' (Anscombe and Wright, 1981, para. 229) For Schütz (1971, p. 173), we are in touch with the other in the *vivid present*: 'The other's speech and our listening are experienced as a vivid simultaneity. This simultaneity is the essence of intersubjectivity, for it means that I grasp the subjectivity of the alter ego at the same time as I live in my own stream of consciousness'.

The Levels of Interpersonal Construction: Dyads and Triads

Traditionally, between about 9 and 15 months of age, a very important development was said to occur in the infant, which Trevarthen and Hubley (1978) describe as *secondary intersubjectivity*. The child and caretaker were seen to be able to engage in *joint attention* or *referencing*. The child has learned to detect eye-direction (Baron-Cohen, 1997) and can then understand that the other person's attention is directed selectively toward objects (and people) in the world. The child is able to construe that another person is attending to the same thing. This was seen as the beginning of the ability to 'construe the construction processes of another' as Kelly states in the Sociality Corollary (see Procter, 2001).

However, the infant's ability to be aware of another's subjective emotional states much earlier on indicates that sociality is a more multi-layered and complex achievement that is gradually achieved over the first year of life.

But as others point things out and name them, language can now develop at an extraordinary pace. In Kelly's terms, the child is aware of what *element* the other person is *construing*. This allows the child to begin to take on the local way in which the world is divided up. He or she is now immersed in the myriad of constructs that comprise the culture and discourses of the family and the wider society (Procter, 2016b). But for PCP, this is not a passive process. Each individual child develops their own unique construct system through which these constructs are assimilated and given personal associations, meaning, and significance.

The Sociality Corollary, as we saw in Chapter 3, is for Kelly, fundamental in all functional interpersonal relationships. However, in making our relational extensions to PCP, we need to acknowledge the primacy of intersubjectivity. Fivaz-Depeursinge and Corboz-Warnery (1999) have shown that infants as young as three-months-old, 'are already able to alternate their gaze between their two parents, and at nine months almost all children are capable of complex triadic interactions' (Ugazio, 2013, p. 41), implying that the baby already has constructs capable of making sense of dyadic similarities, differences, and interactions between the parents. This provides empirical evidence for an additional corollary that Procter (1978, 2014b), in an extension of the Sociality Corollary, called the Relationality Corollary. This allows for the construing of *relationships* between people, not just the construing of individuals and their positions. It states that, 'to the extent that a person can construe the relationships between the members of a group, he or she may take part in a group process with them' (Procter, 1978, p. 144).

In relating to a group of people, a person construes the others as *individuals* (the *monadic level*), such as whether they are *friendly* or *critical*, or, for example, of a stranger shouting in the street, that he or she is *dangerous* or *vulnerable and needing help* (see Table 4.1). But they will also usually be construing the relationship between pairs of people (for example, whether two people talking are genuinely *agreeing* with each other or just being *polite*). This is *dyadic construing*. Or, they may be

Table 4.1 The levels of interpersonal construing

Levels	Examples of construing
Monadic construing (re A)	*Friendly* (vs. *critical*) *Dangerous* (vs. *vulnerable*)
Dyadic construing (re A and B)	*Genuine agreement* (vs. *politeness*) *Play-fighting* (vs. *genuine conflict*)
Triadic construing (re A, B and C)	A is *introducing* B to C vs. *failing to do so* A and B are *making fun* of C (vs. *respecting* C) C needs to *stay with* A and B to prevent A bullying B (vs. *leaving them alone*)

construing patterns of relating between three people. When 'A *introduces* B to C', this triadic episode cannot be broken down into a pattern involving less than three people. It therefore requires a triadic construct to understand it. Two people, A and B, may be *making fun* in a cruel way of C, versus just joking in a *respectful* way. This is a *triadic construct*. Understanding these differences is necessary in order to know how to relate to the situation.

The members of the dyads or groups here discussed, of course, can include the construer him- or herself. Thus, our client in Fig. 4.2 is dyadically construing the *therapeutic relationship* between him and his therapist as one that can be *helpful*. In Table 4.1, a parent C may need to decide whether to *stay with* her two children A and B, and worries that if she *leaves them alone* together, A may bully B.

Bateson (1972b) noticed that this *definition of the relationship* happens even in dogs or monkeys, when play-fighting can suddenly flip over into genuine fighting. He deduced that they must be exchanging signals which indicate 'this is play'. He argued that in all interaction, there are two aspects: communication about the *content* and about the *relationship*. This was an important inspiration for the development of the Relationality Corollary.

Understanding how people's construing occurs at the three levels in Table 4.1 has important clinical relevance. For example, working with a couple, tensions may arise because one partner is dyadically construing their relationship as 'not how I expect you to treat me' according to expectations of what a marital relationship *should* be. Or at a triadic level one partner may object to how the other is relating to a friend: 'you should not flirt like that, this feels inappropriate'. We can see here the importance of *moral* or *ethical* stances and their centrality in human relating, as emphasised by Harré and van Langenhove's (1999) later elaboration of the notion of 'position'.

The levels of interpersonal construing can be poignantly illustrated by looking at the experiences of personal construct psychologist Dorothy Rowe (2007), in her book on siblings, as she recalls her early family experiences. Table 4.2 is an example of a set of tools called qualitative grids (Procter, 2014b), which will be described in Chapter 6. The ways in which she construes various relationships (the 'elements') in her family

Table 4.2 Dorothy's dyadic and triadic construing in her family

Elements: Dyads			Triad
			Dorothy/Mother/
Dorothy/Mother	Dorothy/Myra	Myra/Mother	Myra
I always felt my existence shamed her (50)	Someone told (Myra) at school on her sixth birthday, 'you are very lucky, you have a baby sister' (51)	Tremendously important for Myra to preserve a picture of mother as being good. Wiped her intense fear of mother from her memory (167)	My sister had been sent away because my mother was not coping:
I had trouble feeding: I do not doubt that she blamed me for her breast abscesses (52)	She resolved that my task in life would be to restore to her everything and more that she had lost: In every aspect of that task I have failed, principally because I never tried (51)		I had caused her to be taken from her mother, her father, her treasured bedroom where I was an intruder (51)

(continued)

Table 4.2 (continued)

Elements: Dyads			Triad
Dorothy/Mother	Dorothy/Myra	Myra/Mother	Dorothy/Mother/ Myra
She complained my coughing disturbed her sleep. She gave me boiled sweets to prevent me coughing when I needed sticky mucus to be coughed up (53) My mother beat me. I soon learned to watch what I said…if anything displeased her, she was likely to retire to her bedroom and not speak to the offender for days or even weeks (52)	She made it clear to me there was something intrinsically contemptible about me I longed for her to take favourable notice of me and be interested in me She either ignored me or used me for her own ends If I caught her attention, she would look at me curiously with fascinated disgust as if I was a loathsome slug under a stone (166)		My sister was always as close to our mother as I was distant (51) Since she did not dare blame her mother for her unhappiness, she blamed me (167) She could get me to do anything by telling me that if I did not, my father would be inconvenienced and upset (166: triad here between the sisters and *father*)

are entered into the table or 'grid'. Here, she is describing the relationships between herself, her mother, and her sister Myra. All examples of her construing of the three dyads are drawn from the text (page numbers are included) together with her construing of the triad as a whole.

She describes a very unhappy situation including memories of frank abuse and rejection at the hands of her mother and sister. There are several examples of intensely difficult experiences at the triadic level. This shows how focussing on how a person construes their family relationships reveals the core dynamics of the difficulties that might bring a person to therapy and is invaluable in deciding who to include in sessions and how to begin to make a therapeutic alliance with the members. Of course, to have a full picture of the construing of the threesome, we would want the direct accounts of the other two witnesses in the situation—the mother's and the sister's voices. This is what we seek in constructing a full Perceiver Element Grid (see Chapter 6). The constructs here are what Ugazio would call *narrated polarities* as opposed to *interactive polarities* (Ugazio & Guanieri, 2017). The latter are constructs governing ongoing dialogue and interactions that we would be able to note when conducting a conjoint interview or in examining a transcript of their conversations together.

Distinguishing the different levels of interpersonal construing throws light on the complex processes of intersubjectivity. Intersubjectivity at its fullest involves a 'You' and a 'We'. Galbusera and Fellin (2014) write, 'The mere use of the "you," is an attitude of openness that involves the recognition and acknowledgment of the other as a person' (p. 6). MacMurray (1961) said, 'I can know another person as a person only by entering into personal relation with him' (p. 28). This involves sociality in Kelly's sense. In the fullest of relationships, it will involve *reciprocal sociality* in which each person's world becomes mutually understood and shared in an ongoing manner, allowing for respectful discussion and cross-checking of the nuances of meaning, a process Mascolo and Kallio (2020) refer to as *corroboration*. For such a relationship, as Leitner (1985a) has written, 'I will tend not to allow you deep access unless I know what sort of human being you are'. This involves 'commitment and the risk of invalidation by placing central aspects of ourselves on the line' (p. 86).

But, in addition to reciprocal sociality, the relationship is mutually and dyadically construed as a 'We'. Husserl wrote, 'something momentous, something that goes beyond empathy, happens the moment I turn towards and start to address the other…both of us become aware that *we* are being experienced…a 'we' is established' (cited in Zahavi, 2015, p. 14). Schütz says, 'when we live in a We-relationship, there is a mutual engagement, where we immediately affect each other. Our respective streams of consciousness are interlocked to such an extent that each of our respective experiences is *coloured* by our mutual involvement' (ibid., p. 15, our italics). Shotter (2011) writes:

> When someone acts, their activity cannot be accounted as wholly their own activity – for a person's acts are, among other influences, partly '*shaped*' by the acts of the others around them – this is what makes joint actions...so special: they are continuously creative of new responses, both to their circumstances and to each other. (p. 2, our italics)

This 'colouring' and 'shaping' indicates the importance of understanding how being in different relationships affects our very construing and actions. We construe differently according to the immediate social context that we are in, either in nuanced form or in quite gross ways. How aware we are of these differences can vary from very low levels of cognitive awareness through to a keen appreciation of the differences that occur.

We can illustrate the full functioning of relationships in Fig. 4.3. Each person is construing the other's actions and constructions (sociality), together with their shared construing (the 'We'), represented by the additional arrows at the top of the diagram, of a shared object or 'element', namely their dyadic *relationship*, the 'Us': how they see its *process* and its *feel*. In our view, it is at this level of construing that profound changes

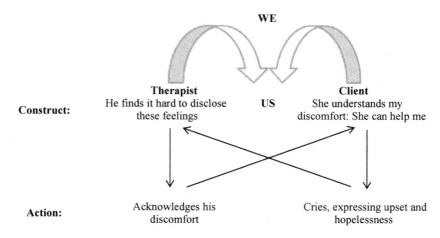

Fig. 4.3 Full intersubjectivity: each construe ('We') the relationship ('Us') in addition to empathy and sociality

in relating can be achieved in therapy, as new ways of construing and experiencing the relationship become available.

Of course, the Individuality Corollary indicates that their constructions of the dyad will not be identical. There is much leeway in how much sharing, agreement and disagreement, understanding and misunderstanding is taking place within the relationship. They may see themselves as holding similar positions (in contrast to a third person or position seen as *other*), or they may construe their two positions as being complementary, different, or in opposition. Having such a clear recognition of these complexities in relationships is an enormous asset in clinical work, both in terms of establishing the therapeutic alliance and helping people with their own relationships with others in their lives.

Polarisation in Relationships: The Family Construct

Kelly's emphasis on the bipolar nature of meaning is an essential principle in understanding the dynamics of human relationships. Because every person is unique, even in the most functional of relationships there will always be differences of view between two people. Normally, this is a resource—combining two different views of a difficulty often leads to a deeper and more comprehensive grasp of a situation (Procter, 2017). This is helpful in moving things forward, as Bateson (1979) pointed out in using the metaphor of having two eyes—the synthesis of the two views in binocular vision transforms our perception into three dimensions, the perception of depth and the accurate apprehension of closeness and distance. When two or more people are living or working together in a well-functioning family or team, the members bring their different views and skills into the collaboration (although there may always be aspects which are withheld). Their complementary differences may be summarised, for example, as the *clear thinker* versus the *practical one* or *the one who takes risks* versus *the cautious one*. Each has something useful to contribute in planning a project or solving a problem. These relatively consistent differences can be labelled *family* or *group* constructs (Procter, 1985a). The family, by its nature, usually consists of people from different genders, stages of life, and sometimes cultures, so it is inherently characterised by a series of very different ways of viewing the world. When two people come together to form a new family, they bring together the traditions and views from their own families of origin. These may be successfully combined or they may remain overtly or covertly unresolved in a conflict of loyalties toward the different cultures and their representative figures.

All too often, though, collaboration can break down or become stuck in arguments and debates, and then *polarisation* occurs. We see this clearly at the political level where views polarise into *left* and *right,* or in the current debate at the time of writing this book, into those who wish the UK to *remain* in, versus those who wish the country to *leave*, the European Union. In complex issues, each has something to contribute but time and energy is devoted to fighting, re-asserting one's view, and proving the other wrong. People take up and enact *positions* at each end of a jointly held construct, a *family* or *group* construct (Procter, 1985a).

Families and teams in difficulty are often beset by these polarised dyadic processes. This may lead family members in the situation to take up a third position of trying to mediate between the two opposing sides, as Ugazio (2013), who has independently developed a very similar model (see Procter & Ugazio, 2017), has emphasised. Therapists and other figures outside the family are also often in a position to take this mediating position. We shall explore in Chapter 8 some useful approaches for helping people to resolve and de-polarise such conflicts.

Family, Group, and Societal Construct Systems

A major outcome of the research conducted on families containing a person diagnosed as schizophrenic (Procter, 1978) was to see that these family constructs are combined together in a family construct system (FCS) (or more generally a group construct system), summarised in Table 4.3. The family becomes governed by a set of commonly held *family constructs* held together in a hierarchical system with properties similar to Kelly's description of individual construct systems. The

Table 4.3 The family construct system (FCS)

- A whole family can be seen as having a construct system, just like an individual has, with a similar hierarchical structure
- Members *negotiate* ways of construing reality
- A few key *family constructs* govern family interaction
- Members move around these streets and avenues, taking *positions* with each other
- More *powerful* members' construing prevails, less powerful views may be subjugated
- Children learn to construe reality in this semantic environment, identifying and contra-identifying with internal and external figures
- The FCS needs to evolve as the family goes through stages of the family life cycle, but in problematic situations may be entrenched
- Therapy involves joining this reality and working for progress within it

FCS's superordinate constructs represent the family's values, their bipolarity differentiating repudiated values from those adhered to and advocated. These may be developed over generations. The FCS provides the members with a finite set of avenues of movement and alternative 'slots' which they are free to utilise. The notion of 'position' that we have been discussing was introduced into the model by Procter (1985a) and may be defined as 'the integrated stance that each member takes in relation to the others' (Feixas, 1992b, p. 225; 1995, p. 321). The FCS may be defined as the 'interlocking set of different family members' positions' (Procter, 1985a, p. 330). The positions that the members take up with each other are dynamically related by contrast to or in agreement with each other. Thus, members will *identify* with other members but also *contra-identify* (Weinreich & Saunderson, 2003). Thus, in Cain and Abel's family, as depicted in Byron's play 'Cain: a mystery', Cain rejects the position of the religious faith to which the others are dedicated, and occupies an opposing position of 'defiance' (Procter & Procter, 2008). The FCS has to change as the family moves through stages of the family life cycle (see Chapters 7 and 9). Therapy may involve helping the family to revise their construing where it has become entrenched. In families with serious psychopathology, Scott and Ashworth (1973) describe how a shared construct of *ill* versus *well* allows the other members, in defining one member as ill, to be able to see themselves as *well* by contrast.

The implications of this proposal broaden our notion of what a 'construct' is into an enormously pervasive and versatile dialogical entity (Procter, 2009a). It is a distinction that governs all aspects of individual functioning as envisaged by Kelly. But he extended it to how cultures and societies divide up the world as discussed in his study of the construct systems held by the different nations of Europe (Kelly, 1996; Procter, 2016b). Here, we are applying the notion of the bipolar construct to the dynamics of interpersonal relationships and the functioning of groups such as families, teams, and organisations. The poles of these interpersonal constructs are the *positions* that people take up and enact in their dialogue. The contrasting meanings of the polarity are continuously created in interaction, modulating and evolving as the conversation proceeds. This has very positive implications for the possibility of change. By having different sorts of conversation, a new path towards problem resolution can be established. This enables therapists in this tradition to maintain an optimistic stance, so important in encouraging hope, which itself contributes toward effective psychotherapy.

Recognising that individuals are intimately embedded in the wider construing of the family and of other important relationships is, for us, of vital importance in the business of helping people in therapy. We need to extend Kelly's compassionate therapeutic stance of *acceptance* and the *credulous approach* (see Chapters 5 and 8) to all the important figures in the client's life or we may be tempted to 'take sides' in a way that is often counterproductive. This may involve actually working with significant others in a family therapy format but, even in individual therapy, it is important to remember that we are always intervening in a family or group situation, even when only working with one person in the drama. When seeing a client or patient one-to-one, we can continue to 'do family therapy' because the FCS is available to the client—the mind is full of, we might say *consists of,* the conversations and voices of significant others, as Vygotsky (1978) argued.

This fits with a dialogical view of self. As we saw in Chapter 2, we are, as personal construct therapist Miller Mair (2015a) insisted, a 'community of selves', a collection of different positions which the self can take up. These different 'selves' are in dialogical relationship with each other. We can experience conversations and debates between these positions and indeed often do so in making important decisions in our lives. Alternatively, a person in difficulty can become paralysed in dilemmas if these 'internal debates' become chronically unresolved. This may be the basis of the experience of auditory hallucinations.

We will now begin, in Chapters 5 and 6, to look at the forms of assessment that flow from Kelly's original theorising together with methods of capturing the interpersonal construing that shapes the interactions and relationships in people's lives.

Notes

1. One of the first critiques of this kind can be found in Procter and Parry (1978).
2. A category error occurs when 'the facts of mental life' are represented as belonging 'to one logical category when they actually belong to another' (Ryle, 1963, p. 17). We will see later that Trevarthen's example here involves seeing *dyadic interactions* wrongly explained as *monadic*.

References

Anscombe, G. E. M., & Wright, G. H. V. (Eds.). (1981). *Ludwig Wittgenstein: Zettel*. Oxford, UK: Blackwell.

Baron-Cohen, S. (1997). *Mindblindness: An Essay on Autism and Theory of Mind*. London: MIT Press.

Bateson, G. (1972a). *Steps to an Ecology of Mind*. Chicago: University of Chicago Press.

Bateson, G. (1972b). A theory of play and fantasy. Reprinted in Bateson, G. (Ed.). *Steps to an Ecology of Mind* (pp. 177–193). Chicago: University of Chicago Press.

Bateson, G. (1979). *Mind and Nature: A Necessary Unity*. London: Fontana/Collins.

Blumer, H. (1966). Sociological implications of the thought of George Herbert Mead. *American Journal of Sociology, 71,* 535–544.

Chiari, G. (2017b). Highlighting intersubjectivity and recognition in Kelly's sketchy view of personal identity. In D. Winter, P. Cummins, H. G. Procter,

& N. Reed (Eds.), *Personal Construct Psychology at 60: Papers from the 21st International Congress* (pp. 54–67). Newcastle upon Tyne, UK: Cambridge Scholars Publishing.

Eron, J. B., & Lund, T. W. (1993). How problems evolve and dissolve. Integrating narrative and strategic concepts. *Family Process, 32,* 291–309.

Esterson, A. (1970). *The Leaves of Spring.* Harmondsworth, UK: Penguin.

Feixas, G. (1992b). Personal construct approaches to family therapy. In G. J. Neimeyer & R. A. Neimeyer (Eds.), *Advances in Personal Construct Psychology* (Vol. 2, pp. 217–255). Greenwich, CT: JAI Press.

Feixas, G. (1995). Personal constructs in systemic practice. In R. A. Neimeyer & M. J. Mahoney (Eds.), *Constructivism in Psychotherapy* (pp. 305–337). Washington, DC: American Psychological Association.

Fivaz-Depeursinge, E., & Corboz-Warnery, J. (1999). *The Primary Triangle.* New York: Basic Books.

Galbusera, L., & Fellin, L. (2014). The intersubjective endeavour of psychopathology research: Methodological reflections on a second-person perspective approach. *Frontiers in Psychology, 5,* 1–14.

Harré, R., & van Langenhove, L. (1999). *Positioning Theory.* Oxford, UK: Blackwell.

Husserl, E. (1929). *Cartesian Meditations.* Dordrecht: Kluwer.

Kelly, G. A. (1955). *The Psychology of Personal Constructs. Vol. I, II.* New York: Norton (2nd printing: 1991, London and New York: Routledge).

Kelly, G. A. (1996). Europe's matrix of decision. In D. Kalekin-Fishman & B. Walker (Eds.), *The Structure of Group Realities: Culture, Society, and Personal Construct Theory* (pp. 27–64). Malabar, Florida: Krieger.

Leitner, L. M. (1985a). The terrors of cognition: On the experiential validity of personal construct theory. In D. Bannister (Ed.), *Issues and Approaches in Personal Construct Theory* (pp. 83–103). London: Academic Press.

MacMurray, J. (1961). *Persons in Relation.* London: Faber and Faber.

Mair, J. M. M. (2015a). The community of self. In D. A. Winter & N. Reed (Eds.), *Toward a Radical Re-definition of Psychology: The Selected Works of Miller Mair* (pp. 102–112). London: Routledge.

Malloch, S., & Trevarthen, C. (2018). The human nature of music. *Frontiers in Psychology, 9,* 1680.

Mascolo, M. F., & Kallio, E. (2020). The phenomenology of between: An intersubjective epistemology for psychological science. *Journal of Constructivist Psychology, 33,* 1–28.

Mead, G. H. (1934/1962). *Mind, Self and Society.* Chicago: University of Chicago Press.

Merleau-Ponty, M. (1962). *The Phenomenology of Perception*. London: Routledge.

Procter, H. G. (1978). *Personal construct theory and the family: A theoretical and methodological Study*. Unpublished PhD thesis, University of Bristol.

Procter, H. G. (1985a). A construct approach to family therapy and systems intervention. In E. Button (Ed.), *Personal Construct Theory and Mental Health* (pp. 327–350). Beckenham, UK: Croom Helm.

Procter, H. G. (2001). Personal construct psychology and autism. *Journal of Constructivist Psychology, 14*, 105–124.

Procter, H. G. (2009a). The construct. In R. J. Butler (Ed.), *Reflections in Personal Construct Theory* (pp. 21–40). Chichester, UK: Wiley-Blackwell.

Procter, H. G. (2014b). Qualitative grids, the relationality corollary and the levels of interpersonal construing. *Journal of Constructivist Psychology, 27*, 243–262.

Procter, H. G. (2016b). PCP, culture and society. In D. A. Winter & N. Reed (Eds.), *The Wiley Handbook of Personal Construct Psychology* (pp. 139–153). Chichester, UK: Wiley-Blackwell.

Procter, H. G. (2017). Comparing PCP with other approaches: Systemic theory, phenomenology and semiotics. *Personal Construct Theory & Practice, 14*, 137–139.

Procter, H. G., & Parry, G. (1978). Constraint and freedom: The social origin of personal constructs. In F. Fransella (Ed.), *Personal Construct Psychology 1977* (pp. 157–170). London: Academic Press.

Procter, H. G., & Procter, M. J. (2008). The use of qualitative grids to examine the development of the construct of good and evil in Byron's play 'Cain: A mystery'. *Journal of Constructivist Psychology, 21*, 343–354.

Procter, H. G., & Ugazio, V. (2017). Family constructs and semantic polarities: A convergent perspective? In D. A. Winter, P. Cummins, H. G. Procter, & N. Reed (Eds.), *Personal Construct Psychology at 60: Papers from the 21st International Congress* (pp. 68–89). Newcastle upon Tyne, UK: Cambridge Scholars Publishing.

Ryle, G. (1963). *The Concept of Mind*. Harmondsworth, UK: Penguin Books.

Rowe, D. (2007). *My Dearest Enemy, My Dangerous Friend: Making and Breaking Sibling Bonds*. London: Routledge.

Scheler, M. (2009). *The Nature of Sympathy*. New Brunswick: Transaction Publishers (Original work, 1913).

Schütz, A. (1971). *Collected Papers Vol I: The Problem of Social Reality*. The Hague: Martinus Nijhoff.

Scott, R. D., & Ashworth, P. L. (1973). The shadow of the ancestor: A historical factor in the transmission of schizophrenia. *British Journal of Medical Psychology, 42,* 13–32.

Sherover, C. M. (1987). Royce's pragmatic idealism and existential phenomenology. In R. S. Corrington, C. Hausman, & T. M. Seebohm (Eds.), *Pragmatism Considers Phenomenology* (pp. 143–165). Lanham, MD: The Center for Advanced Research in Phenomenology.

Shotter, J. (2011). *Language, joint action, and the ethical domain: The importance of the relations between our living bodies and their surroundings.* Paper presented at IIIrd Congreso de Psicologia y Responsabilidad Social, March 5th–9th. Bogota, Colombia.

Spiegelberg, H. (1976). *The Phenomenological Movement: A Historical Introduction* (Vol. 2). The Hague, Netherlands: Martinus Nijhoff.

Trevarthen, C., & Aitken, K. J. (2001). Infant intersubjectivity: Research, theory, and clinical applications. *Journal of Child Psychology and Psychiatry, 42,* 3–48.

Trevarthen, C., & Hubley, P. (1978). Secondary intersubjectivity: Confidence, confiding and acts of meaning in the first year. In A. Lock (Ed.), *Action, Gesture and Symbol*. London: Academic Press.

Trevarthen, C. B. (1979). Communication and cooperation in early infancy: A description of primary intersubjectivity. In B. Bullowa (Ed.), *Before Speech*. Cambridge, UK: Cambridge University Press.

Trevarthen, C. B., & Delafield-Butt, J. (2017). Intersubjectivity in the imagination and feelings of the infant: Implications for education in the early years. In E. Jayne White & C. Dalli (Eds.), *Under-Three Year Olds in Policy and Practice* (pp. 17–39). Singapore: Springer.

Ugazio, V. (2013). *Semantic Polarities and Psychopathologies in the Family: Permitted and Forbidden Stories*. New York: Routledge.

Ugazio, V., & Guanieri, S. (2017). The family semantics grid II: Narrated polarities in couples. *Testing, Psychometrics, Methodology in Applied Psychology, 24,* 1–39.

Vygotsky, L. S. (1978). *Mind in Society: The Development of Higher Psychological Processes*. Cambridge, MA: Harvard University Press.

Watzlawick, P., Beavin, J., & Jackson, D. D. (1968). *Pragmatics of Human Communication*. New York: Norton.

Weinreich, P., & Saunderson, W. (2003). *Analysing Identity: Cross-Cultural, Societal and Clinical Contexts*. London: Taylor and Francis.

Zahavi, D. (2015). You, me, and we: The sharing of emotional experiences. *Journal of Consciousness Studies, 22,* 1–2.

5

Personal and Relational Construct Interviewing

Personal construct psychology is much more than a collection of theoretical ideas, but also offers a set of practical tools. Several of these are methods for the assessment of construing, some designed by Kelly and his students and others by post-Kellian personal construct theorists, including those developed within the personal and relational elaboration of his theory presented in this book. Although there are some ingenious and elaborate formal personal construct assessment techniques, their use is by no means essential in gaining an understanding of another person's view of the world, and in this chapter we shall consider less formal personal construct approaches to interviewing.

Interviewing Methods and Questions

Kelly's (1955) so-called 'first principle' was that 'if you do not know what is wrong with a person, ask him; he may tell you' (pp. 322–323). Implicit in this statement is the 'credulous attitude' advocated by Kelly (1955), in which 'From a phenomenological point of view, the client – like the proverbial customer – is always right' (p. 322). The therapist or

© The Author(s) 2020
H. Procter and D. A. Winter, *Personal and Relational Construct Psychotherapy*,
Palgrave Texts in Counselling and Psychotherapy,
https://doi.org/10.1007/978-3-030-52177-6_5

counsellor who adopts this attitude attempts to show sociality, seeing the world through the client's eyes. This does not necessarily mean that he or she agrees with the client's view of events, only that the principal concern is with gaining a profound understanding of this view while 'suspending' the therapist's own constructions of the events concerned. Such an attitude can therefore be adopted even if the client has engaged in actions, such as serial killing (Winter, 2007a), which may be repugnant to the clinician; or if the client is regarded as delusional, in which case credulous attention to the meaning of the client's 'delusions' may allow the identification of more abstract constructions underlying them that can be a useful focus of therapy (Bannister, 1985).

While parts of the personal and relational construct psychotherapist's initial interview may be relatively unstructured and free-flowing in order to gain a fairly unencumbered picture of the client's construing, at other points it may focus on specific issues. For example, Kelly (1955) suggested the questions shown in Table 5.1 for the 'controlled elaboration of the complaint', essentially asking the client to provide details of what is troubling him or her. One reason for this particular line of questioning is to highlight the transience of the client's complaints. In order to introduce consideration of the perspectives of others, the client may also be asked how their significant others view the complaint, whether he or she knows other people with similar complaints, and how these people have dealt with them. As we have indicated in Chapter 3, the personal and relational construct psychotherapist's interview will also attempt to elicit contrasts. For example, the client who describes a particular self-construction may be asked how the self would be described when he or she is not like this.

Table 5.1 Questions for controlled elaboration of complaint (Kelly, 1955, p. 962)

1. Upon what problems do you wish help?
2. When were these problems first noticed?
3. Under what conditions did these problems first appear?
4. What corrective measures have been attempted?
5. What changes have come with treatment or the passing of time?
6. Under what conditions are the problems most noticeable?
7. Under what conditions are the problems least noticeable?

Particular interview methods and procedures have been suggested for use with certain client groups. For example, as Ravenette (1977, p. 264) pointed out, 'children do not present themselves as having problems for which they require help', but instead it is generally adults who present a child as having problems. In addition to exploring the constructions of the adults concerned, an indirect interviewing approach with children and young people is therefore generally advisable. Ravenette suggested asking the child to describe their troubles with various people, including the self, and viewed these troubles as indicating invalidations of the child's construing. The exploration of the child's 'troubles' need not be conducted in a conventional interview format, and may, instead, incorporate sentence completion tasks and the use of drawings, as described by Ravenette (1977). An example of the former is to ask the child to complete the following sentences in relation to particular people or groups of people (e.g., most boys) : *The trouble with X is…..; They are like that because….; It would be better if….; The difference that would make is…..; The difference that would make to you is….* One way in which Ravenette (1977, pp. 272–273) used drawings was to present a child with a set of drawings depicting 'troubles in school', and to ask: ' *1. What do you think is happening? 2. Who might be troubled and why? 3. How did this come about? 4. If you were there what would you do and why? 5. What difference would that make? 6. What kind of boy* [sic] *is the one picked out in Q.2?'*

To bring the focus onto the interviewee, the child may then be asked:

> In what ways are you and the person in this story different? Are there any other ways in which you are similar to them? (Green, 2005, p. 260)

To explore a child's personal troubles, Ravenette (1977) also invited them to draw pictures of situations which are troubling for them and of one in which everything is fine. The child is asked to say what is happening in each picture, to describe three characteristics of a child who would not be troubled by the situations, to say why they would not be troubled, and to think of when the child himself or herself was like this untroubled child.

Ravenette's (1977) assessment methods did not just focus on the child's troubles but also more generally on 'who are you?'. For example, the child might be asked to tell the interviewer 'three things that best describe' him or her and three things that each of various significant people might say about him or her. These questions elicit various construct poles, the meaning of which can then be explored by asking the child how he or she would know that someone might be described in this way, and how they would describe a person of their acquaintance who is not like this. The child might also be asked to talk about how he or she would be in the future or if he or she decided to be different. In Ravenette's (1980) 'the good and bad of it' technique, dilemmas may be explored by asking the child to describe something bad about himself or herself and what is the preferred state, and then to say something good and bad about each of these.

To elaborate construing of feelings, the 'Portrait Gallery' technique involves asking the child to describe and contrast drawings of a sad and happy face, to complete pictures of blank faces to illustrate other feeling states, and to say three things about each face (Ravenette, 1999a). Finally, another drawing-based technique developed by Ravenette (1999b) to supplement interviews with children was for the child to be given a piece of paper with a curved line drawn on it, and asked to make this into a picture. Consistent with the personal construct theorist's emphasis on bipolarity, the child is then asked to draw the opposite of the first picture, and to explain what the differences between the two pictures are. Many more creative techniques for working with children and young people can be found in Moran (2014).

Various other interview methods have been developed by personal construct psychologists to explore particular aspects of construing. For example, to elicit core constructs, Leitner (1985) suggested asking the person about their earliest memories and significant life events; what their epitaph should be; how they view God; and to describe vivid dreams and fantasies.

Viney and Westbrook (1981), initially largely in exploring the quality of life of people with physical health problems, were primarily concerned with eliciting the transitions in construing reflected in 'positive' and 'negative' emotional states, but also with exploring people's perceived control over their lives, sociality, and level of psychosocial development. They used a simple, open-ended question: 'I'd like you to talk to me for a few minutes about your life at the moment – the good things and the bad – what it is like for you' (Viney & Westbrook, 1981, p. 48). Responses to this question were analyzed using a range of content analysis scales. A further interview method developed by Oades and Viney (2000, 2012) was the Experience Cycle Methodology, which attempts to elucidate a person's construing or actions by taking him or her through the successive stages of this cycle, as indicated in Table 5.2. Interview responses can be categorised into whether an anticipation was tight or loose; whether investment was high or low; whether the anticipation was validated or invalidated; and whether there was significant or minimal construct revision. The areas that this methodology has been used to explore have ranged from selective mutism (Oades & Patterson, 2016) to paternal filicide (Sedumedi & Winter, 2020).

Table 5.2 Interview proforma for Experience Cycle Methodology (from Oades & Patterson, 2016, p. 127)

Anticipation Phase
- *What things were you predicting would happen when you did...?*
- *What options did you see open to yourself at this time?*
- *Were you concerned what others may think of you or what you may think of yourself?*

Investment Phase
- *How much did it matter to you at the time?*

Confirmation/Disconfirmation Phase
- *How did things go compared to what you initially thought would happen?*
- *What feelings did you have about this?*

Construct Revision Phase
- *In general, what did you learn from your experience of....?*
- *Did you change as a result of your experience?*
- *Did you change the way you view....?*

Useful Questions in Interviewing Families and Children

Over many years of working with families in adult and child settings, a list of useful questions was developed (Procter, 2016). This can be found in Appendix A together with, in Appendix B, a list of simpler questions for working with children and people with communication difficulties. Broadening PCP to include the relational makes available the many approaches to interviewing developed by various schools of family therapy, for example, the Mental Research Institute (MRI) (Fisch, Weakland, & Segal, 1982; Watzlawick, Weakland, & Fisch, 1974) and the Milan School of family therapy (Selvini, Boscolo, Cecchin, & Prata, 1980). The list includes many so-called *circular questions* developed by the Milan School (Feixas, Procter, & Neimeyer, 1992). These are specifically designed to reveal the construing of relationships, as discussed in Chapter 4. For example, they evoke awareness and discussion of changes in relationship associated with the presence and absence of issues and difficulties, before and after such occurrences, how a third member intervenes in the process between two other members, and so on. Some of these questions are reminiscent of those involved in the repertory grid (see Chapter 6), for example when a member is asked to rank the family members on a *scale* of who is most through to least worried about a situation (Procter, 1981).

The focus on Kelly's *corrective measures* (see Table 5.1) has been expanded into what the MRI group called *attempted solutions*. This emphasises the *relational nature* of problems. For the MRI, a problem consists of a difficulty met by an attempted solution which does not move things on and yet is reapplied, resulting in a repeating cycle, reminiscent of how Kelly sees '*hostility*' (Chapter 3). A person's attempt to solve a problem is governed by his or her *construing* of the problem, for example, to *punish* in the case of behaviour construed as *done deliberately* as opposed to *console* for the same behaviour seen as *she could not help it*. Establishing the *attempts* to solve a difficulty can therefore reveal the construing involved in the generation and maintenance of problems. This can be charted in the *Bow-Tie Interview*, discussed below.

It is important to note, with all these questions, that the family session should flow in a natural conversation. As Rober (2017, p. 53) has said, 'the focus is on having a rich dialogue with all the family members about their worries'. The therapist's primary aim is to facilitate such a conversation in which each member's voice is heard and respected. We could say, 'if the process is right, the content looks after itself'. The questions and other methods discussed are used in this context when the therapist feels they can add further light on the situation. The numbered stages in Appendix 1 should not therefore be used as a structured interview although they are a useful reminder to ensure that a range of important areas have been considered. As Kelly (1955, p. 48) said, a person is a 'form of motion'. This is no less true of most families, which, when enabled, reveal themselves as enormously creative. A good conversation in a family therapy session often leads to improvements without the need of specific interventions or suggestions from the therapist. We shall look more at this in Chapter 9.

The Zig-Zag Interview and the Bow-Tie Diagram

It is useful to think that the *position* that a person takes on something, as introduced in Chapter 4, has two levels—a construing or meaning level and a behavioural or action level (Feixas, 1995; Procter, 1985a). If a mother construes her son as *disobedient,* this will lead to certain actions, such as reprimand, withdrawal of privileges, and so on. More generally, *constructs* and *stories* or *examples* are in dialectical relationship with each other: A construct such as *obedience* vs. *disobedience* 'carries' a number of stories or examples which the parent will relate. Stories, in their turn, communicate constructs. These two levels can be used as a guideline to interviewing, which we have called the Zig-Zag Interview (Procter, 2007), shown in Fig. 5.1. When listening to a client narrating examples of disobedience we may remain at the lower level and ask for further details of where, when, who was there, and so on (as in Sect. 5 of Appendix A). Or we can seize on a construct in her account, moving to the upper level, asking her more about it, what its contrast pole is, or what other constructs could be used to describe what was happening.

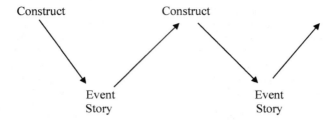

Construct   Construct

Event   Event
Story   Story

Fig. 5.1 The zig-zag interview

This is a way of understanding the natural flow of a conversation, but here we can use it deliberately to guide the interview towards understanding more deeply how clients make sense of a situation, what they do about it, and what further possibilities flow from their positions.

These two levels are reproduced in the bow-tie diagram, introduced in Chapter 4 in Figs. 4.1–4.3, when looking at the interaction between client and therapist in the early stages of a first therapy session. This is a very useful technique for tracing the dynamics of entrenched relationships which get caught in 'escalating cycles of confrontation and retreat' (R. Neimeyer, 2009, p. 42). It is particularly powerful when faced with an argument or conflict in a therapy session where each partner may be trying to recruit the therapist into taking their side. The bow-tie interview consists of tracing out a diagram, asking each participant to provide the details of their construing of the other's actions and their own consequent reactions. The interactional 'loop' is of course *continuous* and so one can start anywhere in the sequence and trace it back or forwards around the arrows of the diagram. Figure 5.2 shows a mother and her 12-year-old son caught in such a predicament.

When the mother says she threatened to put Stuart in care, one can, using the zig-zag interview and going up to the level of construing, ask her how she construes his behaviour: 'What do you make of this situation?'. She replied that he is just like his father, who was violent to her and left the family when Stuart was only two years old. In his turn, Stuart feels she is picking on him unfairly compared to how she treats his two brothers, and we can guess that this resentment is connected to the kind

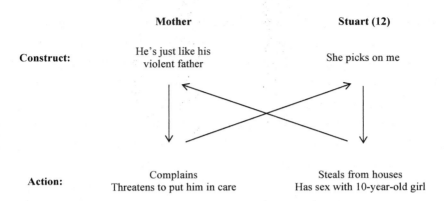

Fig. 5.2 Bow-tie diagram of construing between mother and Stuart (aged 12)

of behaviours that led her to seek therapeutic help. The pattern of inter-action is maintained by the others' actions as confirming or justifying, for each perceiver, the construing being held (diagonal arrows).

The bow-tie is a powerful device for therapeutic intervention as well as for understanding relational process. Constructing such a diagram in the presence of the participants can lead to both feeling understood simulta-neously, cutting through the tendency of each feeling that their version is the only truth, and allowing for them to collaborate in modifying the cycle. A new approach in any of the four corners of the diagram will lead to changes moving through the system. One can therefore negotiate with them where might be the best place to consider changing approach. The diagram allows participants to begin to take responsibility for the pattern as a whole, rather than only their own individual contribution. In one case a mother, trapped in such a cycle with her teenage daughter, who had decided to leave the session and stand outside the room, returned to the next session, saying things were considerably better between them. When asked how this had been achieved, she said, 'I looked at that diagram and decided to do things entirely differently!'

Increasing the Formality of Assessment

While some of the interview methods that we have described are more formal than others, we shall now move on, in the next chapter, to consider much more structured methods of assessment that allow systematic exploration of both the content and structure of a personal or relational construct system.

References

Bannister, D. (1985). The psychotic disguise. In W. Dryden (Ed.), *Therapists' Dilemmas* (pp. 39–45). London: Harper and Row.

Feixas, G. (1995). Personal constructs in systemic practice. In R. A. Neimeyer & M. J. Mahoney (Eds.), *Constructivism in Psychotherapy* (pp. 305–337). Washington, DC: American Psychological Association.

Feixas, G., Procter, H. G., & Neimeyer, G. (1992). Convergent lines of assessment: Systemic and constructivist contributions. In G. Neimeyer (Ed.), *Constructivist Assessment: A Casebook* (pp. 143–178). New York: Sage.

Fisch, R., Weakland, J. H., & Segal, L. (1982). *The Tactics of Change: Doing Therapy Briefly*. San Francisco: Jossey-Bass.

Green, D. (2005). Kids' stuff. In D. A. Winter & L. L. Viney (Eds.), *Personal Construct Psychotherapy: Advances in Theory, Practice and Research* (pp. 256–270). London: Whurr.

Kelly, G. A. (1955). *The Psychology of Personal Constructs. Vol. I, II*. New York: Norton (2nd printing: 1991, London and New York: Routledge).

Leitner, L. M. (1985). Interview methodologies for construct elicitation: Searching for the core. In F. Epting & A. W. Landfield (Eds.), *Anticipating Personal Construct Psychology* (pp. 292–305). Lincoln: University of Nebraska Press.

Moran, H. (2014). *Using Personal construct psychology (PCP) in practice with children and adolescents*. Online eBook: https://issuu.com/pcpinpractice/docs/using_personal_construct_psychology.

Neimeyer, R. A. (2009). *Constructivist Psychotherapy*. London: Routledge.

Oades, L. G., & Patterson, F. (2016). Experience cycle methodology: A qualitative method to understand the process of revising personal constructs. In

D. A. Winter & N. Reed (Eds.), *The Wiley Handbook of Personal Construct Psychology* (pp. 125–136). Chichester, UK: Wiley-Blackwell.

Oades, L. G., & Viney, L. L. (2000). Experience cycle methodology: A new method for personal construct psychologists? In J. W. Scheer (Ed.), *The Person in Society: Challenges to a Constructivist Theory* (pp. 160–173). Giessen, Germany: Psychosozial Verlag.

Oades, L. G., & Viney, L. L. (2012). Experience cycle methodology: Understanding the construct revision pathway. In P. Caputi, L. L. Viney, B. M. Walker, & N. Crittenden (Eds.), *Personal Construct Methodology* (pp. 129–146). Chichester, UK: Wiley-Blackwell.

Procter, H. G. (1981). Family construct psychology: An approach to understanding and treating families. In S. Walrond-Skinner (Ed.), *Developments in Family Therapy: Theories and Applications since 1948* (pp. 350–366). London: Routledge and Kegan Paul.

Procter, H. G. (1985a). A construct approach to family therapy and systems intervention. In E. Button (Ed.), *Personal Construct Theory and Mental Health* (pp. 327–350). Beckenham, UK: Croom Helm.

Procter, H. G. (2007). Construing within the family. In R. Butler & D. Green (Eds.), *The Child Within: Taking the Young Person's Perspective by Applying Personal Construct Theory* (2nd ed., pp. 190–206). Chichester, UK: Wiley.

Procter, H. G. (2016). Useful questions in interviewing families and children. *Rivista Italiana di Costrutivismo, 4,* 124–134.

Ravenette, T. (1977). Personal construct theory: An approach to the psychological investigation of children and young people. In D. Bannister (Ed.), *New Perspectives in Personal Construct Theory* (pp. 251–280). London: Academic Press.

Ravenette, T. (1980). The exploration of consciousness: Personal construct intervention with children. In A. W. Landfield & L. M. Leitner (Eds.), *Personal Construct Psychology: Psychotherapy and Personality* (pp. 36–52). New York: Wiley.

Ravenette, T. (Ed.). (1999a). *Personal Constructs in Educational Psychology: A Practitioner's View.* London: Whurr.

Ravenette, T. (1999b). A drawing and its opposite: An application of the notion of the 'construct' in the elicitation of children's drawings. In T. Ravenette (Ed.), *Personal Constructs in Educational Psychology: A Practitioner's View* (pp. 125–137). London: Whurr.

Rober, P. (2017). *In Therapy Together: Family Therapy as a Dialogue.* London: Palgrave.

Sedumedi, T. P., & Winter, D. A. (2020/in press). I killed my children: Construing pathways to filicide. *Journal of Constructivist Psychology.*

Selvini, M. P., Boscolo, L., Cecchin, G., & Prata, G. (1980). Hypothesizing–circularity–neutrality: Three guidelines for the conductor of the session. *Family Process, 19,* 3–12.

Viney, L. L., & Westbrook, M. T. (1981). Measuring patients' experienced quality of life: The application of content analysis scales in health care. *Community Health Studies, 5,* 45–52.

Watzlawick, P., Weakland, J., & Fisch, R. (1974). *Change: Principles of Problem Formation and Problem Resolution.* New York: Norton.

Winter, D. A. (2007a). Construing the construction processes of serial killers and violent offenders: 2. The limits of credulity. *Journal of Constructivist Psychology, 20,* 247–275.

6

Structured Assessment Methods

Personal construct psychology is perhaps best known for some of the formal assessment methods that it has developed for use by practitioners and researchers. In this chapter, we shall describe, and provide examples of, the major such methods that may be of value to the psychotherapist.

Self-Characterisation

One of the assessment techniques originally developed by Kelly (1955), the self-characterisation, invites the person to write an autobiographical sketch as outlined in the instructions given in Table 6.1. An example of this was provided in the case of Brian in Chapter 1.

Kelly (1955) suggested various aspects of the sketch which it might be useful to consider, including its sequence, organisation, and repetition of themes; and a system by which quantitative scores can be derived from self-characterisations was developed by Jackson and Bannister (1985). However, these specific methods of analysis are rarely used nowadays, and

© The Author(s) 2020
H. Procter and D. A. Winter, *Personal and Relational Construct Psychotherapy*,
Palgrave Texts in Counselling and Psychotherapy,
https://doi.org/10.1007/978-3-030-52177-6_6

Table 6.1 Instructions for self-characterisation (from Kelly, 1955, p. 323)

> I want you to write a character sketch of X, just as if he were the principal character in a play. Write it as it might be written by a friend who knew him very *intimately* and very *sympathetically*, perhaps better than anyone ever really could know him. Be sure to write it in the third person. For example, start out by saying, 'X is…'

the therapist may find it most valuable to use the technique simply as a means of eliciting the construct poles that the person applies to the self, albeit taking particular notice of self-constructions that are used repeatedly. The sketch may also provide a valuable indication of what might be the contrast poles of these constructs. For example, Table 6.2 provides extracts from the self-characterisations of several different clients, all of whom presented with the same complaint. You may be able to identify not only repeated themes in these clients' self-construing but also how they do not see themselves. On the basis of these constructions you may also wish to speculate on the nature of the complaint with which they presented (which will be revealed in Chapter 7).

A useful adaptation of the technique is to ask the client to write a self-characterisation as he or she would be without a particular symptom. This may provide an insight into the client's apparent resistance to losing the symptom. For example, Rodney's characterisation of himself if he were to lose his presenting complaint of inability to ejaculate was as follows:

Table 6.2 Extracts from self-characterisations

- *Shirley is most concerned with others' feelings and would often put herself out to ensure others are happy. She may often feel anger about others' opinions or certain situations—but can only show this emotion to very few people. The happiness and safety of those she loves is upmost (sic) to Shirley*
- *Joan does not like confrontations and is happy that she and her partner rarely have cause to argue seriously…She is very loyal and finds she is able to feel extremely angry on behalf of others but does not often lose her temper on her own account*

(continued)

Table 6.2 (continued)

- *Amanda will do anything for anyone. She tends to put other people first before herself. She will never say anything bad to other people just in case she upsets them, so she keeps it all inside. I feel she needs to be a little selfish for her own good, but Amanda is too good to people*
- *Sarah is warm, friendly, kind and caring. Her desire to please is outstanding. She is fun loving, slow to anger and easily forgiving and would never harm anybody*
- *Hilda is caring and tries hard not to offend people around her*
- *Whenever I've seen Tracy get angry which is very rare, it'll blow over her so quickly it's almost as if she never was angry in the first place*
- *Jean is a very caring person, she cares about people, worries too much about things, never seems to have time for herself*
- *Linda is very patient and sympathetic and generous with her time and attention. She takes a real personal interest in each individual*
- *May is a caring person, who tries to be helpful, supportive, and a loving wife and mother. She is a good listener but cannot confide in her friends as she has been laughed at, so now tends to 'clam up'*

I am relaxed about life. I enjoy life and all its everyday situations. I wake in the morning refreshed from a good revitalizing sleep and look forward the [sic] meet the day ahead...Cheerfully I am preparing my breakfast and make plans for the day. I have many things to do, but I am independent from routine work. I am selling my creative services and have many contracts. I am well paid and name the price.

I am very confident and proud of my achievements. Everyday problems do not irritate me and I face every situation head on.

I enjoy having a body and feel good about my body. My body gives me pleasure instead of aches and pains. I am not ashamed to present my body publicly and I am active in some sports activities.

All the worries that I have are confined to the actual problems of the day.

(Winter, 1992, pp. 203–204)

In Fransella's (1972) terms, Rodney may be considered to be displaying 'if only syndrome', a fantasy that life would be perfect if only the client did not suffer from a particular symptom. In such cases, retention of the symptom may avoid the risk of possible invalidation of this idealistic fantasy.

Other variations of the self-characterisation may facilitate exploration of relational construing. For example, the client might be asked to write characterisations of the self in particular roles in relation to others, couples can be asked to write characterisations of their relationship (Kremsdorf, 1985), and family members can write characterisations of their family or of particular individuals within it (Davis, Stroud, & Green, 1989). Finally, a further illuminating adaptation of the technique is for the client to write self-characterisations as they were (or will be) at various times in their lives, or the titles and abstracts of each chapter of their autobiography (R. Neimeyer, 1985).

Repertory Grid Technique

Repertory grid technique, which is an extension of Kelly's (1955) role construct repertory test, is by far the most widely used of his assessment methods, and was the basis for much of the initial interest in personal construct psychology, particularly in the clinical setting. Its administration consists of three steps, as will now be described.

Administration

Elicitation of Elements

The first decision to make in administering a grid is the nature of the elements on which it will focus. In the clinical setting, these will generally be people, consisting of significant others in the individual's life and aspects of the self, or entirely of different self elements (e.g. *self now, ideal self, self as a parent, self as a son/daughter, self as an employee*) (R. Neimeyer, Klein, Gurman, & Greist, 1983). However, one of the principal advantages of the grid is its flexibility, and grid elements may be drawn from innumerable alternative domains. For example, as we shall see, personal construct work on post-traumatic stress has tended to employ grids in which the elements are life events, including the traumatic event (Sewell et al., 1996); in grids used with couples, the elements may be relationships (Ryle & Lunghi, 1970); and in working with clients with eating disorders, dysmorphophobia, or other somatic complaints, it may be useful to employ a grid in which the elements are body parts (Feldman, 1975). The only rule is that all of the elements should be within the range of convenience of the constructs that will be used in the grid. This will generally mean that elements from two or more different domains (e.g., people, life events, and types of fruit) should not be mixed in a grid.

Having decided on the domain of elements to be included in the grid, the next step is to elicit representative elements from this domain. If the elements are people, this is usually achieved by asking the person completing the grid to provide the names of other people who fit various role titles. Kelly's original role title list is now rarely used, partly because it is very long, consisting of 21 role titles, and partly because some of the role titles used (e.g., *the most successful person whom you know personally*) essentially supplied constructs to the respondent. A list which is likely to be more practicable and useful for the clinician is as follows: *mother; father; partner; child/ren; other close relative/s; a man and woman (other than those given previously) whom I like; a man and woman (other than those given previously) whom I dislike; boss or person in authority; thera-pist; a person I admire; any important others not already included.* This list will be adapted to the client's particular circumstances: for example, if the client is a murderer, the clinician will probably wish to include their victim as one of the elements if not spontaneously provided by the client. If there was or is no one in the client's life fulfilling a particular role (e.g., parent or partner), the client can be asked to think of someone who came or comes closest to fulfilling this role. People who have died do not need to be excluded from the element list.

The name of each of the elements is usually written on a separate card, and the list will normally be supplemented by various aspects of the self, again each written on a card. The most useful self elements are likely to be *self now, how I would like to be (ideal self),* and possibly some of the following: *how others see me (or how a specific other sees me); self in the future (perhaps specifying a particular time point, e.g. 10 years hence); self in the past (again perhaps specifying a particular time, e.g. as a child); self without my symptom.*

Elicitation of Constructs

The next step is to elicit from the respondent a number of their constructs. As with all aspects of repertory grid procedure, there are different ways of doing this, but Kelly's original method is to present the respondent with successive triads (groups of three) of elements and to ask the person, for each triad, to give an important way in which two of them are alike (what is known as the *emergent* pole of the construct) and thereby different from the third. There is some debate about the best way of eliciting the contrast, or *implicit*, pole of the construct if the person does not state this spontaneously. However, since it is more likely to generate bipolar constructs (Epting, Suchman, & Nickson, 1971), we would suggest using the 'opposite method', in which the person is asked how he or she would describe someone who is not characterized by X, the way in which the two chosen elements are alike. If the respondent is unable to think of the contrast pole of a particular construct, this may mean that this pole is 'submerged' (see Chapter 3). The construct does not, however, need to be excluded from the grid as the contrast pole can simply be labelled as 'not X'.

The triads may be formed by initially presenting the person with the first three elements that were elicited, and then successively replacing one of the elements with the next in the list, with no element being retained in more than two successive triads. A variation on this, which may be useful in the clinical context as it is designed to elicit constructs relevant to the self, is Kelly's (1955) Self-Identification Form, in which the *self now* element is included in each triad, with one of the other elements being replaced in every new triad. If the triadic method is too complex for a client (for example, if the client is a child), he or she may be asked, for each of successive pairs of elements, how they are alike or different and then for the opposite of the characteristic thus elicited. Alternatively, the client can be asked to describe each element in turn and again to give the opposites of the elicited characteristics. Constructs included in a grid need not even be elicited by a formal procedure at all, but may be derived from an interview or focus group, although ideally one which allows the elicitation of the contrast poles of constructs. A further alternative is for the constructs used in the grid to be supplied by the clinician rather than elicited from the client. Although this is clearly not within the spirit of personal construct theory, it does at least ensure that the grid includes constructs in which the clinician is interested. A compromise is for the vast majority of the constructs to be elicited from the client, but for the clinician to include in the grid other constructs which seem relevant to the client's presenting problem (e.g., if the client presents with depression, *depressed* versus whatever the client's opposite to this may be) if these are not spontaneously generated in the elicitation procedure.

A variation on the elicitation process which may be useful in exploring subsystems of constructs relating to different aspects of the client's identity is to elicit one set of constructs from triads of elements relating to one such aspect and another set from triads relating to another. For example, this has been used with psychiatric in-patients in a rehabilitation and resettlement programme, where one set of elements concerned the client when in hospital and other in-patients, and the other set consisted of the client when in the outside community and other people outside hospital (Winter, Goggins, Baker, & Metcalfe, 1996). More recently, it has been used in the exploration of radicalisation (Winter & Muhanna-Matar, 2020), allowing comparison of the meaningfulness to the individual of the radicalised and non-radicalised views of the world; and in the study of trainee clinical psychologists' ethical construing, allowing investigation of the relative characteristics of their construct subsystems concerning professional and personal issues (Jenkin, Ellis-Caird, & Winter, 2020; Jenkin & Winter, 2020).

Although a very standardised construct elicitation procedure may be necessary in a research context, this is not the case in the clinical setting. Thus, if the client spontaneously gives more than one construct in comparing and contrasting the elements in a particular triad, the clinician can include all of the constructs concerned in the grid. If the client cannot think of a construct in relation to a certain triad, or only one that has been elicited from a previous triad (since all the constructs in a grid have to be different), he or she can simply go on to consider the next triad. If a construct is given that sounds similar to one that was previously elicited, but does not use the same words, the clinician should ask whether the two constructs have the same meaning for the client. If they do not, both can be included in the grid. The clinician will generally accept all of the constructs given by the client, even if they make little sense, or seem superficial, to the clinician. The procedure is, after all, designed to elicit the client's personal constructs, and, taking a credulous attitude, it is accepted that whatever construct the client gives is an important dimension of meaning for him or her. It does not necessarily have to relate to psychological characteristics of elements: for example, a construct of *tall–short* may represent a superordinate concern for a client who is vertically challenged. There are some constructs, however, that may merit further questioning or that it may be best to exclude from the grid. The former include constructs where the contrast between the two poles seems an unusual one, for example *serious–vegetarian*. In such cases, the clinician would do well to ask whether being vegetarian is really the opposite for the client of being serious. If the client responds in the affirmative, the construct can be accepted, but it may be that the client has used 'serious' to describe two elements in a triad and 'vegetarian' to describe the other element, but without this being the contrast pole of the construct. If this is the case, the clinician should then ask the client how he or she would describe someone who is not serious, and also someone who is not vegetarian. The two constructs thus elicited can then both be included in the grid. The clinician might also wish to question a little further if the client provides a very vague construct, for example saying that two elements are *OK* and that the other is not. In such a case, asking in what way the two elements are OK might be helpful. Finally, constructs that would normally be excluded from the grid are those which concern a relationship between the elements (for example, these two *work together*) or which are dichotomous (for example, *alive–dead*) since, as we shall see, it will be difficult to complete the next step of the grid procedure with such constructs.

As with elements, the only real limit on the number of constructs elicited in the grid is the time available to the clinician and client. However, consideration should be given to the effect of fatigue, if the grid is too large, on the numerous judgements that the client is required to make in the final stage of the grid procedure. Since the more constructs are elicited, the more likely there is to be repetition of themes, and since there is some (McDonagh & Adams-Webber, 1987), although not entirely undisputed (Heckmann et al., 2019), evidence that the earlier constructs elicited are likely to be more superordinate for the client, it is rarely of value for a grid to contain more than 15 elements or constructs (the number of elements and constructs does not need to be equal). In view of the particular statistical procedures that may be used in analysing a grid, it is also inadvisable for the number of constructs and elements to be much less than ten.

Sorting of Elements on Constructs

Kelly's original role construct repertory test only involved the elicitation of elements and constructs, but in the grid form of the test the elements are then sorted on the constructs. The simplest procedure is for the person to assign each element to one or other pole of each construct, with the responses entered as ticks or blanks on a grid form in which the columns represent the elements and the rows the constructs. However, much more commonly used, and able to provide much more information, are ranking and rating procedures. In the former, for each construct in turn, all of the element cards are placed in front of the respondent and he or she is asked to select the one that is most characterised by the emergent pole of the construct. This element is removed, the person is asked which of the remaining elements is best described by this construct pole, and so on. The ranks of the elements on each construct are entered in the corresponding cells on the grid form. Ranking may be found easier by children than the alternative procedure of asking the respondent to rate each of the elements on each of the constructs, for example on a seven-point scale in which one represents one pole of each construct and seven represents the other pole. One of the advantages of the rating method over the use of ranking is that it gives the respondent the freedom to indicate that two elements may be no different in terms of a particular construct. Also, if an odd-numbered rating scale is used, there is the option of assigning an element to the midpoint of the scale, perhaps indicating that the construct cannot really be applied to the element concerned. Since most grid software packages do not accept grids with empty cells, the use of the midpoint is an option that the respondent may be encouraged to take if he or she says that they do not know how a particular element would be described in terms of a particular construct. Some caution should be applied in the use of this option, however, in that if most of the elements are rated extremely at one pole of a construct, a midpoint rating may signify that an element is very different from the other elements. In such cases, the use of the median rating may be more appropriate for elements about which the respondent is uncertain. Other options for imputation of missing values are provided by the IDIOGRID software package (Grice, 2002).

To lessen the likelihood of lengthy deliberation about ratings or rankings, it is usually advisable for the client to be asked not to think too long about the task but instead to give fairly quick first impressions. Sometimes the client may become confused about which pole of a particular construct is designated by a high, and which by a low, rating. The best way of identifying such confusion is when the client comes to rate the ideal self element. If the rating of this element on a particular construct seems strange (e.g., if the ideal self is rated as very *unintelligent*), the client might usefully be asked if this is the way that he or she would really prefer to be. If the answer is yes, no further action need be taken. If no, and the client has consistently rated elements wrongly on the construct concerned, the poles of the construct can simply be reversed on the grid form.

Completion of the grid administration process therefore results in a matrix of numbers, as in Table 6.3. In this grid, the elements were rated on a seven-point scale, with high ratings indicating the left-hand pole of each construct (conventionally, this is the emergent pole, although it does not have to be).

Variations on Grid Procedure

Of the several ingenious variations on grid procedure, we shall now briefly describe some which, mostly with a focus on interpersonal construing, may be of particular interest to the personal and relational construct psychotherapist.

Table 6.3 Geoff's repertory grid

Constructs	Elements														
	A	B	C	D	E	F	G	H	I	J	K	L	M	N	O
1. Confident—self-effacing	7	3	5	7	7	4	7	6	5	4	7	7	3	7	5
2. Nice—nasty	7	7	7	7	2	6	3	7	4	6	7	4	7	4	5
3. Treads on people—caring	2	2	3	2	7	2	3	2	2	2	4	4	2	6	2
4. Satisfied with station—dissatisfied	7	4	5	7	7	7	5	7	6	6	7	5	5	2	4
5. Self-important—self-effacing	3	3	4	2	5	2	7	3	4	2	5	5	2	6	5
6. Doesn't put self first—selfish	5	6	4	7	2	7	5	7	3	4	5	2	6	3	6
7. Argumentative—passive	2	1	5	2	5	2	5	2	6	3	4	5	2	5	2
8. Where they want to be—not where they want to be	7	2	5	7	7	7	4	6	4	5	7	4	3	3	7
9. Attractive—unattractive	7	2	5	7	3	6	2	6	4	5	7	7	6	5	5
10. Wins at all costs—won't win at all costs	5	2	4	2	7	2	4	3	3	4	5	7	2	7	3
11. Suffers from stress—doesn't suffer stress	2	6	4	3	2	3	3	2	2	2	2	4	5	2	7
12. Good promotion material—bad promotion material	6	5	3	2	7	3	5	2	2	3	7	5	2	7	3
13. Hard-working—lets things slide	7	7	5	7	7	6	4	6	2	2	4	7	6	5	7
14. Irritable—even-tempered	2	6	4	2	5	3	2	6	2	4	6	2	2	5	6

Notes Elements: A Man I like; B Self; C Woman I like; D Mother; E Man I dislike; F Father; G Woman I dislike; H Wife; I Son; J Significant other 1; K Ideal self; L Significant other 2; M Significant other 3; N Significant other 4; O Self at work (Elements rated on a 7-point scale, with a high rating indicating that the left-hand pole of a construct describes the element concerned)

Dependency Grid

In this method, originally referred to by Kelly (1955) as the situational resources repertory test, the person is presented with a list of problematic situations and a list of role titles (including the self), for which, as in a conventional grid, he or she is asked to provide the names of specific individuals. The respondent is then asked, for each situation, to which of the people he or she would have turned to for help had they been available. These people are indicated by a cross in the appropriate cell of the grid matrix. This allows exploration of whether a person shows *undispersed dependency*, either focusing all of his or her dependencies on one or two people or depending on everyone for everything, rather than what Kelly (1955) regarded as the more optimal state of depending on some people in some types of situation and on others in other situations.

Double Dyad Grid

In this method, developed by Ryle and Breen (1972a) for use with couples, the grid elements are relationships, each relationship being divided into two reciprocal elements (e.g., *Harry in relation to David; David in relation to Harry*). Each member of the couple completes a grid with the same elements and constructs, and then a second grid as they imagine that their partner will have completed it. While Ryle and Breen supplied the constructs used in the grid, these constructs can be elicited from each member of the couple separately, and then pooled when the couple complete their ratings.

Family Grid

Procter (1985b) developed an approach in which an individual grid is first administered to each member of a family (some results from one family are presented in Table 6.6). Representative constructs are selected from these grids for inclusion in a 'family grid' in which each member rates on these constructs not only all of the family members but also how he or she imagines each of them construes the self and each of the others. These are called 'meta-elements', for example 'how mother sees father', 'how my brother sees me', etc. A computer program, 'Family' (Procter, 1978), was written to derive six measures, including how similarly members are viewed, how much agreement there is between any pair, how much one is able to predict how another sees the members, and so on. A 'common family grid' was then constructed from the four family grids, in which the elements were the four family members seen by each of them (4 × 4 = 16 elements) with the same set of constructs as in the family grid (4 from each member). This was analysed using the same program used for the individual grids, the factors and linkages of elements and constructs giving a view of the overall family construct system.

Reconstruction Grid

One way of tracing the process of reconstruing during therapy is to ask the client to complete ratings of a particular element on a set of supplied constructs at each therapy session, these sessional ratings then being placed in the columns of the grid matrix (Ryle & Lipshitz, 1975; Slater, 1970).

Textual Grid

Most pieces of text contain elements and descriptions of these in terms of particular construct poles. As Feixas and Villegas (1991) have indicated, the elements and construct poles (which need not be single words but can be longer descriptors) may be extracted from a text and entered into a grid matrix, in which a cross is inserted in the appropriate cell if an element is described in the text by a particular construct pole. While it may be particularly interesting to form such a grid from autobiographical material, such as a diary, the method's application is not limited to such material and it may be applied to interview transcripts or even a whole book! (Reed et al., 2014; Winter, Feixas et al., 2007).

Self-Image Profile

Butler's (2001) Self-Image Profile was designed for use with children and young people. It is rather more akin to a questionnaire than a grid, but essentially consists of two elements, 'how I am' and 'how I would like to be' (to which others may be added if required), which the child rates on a 7-point scale on a number of provided items. It thus gives an indication of areas in which the child wishes to change.

Analysis

Classification of Construct Content

While most methods of grid analysis now involve the use of statistical procedures, this is not the case for the analysis of the content of the elicited constructs. A system for such classification, consisting of 22 categories, was devised by Landfield (1971), but nowadays the more commonly used system is that of Feixas, Geldschläger, and Neimeyer (2002), which consists of 45 categories divided into the areas of *moral, emotional, relational, personal, intellectual/operational,* and *values/ interests.* Such systems are likely to be of more interest to the researcher than to the clinician, and instead of using a standard system it is also, of course, possible to develop a system particularly suited to one's own principal area of concern (e.g., Jenkin & Winter, 2020). The clinician may also find it illuminating to make a very broad categorisation of the client's constructs: for example, if a client is found to use very few constructs concerning people's psychological characteristics (Duck, 1973), this may go some way towards explaining his or her interpersonal difficulties. Also of interest to the clinician may be to examine specifically the content of the construct poles that are applied to the self (as indicated by extreme ratings of the self on the constructs concerned).

Quantitative Analyses

There is now a very wide range of software packages available for the analysis of repertory grids, some of which are listed in Table 6.4. The choices available to the grid user in this respect may seem daunting, but in illustrating the analyses that these packages provide we shall focus on one of them, IDIOGRID (Grice, 2002), for such reasons as user-friendliness, cost (in this case freely downloadable), and potential utility of its analyses to the therapist or counsellor. However, most of the packages provide similar methods of analysis, and therapists who are familiar with the statistical package R may prefer OpenRepGrid (Heckmann, 2014); those who are particularly interested in the detection of implicative dilemmas (see Chapter 8) may prefer GRIDCOR (Garcia-Gutierrez & Feixas, 2018); and those who are interested in the amount of conflict in construing associated with, or the predictive power of, particular elements or constructs may prefer GRIDSTAT (Bell, 2009). A further consideration to bear in mind is that currently IDIOGRID only runs on a Windows and not on a Mac operating system.

The steps that we would recommend that the grid user should take in entering data into IDIOGRID, and conducting what is still one of the most useful methods of analysis, originally devised by Slater (1977), are set out in Table 6.5 (alternative options are available for some of these steps but our recommendations are based upon what we have found most useful in clinical practice). We shall now describe some of the main measures that can be derived from such an analysis, with illustrations from the analysis of the grid presented in Table 6.3, completed by a client, Geoff, who was regularly encouraged by his superiors at work to apply for promotion but was then repeatedly unsuccessful at promotion interviews because his 'mind went blank'.

Table 6.4 Grid analysis software

Package	Access details	Particular features	Disadvantages	Cost
Idiogrid (Grice, 2002)	www.idiogrid.com	Includes elicitation procedure and most methods of analysis required by clinician, including dependency grid analysis option and analyses of pairs and groups of grids; user friendly	Does not include cluster analysis. Does not run under Mac OS but if Mac OS is a version that is also Windows enabled, should run under Mac Windows	Free
OpenRepGrid (Heckmann, 2014)	www.openrepgrid.org	Impressive graphics; uses R package. There is also a user-friendly web-based version OpenRepGrid on air (http://www.onair.ope nrepgrid.org/)	Currently only analyses single grids. R-environment package needs to be downloaded (free) to run under a number of operating systems including Windows and Mac	Free
Gridstat (Bell, 2009)	Available from rcbell12345@gmail.com	As well as other methods of analysis, includes analysis of conflict in, and predictive power of, each element and construct; and dependency grid analysis	Only analyses single grids; DOS presentation. Does not run on Mac	Free
GRIDCOR (Garcia-Gutierrez & Feixas, 2018)	https://www.repertory grid.net/en/	As well as other methods of analysis, provides analysis of implicative dilemmas	Only analyses single grids	Not free

Package	Access details	Particular features	Disadvantages	Cost
Webgrid (Gaines & Shaw, 1997)	webgrid.uvic.ca	Allows elicitation of constructs; includes cluster analysis; allows comparison of pairs of grids. As well as the web version, a downloadable version, Rep Plus, is available	Limited range of analysis options	Free
Gridsuite (Fromm & Bacher, 2014)	www.gridsuite.de	Allows elicitation of constructs; includes cluster analysis; allows comparison of pairs of grids; emphasises role of grid user as interpreter of data	Limited range of analysis options	Not free
Flexigrid/ Multigrid (Tschudi, 1993)	Contact the author	As well as single grid analysis, includes analysis of groups of grids	DOS presentation; requires installation of a programme in order to run it; does not run under current version of Windows	Not free
Hiclas (De Boeck & Rosenberg, 1988)	Contact the author	Provides hierarchical class analysis, which has been used in PCP work on post-traumatic stress	Does not offer other analyses. Does not run on Mac	Not free

Table 6.5 Steps in using Idiogrid to conduct Slater Single Grid Analysis

Grid data

Change
- Grid label to a particular label for your grid
- Grid file name to a new name, which can be the same as the grid label
- Number of constructs to the number in your grid
- Number of elements to the number in your grid
- Grid type (usually to rating: minimum 1; maximum 7)

After each change, click 'activate changes'

Edit
- Enter/edit constructs or elements
- Enter emergent (high rating) and implicit (low rating) poles of constructs and names of elements
- Click OK
- Double click on first empty cell, enter rating/ranking, press return, enter next rating/ranking, and so on, pressing return following last entry

Analyses

Slater analysis: Single grid

Tick
- Display grid in output
- Principal components analysis
- Graphing options
- Emergent and implicit
- OK
- Element descriptive statistics
- Element Euclidean distances
- Standardise
- Construct descriptive statistics
- Construct correlations
- OK

Element Measures

In the final column of the first table in the output from the IDIO-GRID Slater analysis, headed *Descriptive Statistics for Elements,* may be found the percentage sum of squares accounted for by each of the elements. It may be regarded as indicating the salience of each element to the individual. For Geoff, this table indicated that by far his most salient element, accounting for 13.06 per cent of the sum of squares (as compared with the 6.67 per cent that would be expected if the sums of squares were equally divided between the elements), was the man he disliked. If the sum of squares accounted for by the self-element were relatively low (which was not the case with Geoff), this might indicate a high degree of uncertainty concerning the self and that therapy might appropriately focus on elaboration of the person's self-construing. Somewhat similar information can be derived from simply counting the number of midpoint ratings (i.e., 4s if a 7-point scale is used) applied to a particular element. This has been regarded as a measure of constriction of construing (Winter, Bell, & Watson, 2010), but more simply elements which receive a high number of midpoint ratings may be regarded as relatively unconstruable, or lacking in salience, for the person completing the grid.

Following this table are two tables labelled *Element Euclidean Distances*, indicating the degree of construed dissimilarity of each pair of elements. In the second table (which is the only one that need be looked at), the distances are standardised and are on a scale from 0 to 2, with distances below 0.8 indicating that the elements concerned are construed as very similar (and identical if the distance between them is 0), whereas distances above 1.2 indicate that they are seen as very dissimilar (Winter, 1992). Of particular interest to the psychotherapist, and of use in monitoring change if a grid is readministered at a later date, is the distance between the self and ideal self. For Geoff this was 1.30, indicating a low level of self-esteem, and it was also apparent that he viewed himself as dissimilar to other people in general, the distance between only one other element and the self being less than 0.80 (and only marginally so: 0.76).

Construct Measures

In the table entitled *Descriptive Statistics for Constructs* (which is only relevant for grids that employ ratings), the first column gives the mean rating of the elements on each construct. If the mean is towards one or other pole of the construct, the construct is being used in a 'lopsided' way, which, as we shall see in Chapter 7, may be of clinical significance.

The final column of the table, providing the percentage sum of squares for each construct, indicates the extent to which the construct discriminates between the elements. For Geoff, his preoccupation with his complaint of failing at interviews was perhaps reflected in his construct *good–bad promotion material* having the highest percentage sum of squares (9.31%).

The next table, presenting correlations between constructs, is often of considerable clinical interest as it indicates the meaning of each construct for the client. As with all correlation coefficients, they range from −1.00 to +1.00, with a negative correlation indicating that the high-rating pole of one construct is associated with the low-rating pole of the other, a positive correlation indicating that the high-rating poles of the constructs are related to each other, and a correlation of 0 indicating that the constructs are unrelated. Although in clinical practice there is no need to be over-concerned with the statistical significance of these correlations, the clinician who is interested in this can check significance tables, remembering that the number of degrees of freedom equals the number of elements minus one. The therapist or counsellor may be particularly interested in the correlations between a construct relating to the client's presenting complaint and other constructs. For example, in Geoff's grid, it is of note that the correlations between the constructs *good–bad promotion material* and *treads on people–caring, doesn't put self first–selfish*, and *nice–nasty* are 0.74, −0.39, and −0.33 respectively. Given that this indicates that he construes people who are good promotion material as likely to tread on other people and be selfish and nasty, it is perhaps small wonder that he sabotaged his promotion interviews.

A quick way of identifying whether the correlations between constructs reveal *implicative dilemmas*, in which the preferred pole of one construct is related to the non-preferred pole of another, is to use a method of analysis devised by Feixas and Saúl (2004), which is provided by the GRIDCOR package but has now also been incorporated into IDIOGRID. It can be accessed by selecting the 'implicative dilemmas' analysis option in IDIOGRID, following which *self now* should be selected as the 'target element' and *ideal self* as the 'ideal element'. It first identifies congruent constructs, those on which the self and ideal self are construed similarly; discrepant constructs, on which these elements are construed differently; and dilemmatic constructs, those on which the ideal self is at the midpoint. An implicative dilemma is defined as a correlation (above a chosen cut-off point) between a congruent and a discrepant construct such that the preferred pole of one is related to the non-preferred pole of the other. This would indicate that were the person to move towards the preferred pole of the discrepant construct, he or she would have to move away from the preferred pole of the congruent construct. Applying this analysis with Geoff's grid, dilemmas would have been identified involving the discrepant constructs *confident–self-effacing, self-important–self-effacing, wins at all costs–won't win at all costs,* and *suffers from stress–doesn't.* Specifically, while on these constructs he would prefer to move away from his current self-construction as self-effacing, not winning at all costs, and not suffering from stress, correlations with the congruent construct *doesn't put self first–selfish* indicate that to do so would imply seeing himself as more selfish, which he would not want to do. Similarly, correlations of the first three of these discrepant constructs with the congruent construct *nice–nasty* indicate that moving to the preferred poles of these constructs would also entail viewing himself as more nasty. Incidentally, the analysis would not have revealed the possibly problematic relationships of the construct *good–bad promotion material* with other constructs identified above as, although Geoff would like to be better promotion material, his self and ideal self ratings on this construct were not sufficiently different for the construct to be regarded as discrepant. Also, the construct *treads on people–caring* presents Geoff with a dilemma, in the terms of Feixas and Saúl, as the placement of the ideal self at the midpoint indicates that he cannot decide which pole of the construct he would prefer to characterise him.

Principal Component Analysis

Returning to the output from the IDIOGRID Slater analysis, the next section that may be of interest to the therapist or counsellor is the table headed Eigenvalue Decomposition. This presents results of a form of principal component analysis, which essentially breaks the grid down into its major groups of interrelated constructs, or components, each of which is relatively unrelated to other such groups. All that need concern the clinician is that the higher the percentage of variance in a grid accounted for by the first principal component (the number in the middle column of the first row of the table), the less differentiated, or more unidimensional, is the person's construing. This has been regarded as a measure of 'tightness' of construing and is highly correlated with another frequently used grid measure, Intensity, the sum of squares of intercorrelations between constructs (which may be calculated through the 'summary indices' analysis option in IDIOGRID). Of more relevance to the therapist, there is some evidence that the higher the percentage of variance accounted for by the first component, the less likely is the person to respond to exploratory (rather than directive) psychotherapy (Winter, 1983). This may be because in a person whose construct system is very tightly organised, the invalidation of any one construct, as may occur in psychotherapy, is likely to carry implications for most other constructs, including core constructs. Therefore, in Kelly's terms, for such a person, psychotherapy is likely to be threatening. As we shall see in Chapter 7, however, a very loosely organised construct system is likely to pose at least as many problems as one that is very tightly organised. A common question regarding the percentage of variance accounted for by the first principal component, and indeed other grid measures, is what constitutes a high or low score. The answer, perhaps frustratingly, is that it depends. This is because there is no standard form of grid and, for example, the larger the grid the lower the percentage of variance that is likely to be accounted for by the first component. Nevertheless, in a study using a grid with 16 constructs and 16 elements, the average percentage of variance of the first component was found to be 39.4 per cent in people not presenting with psychological problems (Ryle & Breen, 1972b).

In the remaining tables in the IDIOGRID output, those of construct and element loadings on the components enable the components to be defined. This is in terms of the constructs and elements that have the highest positive and negative loadings on the components, with those that load positively on a component (where in the case of constructs, the loading indicates the position of the construct's emergent pole) being contrasted with those that load negatively. For Geoff, these loadings indicate that the first principal component, essentially his major way of construing his world, contrasts people who *win at all costs,* are *selfish, nasty, tread on people, self-important, argumentative,* and are *good promotion material,* like the man he dislikes, with people who *won't win at all costs, don't put themselves first,* and are *nice, don't tread on people,* and are *self-effacing, passive,* and *bad promotion material,* like his parents and to some extent his wife. His second principal component contrasts people who are *where they want to be* and *attractive,* like his ideal self, with those who are *not where they want to be* and *unattractive,* like himself. The loadings, usually just those on the first and second component, are plotted to provide a visual depiction of the individual's construct system (which will be found in a screen below that containing the textual output) in which the horizontal axis of the plot represents the first principal component and the vertical axis the second component. The elements are indicated by points on the plot, with physical distance between them indicating psychological distance, those in opposite quadrants being the most dissimilar, and proximity to the origin of the plot indicating that an element is not very meaningful. The constructs are indicated by lines passing through the origin of the plot, with their poles specified at the borders of the plot.

The therapist or counsellor who analyses a grid may find it useful to turn initially to the plot, which will provide a good indication of what aspects of the textual output to inspect in more detail (although it should be borne in mind that the plot does not provide an entirely accurate picture of the grid since it only accounts for the percentage of variance equivalent to the first two principal components). The plot may also be usefully shared with the client who completed the grid. In Geoff's plot (see Fig. 6.1), several of the features of his construing that we have noted above are immediately apparent. These include the contrast in his views of himself and his ideal self; the extreme construing of the man he dislikes; and the closeness of being good promotion material to winning at all costs, treading on people, and being argumentative, selfish, self-important, and nasty. Also apparent is the similarity in his construing of his parents and his wife, which, if a focus of therapy were on his marital relationship, might lead to consideration of whether this relationship is similar to a parental one and, if so, what the implications of this might be.

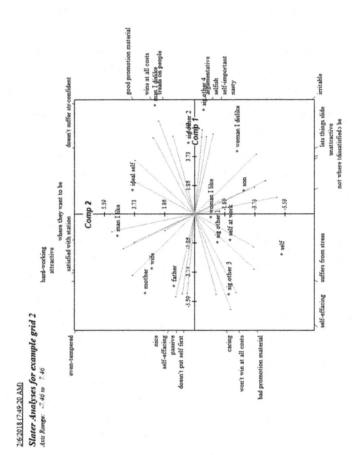

Fig. 6.1 Plot of elements in construct space for Geoff's grid

Comparison of Grids

IDIOGRID also provides useful options for the analysis of pairs and groups of grids (accessed by the Slater analysis 'two grids' and 'multiple grids' options respectively) if these grids use the same elements and constructs. Amongst the measures that can be derived from the comparison of two grids are an index of their overall similarity (general degree of correlation) and indices of similarity in the use of individual constructs and in the construing of particular elements (high similarity indicated by low percentage sum of squares in the descriptive statistics from the grid for differential changes). Such analyses may be particularly useful in comparing pre- and post-therapy grids; and also the grids of couples (Ryle & Breen, 1972a; Winter & Gournay, 1987), including each partner's accuracy in predicting the grid that the other has completed or the correlations between each partner's individual grid and a grid that they complete together, this indicating which partner's construing is dominant (Bannister & Bott, 1973).

The analysis of a group of grids provides the option of deriving the average grid of the group, which may then be subjected to a single grid Slater analysis. Each of the individual grids in the group may then be compared with the average grid using the two grids analysis option, thus providing an indication of the extent to which each member's construing deviates from that of the group as a whole. Amongst the areas in which this method of analysis has proved useful is the investigation of the process of group psychotherapy (Winter & Trippett, 1977).

Dependency Grid Analysis

IDIOGRID contains an analysis option for dependency grids. The main measure that can be derived from this is the dispersion of dependency index (Walker, Ramsey, & Bell, 1988), which does what it says on its label, namely measuring the extent to which dependencies are dispersed across the elements in the grid.

Qualitative Grids

The Perceiver Element Grid

There are a number of different forms of qualitative grid (Procter, 2002, 2014b; Procter & Cummins, 2014) which prove to be powerful methods of capturing construing in situations, in families, and groups as well as in an individual's construing of self. We have already seen the most well-known of these, the Perceiver Element Grid or 'PEG', a version of which we used in looking at Dorothy Rowe's family in Chapter 4. The PEG has its origin in the process of summarising how people in families see themselves and each other, using the results of individual repertory grids given to each member (Procter, 1978, 1985b). An example is shown in Table 6.6 of a family in which the parents came to the UK from Eastern Europe. They have two sons aged 19 and 17 years old, the older one having been diagnosed with schizophrenia. Each of the four perceivers' construing is contained in the rows. How each is construed can be seen

Table 6.6 Perceiver Element Grid: How each member sees self and the others (Procter, 1985b)

		Elements			
	PEG →	Mother	Father	Identified Patient	Brother
Perceivers	Mother	Placid, happy quiet, doesn't like football	Unhappy, temper, likes football	Placid, happy	Placid, happy
	Father	Sad, argumentative, shy, proud	Sad, argumentative, modest	Sad, argumentative, shy, modest	Proud, sociable, happy, modest
	Identified patient	Hard to please, warm, loving, babyish	Cold, not loving	Warm, shows feeling	Cold, not loving
	Brother	Depressed, introvert, gentle	Extrovert, rough, not clever	Depressed, introvert, gentle, not generous	Extrovert

in the columns. The diagonal boxes show how each member construes self. The arrow is a reminder to read the grid from left to right, otherwise confusion between rows and columns can easily occur. There is evidence in the grid of differences in views and values and of sadness, conflict, and frustration although mother sees both her sons as placid and happy.

It was soon realized that the PEG can be filled out directly by people, or by the therapists and researchers drawing the material from interviews and transcripts, without the need of administering repertory grids to the individuals in the first place. In individual therapy, a person can be asked to fill in a PEG, guessing how the other members in the family or in a situation would fill it in. (Rather than just writing words, people can also use drawings or cartoons, perhaps including 'thought bubbles'). People usually experience this as an enlightening exercise as it encourages them to 'get into the shoes' of the other people, as covered in Kelly's Sociality Corollary. It exposes gaps in people's knowledge: 'You know, I have no idea of how she was seeing him!' This encourages a stance of curiosity and questioning rather than making assumptions. But gaps may be evidence of construing which is suspended, submerged, or the result of invisibility of one member to another.

A particularly powerful use of PEGs is when individuals in a family or group are each asked to fill in an identical PEG independently, guessing how the others would fill in their sections, and then bringing them together to share and compare what they have written or drawn in a discussion (Procter, 2007a). This was used in a study of sons diagnosed with Attention Deficit Hyperactivity Disorder and their fathers (Stewart, Procter, & Dallos, 2011, see Table 6.7 for the son's PEG). The grid was given to the fathers and sons as four sheets labelled with the four views, giving ample room for text and/or drawings.

Aaron draws himself as seen as a protector of victims, standing up angrily to bullies in the school playground, and writes 'I can be a grumpy old man'. He sees his Dad in two different moods—an 'ogre' on a bad day and happy on a good day. He guesses his father would describe him as 'troublemaker' and 'distructive' (sic), in tiny writing, perhaps reflecting his shame or fear of being viewed this way by his father. He draws his father's self-construing as 'boss of the house', 'big and bluff', 'boss of us', and 'bill payer' with cartoons showing him as triumphant and

Table 6.7 Aaron's PEG showing how he sees himself and his father and how he guesses father sees himself and his son

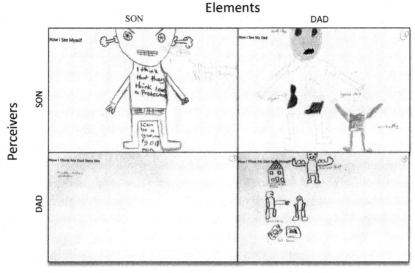

giving instructions. Father, in his turn, describes himself in his PEG as a disciplinarian and that Aaron sees him as 'a bit of a bully'.

The discussion of their grids (which, of course, they were both aware would take place before the exercise) was video recorded and transcribed. It was notable in being heated but led to an increased understanding between father and son. In this way the method proves to be of therapeutic value as well as being a powerful assessment technique. By its nature, the PEG gives equal weight to all the members. As they both look at the material in front of them, it is clear that two persons and their worlds are being represented, and both can feel understood. This can correct the power imbalance that results when only one participant's voice predominates.

The PEG is a flexible instrument and indeed can be adapted 'on the fly' in clinical situations, for example, by adding further rows and columns as new figures are introduced into the account. It has been used to explore different selves in the 'Community of Selves' (Mair, 2015a) and how these relate in different situations and relationships

(Stojnov & Procter, 2012). Pavlović (2011), for example, offers a grid in which a young woman explores how her sub-selves labeled as 'hard-worker', 'negotiator', and 'children' relate. In situations of high tension and conflict, people can be asked what their *goals* would be, in filling out the boxes: 'How would you/she *like to be able to see* self and others, after a successful resolution of the difficulties' (Procter, 2007b). This helps to focus on positive ways forward and was used in working with a dysfunctional team of therapists (Procter, 2007b). Other uses of the PEG have concerned relations in foster families (Cooper, 2011), family adjustment to acquired brain injury and dementia (Coppock et al., 2017; Davis, 2012), attitudes to mothers in health-care settings (Holder, 2018), and paternal filicide (Sedumedi, 2018). More generally, it has found use in situations of intercultural conflict (Barbour & Bourne, 2020; Burr et al., 2014; Naffi & Davidson, 2017), which can valuably inform clinical work with dual-heritage families.

Dyads and Triads

It is notable that all the constructs in Table 6.6 are monadic, they only refer to the individuals concerned. As we saw in Chapter 4, much crucial construing in situations occurs at the dyadic and triadic levels, as shown in the grid used to capture Dorothy Rowe's experiences (Table 4.2). The flexibility of the PEG allows us to add columns (and rows) to the grid as the discussion in therapy considers the *relationships between the members* as elements, in general or in specific situations. It is even possible to include dyads, for example, as perceivers and to include them as *rows* in the grid. A useful grid in working with couples and other pairs is shown in Table 6.8.

In this 'I-Me-You-Us' grid, or 'IMYU', Carol is asked to fill the grid in about the tensions that exist with her brother. She feels that as a woman and older sister, the daily burdens of care for their elderly and dementing parents are largely resting on her shoulders. She feels stuck in her efforts to get a fairer balance of input, but fears the results of escalating conflict or a split if she were to insist that he do more for them. In spite of being a dyadic situation, it is a triadic problematic situation that is being

Table 6.8 IMYU Grid: Carol (63) considers the relationship with her younger brother regarding looking after their ageing parents

→	Me	You	Us
I	Engaged with family Keep everyone going	Disengaged with family at times Keeping self going	Trying to find a balance without talking about it. Trying to find common ground
You	Doing too much	Not doing enough	Too busy to discuss a better balance between competing responsibilities
We	Doing more than my fair share	Meeting the needs of your new family at the expense of your old one from birth	Getting through this traumatic time in any way we can

described, as in the final column in Table 4.2. One could add a column to ask for the construing of the triad (including the parents) if this were felt to be useful. Carol was surprised when asked to do this exercise. She suddenly realised in filling in the bottom row that this 'We' relationship was the most important thing and that it was worth developing and building on it after their many years of very independent lives.

Event or Episode Grids

The Perceiver Element Grid captures the construing occurring between a group of people in general or at a particular point in time. If one wishes to capture changes over time, one can of course repeat the grid at a later point in time. This is useful in plotting changes over a course of therapy or with a change in circumstances, such as the onset of illness or a set of problems. For example, Davis (2012) looked at changes in dyadic relationships in a family with the onset of dementia in one of the members. However, one can look at changes over long or short periods of time in one grid by devoting the rows to events, episodes, or eras. In the last, for example, we may look at an adult's life and have them fill in a grid with rows devoted to *childhood, adolescence,* and *the current situation.* One could add a fourth row for 'how I would like things to be in the future'. The columns are then devoted to how the person sees various people, or how various people are seen to construe events or issues.

It is also possible to use these grids for tracing construing over a rapid sequence of events. This is valuable, for example, in tracing the construing involved in a traumatic or crisis situation, or a repeating pattern of conflict in a couple or between a parent and child. Procter and Procter (2008) used an Event or Episode Perceiver Grid (EPG) to examine how the argument between Cain and Abel developed over a period of minutes, culminating in the latter's murder, as depicted in a play by Byron. Table 6.9 shows an EPG depicting a traumatic and life-changing series of events described by Dorothy Rowe (2007) at a family party when she was five years old.

In this grid, the events or episodes are given in each row, and the columns show the perceivers' construings or utterances. Again, this is all given in the account of one participant – Dorothy (Dot). In therapy or research, the actual views of the people involved can be entered into the grid, allowing for a record that represents each person's view of the situation. Dorothy recounts here an experience of rejection and discon-firmation that she feels shaped her whole future life path and perhaps led to her making the significant contribution that she has in psychology and the understanding of and therapy for depression and other difficulties.

Methods of Exploring Construct Implications

Laddering

Probably the best-known method of investigating the implications of constructs is laddering, devised by one of Kelly's students, Dennis Hinkle (1965), and only ever presented by him in a very extensively quoted Ph.D thesis. In this procedure, the person is asked, for one of their constructs, which pole he or she would prefer to be described by and why. This question elicits the preferred pole of a new construct, the contrast pole of which, if not spontaneously provided, may be elicited by asking what is the opposite of the preferred pole. This process is repeated with the new construct that has been elicited, and continued until the

Table 6.9 Episode Perceiver Grid (EPG) depicting crucial events in Dorothy's childhood (text taken from Rowe, 2007, p. 158)

EPG		Perceivers	
		Dorothy aged 5	Family members
Episodes	Granma's 75th Birthday Party	I spent all day with my mother and my aunts with the preparations I fetched and carried	It should have been obvious to any adult that the party was very important to me
	A person I did not know arrived but there was no more room at the table		My mother said, "He can have Dot's place. She doesn't need to sit at the table"
	Dorothy runs out	My heart stood still. I had to get away, to hide. I ran down the hall and out the front gate and into the night and hid in my father's car	No one came to search for me. I could not expose myself to all those eyes and the clucking about how I had got over my little upset
	Eventually my father appeared at the side of the car asking if I would like something to eat	I shook my head and shrank back into the corner of the back seat	
	After	But I did not forget. That night I began my journey away from my family. 'You've got to learn to leave the table when love's no longer being served' (Nina Simone)	No mention was ever made of this event

person cannot think of a reason for their preference or this reason is self-evident. Laddering was designed to elicit increasingly superordinate constructs, and Hinkle (1965) provided some evidence for this, although it has not gone entirely unchallenged (Bell, 2014; Butt, 1995). However, whether or not laddering produces a clear hierarchy of constructs, it often reveals interesting relationships between constructs.

Of particular interest in indicating possible dilemmas is a situation in which the preferred pole of a construct switches from one to the other side of the ladder. This was the case with a client who was experiencing difficulties in his work situation, and who produced the ladder presented in Table 6.10, in which the preferred pole of *selfless* in the first rung of the ladder led up to the non-preferred pole of *not employable* in the last. This dilemma subsequently became a focus of therapy with the client (Winter, 2008).

The construct in the bottom rung of the ladder will often be much more concrete than the one in the last example. For example, consider the ladders in Table 6.11, completed by the members of a couple who were having constant heated arguments about seemingly trivial matters. In this case, one of these subordinate issues, concerning where to squeeze a toothpaste tube, is seen to have fundamentally different implications for them.

Table 6.10 Example of a ladder

Not employable	Versus	Employable
Always thinks about the consequences of their behaviour on other people	versus	Successful and held in high regard
Feels better about self from a moral perspective	versus	Able to live with self
Selfless	versus	Calculating

Table 6.11 Example of ladders completed by a couple

Husband	Wife
Exploits the planet–Respects the planet	Free–Repressed
Thoughtless–Conserves resources	Authentic–Rule-bound
Wasteful–Thrifty	Spontaneous–Inhibited
Squeezes tube from the middle-Squeezes from the end	Squeezes tube from the middle-Squeezes from the end

Pyramiding

In contrast to laddering, pyramiding, developed by another of Kelly's students, Landfield (1971), aims to elicit the subordinate implications of constructs. It involves asking, for each pole of a construct, what kind of a person is someone so described and/or how does one know that a person is like this.

Implications Grid

Laddering was not the only construct assessment technique devised by Hinkle. In another, the implications grid, constructs are elicited from an individual in the usual way and a grid is constructed in which each construct is represented in both a row and a column of the grid. The person is then asked, for each construct, 'if you woke up one morning and realized that you were best described by one side of this construct while the day before you had been best described by the opposite side – if you realized that you were changed in this *one* respect - what other constructs…would be *likely* to be changed by a change in yourself on this one construct alone?' (Hinkle, 1965, p. 37, italics in original). A tick is inserted in each cell of the grid in which a change in the construct in the corresponding row implies a change in the construct in the corresponding column.

A variation on this procedure is Fransella's (1972) bi-polar implications grid, in which each pole of each of a person's elicited constructs is written on a card and the person is asked for each card, one at a time, if all that he or she knew about someone was that they had the characteristic described on the card, which other cards would apply to them. The rows and columns of the grid matrix consist of the construct poles, and ticks are inserted in those cells where if a person were described by the construct pole in the corresponding row he or she would also be described by the pole in the corresponding column.

Simple methods of analysing implications grids include counting the number of implications of each construct (or construct pole in the bi-polar implications grid), which Hinkle considered to indicate the construct's superordinacy. More complex methods of analysis have been proposed by Caputi, Breiger, and Pattison (1990).

Resistance to Change Grid

Yet another new procedure described in Hinkle's Ph.D. thesis is the resistance to change grid. Here, the person is asked, for each elicited construct, which pole he or she would prefer to be described by. Each construct is then paired with every other and the person is asked, for each pair, on which construct he or she would rather shift from the preferred to the non-preferred pole if such a shift had to be made on one of the constructs. A construct's resistance-to-change score is obtained by counting the number of times that the person would prefer not to change on the construct, and again Hinkle (1965) associated this with the construct's superordinacy.

ABC Model

Tschudi's (1977) ABC model explores the positive and negative implications of each pole of a construct (construct A), and, as in its original major applications, may be particularly useful when this construct concerns a symptom and its contrast (Tschudi & Winter, 2011). This construct, the problem construct, is first elicited, one of its poles (a1) representing the problematic position and the other (a2) the desired position. The person is then asked for the negative consequences of a1 and the positive consequences of a2, this providing the poles b1 and b2 of a new construct, B. Finally, the person is asked for the desirable consequences of a1 and the undesirable consequences of a2, their answers providing the poles c2 and c1 respectively of a 'payoff construct', C. It is this latter construct which can be viewed as preventing movement from a1 to a2, for example the loss of the client's symptom.

Table 6.12 provides the ABC responses of Tom, who attended a social skills group because he wanted to be more assertive, but whose scores on a range of outcome measures deteriorated over the course of the group sessions. His 'problem construct' is of interest as he gave his

Table 6.12 Example of an ABC

a1. Reasonable (unassertive)	a2. Stands up for himself and asserts his opinion
b1. Mixed up inside and withdrawn	b2. Relieves tension
c2.1. Perceived as a good bloke	c1.1. Perceived as a pain in the neck
c2.2. Would not risk losing argument	c1.2. Might lose an argument
c2.3. Would not become attacking or violent	c1.3. Might become personally attacking or physically violent

problematic position as not only being *unassertive* but also being *reasonable*. While the negative consequence of being unassertive and reasonable was to be *mixed up inside and withdrawn*, its positive consequences, or payoffs, were to be *perceived as a good bloke*, who *would not risk losing an argument*, and *would not become attacking or violent*. It was small wonder, then, that he responded poorly to a therapeutic intervention that aimed to make him behave more assertively but did not consider the implications that such a change might carry for him (Winter, 1987).

A Wealth of Methods

Personal construct psychology has generated a large number of methods for the assessment of construing and, in keeping with the underlying theory, there are various alternative forms of each of these methods and numerous specific measures that can be derived from many of them. We have given detailed attention to some of the methods in this chapter since they may be central to the diagnostic process in personal and relational construct psychotherapy (as we shall see in Chapter 7), may be used in the therapeutic process itself, and can also provide sensitive measures of therapeutic outcome which, unlike standard questionnaires, can be tailored to the individual client (Winter, 2003c). Since they use individuals' own constructs rather than imposing particular constructs upon them, they are also well suited to work in different cultural settings (e.g., Winter, Brown, Goins, & Mason, 2016). However, we have still not been able to give more than a flavour of personal construct assessment methodology, and the reader who wishes to explore this area further is recommended to turn to Caputi, Viney, Walker, and Crittenden (2012), Bell (2016), G. Neimeyer (1993), and Fransella, Bell, and Bannister (2004).

References

Bannister, D., & Bott, M. (1973). Evaluating the person. In P. Klein (Ed.), *New Approaches to Psychological Medicine* (pp. 157–177). Chichester, UK: Wiley.

Barbour, P. J., & Bourne, D. (2020/in press). Developing sociality in a post-conflict Northern Ireland: An application of the Perceiver Element Grid. *Journal of Constructivist Psychology*.

Bell, R. C. (2009). *GRIDSTAT, Version 5: A Program for Analyzing the Data of a Repertory Grid* (computer software). Department of Psychology, University of Melbourne.

Bell, R. C. (2014). Did Hinkle prove laddered constructs are superordinate? A re-examination of his data suggests not. *Personal Construct Theory and Practice, 11,* 1–4.

Bell, R. C. (2016). Methodologies of assessment. In D. A. Winter & N. Reed (Eds.), *The Wiley Handbook of Personal Construct Psychology* (pp. 71–87). Chichester, UK: Wiley-Blackwell.

Burr, V., Giliberto, M., & Butt, T. (2014). Construing the cultural other and the self: A personal construct analysis of English and Italian perceptions of national character. *International Journal of Intercultural Relations, 39,* 53–65.

Butler, R. J. (2001). *The Self Image Profiles for Children and Adolescents.* London: The Psychological Corporation.

Butt, T. (1995). Ordinal relationships between constructs. *Journal of Constructivist Psychology, 8,* 227–236.

Caputi, P., Breiger, R., & Pattison, P. (1990). Analyzing implications grids using hierarchical models. *International Journal of Personal Construct Psychology, 3,* 77–90.

Caputi, P., Viney, L. L., Walker, B. M., & Crittenden, N. (Eds.) (2012). *Personal Construct Methodology.* Chichester, UK: Wiley-Blackwell.

Cooper, E. (2011). *Exploring the personal constructs of looked after children and their foster carers: A qualitative study.* Unpublished DClinPsy thesis, University of Hertfordshire.

Coppock, C., Winter, D., Ferguson, S., & Green, A. (2017). Using the Perceiver Element Grid (PEG) to elicit intrafamily construal following parental Acquired Brain Injury. *Personal Construct Theory and Practice, 14,* 25–39.

Davis, C. (2012). *Women's narratives of dementia: An exploration of the impact of male dementia on families.* Unpublished DClinPsych thesis, University of Surrey.

Davis, H., Stroud, A., & Green, L. (1989). Child characterization sketch. *International Journal of Personal Construct Psychology, 2,* 323–337.

De Boeck, P., & Rosenberg, S. (1988). Hierarchical classes: Model and data analysis. *Psychometrika, 53,* 361–381.

Duck, S. (1973). *Personal Relationships and Personal Constructs: A Study of Friendship Formation.* London: Wiley.

Epting, F. R., Suchman, D. L., & Nickeson, C. J. (1971). An evaluation of elicitation procedures for personal constructs. *British Journal of Psychology, 62,* 513–517.

Feixas, G., Geldschläger, H., & Neimeyer, R. A. (2002). Content analysis of personal constructs. *Journal of Constructivist Psychology, 15,* 1–20.

Feixas, G., & Saúl, L. A. (2004). The Multi-Center Dilemma Project: An investigation on the role of cognitive conflicts in health. *Spanish Journal of Psychology, 7,* 69–78.

Feixas, G., & Villegas, M. (1991). Personal construct analysis of autobiographical text: A method presentation and case illustration. *International Journal of Personal Construct Psychology, 4,* 51–83.

Feldman, M. M. (1975). The body image and object relations: Exploration of a method utilizing repertory grid technique. *British Journal of Medical Psychology, 48,* 317–332.

Fransella, F. (1972). *Personal Change and Reconstruction: Research on a Treatment of Stuttering.* London: Academic Press.

Fransella, F., Bell, R., & Bannister, D. (2004). *A Manual for Repertory Grid Technique.* Chichester, UK: Wiley.

Fromm, M., & Bacher, A. (2014). *GridSuite 4* (Windows and Mac Ed.). Stuttgart: University of Stuttgart.

Gaines, B. R., & Shaw, M. L. G. (1997). Knowledge acquisition, modelling and inference through the World Wide Web. *International Journal of Human-Computer Studies, 6,* 729–759.

Garcia-Gutierrez, A., & Feixas, G. (2018). *GRIDCOR: A Repertory Grid Analysis Tool* (Version 6.0) [Web application]. Retrieved from http://www.repertorygrid.net/en.

Grice, J. W. (2002). IDIOGRID: Software for the management and analysis of repertory grids. *Behavior, Research Methods, Instruments, and Computer, 34,* 338–341.

Heckmann, M. (2014). *The OpenRepGrid project—Software tools for the analysis and administration of repertory grid data.* Workshop held at the 12th. Biennial Conference of the European Personal Construct Association (EPCA), Brno, Czech Republic.

Heckmann, M., Pries, J. C., Engelhardt, T.-C., Meixner, J., Saúl, L. A., Perea-Luque, J. R. & López-González, M. A. (2019). On the relation between order of elicitation and subjective construct importance. *Journal of Constructivist Psychology, 32,* 18–32.

Hinkle, D. N. (1965). *The change of personal constructs from the viewpoint of a theory of construct implications.* Unpublished PhD thesis, Ohio State University.

Holder, E. (2018). *Mothers' and professionals' construal of the role of mother in health care settings.* Unpublished DClinPsy. thesis, University of Hertfordshire.

Jackson, S. R., & Bannister, D. (1985). Growing into self. In D. Bannister (Ed.), *Issues and Approaches in Personal Construct Theory* (pp. 67–82). London: Academic Press.

Jenkin, A. C., Ellis-Caird, H., & Winter, D. A. (2020/in press). Moral judgments and ethical constructs in clinical psychology doctoral students. *Ethics and Behavior.*

Jenkin, A. C., & Winter, D. A. (2020/in press). Exploration of ethical construing in clinical psychology doctoral students: An adaptation of repertory grid technique. *Journal of Constructivist Psychology.*

Kelly, G. A. (1955). *The Psychology of Personal Constructs. Vol. I, II.* New York: Norton (2nd printing: 1991, London and New York: Routledge).

Kremsdorf, R. (1985). An extension of fixed-role therapy with a couple. In F. Epting & A. W. Landfield (Eds.), *Anticipating Personal Construct Psychology* (pp. 216–224). Lincoln: University of Nebraska Press.

Landfield, A. (1971). *Personal Construct Systems in Psychotherapy.* Chicago: Rand McNally.

Mair, J. M. M. (2015a). The community of self. In D. A. Winter & N. Reed (Eds.), *Toward a Radical Re-Definition of Psychology: The Selected Works of Miller Mair* (pp. 102–112). London: Routledge.

McDonagh, D., & Adams-Webber, J. (1987). The implication potential of personal constructs in relation to their subjective importance and order of elicitation. *Social Behavior and Personality, 15,* 81–86.

Naffi, N., & Davidson, A.-L. (2017). Engaging host society youth in exploring how they construe the influence of social media on the resettlement of Syrian refugees. *Personal Construct Theory and Practice, 14,* 116–128.

Neimeyer, G. J. (Ed.). (1993). *Constructivist Assessment: A Casebook.* Newbury Park, CA: Sage.

Neimeyer, R. A. (1985). Personal constructs in clinical practice. In P. C. Kendall (Ed.), *Advances in Cognitive-Behavioural Research and Therapy* (Vol. 4, pp. 275–339). New York: Academic Press.

Neimeyer, R. A., Klein, M. H., Gurman, A. S., & Greist, J. H. (1983). Cognitive structure and depressive symptomatology. *British Journal of Cognitive Psychotherapy, 1,* 65–73.

Pavlović, J. (2011). Personal construct psychology and social constructionism are not incompatible: Implications of a reframing. *Theory and Psychology, 21,* 396–411.

Procter, H. G. (1978). *Personal construct theory and the family: A theoretical and methodological Study.* Unpublished PhD thesis, University of Bristol.

Procter, H. G. (1985b). Repertory grid techniques in family therapy and research. In N. Beail (Ed.), *Repertory Grid Technique: Application in Clinical and Educational Settings* (pp. 218–242). Beckenham, UK: Croom Helm.

Procter, H. G. (2002). Constructs of individuals and relationships. *Context, 59,* 11–12.

Procter, H. G. (2007a). Construing within the family. In R. Butler & D. Green (Eds.), *The Child Within: Taking the Young Person's Perspective by Applying Personal Construct Theory* (2nd ed., pp. 190–206). Chichester, UK: Wiley.

Procter, H. G. (2007b). *Manual for Using the G-PEG (Goals Perceiver Element Grid) in Team Building and Consultation.* Retrieved April 2018, from: http://www.pcp-net.org/tools/G-PEG%20Manual%202015.pdf.

Procter, H. G. (2014b). Qualitative grids, the relationality corollary and the levels of interpersonal construing. *Journal of Constructivist Psychology, 27,* 243–262.

Procter, H. G., & Cummins, P. (2014). *Personal Construct Psychology and Qualitative Grids: A series of 5 videos introducing the methods.* Retrieved October 2019, from: https://www.youtube.com/watch?v=z3uS7UA0P9M&feature=youtu.be&list=PLQwfkFsf7l9dg5Q2afwWkWflfbQGYCVwX.

Procter, H. G., & Procter, M. J. (2008). The use of qualitative grids to examine the development of the construct of good and evil in Byron's play 'Cain: a mystery'. *Journal of Constructivist Psychology, 21,* 343–354.

Reed, N., Winter, D., Schulz, J., Aslan, E., Soldevilla, J. M., & Kuzu, D. (2014). An exemplary life? A personal construct analysis of the autobiography of Rudolf Hoess, commandant of Auschwitz. *Journal of Constructivist Psychology, 27*, 274–288.

Rowe, D. (2007). *My Dearest Enemy, My Dangerous Friend: Making and Breaking Sibling Bonds.* London: Routledge.

Ryle, A., & Breen, D. (1972a). A comparison of adjusted and maladjusted couples using the double dyad grid. *British Journal of Medical Psychology, 45*, 375–382.

Ryle, A., & Breen, D. (1972b). Some differences in the personal constructs of neurotic and normal subjects. *British Journal of Psychiatry, 120*, 483–489.

Ryle, A., & Lipshitz, S. (1975). Recording change in marital therapy with the reconstruction grid. *British Journal of Medical Psychology, 49*, 281–285.

Ryle, A., & Lunghi, M. (1970). The dyad grid—A modification of repertory grid technique. *British Journal of Psychiatry, 117*, 323–327.

Sedumedi, P. (2018). *I killed my child(ren): A qualitative study exploring the phenomenon of paternal filicide in the South African context.* Unpublished PhD thesis, University of Hertfordshire.

Sewell, K. W., Cromwell, R. L., Farrell-Higgins, J., Palmer, R., Ohlde, C., & Patterson, T. W. (1996). Hierarchical elaboration in the conceptual structure of Vietnam veterans. *Journal of Constructivist Psychology, 9*, 79–96.

Slater, P. (1970). Personal questionnaire data treated as a form of repertory grid. *British Journal of Social and Clinical Psychology, 9*, 357–370.

Slater, P. (1977). *The Measurement of Intrapersonal Space by Grid Technique. Vol. 2. Dimensions of Intrapersonal Space.* London: Wiley.

Stewart, S., Procter, H. G., & Dallos, R. (2011). Fathers, sons and ADHD: A qualitative personal construct study. In D. Stojnov, V. Džinović, J. Pavlović, & M. Frances (Eds.), *Personal Construct Psychology in an Accelerating World* (pp. 109–126). Belgrade, Serbia: Serbian Constructivist Association, EPCA.

Stojnov, D., & Procter, H. G. (2012). Spying on the self: Reflective elaborations in personal and relational construct psychology. In M. Giliberto, F. Velacogna, & C. Dell'Aversano (Eds.), *PCP and Constructivism: Ways of Working, Learning and Living.* Firenze, Italy: Libri Liberi.

Tschudi, F. (1977). Loaded and honest questions: A construct theory view of symptoms and therapy. In D. Bannister (Ed.), *New Perspectives in Personal Construct Theory* (pp. 321–350). London: Academic Press.

Tschudi, F. (1993). *Manual FLEXIGRID 5.21.* Oslo: Tschudi System Sales.

Tschudi, F., & Winter, D. (2011). The ABC model revisited. In P. Caputi, L. L. Viney, B. M. Walker, & N. Crittenden (Eds.), *Personal Construct Methodology* (pp. 89–108). Chichester, UK: Wiley-Blackwell.

Walker, B. M., Ramsay, F. L., & Bell, R. C. (1988). Dispersed and undispersed dependency. *International Journal of Personal Construct Psychology, 1,* 63–80.

Winter, D. A. (1983). Logical inconsistency in construct relationships: Conflict or complexity? *British Journal of Medical Psychology, 56,* 79–88.

Winter, D. A. (1987). Personal construct psychotherapy as a radical alternative to social skills training. In R. A. Neimeyer & G. J. Neimeyer (Eds.), *Personal Construct Therapy Casebook* (pp. 107–123). New York: Springer.

Winter, D. A. (1992). *Personal Construct Psychology in Clinical Practice: Theory, Research and Applications.* London: Routledge.

Winter, D. A. (2003c). Repertory grid technique as a psychotherapy research measure. *Psychotherapy Research, 13,* 25–42.

Winter, D. A. (2008). Personal construct psychotherapy in a national health service setting: Does survival mean selling out? In J. D. Raskin & S. K. Bridges (Eds.), *Studies in Meaning: 3. Constructivist Therapy in the 'Real' World* (pp. 229–252). New York: Pace University Press.

Winter, D. A., Bell, R. C., & Watson, S. (2010). Midpoint ratings on personal constructs: Constriction or the middle way? *Journal of Constructivist Psychology, 23,* 337–356.

Winter, D. A., Brown, R., Goins, S., & Mason, C. (2016). *Trauma, Survival and Resilience in War Zones: The Psychological Impact of War in Sierra Leone and Beyond.* Hove, UK: Routledge.

Winter, D. A., Feixas, G., Dalton, R., Jarque-llanazares, L., Laso, E., Mallindine, C., & Patient, S. (2007). Construing the construction processes of serial killers and violent offenders: 1. The analysis of narratives. *Journal of Constructivist Psychology, 20,* 1–22.

Winter, D. A., Goggins, S., Baker, M., & Metcalfe, C. (1996). Into the community or back to the ward? Clients' construing as a predictor of the outcome of psychiatric rehabilitation. In B. M. Walker, J. Costigan, L. L. Viney, & B. Warren (Eds.), *Personal Construct Theory: A Psychology for the Future* (pp. 253–276). Sydney: Australian Psychological Society.

Winter, D., & Gournay, K. (1987). Constriction and construction in agoraphobia. *British Journal of Medical Psychology, 60,* 233–244.

Winter, D. A., & Muhanna-Matar, A. (2020). Cycles of construing and self-constitution in radicalization and deradicalization: A study of Salafist Muslims. *Journal of Constructivist Psychology, 33,* 58–88.

Winter, D. A., & Trippett, C. J. (1977). Serial change in group psychotherapy. *British Journal of Medical Psychology, 50,* 341–348.

7

Personal and Relational Construct Formulation

Diagnosis and Formulation

The word formulation as applied to psychotherapy is often said to originate with the cognitive-behavioural tradition (Bruch, 1998), and formulation is currently championed by clinical psychologists as an alternative to psychiatric diagnosis (Division of Clinical Psychology, 2011). However, many years before these developments, Kelly was making extensive use of the term. It is central to his approach to psychotherapy and indeed it appears nearly 200 times in his two 1955 volumes. His contribution here was revolutionary and included a radical critique of the categorical approach to diagnosis, initiated by Kraepelin, which is still very much the dominant model today in, for example, the form of the DSM-V, a system based on categories or 'pigeon-holes' in which the client's difficulties are classified along the lines of the diseases of general medicine. Kelly proposes instead that our understanding of the person's problems, our *formulation*, needs to be based on the view, as we saw earlier, that a person is a 'form of motion': 'The client does not sit cooped up in a nosological pigeonhole, he proceeds along his way' (Kelly, 1955, p. 775). Rather than using fixed *categories* of disorder, therefore, we think

© The Author(s) 2020
H. Procter and D. A. Winter, *Personal and Relational Construct Psychotherapy*,
Palgrave Texts in Counselling and Psychotherapy,
https://doi.org/10.1007/978-3-030-52177-6_7

in terms of axes or *avenues of movement* along which we will help the person move towards a resolution of their difficulties, a process Kelly refers to as *transitive diagnosis*. Kelly (1955) considered that 'Transitive diagnosis is not complete until a plan for management and treatment has been formulated' (p. 810). However, 'transitive formulation' does not stop at this point but continues into the therapeutic conversation in a process of collaboration, rather than the therapist acting as expert delivering knowledge from on high. It goes without saying, of course, that when a client does present with a condition involving an organic or physiological process, such as stroke, dementia, neurological or developmental disorders, the therapist should have sufficient knowledge to be able to refer to the appropriate professional, but everything that we have to say about formulation continues to have relevance in the management of biological conditions as well.

Current definitions of formulation in psychotherapy usually involve *explanation*, in which 'causes' or 'factors' are identified as to *why* a problem is occurring, the assumption being that this will help the therapeutic process. For example, Eells (2006, p. 4) writes, 'a psychotherapy case formulation is a hypothesis about the causes, precipitants and maintaining influences of a person's psychological, interpersonal and behavioural problems'. This reflects the predominant determinism that, as we saw in our first chapter, Kelly was at pains to transcend, maintaining that construct dimensions do constrain us but also provide us with choice and avenues of free movement, degrees of freedom. A construct such as *normal* versus *ill* does not *cause* us to act in a certain way; it helps us to make sense of events and to choose certain alternatives. A parent may ask, 'If our son is *ill*, we want to know what treatment is available, what medication he should have? If he is not ill, he clearly needs to pull his socks up and stop behaving in these ridiculous ways'. As the construct theorist Butt (2013, p. 223) said, 'we should be content with a psychology of understanding rather than causal explanation'. PRCP formulation is concerned to *understand* situations and problems by identifying the constructs held by the client and others governing and structuring the behaviours, symptoms, and interactions which comprise the difficulties. The constructs act as a gateway to the client's world and open the possibility of discovering new ways of construing and moving forward.

For Kelly (1955), to formulate is very close to the term 'to construe'. The simplest formulation is the application of a construct: 'A construct is a *single* formulation of a likeness and a difference' (p. 133). He advises us to start the process of formulation by listening to how the client and others are formulating his or her complaint. Kelly writes, 'The manner in which it is formulated throws important light upon the complainant's basic framework of ideas' (p. 788). We are looking to understand what the Brief Therapy group call the *position on the problem* and the associated *position on therapy* (Fisch, Weakland, & Segal, 1982). Questions to throw light on this are given in Sects. 7 and 9 of Appendix A. The parent's construct mentioned above, 'is he ill or normal?', represents two general positions on the problem, a *medical* or a *moral* construction. The therapist attempts, in as faithful a way as possible, to understand the sets of constructs being applied by the client and others, including family members and professionals. By accepting and utilising these terms, the '*credulous approach*', the client and family will feel understood, opening the way for a productive therapeutic alliance.

But the therapist, in accepting these constructions, does not passively swallow them whole. He or she will begin to question in detail what they mean, including what the contrasting meaning is for the person. If appropriate, this may be done quite playfully. If the client is using the construct 'depression' to describe the problem, we may *deconstruct* it by shifting it to other similar words, for example *dejection* or *oppression*. As shown in Sect. 5 of Appendix A, we will ask for occasions when these feelings are most and least noticeable. We may ask for how strong the feelings are on a scale, or what was happening when the feeling was *not* present, what words are used to describe these 'exceptions' (White & Epston, 1990), beginning to elaborate the *contrast pole* and creating a new dimension or *pathway* along which it is possible to move. This is the shift from a categorical to a transitive formulation of the problem.

Problems typically become the subject of very elaborated construing, with many implications, examples, and shades of meaning, as the person and others struggle with the difficulties, whereas the contrast poles, the exceptions and goals, may remain quite idealised and impoverished in terms of implications, as our mention of Fransella's work on stuttering in Chapter 3 indicated. The therapist will want to counter this by elaborating examples of the contrast poles by asking for goals and when these have already been experienced, encouraging vivid imagery of these occasions by asking for examples of the actions and situations associated with them (see Sect. 4 of Appendix A for ways of approaching this). Sometimes the client, perhaps as a result of being referred, has already experienced some examples of 'improvement' or 'progress', shifts to the contrast pole of the construct. In this case, a switch to a discussion of these experiences may be made, even in a first session, to examine the changes in detail and how the person achieved them, as shown by the questions in Sect. 10 of Appendix A.

Formulation is a *process*, a collaborative joint inquiry, in which sense is made of the situation by both client and therapist, testing out the hypotheses and reformulating progressively. This equalisation of the power relationship in therapy is vital in helping people to get back in touch with their own *agency*, to begin to realise that it is possible to make changes in the pattern of life. Both client and therapist bring their own kinds of expertise to the alliance—the client is an expert on his or her own life, the therapist an expert on helping people in general—a relationship Kelly (1969b) likens to that between a research supervisor and person doing the front-line research, and which Feixas (1995) described as the expert-to-expert relationship.

The richness of the therapeutic dialogue can be overwhelming. Kelly (1955) writes, 'within an hour's psychotherapeutic interview the clinical psychologist may have successfully formulated and accepted approximate answers to dozens of issues' (p. 192). He advises us to see formulation as taking place in two stages, *structuration* and *construction*. One of the problems in this work is becoming attached to a particular hypothesis and thus becoming impermeable to other ways of looking at the situation. He warns us that, 'every clinician tends to be biased by what he hears' (p. 798). Structuration minimises the risk of this. It consists of a rough classification of all of the details of the case placed under temporary headings. In the first author's practice, he would reserve a few minutes before every session to write these at the top of the sheet of paper designated for the session notes. Typical headings would be clients' interests, plans, examples of construing, life events, referral details, previous therapy, family members, school/work experiences, goals, hunches, possible strategies, and so on. Included in this would be details of diagnoses and other normative constructions of the case. The 'facts' of the case would be listed with no attempt to link them together yet into a coherent story. This reduces the tendency to start making sense of them prematurely, although they would inevitably be organised under the therapist's system. The therapist combines a 'not-knowing' stance with a keen awareness of all the details of the case, even if at this point they do not seem significant. The frame of mind of structuration can actually be maintained throughout the course of therapy.

As the therapist begins to grasp the situation better, he or she is able to 'subsume' the construing of the client and significant others in the situation and organise the material according to how the therapist considers that *they* construe it. We then enter the phase of *construction*. Kelly (1955, p. 1005) writes, 'As therapy progresses and the therapist acquires a better overview of the case, he may be able more and more to substitute construction for structuration of material arising during the course of the day-by-day sessions…permit(ting) him to see the client in perspective: past, present and future' (p. 765). The construction phase of formulation is aided by using Kelly's set of 'professional diagnostic constructs', presented in Chapter 3. It is important to recognise that these constructs are not in themselves problem-oriented—they are as applicable to any other individual as they are to our client. As Kelly (1955) said, 'In themselves, they are neither good nor bad, healthy nor unhealthy, adaptive nor maladaptive' (p. 453).

Psychological Disorder

Despite his rejection of psychiatric nosology, Kelly (1955) did use the term disorder, defined as 'any personal construction which is used repeatedly in spite of consistent invalidation' (p. 831), and provided a rudimentary classification of disorders in terms of his diagnostic constructs.

While most of these categories of disorders relate to aspects of the structure or process of, or transitions in, construing, Kelly also indicated that some disorders may arise from the content of the construct system. In view of its mechanistic connotations, it has been suggested that the term 'disorder' be replaced by 'imbalance', reflecting the fact that disorders may reflect the persistent use of a particular strategy (for example, tightening, loosening, constriction, or dilation) to avoid invalidation rather than the cyclical interplay of contrasting strategies (Winter, 2003a, 2009). More generally, in a disorder the person's completion of Experience Cycles effectively becomes blocked, so that the person no longer tests out, and risks the invalidation of, their constructions. This state has been referred to as one of *non-validation* (Walker, 2002).

The relational and developmental aspects of disorders have also received increasing attention. As we have seen in Chapter 6, Kelly (1955) himself indicated that some disorders involve failure to disperse one's dependency relationships appropriately. Chiari et al. (1994) went on to identify dependency paths 'channelized' by aggression, threat, and guilt (in Kelly's sense of these terms), these having a basis in the child's early relationships with their parents. Chiari's (2017b) later elaboration of this model included the addition of a developmental path channelised by anxiety and a focus on the development of identity in childhood, a process which requires 'mutuality of intersubjective recognition...the willingness to recognize each other as *dependent on each other,* but at the same time as *fully individualized*' (p. 185). In disorders, there is considered to be uncompleted recognition in the form either of fusion, contempt, or negligence, associated with the dependency paths of threat, guilt, and anxiety respectively and with the likelihood of being assigned to particular psychiatric diagnostic categories. An alternative perspective, complete with a triaxial diagnostic system, has been provided by Leitner, Faidley, and Celentana (2000). Their first axis concerns the 'developmental/structural arrests' in a person's construing of self and others that may arise as a result of traumas experienced in childhood. Specifically, these arrests may involve failure to develop a distinction between, or senses of the permanence and constancy of, the self and others. Disorders are viewed by Leitner and his colleagues as involving a retreat from role relationships, those involving construing of the other person's construction processes, in order to avoid the risk of core role invalidation. The second axis of the system concerns interpersonal styles that may be used to avoid, or develop alternatives to, such relationships. These styles are undispersed, excessively dispersed, or avoidance of, dependencies; and physical or psychological distancing of the self from others. The third axis concerns limitations or strengths in nine aspects of the construing of others' construction processes, namely discrimination, flexibility, creativity, responsibility, openness, commitment, courage, forgiveness, and reverence.

Personal Construct Research on Psychological Disorders

The personal construct formulation of psychological problems is not just theoretically based but is supported by a not inconsiderable amount of research evidence. The studies concerned, most of which employ repertory grid technique, have examined differences in construing between client and non-client groups, relationships between construing and severity of symptomatology, and changes in construing associated with successful therapy. Some of this research may be criticised for its use of traditional psychiatric diagnostic categories to define its groups of participants, which are then compared in terms of aspects of their construing. This arguably only results in a reframing of the traditional diagnoses in personal construct terms, rather than any more fundamental paradigm shift. Nevertheless, it has been of value in demonstrating that the problems of people who receive psychiatric diagnostic labels can be explained in terms of exactly the same processes of construing as operate in people who escape such labels. It has also provided a basis for the development of personal construct psychotherapeutic approaches for the people concerned. It is beyond the scope of this book to provide a comprehensive review of the research, but we shall now outline some of its principal findings.

Construct System Structure and Construing Processes

The above critique of personal construct research on psychological disorders is perhaps most clearly illustrated by the first major research programme in this area, conducted by Bannister and his colleagues on clients diagnosed with schizophrenic thought disorder. In his original studies, using repertory grid technique, Bannister (1960, 1962) provided evidence that such clients were characterised by loose construing, as reflected in weak and unstable relationships between constructs. This research resulted in the development of a grid test for the diagnosis of schizophrenic thought disorder (Bannister & Fransella, 1966), much to the later regret of at least one of its authors (Fransella, 2001). It was nevertheless valuable in generating a hypothesis, supported by further research (Bannister, 1963, 1965; Cipolletta & Racerro, 2003), that loosening in clients who receive this diagnosis is a response to serial invalidation of construing; and, as we shall see in Chapter 7, a therapeutic intervention to reverse this process. It also stimulated a number of other research studies on construing in people diagnosed as psychotic (Garcia-Mieres et al., 2019; Winter, 1992), the findings of which have not been entirely consistent[1] but which at least have provided a message that talk and behaviour that might appear bizarre may reflect a perfectly understandable process of construing rather than being the symptoms of an illness. Bannister's 'serial invalidation hypothesis', together with research indicating relationships between the structure of construing of clients diagnosed as schizophrenic and that of their parents (Winter, 1975), have also pointed to the importance of taking a relational perspective on the construing of people so diagnosed. Indeed, when Bannister first advanced his hypothesis, it was considered to be consistent with theories of schizophrenia that emphasised processes of family interaction, such as the 'double bind' (Bateson, Jackson, Haley, & Weakland, 1956).

Another body of research concerned with general structural characteristics of the construct system has provided evidence, albeit again not entirely consistent, of tight, undifferentiated construing in clients diagnosed with depressive or anxiety disorders (Winter, 1992). Of arguably greater interest and therapeutic relevance, though, are studies that, rather than examining the structure of the entire construct system, have focused on subsystems within it. As mentioned in Chapter 3, one of the earliest such studies was Fransella's (1972) research, which has received some subsequent support (DiLollo, Manning, & Neimeyer, 2005), demonstrating that the 'stuttering' construct subsystems of people who stutter are more structured than their 'fluency' construct subsystems. Stuttering is central to these individuals' core roles, and is in effect their 'way of life', just as, for example, addiction may be to the core role of the person who is chemically dependent (Klion, 1993).

In research on people who have suffered post-traumatic stress, the focus has been on the subsystem of constructs applied to the traumatic event. This work was pioneered by Sewell (1997), who found construing of the traumatic event to be significantly less elaborated in people who were diagnosed with post-traumatic stress disorder than in those not so diagnosed despite experiencing the same, or similar, events. In Sewell's view, the former people were in a state of 'constructive bankruptcy' in that their constructs did not allow them to make sense of the traumatic event. However, Sermpezis and Winter (2009) have provided evidence for the contrary view that in people diagnosed with post-traumatic stress disorder the traumatic event is over-elaborated and thus comes to dominate their lives. Other studies have focused upon characteristics of construing associated with particular traumatic experiences, such as childhood sexual abuse (Bhandari, Winter, Messer, & Metcalfe, 2011; Erbes & Harter, 2002).

Turning to another of Kelly's diagnostic constructs, constriction, there is some research indicating constrictive processes in particular types of psychological disorder. Such processes, involving the delimiting of the person's world to avoid events that are difficult to construe, may find expression in various complaints with which clients present but perhaps no more vividly than in agoraphobia. It can now be revealed that this was the presenting complaint of all of the clients extracts of whose self-characterisations are provided in Table 6.2. These self-characterisations, similarly to those in a study by Hopkins (2012), indicated that the clients tended to view themselves as very caring and to avoid situations of interpersonal conflict, and further repertory grid findings revealed that such conflict, and the emotions associated with it, was an area in which their construing was poorly elaborated (Winter & Gournay, 1987). Furthermore, their partners tended to share these features of construing, and the greater the commonality of construing between the clients and their partners, the less likely were the clients to go out of the house. In effect, they were constricting their interpersonal worlds to partners with whom their relationships were ones of mutual validation rather than facing the anxiety, and possible invalidation, occasioned by going out into a world in which they might encounter conflict situations that they were ill-equipped to construe. This once again indicates how crucial it is in understanding a client's predicament and providing appropriate therapeutic interventions to consider not only their own personal construct system but also the broader relational construct system or systems by which they are influenced. Similar issues have been addressed in personal construct and related research on other types of disorder: for example, an eating disorder may involve a constrictive strategy (Button, 1993) and express a particular type of construing within a family, which has been described as 'the semantics of power' (Castiglioni, Faccio, Veronese, & Bell, 2013).

Kelly (1961) regarded suicide as 'the ultimate constriction'. He produced a taxonomy of suicide, one of the categories in which was 'suicide as a dedicated act', which is designed to validate one's life...to extend its essential meaning' (p. 260). This was the type of suicide committed by Socrates, who decided to drink hemlock rather than renouncing his beliefs in civil obedience by fleeing after his death sentence for corruption and impiety. Kelly contrasted this type of suicide with 'mere suicide', which is of two types: 'deterministic suicide', in which 'the course of events is so obvious that there is no point in waiting around for the outcome'; and 'chaotic suicide', in which 'the only definite thing one can do is abandon the scene altogether' (p. 260). This taxonomy has been extended to other acts of self-harm, and some evidence has been provided that it has a reasonable level of inter-rater reliability when applied to interviews with people who have self-harmed (Winter et al., 2007). This research also found evidence that a constricted view of the future self was associated with high levels of hopelessness, consistent with some previous research that has associated constriction of construing with suicide risk (Dzamonja-Ignjatovic, 1997; Landfield,

1971), although Hughes and Neimeyer (1990, 1993) found the best predictor of such risk to be polarised and disorganised construing.

Self-Construing

A particular focus of research on aspects of construing associated with psychological disorder has been how the self is construed. Extreme and negative self-construing, including viewing the self as different from others, have been found in clients diagnosed with depression and anxiety disorders (Feixas, Erazo-Caicedo, Harter, & Bach, 2008; Winter, 1992), as well as in some studies of those diagnosed as psychotic (Garcia-Mieres et al., 2019). There is also evidence of negative self-constructions in clients presenting with eating disorders (Feixas et al., 2010) and those who have self-harmed and have high levels of suicidal ideation and hopelessness (Winter, Sireling et al., 2007). In clients diagnosed as schizophrenic, a weak sense of identity has been indicated by low elaboration of self-construing (Gara, Rosenberg, & Mueller, 1989).

Dilemmas

Another growing body of research focusing on the content, rather than the structure, of construing concerns *implicative dilemmas*, in which, as we have seen in Chapter 6, the preferred pole of one construct is associated with the non-preferred pole of another. Such dilemmas have now been observed in a range of client groups, to a greater extent than in non-clients (Feixas et al., 2014a; Feixas, Montesano, Erazo-Caicedo, Compañ, & Pucurull, 2014b; Feixas, Saúl, & Ávila-Espada, 2009; Montesano, Feixas, Erazo-Caicedo, Saúl, & Dada, 2014; Montesano, López-González, Saúl, & Feixas, 2015).

Formulation in the Relational Extension of PCP

In the 1950s, when Kelly's two volumes appeared, writers in the systemic family therapy tradition were developing what they claimed to be a new paradigm, a completely new way of understanding human problems. Haley, for example, was critiquing psychiatry and psychoanalysis, the dominant clinical approaches at the time, for situating problems inside the individual, contrasting this 'intrapsychic' view with an *interpersonal* formulation, which saw psychological difficulties as intimately tied up with changes, patterns of interaction, and conflicts in the identified patient's family relationships. He saw a gap, a 'discontinuous change' (Haley, 1963, p. 152) between the two levels of description. He criticised attempts to combine them and see both as 'true', for example, by seeing that the family relationships are mirrored inside the individual[2] or by focussing on how each individual perceives the relationships:

> Investigators continue to use concepts of the individual when attempting to describe family relationships…For example, individual family members are tested to discover how each perceives the relationships in his family. This is apparently a study of relationships, but essentially it is merely a study of individual perception. (Haley, 1963, p. 154)

Haley is willing to say that the family point of view does not *refute* intrapsychic descriptions, but his argument clearly constitutes a challenge to our own attempt to synthesise the personal and relational. However, Haley fails to see that when members are caught in repeating problematic patterns of interaction, their actions must be governed by how each is construing the immediate situation. To think otherwise would seem to imply a return to a behavioural stimulus-response view: a 'black box' model.[3] For us, of course, it is these very constructs which govern and maintain the interactional scenarios and that are revised in successful therapeutic change. The closing of the gap between the levels of description is made possible because our unit of analysis, the construct, functions across personal, relational, and cultural levels of description (Procter, 2016b). That Kelly was restricted to an intrapsychic level of understanding is belied by his statement that we must depart from 'the common notion that diagnosis involves an analysis of the client only... *both* the client and his milieu must be understood' (1955, p. 804).

The experience of interviewing family members together, when the chief protagonists in the drama are all present, frequently shows that each member is acting in an understandable way, given the context of the situation. If a person is faced, for example, with an apparently irreconcilable conflict, mutual misunderstanding, or power asymmetry between two other members, we may think, 'anyone in this situation would respond with the desperation, anger, anxiety, depression, or madness that this person is experiencing'! But it is not a question of blaming the other two. If one steps into the shoes of either of the others, one can arrive at a similar conclusion. The upshot of this observation is that *there does not have to be anything wrong with a member's functioning* at the intrapsychic level, with their physiological state, or with their manner of construing. Systems of relationships stuck in an unhelpful track can have a tendency to escalate, demonstrating the 'great effects of small causes' as Watzlawick, Weakland, and Fisch (1974, p. 127) put it. Extreme reactions such as violence, murder, suicide, or serious psychopathology can emerge from these apparently small beginnings. This does not mean, however, that Kelly's contributions to understanding disorders of construction and transition, discussed in the previous section, cannot at the same time apply. They can throw light on the state of shared construct systems and the FCS, just as they do on personal construct systems. In this framework, both levels of description complement each other seamlessly. This is enabled by Kelly insisting that his dimensions are not restricted to psychopathology but are applicable to anyone's construing, to all the family members, and to the therapist as well (see Chapter 11 on reflexivity for more on this).

Construing in the Family and in the Wider Culture

Comprehending the family's construing must involve understanding the cultural background and traditions in which the family is situated.

Kelly (1955, p. 93) takes a 'similarity-of-expectations view' of culture, rather than looking for its characteristics. He exhorts us to keep 'clearly aware of the cultural context in which deviant behaviour arises', the culture providing people with evidence of what they regard as 'true' (1955, p. 792). He lists many areas of questioning to help throw light on cultural construing including social class, ethnicity, identification with occupational, educational and religious groups, attitudes to people regarded as strangers, failures and successes, and the use of conventional terms for symptoms and difficulties. Kelly underlines the importance of finding out how clients themselves view their own cultural backgrounds and listening out for the 'we's' and 'they's' which indicate identification and contra-identification with belief systems and groupings in their milieu (1955, p. 718). The maternal and the paternal families of origin are often rooted in very different cultures and ways of making sense of life, relationships, problems, and how to set about resolving them. How do these two cultural languages and practices come together in the new family? They may have succeeded in creating a rapprochement between them, but often the situation remains one of a conflict of loyalties or a suppression or withholding of construing from one side of the family heritage. This situation is made more complex when both parents originate in different cultures to the host society, in which the children are learning the language and mores, setting up different expectations and tensions between the generations.

Central for formulation here is the concept of the *family construct system*, introduced at the end of Chapter 4. All groups develop a shared construing system but the family is unique in being tied to the lifelong realities of biological relatedness and the fact that we are all born of sexual relationships. A girl may never have met her father, who has no connection with the family, and yet he is still 'my father' and therefore occupies an important slot in the FCS (Procter, 1981). Closely tied to this notion is a concept introduced by Haley (1973), the *Family Life Cycle*. The family as a whole goes through the transitions of birth, going to school, adolescence, leaving home, retirement, divorce, death, and bereavement, changes requiring major adjustment in the FCS as new roles and relationships are demanded. Haley argued convincingly that problems are often associated with arrested adjustment or difficulties in making these transitions. In a key paper, the Milan family therapy team describe a formulation made of a divorced mother and her 13-year-old son, who is presenting with rebellious and delinquent behaviour. Their first hypothesis, that the function of the difficulties is to get the father back into the family, is quickly dispelled in the interview. A second formulation, that the mother has met another man and the son is finding her 'not the same any more', is soon established to be the case (Selvini, Boscolo, Cecchin, & Prata, 1980). Understanding these transitions ties in nicely with Kelly's notion of transitional formulation and finding a pathway forward for the family members. We will look more at managing this in Chapter 9. Light will be thrown on the FCS in finding the answers to questions of the type summarised in Sect. 8 of Appendix A and by using qualitative grids and bow-ties (see Tables 2.2, 4.2, 6.6, and 6.7 and Figs. 5.2 and 7.1).

In integrating the personal and systemic-relational levels of understanding, we can extend Kelly's idea of 'professional diagnostic constructs', outlined in the previous section, to examining the construing involved in interpersonal scenarios. Table 7.1 shows examples of a series of these, concentrating on the possibilities in dyadic relationships. The questions help focus the family members at the relational level of construing. This will be followed up by asking for detail about the conversations and exchanges between them. We thus build up a picture

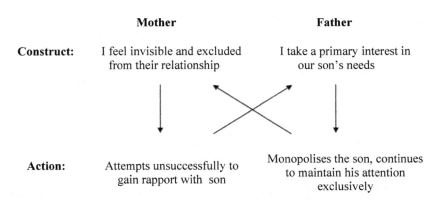

Fig. 7.1 Bow-tie tracing the maintenance of construing between a boy's parents

Table 7.1 Professional dyadic constructs with associated sample questions

Dyadic construct	Sample question
Dyad in general	How do you see the relationship between you and your father?
Similarity/Difference	Which of you does she take after more?
Closeness/Distance	Who do you feel closest to?
Agreement/Disagreement	Do you agree with her on that?
Understanding/Misunderstanding	Does she tend to get what you were saying?
Up/Down in Hierarchy	Did she go along with him on that?

and understanding of how the family construct system is functioning, with the ongoing positions that members take up and how these are sustained by the interactional evidence that they see facing them.

Establishing dyadic patterns can then be built upon by looking at how third parties fit in, thereby investigating triadic patterns such as exclusion, jealousy, rivalry, mediation, and coalition (these terms could be regarded as 'professional diagnostic constructs' covering triadic situations). Haley (1967) outlines a problematic triadic pattern which he calls the 'perverse triangle'. This may be found in families, teams, and any group involving a construed hierarchy. In this pattern, two members at different levels of hierarchy form a *coalition*—a process of joint action or construing at the expense of a third party. For example, a parent or grandparent may join with a child to criticise and undermine the other parent or a sibling. The result is an unstable and contradictory scenario which can be observed in many problematic situations in families and organisations. The pattern shown in Fig. 7.1 is a good example of this process. The bow-tie gives us a picture of problem maintenance at the dyadic level (Fig. 7.1) but can also capture triadic patterns as shown where a mother, presenting with depression, feels excluded from the father-son pair, her experiences of depression and withdrawal serving to maintain the unbalanced parental roles.

Triadic patterns have been seen as central to problems in many approaches to family therapy. As we saw in Chapter 4, members tend to take up opposing positions in relation to each other along a dimension we called a *family construct*. For example, in Byron's play *Cain: a mystery,* Cain opposes the rest of the family with *defiance* against their shared position of *reverence* for God (Procter & Procter, 2008). In a parallel development to our own,[4] deriving from social constructionism and conversational analysis, Ugazio (2013) describes a similar process to our own *family construct*, which is dyadic, but adds a mediating position taken up by a third member. She labels this triadic structure a *semantic polarity,* insisting that any polarisation taking place in a family will tend to encourage others to try and mediate between them. An example from Byron's play is where Adah, Cain's sister and wife, tries to reconcile their conflict, insisting that *love between family members is paramount* (see Fig. 7.2).

Ugazio's work is important in that she finds a link between commonly held family constructs or semantic polarities and different types of psychological difficulties. She describes four ubiquitous shared polarities which will appear in most family construct systems but one of which tends to dominate in particular families. Three of them were described by Dallos and Procter (1984) as *Far/Near, Up/Down,* and *In/out,* dimensions of the closeness/distance, hierarchy, and inclusion/exclusion constructs that we have been discussing. Ugazio adds a fourth polarity, *Good/Bad,* to this list (see Table 7.2).

For Ugazio, the positions taken up by family members are governed by *values,* similar to Kelly's superordinate constructs. The social actions

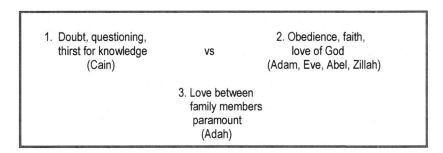

Fig. 7.2 Superordinate family construct or semantic polarity (from Procter and Procter, 2008)

Table 7.2 Ugazio's four semantic polarities (selected from Ugazio, 2013)

	Semantics of freedom Far–Near		Semantics of goodness Good–Bad		Semantics of Power Up–Down		Semantics of belonging In–Out	
Values	Freedom	Dependence	Good	Evil	Achievement	Failure	Inclusion	Exclusion
Relational movements	Keeping distance	To move closer	Self-sacrifice	To exploit	To win	To lose	To welcome	To reject
Emotions	Courage	Fear	Innocence	Guilt	Pride	Shame	Gratitude Joy	Rage Desperation
Personal attributes	Unattached	Bound	Restrained	Spontaneous	Determined	Pliable	Worthy	Unworthy
Typical disorders	Phobias		Obsessive-Compulsive		Eating Disorder s		Depression	

of the person toward the other within the polarity are exemplified as *relational movements*, and examples are given of particular *emotions* typically associated with each position. The family member habitually occupying and growing into a position tends to develop characteristic *personal attributes* and stances congruent with it. The implication is that family members suffering from these problems tend to have, somewhere in the current or historical family, relatives who have played out a role at the opposite end of the polarity, for example someone diagnosed with agoraphobia may have a sibling who lives a wild life, confronting danger. As we see in Table 7.2, Ugazio and her team have found evidence that phobias, obsessive-compulsive, eating, and mood disorders tend to be associated with these four different polarities (Ugazio, Negri, & Fellin, 2015). This research obviously needs replicating in other centres but it would imply a set of highly suggestive findings with important implications for our understanding of these common disorders. In the process of formulation, hypotheses from this work can be generated but from a Kellian point of view, we remain cautious about the use of conventional diagnostic categories. We must remember to 'start from scratch' with each case, only using normative construing to alert us to the presence of patterns and correlations we may otherwise have missed.

Critiques of Formulation

Johnstone (2014) lists horror stories of situations where therapists have caused great harm by rigidly imposing formulations and explanations and refusing to modify them despite protest and discomfiture by clients. Some practitioners have questioned the need for formulation at all. Rogers (1951) saw what he referred to as 'psychological diagnosis' as unnecessary and even damaging. Smail (1996) was concerned that psychotherapy itself is in danger of diverting us away from a recognition of the struggles and oppression of the social and political context. Rosenbaum (1996, p. 110) advised us to let go of all conceptions and to 'cultivate compassion, kindness, acceptance and joy for the client'. Whilst this is a laudable stance, in reality we cannot help but begin to make constructions and formulations even if these remain unverbalised. We believe that by accepting this, we are more likely to discover and confront our own preconceptions and prejudices. By basing our formulation on the construing of clients and others in their network, we minimise the danger of imposing extrinsic and alien judgments upon them. This is further helped by PRCP itself being more of a *method* of accessing clients' construing rather than a *picture* or set of explanations about problem formation such as psychoanalysis. It is *open* to unearthing any set of construing in any culture with a minimum of 'content' in its framework. We do give emphasis to the bipolarity of construing, but the content of the poles of constructs is that of the clients rather than the therapist.

It is true that sometimes we can achieve therapeutic change without formulation. Because people and their families are inherently a 'form of motion', it is quite common that the rich dialogue of a first session, with its sympathetic and detailed focus on the experiences and construings of the client/s, can lead to them returning to the next session already with news of progress and improvement in the situation and comments that the previous meeting had been very thought-provoking. But we think that the complex and unique nature of any particular problematic situation calls for the methods of formulation that we have covered in this chapter. The integration of the personal and the systemic-relational in our framework gives us the choice of focussing either on the individual level or the relational level as seems appropriate to the particular case and often on a combination of the two. Chapter 8 will focus on interventions at the individual level and Chapter 9 will cover therapeutic approaches to working with families and other relationship systems.

Notes

1. Although it is beyond the scope of this book to review the evidence concerned, attempts to explain Bannister's findings on the basis of general cognitive deficits, such as attentional difficulties, have been refuted by findings that loose construing in clients diagnosed as thought disordered schizophrenics is specific to their application of psychological (as opposed

to physical) constructs to people (as opposed to objects) (for a review, see Winter [1992]). Also, it should be noted that it may be unsurprising that findings of research on 'schizophrenia' are inconsistent since this diagnosis may itself be regarded as loose and unreliable.

2. A clear example of this view can be found in Laing (1971).
3. In wishing to dissociate from internal conflict models of problems, Watzlawick, Beavin, and Jackson (1968) blessed such a model, although they gave a role to 'punctuation' as we noted in Chapter 4.
4. See Procter and Ugazio (2017).

References

Bannister, D. (1960). Conceptual structure in thought-disordered schizophrenics. *Journal of Mental Science, 106,* 1230–1249.

Bannister, D. (1962). The nature and measurement of schizophrenic thought disorder. *Journal of Mental Science, 108,* 825–842.

Bannister, D. (1963). The genesis of schizophrenic thought disorder: A serial invalidation hypothesis. *British Journal of Psychiatry, 109,* 680–686.

Bannister, D. (1965). The genesis of schizophrenic thought disorder: Re-test of the serial invalidation hypothesis. *British Journal of Psychiatry, 111,* 377–382.

Bannister, D., & Fransella, F. (1966). A grid test of schizophrenic thought disorder. *British Journal of Social & Clinical Psychology, 5*(2), 95–102.

Bateson, G., Jackson, D. D., Haley, J., & Weakland, J. (1956). Toward a theory of schizophrenia. *Behavioral Science, 1,* 251–264.

Bhandari, S., Winter, D. A., Messer, D., & Metcalfe, C. (2011). Family characteristics and long-term effects of childhood sexual abuse. *British Journal of Clinical Psychology, 50,* 435–451.

Bruch, M. (1998). The development of case formulation approaches. In M. Bruch & F. W. Bond (Eds.), *Beyond Diagnosis: Case Formulation Approaches in Cognitive-Behavioural Therapy* (pp. 1–23). Chichester, UK: Wiley.

Butt, T. (2013). Toward a pragmatic psychology. *Journal of Constructivist Psychology, 26,* 218–224.

Button, E. J. (1993). *Eating Disorders: Personal Construct Therapy and Change.* Chichester, UK: Wiley.

Castiglioni, M., Faccio, E., Veronese, G., & Bell, R. C. (2013). The semantics of power among people with eating disorders. *Journal of Constructivist Psychology, 26,* 62–76.

Chiari, G. (2017b). Highlighting intersubjectivity and recognition in Kelly's sketchy view of personal identity. In D. Winter, P. Cummins, H. G. Procter, & N. Reed (Eds.), *Personal Construct Psychology at 60: Papers from the 21st International Congress* (pp. 54–67). Newcastle upon Tyne, UK: Cambridge Scholars Publishing.

Chiari, G., Nuzzo, M. L., Alfano, V., Brogna, P., D'Andrea, T., Di Battista, G., ... Stiffan, E. (1994). Personal paths of dependency. *Journal of Constructivist Psychology, 7,* 17–34.

Cipolletta, S., & Racerro, G. (2003). Testing the serial invalidation hypothesis in the genesis of schizophrenic thought disorder: A research with repertory grids. In G. Chiari & M. L. Nuzzo (Eds.), *Psychological Constructivism and the Social World* (pp. 353–368). Milan, Italy: Franco Angeli.

Dallos, R., & Procter, H. G. (1984). *Family Processes: An Interactional View.* D307 Social Psychology Course, Open University, Milton Keynes.

DiLollo, A., Manning, W. H., & Neimeyer, R. A. (2005). Cognitive complexity as a function of speaker role for adult persons who stutter. *Journal of Constructivist Psychology, 18,* 215–236.

Division of Clinical Psychology. (2011). *Good Practice Guidelines on the Use of Psychological Formulation.* Leicester, UK: British Psychological Society.

Dzamonja-Ignjatovic, T. (1997). Suicide and depression from the personal construct perspective. In P. Denicolo & M. Pope (Eds.), *Sharing Understanding and Practice* (pp. 222–234). Farnborough, UK: EPCA Publications.

Eells, T. D. (2006). History and current status of psychotherapy case formulation. In T. D. Eells (Ed.), *Handbook of Psychotherapy Case Formulation* (2nd ed., pp. 3–32). New York: Guilford.

Erbes, C. R., & Harter, S. L. (2002). Constructions of abuse: Understanding the effects of childhood sexual abuse. In J. D. Raskin & S. K. Bridges (Eds.), *Studies in Meaning: Exploring Constructivist Psychology* (pp. 27–48). New York: Pace University Press.

Feixas, G. (1995). Personal constructs in systemic practice. In R. A. Neimeyer & M. J. Mahoney (Eds.), *Constructivism in Psychotherapy* (pp. 305–337). Washington, DC: American Psychological Association.

Feixas, G., Erazo-Caicedo, M. I., Harter, S. L., & Bach, L. (2008). Construction of self and others in unipolar depressive disorders: A study using repertory grid technique. *Cognitive Therapy and Research, 32,* 386–400.

Feixas, G., Montebruno, C., Dada, G., Del Castillo, M. & Compañ, V. (2010). Self construction, cognitive conflicts and polarization in bulimia nervosa. *International Journal of Clinical and Health Psychology, 10*, 445–457.

Feixas, G., Montesano, A., Compan, V., Salla, M., Dada, G., Pucurull, O., ... Guardia, J. (2014a). Cognitive conflicts in major depression: Between desired change and personal coherence. *British Journal of Clinical Psychology, 53*(4), 369–385.

Feixas, G., Montesano, A., Erazo-Caicedo, M. I., Compañ, V., & Pucurull, O. (2014b). Implicative dilemmas and symptom severity in depression: A preliminary and content analysis study. *Journal of Constructivist Psychology, 27*, 31–40.

Feixas, G., Saúl, L. A., & Ávila-Espada, A. (2009). Viewing cognitive conflicts as dilemmas: Implications for mental health. *Journal of Constructivist Psychology, 22*, 141–169.

Fisch, R., Weakland, J. H., & Segal, L. (1982). *The Tactics of Change: Doing Therapy Briefly*. San Francisco: Jossey-Bass.

Fransella, F. (1972). *Personal Change and Reconstruction: Research on a Treatment of Stuttering*. London: Academic Press.

Fransella, F. (2001). The making of a psychologist: A late developer. In G. C. Bunn, A. D. Lovie, & G. C. Richards (Eds.), *Psychology in Britain: Historical Essays and Personal Reflections* (pp. 372–380). London: BPS Books and Science Museum.

Gara, M. A., Rosenberg, S., & Mueller, D. R. (1989). Perception of self and others in schizophrenia. *International Journal of Personal Construct Psychology, 2*, 253–270.

García-Mieres, H., Niño-Robles, N., Ochoa, S., & Feixas, G. (2019). Exploring identity and personal meanings in psychosis using the repertory grid technique: A systematic review. *Clinical Psychology & Psychotherapy, 26*, 717–733.

Haley, J. (1963). *Strategies of Psychotherapy*. New York: Grune and Stratton.

Haley, J. (1967). Toward a theory of pathological systems. In J. Zuk & I. Nagy (Eds.), *Family Therapy and Disturbed Families* (pp. 11–27). Palo Alto, CA: Science and Behavior Books.

Haley, J. (1973). *Uncommon Therapy: The Psychiatric Techniques of Milton H. Erickson*. New York: W. W. Norton.

Hopkins, N. J. (2012). Is there a typical agoraphobic core structure? *Personal Construct Theory and Practice, 9*, 19–27.

Hughes, S. L., & Neimeyer, R. A. (1990). A cognitive model of suicidal behavior. In D. Lester (Ed.), *Understanding Suicide: The State of the Art* (pp. 1–28). New York: Charles Press.

Hughes, S. L., & Neimeyer, R. A. (1993). Cognitive predictors of suicide risk among hospitalized psychiatric patients: A prospective study. *Death Studies, 17,* 103–124.

Johnstone, L. (2014). Controversies and debates about formulation. In L. Johnstone & R. Dallos (Eds.), *Formulation in Psychology and Psychotherapy* (2nd ed., pp. 260–289). London: Routledge.

Kelly, G. A. (1955). *The Psychology of Personal Constructs. Vol. I, II.* New York: Norton (2nd printing: 1991, London and New York: Routledge).

Kelly, G. A. (1961). Theory and therapy in suicide: The personal construct point of view. In M. Farberow & E. Shneidman (Eds.), *The Cry for Help* (pp. 255–280). New York: McGraw-Hill.

Kelly, G. A. (1969b). Personal construct theory and the psychotherapeutic interview. In B. Maher (Ed.), *Clinical Psychology and Personality: The Selected Papers of George Kelly* (pp. 224–264). New York: Wiley.

Klion, R. E. (1993). Chemical dependency: A personal construct theory approach. In A. W. Landfield & L. M. Leitner (Eds.), *Critical Issues in Personal Construct Psychotherapy* (pp. 279–301). Melbourne, FL: Krieger.

Laing, R. D. (1971). The family and the 'family'. In R. D. Laing (Ed.), *The Politics of the Family and Other Essays* (pp. 3–18). Harmondsworth, UK: Penguin.

Landfield, A. (1971). *Personal Construct Systems in Psychotherapy.* Chicago: Rand McNally.

Leitner, L. M., Faidley, A. J., & Celentana, M. A. (2000). Diagnosing human meaning-making: An experiential constructivist approach. In R. A. Neimeyer & J. D. Raskin (Eds.), *Construction of Disorders: Meaning Making Frameworks for Psychotherapy* (pp. 175–203). Washington, DC: American Psychological Association.

Montesano, A., Feixas, G., Erazo-Caicedo, M. I., Saúl, L. A., Dada, G., & Winter, D. (2014). Cognitive conflicts and symptom severity in Dysthymia: "I'd rather be good than happy". *Salud Mental, 37,* 41–48.

Montesano, A., López-González, M. A., Saúl, L. Á., & Feixas, G. (2015). A review of cognitive conflicts research: A meta-analytic study of prevalence and relation to symptoms. *Neuropsychiatric Disease and Treatment, 12,* 2997–3006.

Procter, H. G. (1981). Family construct psychology: An approach to understanding and treating families. In S. Walrond-Skinner (Ed.), *Developments in Family Therapy: Theories and Applications since 1948* (pp. 350–366). London: Routledge and Kegan Paul.

Procter, H. G. (2016b). PCP, culture and society. In D. A. Winter & N. Reed (Eds.), *The Wiley Handbook of Personal Construct Psychology* (pp. 139–153). Chichester, UK: Wiley-Blackwell.

Procter, H. G., & Procter, M. J. (2008). The use of qualitative grids to examine the development of the construct of good and evil in Byron's play 'Cain: A mystery'. *Journal of Constructivist Psychology, 21,* 343–354.

Procter, H. G., & Ugazio, V. (2017). Family constructs and semantic polarities: A convergent perspective? In D. A. Winter, P. Cummins, H. G. Procter, & N. Reed (Eds.), *Personal Construct Psychology at 60: Papers from the 21st International Congress* (pp. 68–89). Newcastle upon Tyne, UK: Cambridge Scholars Publishing.

Rogers, C. R. (1951). *Client-Centered Therapy: Its Current Practice, Implications, and Theory.* Boston: Houghton Mifflin.

Rosenbaum, R. (1996). Form, formlessness and formulation. *Journal of Psychotherapy Integration, 6,* 107–117.

Selvini, M. P., Boscolo, L., Cecchin, G., & Prata, G. (1980). Hypothesizing–circularity–neutrality: Three guidelines for the conductor of the session. *Family Process, 19,* 3–12.

Sermpezis, C., & Winter, D. A. (2009). Is trauma the product of over or under-elaboration? A critique of the personal construct model of post-traumatic stress disorder. *Journal of Constructivist Psychology, 22,* 306–327.

Sewell, K. W. (1997). Posttraumatic stress: Towards a constructivist model of psychotherapy. In G. J. Neimeyer & R. A. Neimeyer (Eds.), *Advances in Personal Construct Psychology* (pp. 207–235). Greenwich, CT: JAI Press.

Smail, D. (1996). *How to Survive Without Psychotherapy.* London: Constable.

Ugazio, V. (2013). *Semantic Polarities and Psychopathologies in the Family: Permitted and Forbidden Stories.* New York: Routledge.

Ugazio, V., Negri, A., & Fellin, L. (2015). Freedom, goodness, power, and belonging: The semantics of phobic, obsessive-compulsive, eating, and mood disorders. *Journal of Constructivist Psychology, 28,* 293–315.

Walker, B. M. (2002). Nonvalidation vs. (In)validation: Implications for theory and practice. In J. D. Raskin & S. K. Bridges (Eds.), *Studies in Meaning: Exploring Constructivist Psychology* (pp. 49–61). New York: Pace University Press.

Watzlawick, P., Beavin, J., & Jackson, D. D. (1968). *Pragmatics of Human Communication.* New York: Norton.

Watzlawick, P., Weakland, J., & Fisch, R. (1974). *Change: Principles of Problem Formation and Problem Resolution*. New York: Norton.

White, M., & Epston, D. (1990). *Narrative Means to Therapeutic Ends*. Adelaide, Australia: Dulwich Centre Publications.

Winter, D. A. (1975). Some characteristics of schizophrenics and their parents. *British Journal of Social and Clinical Psychology, 14*, 279–290.

Winter, D. A. (1992). *Personal Construct Psychology in Clinical Practice: Theory, Research and Applications*. London: Routledge.

Winter, D. A. (2003a). Psychological disorder as imbalance. In F. Fransella (Ed.), *International Handbook of Personal Construct Psychology* (pp. 201–209). Chichester, UK: Wiley.

Winter, D., & Gournay, K. (1987). Constriction and construction in agoraphobia. *British Journal of Medical Psychology, 60*, 233–244.

Winter, D. A. (2009). The personal construct psychology view of psychological disorder: Did Kelly get it wrong? In L. M. Leitner & J. C. Thomas (Eds.), *Personal Constructivism: Theory and Applications* (pp. 279–295). New York: Pace University Press.

Winter, D., Sireling, L., Riley, T., Metcalfe, C., Quaite, A., & Bhandari, S. (2007). A controlled trial of personal construct psychotherapy for deliberate self-harm. *Psychology and Psychotherapy, 80*, 23–37.

8

Individual Psychotherapy

The process of assessment and formulation was, for Kelly (1955), 'the planning stage of therapy' (p. 203), and there is usually a seamless transition between these different phases of the clinician's interaction with a client. Thus, the credulous attitude shown in the assessment process, which we have described in Chapter 5, is maintained during therapy, as is the stance of therapist and client being co-experimenters rather than the therapist making expert pronouncements or prescribing particular ways of construing and behaving. The changes in construing that may occur during therapy, and the processes and techniques by which they may be achieved, will now be described, before considering some specific varieties of personal construct psychotherapy.

Reconstruction

If psychological disorder essentially represents a block in the process of construing, psychotherapy, as Kelly (1955) described, may be regarded as involving reconstruction. The aim is to get the client's Experience Cycles moving again, and thereby to 'make one feel that he has come

© The Author(s) 2020
H. Procter and D. A. Winter, *Personal and Relational Construct Psychotherapy*,
Palgrave Texts in Counselling and Psychotherapy,
https://doi.org/10.1007/978-3-030-52177-6_8

alive' (Kelly, 1980, p. 29). Therapeutic reconstruction may take many forms, which Kelly (1969b, p. 231) described in terms of the following approaches that the therapist and client might take:

'1. The two of them can decide that the client should reverse his position with respect to one of the more obvious reference axes'.

   This is a superficial and unstable type of reconstruction, described by Kelly as 'slot rattling', because, with no fundamental change in the construct involved, the client can easily slot rattle back to their original position. Nevertheless, it may occasionally be useful in order at least to allow the client to experiment with a contrasting view of the self or of events. For example, the client who construes the self as trapped might be invited to experiment with a self-construction as a free person.

'2. Or they can select another construct from the client's ready repertory and apply it to matters at hand'.

   For example, the client who construes their partner as argumentative might be encouraged to consider the partner's behaviour in terms of another of the client's construct poles, such as 'passionate'.

'3. They can make more explicit those preverbal constructs by which all of us order our lives in considerable degree'.

   Increasing the client's awareness of their preverbal constructs may allow these constructs to be put to the test and, at the very least, should allow the client to feel more in control of their behaviour in domains where these constructs previously operated.

'4. They can elaborate the construct system to test it for internal consistency'.

   Consideration of the relationships between a client's constructs may, as we have seen, reveal dilemmas that are making the client resistant to change.

'5. They can test constructs for their predictive validity'.

   As we have noted, Kelly viewed the relationship between therapist and client as similar to that between a research supervisor and their student. The therapist may, for example, help the client design experiments by which their constructions of the world can be tested both within and outside the therapy room.

'6. They can increase the range of convenience of certain constructs, that is apply them more generally. They can also decrease the range of convenience and thus reduce a construct to a kind of obsolescence'.

An example of increasing the range of convenience of a construct is Karst's (1980) encouragement of a client to extend the use of her construct concerning creativity from the kitchen to the bedroom. The converse approach of decreasing a construct's range of convenience was used by Winter (2003) with a police officer whose construct of being constantly vigilant, which had led to him intrusively questioning members of the public about quite innocuous activities when off duty, was limited in its application to law enforcement situations when he was at work.

'7. They can alter the meaning of certain constructs; rotate the reference axes'.

Altering the meaning of constructs, or as Kelly (1955, p. 1033) put it, 'getting him to shuffle some of his ideas into new combinations', may be a step in the resolution of dilemmas with which a client is faced.

'8. They can erect new reference axes'.

This is the most fundamental type of reconstruction that can occur during therapy, effectively allowing the client to view the world through a fresh pair of spectacles. For example, consider the client whose previous view of their interpersonal world was solely in terms of value-laden constructs concerning the goodness or badness of others, but who then comes to develop a superordinate construct concerning whether others are easy or hard to understand.

The Therapeutic Process

The process of personal construct psychotherapy, as indeed of any optimal therapeutic experience, essentially involves a delicate balance of validation and invalidation of the client's construing. If there is no invalidation, there is little or no likelihood that therapy will lead to any change in the client. However, as Kelly (1955) pointed out, the client will require 'a broad base of confirmation' so as to have sufficient trust to engage in major reconstruction. Invalidation should therefore occur within an overall climate of validation, which to some extent will be provided by the therapist's credulous attitude. As we shall see, several of the therapeutic techniques employed by the personal construct psychotherapist involve a subtle mixture of validation and invalidation in which the validity of a client's constructions is not denied but instead he or she is invited to suspend these constructions while experimenting with alternative constructions. Of particular concern to the therapist will be to avoid invalidation that impacts on the client's core constructs because this will only be likely to cause threat and possibly guilt, and to increase the client's resistance to therapy or, at worst, to lead to adverse consequences of therapy, including exacerbation of the problems for which the client sought help in the first place (Winter, 1996). Whereas in some therapeutic approaches, the client who is construed as resistant may be regarded as stubbornly or inexplicably thwarting the therapist's best efforts, the personal construct view would be that such clients, by essentially protecting their core constructs, are 'behaving perfectly reasonably from their own perspective' (Fransella, 1985, p. 300). Rather than continuing to apply their original approach to a 'resistant' client, perhaps with even greater force, the therapist should acknowledge that this approach is likely to have been too invalidating and should modify it accordingly.

Before leaving the topic of validation and invalidation during therapy, it is worth remembering that, unlike in some other therapeutic approaches, these terms are not equated with the respective expression of approval or disapproval of the client. For example, the client who feels blameworthy for abuse that they have suffered may be profoundly invalidated by a therapist telling them that they were not to blame. Similarly, as we have seen in Chapter 3, the client who feels deserving of rejection may be invalidated by the therapist's acceptance. In such cases, the maintenance of an appropriate balance of validation and invalidation may place particular demands on the therapist's juggling skills!

Therapeutic Techniques

Although personal construct psychotherapy involves a particular approach to the therapeutic process rather than being especially technique-laden, numerous different techniques can be used to achieve the various types of reconstruction that we have outlined above. These do not necessarily have to be derived from personal construct theory, but if a technique is borrowed from another theoretical approach, its mode of action will be conceptualised in personal construct terms. For example, a cognitive-behavioural technique may be employed in order to help the client to test the predictive validity of particular constructs. The broad classes of techniques employed in personal construct psychotherapy will now be considered, with particular reference to their primary focus.

Palliative Techniques

These techniques may be used at times when the focus is on providing some validation of the client's construing, for example when the pace of therapy is feeling too rapid or events too out of control for the client. That they should only be employed sparingly is indicated by Kelly's (1955) comment that they 'should be localized....and not allowed to form an addiction' (p. 662). One such technique, *reassurance*, involves providing the client with a temporary superordinate construction of their situation, such as indicating that the anxiety that he or she has been experiencing may be due to the difficult issues that have been discussed in therapy sessions. Another palliative technique, *support*, involves helping the client to experiment successfully and offering some validation for their anticipations.

Elaborative Techniques

Therapy is likely to involve continuation of the process of elaboration of construing that began when the client was being assessed. The therapist may, for example, explore, and perhaps try to resolve, inconsistencies in the client's construing or ask them to spell out the courses of action that might arise from construing events in particular ways. The primary focus of elaboration may initially be the client's complaint, but it is then likely to shift to other areas of the client's construing and material that arises over the course of therapy. Indeed, if the client effectively knows too much about their complaint already, it may be advisable, instead of discussing the complaint, to focus on elaborating an alternative role to being a person with this particular complaint. This was the case in Fransella's (1972) treatment of people who stuttered, for whom stuttering had been their 'way of life' but whose construing of themselves as fluent was elaborated in therapy by a focus on their occasional episodes of fluency.

Elaboration may be aided by the use of some of the assessment techniques that we have described in Chapters 5 and 6, which may be employed for therapeutic as well as for diagnostic ends. For example, as we have seen, elaboration of the contrast to being a person with a particular complaint may be facilitated by the client writing a self-characterisation as they would be without the complaint. Another effective aid to elaboration is what Kelly (1955) termed *casual enactment*, brief informal role-playing in which therapist and client take the roles of people about whom the client has been talking, such as the client and their partner. In playing a particular part, the therapist should use some of the words that the client attributed to the person concerned when they described the incident that is being portrayed. Kelly's (1955) four principles of casual enactments were that there should be '*no long preliminary discussions*' (p. 1026, italics in original); that they should only last a few minutes; that they should involve exchange of parts, thus facilitating sociality (see Chapter 3) with the other person portrayed in the interaction; and that they should '*avoid caricature*' (p. 1028, italics in original).

Loosening and Tightening

A productive course of therapy is likely to involve the client completing several Creativity Cycles (see Chapter 3), oscillating between processes of loosening and tightening of construing. The therapist may at times wish to promote one or other of these processes, particularly if the client's disorder is characterised by excessively tight or loose construing.

Loosening was viewed by Kelly (1955) as 'one of the most important procedures in the psychotherapist's armamentarium' (p. 1060) since it 'may set the stage for rotation of the personal-construct axes, for an eventual tightening of constructions along new lines, for a more spontaneous elaboration, and for experimentation' (p. 1033). He considered that it may be achieved in four main ways, namely by relaxation exercises; chain association, in which the client is asked to say whatever comes into their mind; recounting of dreams, since they 'represent about the most loosened construction that one can put into words' (p. 1037); and the therapist's uncritical acceptance of the client's construing. R. Neimeyer (1988) extended this list by including additional techniques, such as guided imagery, artistic expression, brainstorming, and hypnotherapy; 'environmental conditions' in the therapy room, such as subdued lighting and comfortable seats; and such therapist behaviour as an open posture, slow and quiet speech, which lacks precision and contains metaphors, and the use of open-ended questions.

Tightening of construing is necessary if the client is to define their predictions and put these to the test. It therefore sets the stage for experimentation as well as facilitating the hierarchical organisation of the client's construct system. Like loosening, tightening may be achieved in various ways, and these include the use of elaborative techniques and assessment methods such as the repertory grid; preparation by the client of summaries of therapy sessions; and the client being asked to provide validational evidence for particular constructions. R. Neimeyer (1988) has again extended this list to include such techniques as behavioural monitoring, practising new skills, and provision of interpretations; environmental conditions such as bright lights and upright chairs; and therapist behaviour such as maintenance of eye contact, note-taking, loud and fast speech, with precise sentences, and closed questions. With a client for whom there are residual islands of structure in a construct system that is generally loosely organised, the therapist may also attempt to arrange their environment so that predictions in these areas of tighter construing are validated. This was the approach taken by Bannister, Adams-Webber, Penn, and Radley (1975) in their 'serial validation' of in-patients diagnosed with schizophrenic thought disorder, with whom, for example, nursing staff were instructed to behave in such a way with each client that would validate, and supposedly therefore tighten, the client's construing. Difficulties faced in achieving this outcome included insufficient control over the clients' environments and their other sources of validation and invalidation; and problems in operationally defining the clients' constructs in a way which appropriately reflected their personal meaning. It was therefore perhaps not surprising that, although some changes in the predicted direction were apparent in the clients receiving the intervention, Bannister and his colleagues concluded that the effectiveness of their approach was 'not proven'.

A specific subset of tightening techniques designed to reduce particular constructs to a state of impermeability are *word binding*, in which the client has to name a construct and stick to the chosen name; *time binding*, in which the time when a construct was formed is identified and the construct is viewed as only applicable at this time; and *person binding*, in which the construct is tied to anticipation of a particular person. Binding techniques are a good example of the mixture of validation and invalidation mentioned previously as they do not deny the validity of a client's construing, but merely attempt to limit the situations in which the constructs concerned are deemed applicable. An example of the use of time and person binding is the case of Stanley, who presented with difficulties of four years' duration in obtaining an erection. An understanding of these problems was provided when he completed a repertory grid, which indicated that he anticipated that if he were to lose his sexual problem he would become less honest and lovable, and more like his father. Discussion of his grid results led him to recall the invalidation of his construction of his father as very moral by events in which, as a child, he witnessed his father flirting with other women in front of his mother. Interestingly, in view of his presenting complaint, he contrasted times when his father was 'hard' and 'unloving' with those when he was 'soft and malleable'. In therapy, the approach was taken that constructs concerning sexual responsiveness which had once been useful in making sense of his father's behaviour could be regarded as anachronisms which had outlived their usefulness and were not relevant to other people or current events. At the end of six sessions of therapy, he was again able to obtain an erection, and a second repertory grid indicated that he construed himself without sexual problems much more favourably and that being sexually attractive held fewer negative implications for him (Winter, 1988).

Experimentation

Personal construct psychotherapy will always, to some degree, involve experimentation with new constructions, in which 'the therapy room can be a laboratory and the client's community a field project' (Kelly, 1955, p. 1067). This experimentation can even be made very explicit, with the client keeping a diary of their hypotheses and experimental results (Epting & Amerikaner, 1980), some of these derived from homework assignments (R. Neimeyer & Winter, 2006). More generally, the process is facilitated by therapy being conducted in an *invitational mood* (Kelly, 1964) in which the client is invited to try out certain constructions as if they were correct. Thus, the client may be invited to enact a particular scenario as if one or both of the protagonists were construed in a different way (for example, as if the client's partner's persistent questioning reflected an attempt to understand rather than to control him or her). Alternatively, as Mair (2015b) has described, he or she may be invited to use metaphor, perhaps considering their complaint as if it were a person or creature (as in Winston Churchill's view of his depression as a 'black dog' [Lovell, 2011]), as a way of facilitating elaboration of, and experimentation with, construing. Although Mair (2015b) noted that constructs and metaphors are not identical, he identified several similarities between the use of metaphor and construing,[1] not least that 'metaphor….is a means of entering the unknown through the gateway of the known' (p. 84). Of particular therapeutic use may be Mair's (2015a) metaphor of the 'community of self' (see Chapter 2), in which the client is encouraged to experiment with the parts played by their different selves as if they were the members of a particular type of community of the client's choosing. For example, the client who views their selves as if they were the members of a football team might experiment with whether more effective teamplay could be achieved by the forwards helping out more with defence, the creative midfielder sometimes taking the simple option rather than over-elaborating, the goalkeeper communicating more with the defenders, or the manager giving the players more freedom to express themselves. There can also be experimentation with the changes that could take place in the community if a new character, perhaps representing a previously unelaborated aspect of the self, were to join it. For example, in a client whose metaphor of her community of selves was a village (the residents of which included a 'bakery girl', a 'school teacher', a 'retired professor', and a 'crazy painter'), relationships within the community were dramatically reshuffled by the arrival in the village of a new character, an 'ex-soldier' who had returned from the war. The client was subsequently able to make some major changes in her personal life.

It will be apparent that the experimentation in personal construct psychotherapy may involve a certain amount of playfulness, and as such it may be particularly appropriate with children and adolescents, who can be regarded as natural experimenters (Agnew, 1985). As illustrated by Bendinelli and Lui (2014), 'play can be considered a highway to the child's world' (p. 96). It may, for example, help the child to verbalise preverbal constructs. Its therapeutic use can be facilitated by the provision of a variety of props, including puppets, drawing materials, games, and Lego bricks (Moran, 2014; Stein, 2007).

Varieties of Personal Construct Psychotherapy

Fixed-Role Therapy

Perhaps the most well elaborated of the therapeutic techniques devised by Kelly (1955), fixed-role therapy can be used as a means of encouraging experimentation within a phase of personal construct psychotherapy or as a therapeutic approach in its own right. In its traditional form, as illustrated in the case of Brian in Chapter 1, it involves the client enacting a new role portrayed in a character sketch written by the therapist, who will generally be informed not only by previous conversations with, but also by a self-characterisation written by, the client. Kelly outlined six considerations which should be taken into account in writing the sketch. Firstly, it should demonstrate an acceptance of the client while at the same time developing a major theme for the client to explore, rather than trying to correct the client's 'minor faults'. Secondly, it should use sharp contrast, although this should not generally involve asking the client simply to 'slot rattle' to the opposite of his or her current self-construction. Rather, the sketch will be more likely to be useful if the theme that it develops is orthogonal to (relatively independent from) the major construct dimensions that the client generally applies to him/herself. The third consideration is that the sketch should set '*ongoing processes in motion rather than creating a new state*' (Kelly, 1955, p. 371, italics in original). This may be achieved by the sketch including more permeable constructs (i.e., which are more easily applied to new elements) than those in the client's self-characterisation. The fourth consideration is that the sketch should present testable hypotheses; while the fifth is that it should provide constructs which may enable the client to construe other people's construction processes, which as we have seen in Chapter 3 was regarded by Kelly as the basis of role relationships. Finally, the sketch should provide the client with 'the full protection of "make-believe"' (Kelly, 1955, p. 373), aided by such features as the character portrayed being given a new name, which is often symbolic of a major dimension introduced in the sketch. The client may thus be enabled to experiment with new constructions and behaviour in a playful manner without the danger of experiencing the threat and guilt that would be likely to result from feeling committed to undergoing a total metamorphosis into the new character.

These features of a fixed-role sketch may be demonstrated by the sketch that was written for Tom, a client who presented with interpersonal problems, particularly in relation to assertiveness, and whose ABC was presented in Table 6.12. His self-characterisation, written from the perspective of a sympathetic friend, was dominated by his difficulties in social situations and his search for a girlfriend, as in the following extract describing the period after he left university:

Tom became an outsider who would try to mix in but found it difficult…I think he was trying to sort his life out and was trying and aiming
for all sorts of things and never really settling down. I remember making
a comment that I thought he was screwed up. By this time was was (sic)
settled, earning good money and really enjoying life. Tom on the other
hand was never good company. My social life was really going well but
Tom seemed to be wanting something different. I was content in mixing
mostly with blokes and socializing with their girlfriends. I think Tom
was fed up with male company and longed for a girlfriend…When met
(sic) a girl called Kate I hardly saw him but presumed he was happy and
perhaps more settled…When he finished with her he came back into my
social scene but more often than not was quiet, depressed and somehow
we couldn't talk about the same things again…He seems to worry a lot
particularly over if he will ever get married and have children. I tell him
that is not worth worrying about. (Winter, 1992, pp. 269–270)

The fixed role that was written for Tom was informed not only by
his self-characterisation but also by his ABC and repertory grid results,
which indicated that assertiveness and extraversion carried various negative implications for him, including being demanding and unreasonable.
Also taken into account were his descriptions of interpersonal relationships. For example, he tended to view social interactions in terms of
there being 'a winner and a loser' and 'a right and wrong opinion'. Since
he could rarely countenance anyone else being 'right' unless they agreed
with him, he usually did not bother to consider the opinions of others.
He also attributed his feeling of social isolation at work to his being more
'refined' and 'of a higher social class' than his colleagues, and, demonstrating Kellyan hostility (see Chapter 3), he was able to maintain this
view of himself as superior by taking jobs, such as labouring, which did
not match his university education. Tom's fixed role sketch presented a
new character, Jim Nastic, who was described as follows:

Jim Nastic's philosophy of life very much reflects his approach to his
favourite sport, tennis: it's not whether a player wins or loses that's important but whether they've played the game to the best of their ability.
Whether at work or at play, he believes that if a job is worth doing it's
worth doing well, and he brings to everything that he does a certain

passion and conviction, which cannot fail to earn your respect. Although you might perhaps think that this would make him appear a little too serious and intense, once you get to know him you soon realise that his main concern is to live life to the full and that this includes having fun as well as working hard. Life doesn't always run smoothly for him, of course, but when he has a disappointment he always seems able to learn something from it, and to look to the future rather than brooding on his present or past misfortunes.

One of his greatest strengths at tennis is his ability to anticipate the moves of the other players, be they his opponents or doubles partners. In other areas of his life, he also always tries to see the world through the eyes of the people with whom he comes into contact, perhaps because he has mixed with people from so many different walks of life. His lively curiosity in what makes other people tick is usually reciprocated and leads him, almost before he knows it, into some very rewarding relationships. He also, of course, has his fair share of disagreements with others, but when this happens, he always makes an effort to understand the other person's point of view, even though he might not accept it. Because of this, he has a reputation both for commitment to those causes that are close to his heart and tolerance of the right of others to hold different opinions. (R. Neimeyer & Winter, 2006, p. 166)

The ways in which this sketch took into account the six considerations outlined by Kelly (1955), and described above, are indicated in Table 8.1. These considerations once again demonstrate the delicate balance of validation and invalidation that characterises personal construct psychotherapy, as does the way in which the sketch and the therapeutic process are presented to the client. After writing the sketch, the therapist carries out an acceptance check by asking the client whether the character portrayed seems plausible and is the sort of person that the client would like to know. If not, the sketch is modified until it is acceptable to the client. Then, in introducing the therapeutic procedure, the therapist reassures the client that, rather than being banished into permanent exile, his or her old self is merely being asked to go on holiday for a couple of weeks. This is well illustrated in the form of words that Kelly (1955, pp. 384–385) used when inviting a client, Ronald Barrett, to experiment with being a new character, Kenneth Norton:

Table 8.1 Kelly's six considerations as demonstrated in a fixed-role sketch

Acceptance of client and development of a major theme rather than correcting faults
The major theme (passion and conviction associated with living life to the full and 'playing the game' to the best of one's ability) reframed some of Tom's perceived impediments as possible strengths and drew upon some of his acknowledged skills (e.g. tennis). The sketch described someone whose life 'doesn't always run smoothly' but indicated possible alternative ways of dealing with problems, such as disagreements with others

Use of contrasts expressed in constructs orthogonal to client's main construct dimensions
Contrasts involved in the new role were clearly stated (e.g. importance of winning vs. playing the game to the best of one's ability; looking to the future vs. brooding on misfortunes), and constructs regarding relationships with the opposite sex were deliberately omitted in an attempt to introduce new constructs relatively independent of this initial area of concern

Setting ongoing processes in motion by use of more permeable constructs
It is indicated that the new constructs introduced could be applied in a range of situations ('at work or at play')

Presentation of testable hypotheses
Hypotheses testable in his normal social environment are presented (e.g. 'lively curiosity' in others will usually be reciprocated)

Provision of constructs enabling the construing of others' construction processes
There is emphasis on trying to see the world through others' eyes, transferring skills from the tennis court to interpersonal relationships

Protection of 'make-believe'
The character has a playful new name, and is not explicitly compared with the client

---

"For the next two weeks I want you to do something unusual. I want you to *act* as if you were (Kenneth Norton). We will work it out together. For two weeks try to forget that you are (Ronald Barrett) or that you ever were. You *are* (Kenneth Norton)! You *act* like him!

You *think* like him. You talk to your friends the way you think he would talk! You *do* the things you think he would do! You even *have his interests* and you *enjoy* the things he would enjoy!

"Now I know this is going to seem very artificial. We expect that. You will have to keep thinking about the way (Kenneth) would do things rather than the way (Ronald) might want to do them.

"You might say that we are going to send (Ronald) on a two weeks' vacation and let him rest up. In the meantime (Kenneth) will take over. Other people may not know it but (Ronald) will not even be around. Of course, you will have to let people keep calling you (Ronald), but you will think of yourself as (Kenneth). After two weeks we will let (Ronald) come back and then see what we can do to help him.

"Let us arrange to talk this over every other day." (The clinician sets up the schedule of appointments.)

"Now that copy of Kenneth's character sketch is for you to keep. Keep it with you all the time and read it over at least three different times a day, say, when you get up, some time during the day – perhaps when you eat lunch – and when you go to bed.

"Now let us do some rehearsing."

Rehearsals of the role in the therapy room follow the general principles of enactment, with client and therapist alternating in playing the fixed role or a person with whom the character portrayed in the role is interacting. The initial focus will be on relatively superficial interactions before moving on to those involving more significant relationships and topics. After each particular scenario has been rehearsed with the therapist, the client will generally seek to play the role in a similar situation in real life. At the end of the role play period, when the client's old self returns from 'holiday', he or she may or may not decide to continue to adopt some of the characteristics of the fixed role. Whatever happens, though, the client will at least have experimented with new constructions, others will be likely to have reacted to him or her differently, and he or she will have had 'one good rousing, construct-shaking experience' (Kelly, 1955, p. 412).

Several variations on Kelly's original fixed-role procedure have now been developed. For example, a series of mini fixed roles may be used, each designed to help the client deal with a particular problem (Epting, 1984; Epting & Nazario, 1987). In the spirit of co-experimentation, one of us has also found it valuable, in addition to writing a fixed-role sketch for a client, to ask the client to write their own sketch, the two sketches then being amalgamated into the role that the client eventually plays (Winter, 2008).

Dilemma-Focused Intervention

We now turn to another type of personal construct intervention that may be used as a full-blown therapeutic approach or as a treatment module that can be added to an overall course of therapy of any orientation. As we have seen, personal construct psychotherapy will often involve identification and resolution of inconsistencies in a client's construing, but dilemma-focused intervention, which has been developed on the basis of an extensive research programme, does this in a very systematic way, supported by a treatment manual (Feixas & Compañ, 2016). Although it has particularly been used with clients presenting with depression, it is applicable with any client who has at least one implicative dilemma (in which a desired characteristic is associated with an undesired characteristic), identified by a repertory grid as we have described in Chapter 6.

Having identified a client's dilemma/s, the first step in therapy is to reformulate their problem in terms of the dilemma/s, with a view to helping the client to make sense of the impasse to their desired change. For example, with Geoff, whose grid we presented in Chapter 6, understanding that he struggled to be confident because he associated confidence with selfishness might have brought a sense of coherence to his predicament. A dilemma can be made more evident by the 'magic wand technique',[2] asking the client to imagine how their life would be if the therapist could change them to their desired state (e.g., in Geoff's case, becoming confident) immediately by waving a magic wand. Exploration of the imagined scenario will often reveal negative implications of change. The dilemma can also be made more vivid by identifying prototypical people in the client's life who represent each pole of the dilemma.

As well as repertory grid technique, various other assessment techniques that we have described in Chapter 6 may be used to elaborate a dilemma. These include the ABC model, self-characterisation, laddering, and pyramiding. One particular variety of laddering which may be especially useful in exploring, and effecting some change in, dilemmatic constructs (those in which in a grid the ideal self is located at the midpoint of the rating scale) is dialectical laddering (R. Neimeyer, 1993).

Here, the therapist helps the client to develop a new construct that integrates two construct poles that had previously seemed irreconcilable and provides an alternative to these. For example, with a client's construct *dominating* versus *dominated*, in which there is no preference for either pole, the client could merge the two poles into one of *views relationships in terms of power*, which could be contrasted, for example, with *views relationships in terms of opportunities for growth*.

Dilemma-focused intervention will generally proceed with a focus on 'reconstruction of immediate experience', drawing upon Kelly's (1970a) notion of the Experience Cycle to explore particular examples of the client's anticipations relevant to the dilemma, the validational fortunes of these, and whether any reconstruction seems necessary. For example, considering situations in which he had managed to be assertive, Tom (whose ABC we presented in Table 6.12) acknowledged that these had not eventuated in his anticipated outcome of physical violence, and was thus enabled to begin to reconstrue assertiveness.

The strong relational emphasis of dilemma-focused intervention generally becomes increasingly apparent as therapy progresses. For example, there will be an attempt to identify 'accomplices of the dilemma', significant others who essentially validate the constructions involved in the dilemma (as might be the case, for example, if Geoff's partner were to remark on his selfishness at times when he acted confidently). Having identified such individuals, therapy might usefully focus on ways in which the client's relationship with them could change. Other people whom it might prove useful for the client to identify are those who are 'exceptions to the dilemma' in that they manage to combine the seemingly irreconcilable characteristics represented by the desired poles of the two constructs involved in a dilemma (i.e., in Geoff's case, confidence and unselfishness). By discussing how these people might act in difficult situations, such as those involving the accomplices of the dilemma, the client might find possible ways of resolving the dilemma.

Another component of dilemma-focused intervention, historical reconstruction of the dilemma, can be illustrated by returning to the case of Tom. In trying to identify prototypical people representing the poles of his dilemma, it became apparent that Tom's mother when he was a child represented each pole at different times. Thus, he recalled that she was generally meek and gentle, but that on the rare occasions when she did assert her opinions, she became violent towards him and his father. This facilitated the 'binding' of his dilemma concerning assertiveness to his construing of his mother at that particular time (Winter, 1987). Historical reconstruction of the dilemma can be aided by writing assignments, including asking the client to write a history of their dilemma and to write the titles of the chapters of their autobiography, including one concerning a future in which their dilemma is resolved, which can lead to discussion of their position in the dilemma in each of these chapters.

In order to experiment with being someone who is an 'exception to the dilemma', the client might be asked to enact a fixed role of someone in whom the dilemma is resolved. However, as one of us (DW) has found, simply asking the client to write a self-characterisation as if they could combine the desired poles of the constructs in the dilemma may be sufficient to facilitate the elaboration of ways of resolving the dilemma. Another dramatisation method commonly used in dilemma-focused intervention is an adaptation of Gestalt therapy's two-chair technique, in which the client engages in a dialogue between, and attempts to integrate, the two poles of a dilemma while switching backwards and forwards between chairs representing these poles.

As therapy progresses, the emphasis is on 'future projection' and how to live without the dilemma. The magic wand technique may be used again to explore in detail how specific situations would be if the dilemma were resolved. There will also be a focus on occasions when the client has been able to act as if the dilemma were resolved, thus enabling the client to elaborate further how to be such a person.

Experiential Personal Construct Psychotherapy

The primary goal of experiential personal construct psychotherapy is to help the client form role relationships, those which, as described in Kelly's Sociality Corollary, involve construing the construction processes of others.[3] As we have seen in Chapters 3 and 7, Leitner (1985a) considers that such relationships may be terrifying, and that therefore people may retreat from them but as a result feel empty and alienated, often expressing their struggles with role relationships in particular symptoms. In experiential personal construct psychotherapy, the relationship between client and therapist is central as it provides a way of understanding and exploring how the client engages in and retreats from role relationships more generally. This is likely to be achieved by focusing on the client's experience of transference, which Kelly (1955) viewed simply as a process in which the client transfers on to the therapist constructs from the client's existing repertoire. The experiential personal construct psychotherapist needs to be aware of his or her own countertransference in order to maintain an 'optimal therapeutic distance' with the client so that they are not so distant as to be 'therapeutic strangers', nor so fused as to be in a state of 'therapeutic unity', in which there is little or no differentiation between the client's and therapist's experiences (Leitner, 1985a). This can arguably be related to our previous discussion of the optimal therapeutic process as involving an appropriate balance of experiences of invalidation and validation.

Experiential personal construct psychotherapy does not use a specific set of techniques, but its primary tool is the therapist himself or herself. The therapist's attitude to the client is not just credulous but *reverent*, a term that is used to describe the awe of being aware that one is being allowed to affirm the other's core meanings (Leitner & Pfenninger, 1994). The therapist also needs to display 'creative artistry' (Leitner & Faidley, 1999), cyclically loosening and tightening their own construing, and being open to the use of a range of different interventions, including those, such as music, drawing, or dance, that focus on, and may increase the level of awareness of, non-verbal construing. The therapist who is sensitively attuned to the client's experiences and sufficiently flexible in his or her approach should thereby be able to evoke the client's 'experiential truths' (Leitner et al., 2005).

Narrative Hermeneutic Personal Construct Psychotherapy

The therapeutic relationship is also of central importance in narrative hermeneutic personal construct psychotherapy (Chiari & Nuzzo, 2010), which, while based upon personal construct theory, also draws, amongst others, upon narrative approaches; Gadamer's (1989) notion of the hermeneutic dialogue, with its emphasis on the linguistic construction of the world; and the biological theory of autopoiesis (Maturana & Varela, 1987), which views an organism's 'organization of living' as realised through particular structures. Care is taken to ensure that psychotherapy promotes structural changes that foster the restoration or conservation, rather than disintegration, of the organisation of self. To give just one way in which this may be achieved, and which, like Leitner's (1985a) 'optimal therapeutic distance', involves a delicate balance of validation and invalidation, the therapist will aim to develop an 'orthogonal therapeutic relationship'. In such a relationship, the therapist takes a position that cannot easily be understood in terms of the constructs that the client normally applies to his or her relationships, and that therefore requires the application of new constructs that are independent of these. An example of such a relationship can be drawn from the work of one of us with a client who had been through the therapeutic mill, having previously experienced little or no benefit from cognitive-behavioural, psychodynamic, and humanistic therapies (Winter, 2008). He regarded himself as a 'critical user' of psychotherapy, and his serial seeking out of different forms of therapy could have been seen as a hostile (in Kelly's sense) attempt to validate constructions of psychotherapy as, at best, ineffective. When reporting on a fixed-role therapy homework exercise during our course of personal construct psychotherapy, he said that he had 'once again...sabotaged the therapy', an accusation, coupled with 'resistance', that previous therapists had levelled against him. However, on this occasion the therapist's response was not in terms of a construct of criticism and rejection versus acceptance but instead to show curiosity in the novel approach that the client had taken to the exercise (involving having conversations between the fixed role and a character representing his angry self).

While narrative hermeneutic psychotherapy may use all of the personal construct therapeutic techniques that we described earlier in this chapter, these are regarded as 'conversational acts'. The first phase of therapy involves 'the arrangement for a therapeutic conversation', in which the client's willingness to participate is facilitated by such means as the therapist's credulous approach. There is then a search for further meaning, which may involve constantly returning to particular topics, with ever increasing understanding. This turns into a search for alternative narratives through a dialectical process of questions and answers. The therapist's questions may be particularly guided by the notions of personal paths of dependency, notably those involving threat and guilt, and forms of uncompleted recognition (see Chapter 7).

Applications with Particular Client Groups

As we have seen, specific personal construct psychotherapy approaches have been developed for use with particular client groups, some of the earliest examples of this being Fransella's (1972) work with people who stutter and that of Bannister et al. (1975) with clients diagnosed with schizophrenic thought disorder. It is beyond the scope of this book to describe all of these specific applications of personal construct psychotherapy, but descriptions may be found in Button (1985), R. Neimeyer and G. Neimeyer (1987), Winter (1992), and Winter and Viney (2005). We shall now briefly present two examples of such approaches.

A Personal Construct Psychotherapy Intervention for People Who Self-harm

As mentioned in Chapter 7, Kelly's taxonomy of suicide as either a 'dedicated act', 'deterministic', or 'chaotic' has been extended to encompass non-fatal acts of self-harm (R. Neimeyer & Winter, 2006; Winter et al., 2000). For some people, their self-harm may be viewed as a 'way of life' that provides them with some structure at times of apparent chaos. For others, it can be seen as a foreshortening of the Circumspection-Preemption-Control (CPC) Cycle (see Chapter 3), in which the person acts with little or no prior circumspection. In other cases, it might help to absolve guilt, while for yet others it might be a hostile act in which the person attempts to extort evidence for some construction. There are therefore several different possible routes to self-harm, and the particular approaches taken in the therapeutic intervention developed by Winter, Sireling et al. (2007) will vary accordingly, being dependent on the personal construct formulation of the self-harm of each individual client.

The intervention is offered on a six-session renewable contract, beginning a few weeks after the act of self-harm (Winter, 2005). The first two sessions adopt a credulous approach, viewing the self-harm as an experiment and exploring what the client was anticipating would happen and whether their anticipations were validated or invalidated. In some cases, the invalidation is massive, as in a client who anticipated that her self-harm would elicit some sympathy from her husband, only to find that he 'just beat the shit out of me' (Winter, 2018a, p. 11). Exploration of the reasons for a client's self-harm may help to elaborate construing that was at a low level of awareness and to bind in words constructions that previously only received non-verbal expression. It may also facilitate the viewing of self-harm as a strategy that is possibly open to replacement by other strategies. The client may be asked to invite a significant other to the second session so that this person's perspective on the self-harm can be compared with that of the client. There may also be the use of formal personal construct assessment procedures, such as the repertory grid.

Following the first two sessions, the self-harm is formulated in personal construct terms, thus providing the focus for the remaining sessions. The approach adopted in these will be very different, for example, in a client whose self-harm occurred in the context of a deterministic view of the world than in one whose view appeared chaotic. In the former, a particular focus may be on loosening, and in the latter on tightening, the individual's construing. Some instances of 'deterministic' self-harm may be associated with undispersed dependency, as when there has been the loss of a person on whom the client focussed all, or most, of their dependencies. In such cases, the client may be helped to experiment gradually with dispersing their dependencies. In some instances of 'chaotic' self-harm, events may appear unpredictable because the client has difficulty with sociality, construing other people's construction processes, and this may then be a focus of therapy, perhaps making particular use of enactment techniques.

If self-harm appears to be the person's way of life, therapy is likely to focus upon developing alternative ways of anticipating the world. If it reflects a foreshortening of the CPC Cycle, exercises in applying this cycle in decision-making may be used. If the self-harm seems to involve absolution of guilt, therapy may focus on elaborating a core role that does not involve self-harm. Finally, in cases of self-harm that involves hostility, the therapeutic focus is likely to be on non-hostile experimentation.

Constructivist Grief Therapy

Our second example is of an approach that, while drawing upon personal construct theory, is most commensurate with those elaborations of the theory that have a narrative emphasis and focus on the stories by which we live our lives (Mair, 1988). This approach was developed by R. Neimeyer (2005, 2016) to facilitate the reconstruction of meaning in people who are struggling with experiences of loss. Such experiences, in R. Neimeyer's (2000, 2005) view, involve narrative disruption, of which there are three major types. The first, involving 'disorganised narratives', is often associated with traumatic loss, as when a 'micro-narrative' concerning the traumatic experience cannot be integrated with the 'macro-narrative' of the person's life. The second involves 'dissociated narratives', stories about the loss that the individual has not revealed to others, and perhaps also not to the self. The third type of narrative disruption involves 'dominant narratives' that may marginalise the individual's own personal accounts. In these three types of narrative disruption, therapy will be likely, respectively, to focus upon integration of disorganised narratives; selective disclosure of dissociated narratives; and elaborating alternatives to a dominant narrative.

A further distinction made by R. Neimeyer (2016) is between two narrative strands that may be constructed by a bereaved person, one concerning the 'event story' of a loved one's death, and the other concerning the 'back story' of the relationship with the deceased. A particular focus of constructivist grief therapy may be on reconstructing this latter relationship in a way that it may be continued, a process that may be aided by the use of a variety of methods, including two chair technique, narrative, ritual, and expressive approaches, and having a photograph of the lost loved one present (R. Neimeyer, 1999).

Beyond Individual Personal Construct Psychotherapy

It should be apparent that, even when conducted on an individual basis, personal construct psychotherapy will usually have a very relational emphasis. We shall now turn in the next two chapters to applications that are explicitly relational in that they involve working with couples, families, systems, or groups.

Notes

1. Mair (2015b)went so far as to say that 'It could almost be argued that personal construct psychology is a psychology of man as a maker and user of metaphor' (p. 86).
2. This is essentially similar to the 'miracle question' in solution-focused therapy (De Shazer, 1994).
3. The word ROLE is capitalised by experiential personal construct psychotherapists to differentiate Kelly's notion of it from more conventional usage.

References

Agnew, J. (1985). Childhood disorders or the venture of children. In E. Button (Ed.), *Personal Construct Theory and Mental Health* (pp. 224–245). London: Croom Helm.

Bannister, D., Adams-Webber, J. R., Penn, W. I., & Radley, A. R. (1975). Reversing the process of thought disorder: A serial validation experiment. *British Journal of Social and Clinical Psychology, 14,* 169–180.

Bendinelli, G., & Lui, C. (2014). Play as a way of knowing, learning and changing. In H. Moran (Ed.), *Using Personal Construct Psychology (PCP) in Practice with Children and Adolescents* (pp. 88–98). https://issuu.com/pcp inpractice/docs/using_personal_construct_psychology.

Button, E. (Ed.). (1985). *Personal Construct Theory and Mental Health*. Beckenham, UK: Croom Helm.

Chiari, G., & Nuzzo, M. L. (2010). *Constructivist Psychotherapy: A Narrative Hermeneutic Approach*. London: Routledge.

De Shazer, S. (1994). *Words Were Originally Magic*. New York: Norton.

Epting, F. R. (1984). *Personal Construct Counseling and Psychotherapy*. New York: Wiley.

Epting, F. R., & Amerikaner, M. (1980). Optimal functioning: A personal construct approach. In A. Landfield & L. M. Leitner (Eds.), *Personal Construct Psychology: Psychotherapy and Personality* (pp. 55–73). New York: Wiley.

Epting, F. R., & Nazario, A., Jr. (1987). Designing a fixed role therapy: Issues, techniques, and modifications. In R. A. Neimeyer & G. J. Neimeyer (Eds.), *Personal Construct Therapy Casebook* (pp. 277–289). New York: Springer.

Feixas, G., & Compañ, V. (2016). Dilemma-focused intervention for unipolar depression: A treatment manual. *BMC Psychiatry, 16*, 235.

Fransella, F. (1972). *Personal Change and Reconstruction: Research on a Treatment of Stuttering*. London: Academic Press.

Fransella, F. (1985). Individual psychotherapy. In E. Button (Ed.), *Personal Construct Theory and Mental Health* (pp. 277–301). London: Croom Helm.

Gadamer, H.G. (1989) *Truth and Method* (J. Weinsheimer & D. G. Marshall, Trans., 2nd ed.). New York: Seabury Press.

Karst, T. O. (1980). The relationship between personal construct theory and psychotherapeutic techniques. In A. W. Landfield & L. M. Leitner (Eds.), *Personal Construct Psychology: Psychotherapy and Personality* (pp. 166–184). New York: Wiley.

Kelly, G. A. (1955). *The Psychology of Personal Constructs. Vol. I, II*. New York: Norton (2nd printing: 1991, London and New York: Routledge).

Kelly, G. A. (1964). The language of hypothesis: Man's psychological instrument. *Journal of Individual Psychology, 20*, 137–152.

Kelly, G. A. (1969b). Personal construct theory and the psychotherapeutic interview. In B. Maher (Ed.), *Clinical Psychology and Personality: The Selected Papers of George Kelly* (pp. 224–264). New York: Wiley.

Kelly, G. A. (1970a). A brief introduction to personal construct theory. In D. Bannister (Ed.), *Perspectives in Personal Construct Psychology* (pp. 3–20). London: Academic Press.

Kelly, G. A. (1980). A psychology of the optimal man. In A. W. Landfield & L. M. Leitner (Eds.), *Personal Construct Psychology: Psychotherapy and Personality* (pp. 18–35). New York: Wiley.

Leitner, L. M. (1985a). The terrors of cognition: On the experiential validity of personal construct theory. In D. Bannister (Ed.), *Issues and Approaches in Personal Construct Theory* (pp. 83–103). London: Academic Press.

Leitner, L. M., & Faidley, A. J. (1999). Creativity in experiential personal construct psychotherapy. *Journal of Constructivist Psychology, 12,* 273–286.

Leitner, L. M., Faidley, A. J., Dominici, D., Humphreys, C., Loeffler, V., Schlutsmeyer, M., & Thomas, J. (2005). Encountering an other: Experiential personal construct psychotherapy. In D. A. Winter & L. L. Viney (Eds.), *Personal Construct Psychotherapy: Advances in Theory, Practice and Research* (pp. 54–68). London: Whurr.

Leitner, L. M., & Pfenninger, D. T. (1994). Sociality and optimal functioning. *Journal of Constructivist Psychology, 7,* 119–135.

Lovell, M. S. (2011). *The Churchills: A Family at the Heart of History—From the Duke of Marlborough to Winston Churchill.* London: Little, Brown.

Mair, J. M. M. (1988). Psychology as storytelling. *International Journal of Personal Construct Psychology, 1,* 125–137.

Mair, J. M. M. (2015a). The community of self. In D. A. Winter & N. Reed (Eds.), *Toward a Radical Re-definition of Psychology: The Selected Works of Miller Mair* (pp. 102–112). London: Routledge.

Mair, J. M. M. (2015b). Metaphors for living. In D. A. Winter & N. Reed (Eds.), *Toward a Radical Re-definition of Psychology: The Selected Works of Miller Mair* (pp. 73–101). London: Routledge.

Maturana, H. R., & Varela, F. J. (1987). *The Tree of Knowledge: The Biological Roots of Human Understanding.* Boston: Shambhala.

Moran, H. (2014). *Using Personal construct psychology (PCP) in practice with children and adolescents.* Online eBook: https://issuu.com/pcpinpractice/docs/using_personal_construct_psychology.

Neimeyer, R. A. (1988). Integrative directions in personal construct therapy. *International Journal of Personal Construct Psychology, 1,* 283–297.

Neimeyer, R. A. (1993). Constructivist approaches to the measurement of meaning. In G. J. Neimeyer (Ed.), *Constructivist Assessment: A Casebook* (pp. 58–103). Newbury Park, CA: Sage.

Neimeyer, R. A. (1999). Narrative strategies in grief therapy. *Journal of Constructivist Psychology, 12,* 65–85.

Neimeyer, R. A. (2000). Narrative disruptions in the construction of self. In R. A. Neimeyer & J. A. Raskin (Eds.), *Constructions of Disorder: Meaning Making Frameworks for Psychotherapy* (pp. 207–241). Washington, DC: American Psychological Association.

Neimeyer, R. A. (2005). Growing through grief: Constructing coherence in narratives of loss. In D. A. Winter & L. L. Viney (Eds.), *Personal Construct Psychotherapy: Advances in Theory, Practice and Research* (pp. 111–126). London: Whurr.

Neimeyer, R. A. (2016). Reconstructing meaning in bereavement. In D. A. Winter & N. Reed (Eds.), *The Wiley Handbook of Personal Construct Psychology* (pp. 254–264). Chichester, UK: Wiley.

Neimeyer, R. A., & Neimeyer, G. J. (Eds.). (1987). *Personal Construct Therapy Casebook*. New York: Springer.

Neimeyer, R. A., & Winter, D. A. (2006). To be or not to be: Personal constructions of the suicidal choice. In T. Ellis (Ed.), *Cognition and Suicide: Theory, Research and Practice* (pp. 149–169). Washington, DC: American Psychological Association.

Stein, M. (2007). Non-verbal techniques in personal construct psychotherapy. *Journal of Constructivist Psychology, 20,* 103–124.

Winter, D. A. (1987). Personal construct psychotherapy as a radical alternative to social skills training. In R. A. Neimeyer & G. J. Neimeyer (Eds.), *Personal Construct Therapy Casebook* (pp. 107–123). New York: Springer.

Winter, D. A. (1988). Reconstructing an erection and elaborating ejaculation. *International Journal of Personal Construct Psychology, 1,* 81–100.

Winter, D. A. (1992). *Personal Construct Psychology in Clinical Practice: Theory, Research and Applications*. London: Routledge.

Winter, D. A. (1996). Psychotherapy's contrast pole. In J. W. Scheer & A. Catina (Eds.), *Empirical Constructivism in Europe: The Personal Construct Approach* (pp. 149–159). Giessen, Germany: Psychosozial Verlag.

Winter, D. A. (2003). Stress in police officers: Personal construct theory perspectives. In J. Horley (Ed.), *Personal Construct Perspectives on Forensic Psychology* (pp. 121–142). London: Routledge.

Winter, D. A. (2005). Self harm and reconstruction. In D. A. Winter & L. L. Viney (Eds.), *Personal Construct Psychotherapy: Advances in Theory, Practice and Research* (pp. 127–135). London: Whurr.

Winter, D. A. (2008). Personal construct psychotherapy in a national health service setting: Does survival mean selling out? In J. D. Raskin & S. K. Bridges (Eds.), *Studies in Meaning: 3. Constructivist Therapy in the 'Real' World* (pp. 229–252). New York: Pace University Press.

Winter, D. A. (2018a). Self-harm and reconstruction: A personal construct theory perspective. *Journal of Psychotherapy and Counselling Psychology Reflections, 3,* 9–14.

Winter, D., Bhandari, S., Lutwyche, G., Metcalfe, C., Riley, T., Sireling, L., & Watson, S. (2000). Deliberate and undeliberated self harm: Theoretical basis and evaluation of a personal construct psychotherapy intervention. In J. W. Scheer (Ed.), *The Person in Society: Challenges to a Constructivist Theory* (pp. 351–360). Giessen, Germany: Psychosozial-Verlag.

Winter, D., Sireling, L., Riley, T., Metcalfe, C., Quaite, A., & Bhandari, S. (2007). A controlled trial of personal construct psychotherapy for deliberate self-harm. *Psychology and Psychotherapy, 80,* 23–37.

Winter, D. A., & Viney, L. (Eds.). (2005). *Personal Construct Psychotherapy: Recent Advances in Theory, Practice and Research.* London: Whurr.

9

Working with Families and Couples

When we work with the family or partner together with a person in difficulty, we are able to see the members relating directly—their construing in action—and to observe the relational situation which forms such a vital context to most problems being presented, rather than relying on just the client's individual account of that situation. This opens doors to many new possibilities: richer information obtained from the construing of several closely involved different observers; the opportunity to intervene in relational processes with the parties concerned simultaneously; and to work with members who are most able and motivated to help resolve difficulties. It allows a piece of work to take place which draws on the experience, ideas, and creativity of several minds, whilst the therapist ensures that the members collaborate in the most constructive and productive way possible. Advantages of working with families are listed in Table 9.1. All these additional factors also tend to allow for briefer effective involvement in mental health than working only with the individual client (Crane & Payne, 2011; Stratton, 2010). We do not, however, need to set these modes of treatment against each other—indeed, we will often use a combination of individual and family sessions,

© The Author(s) 2020
H. Procter and D. A. Winter, *Personal and Relational Construct Psychotherapy*,
Palgrave Texts in Counselling and Psychotherapy,
https://doi.org/10.1007/978-3-030-52177-6_9

Table 9.1 Advantages of working with families and couples

- Direct contact with the important people in the situation
- Richer information obtained from the construing of several closely involved different observers
- Therapist can develop alliances with all members present
- Convening the whole group to act as one toward shared goals
- Opportunity to work with the most motivated members
- The treatment of choice with people who cannot or will not communicate
- Interaction between people directly observable
- Disagreements and misunderstandings addressed directly
- All members can reflect on therapy and progress between sessions
- Shared experiments and new perspectives

although it is good to start with a family meeting, so that an agreement with them to participate in a course of therapy can be made.

Rober (2017) wrote of a child in one of his sessions wondering about his therapist: 'Is he kind? Is he severe or judgemental? Does he have respect for children? Does he show that he is interested? Does he attach importance to drawings, or is he only interested in words and explanations?' (p. 159). PCP is well able to fulfil all these values, with its emphasis on acceptance, the credulous approach, support, respecting and working with a client's ways of experiencing and construing the world, and its avoidance of the therapist 'colonising' the family with too much investment in change, imposing explanatory frameworks and how things *ought* to be (Cade, 1998). But in addition to these general values, as we have seen in earlier chapters, PCP has many tools and approaches for compassionately entering people's worlds and doing justice to their unique ways of making sense of things, and is particularly strong on methods for engaging and working with children (Burnham, 2008; Butler & Green, 2007; Moran, 2014; Procter, 2007a; Ravenette, 1999a). Of course, family therapy can be practised with difficulties arising at any stage of life and indeed the service led by one of us (HP) in Somerset, UK, was the first to offer comprehensive family therapy for adult, and older adult, mental health in the country (Pottle, 1984; Procter & Pieczora, 1993; Procter & Stephens, 1984; Walker & Procter, 1980).

If, as Kelly said, people are a bit like scientists, then we can see the family as a *team of scientists*, engaged in a process of inquiry as the members struggle together to make sense of the world, their experiences

Table 9.2 The process of PRCP family therapy

- Constructive alternativism in the family as a resource
- Relating to each member as a whole person—their construing in the area of their interests, work, school, etc.
- Countering pathologising conflict and disempowerment by emphasising each member's experience
- Steering the conversation to the constructive and functional
- Broadening the range and overlap in construing
- Enhancing sociality and mutual understanding
- Moving from individual to relational construing
- All this leads to new dialogue, enabling the family to move forward

and the difficulties that they are facing (Procter, 1987). Any group that we work with consists of a set of unique individuals, each with a different way of construing, but families, by their nature, as well as having their own construct system, tend to include people strikingly disparate in their positions and concerns, the members being, usually, of contrasting gender, different ages, and facing the different challenges associated with their particular stages of life. As we come together as therapists with the family members, the challenge is simultaneously to make an alliance with them all in spite of these differences and what may be significant disagreements and tensions between them.[1] But we see this situation as an advantage: As we join them in their process of inquiry, the differences become a creative resource helping us to generate new ways of seeing things and finding new paths forward (see Table 9.2).

Interviewing Families

As the therapist accompanies the family into the meeting room, he or she will already notice from things like how they seat themselves some aspects of their habitual relating, for example their power hierarchy and affiliations between members. Ideally, the therapist will already have spoken to one or more of them on the phone, explaining how useful it is to have a family meeting and urging them to attend. The environment should be comfortable, with toys and other materials[2]; and it is good to greet and settle the youngest members, already starting informal and playful conversation with them. In working with families, the therapist tends to be quite active, in contrast to traditional forms of group psychotherapy, where he or she may tend to wait for group members to start talking and to intervene more minimally. Because family members know each other extremely well, their patterns of relating may tend to dominate the session if they are left to interact spontaneously, and this can lead to problematic impasses and tensions being aired too soon. Questioning plays a central role in the process. We have already covered some aspects of the list of questions for families and children in Appendices A and B (see Chapters 5 and 6). If the problem is raised early on, it is useful to say that we shall be coming to these issues soon, but firstly the therapist would like to get to know them all a little as individuals. Sometimes, a considerable amount of time is devoted to this stage (Sects. 1–3 in Appendix A). Asking about their interests, friends, school, work, and so on settles them well but also allows the therapist to begin to develop rapport and alliances, and to get in touch with each person's construing. This will frequently allow the therapist to use members' constructs and language as metaphors in making observations and useful comments about their situation. We will be interested in their experiences of family life, how the parents met, their families of origin, grandparents and other figures who are interested in them, what it is like, for example, to be first, middle, or last born, and comparing how life is for children with how the parents experienced life in their childhoods and so on.

Often, during these discussions, difficulties quite different from the original referral emerge, such as illness, bereavement, and worries or conflicts with or about other members of the family. We are not tied to working only with the referred problem,[3] and it is not uncommon for the latter to be seen as secondary to other more serious issues for the family. Occasionally, the entire course of therapy is conducted without addressing the referred problem, which quietly vanishes or resolves itself spontaneously! The therapist will be making a mental list of all the worries and stresses that the family are experiencing. Already, during this phase, we can be looking for times when the family is at its most happy and functioning. Examples of times when everyone is getting on with life can be tied to the therapy: 'if we were to meet together a few times to make things better, are *those the kind of experiences* that you would like us to be aiming for?' This defines the therapy as being primarily about making changes. Problems have the tendency to expand and fill the whole universe of concern, so already we will be countering that escalation and giving at least equal weight to goals and memories of times when the problems are least noticeable, including memories of before the onset of the difficulties (see Appendix A, Sec. 4).

'Problems' versus 'Goals' is a central construct in therapy and represents the pathways of Kelly's 'transitive diagnosis' discussed in Chapter 7. In Fig. 9.1, the metaphor of a magnetic field (which aligns iron filings between North and South) represents the negotiation of different family members' constructions of problems and goals. In the upper panel the arrows represent the different versions of their troubles held by the different family members. Part of what brought them to therapy may be that they are pursuing different priorities and so nothing is getting ironed out. There may be contradictions between the different members'

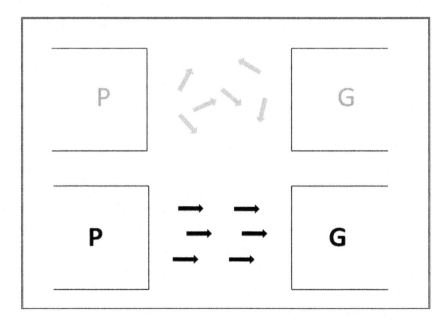

Fig. 9.1 The 'Problem-Goal Magnet': aligning different members' goals

concerns. In Kelly's terms, we could see this as a 'looseness' or a 'fragmentation' of the family construct system (FCS). By assembling problems and goals, we are setting up a 'magnetic field' in which aligned transitive pathways forward are assembled. The therapist will gather all the concerns together in a list. It is common towards the end of the session to give a summary, saying, 'Things have been very difficult for you. You are all suffering with the sad loss of maternal grandmother; the difficult conflict occurring with your elder daughter; your son getting involved with drugs; as well as the bedwetting of your younger daughter. Given all these things, I think you have been dealing with the situation extremely well and it is not surprising that you, Susan, have been feeling so desperate, getting so anxious and exhausted. Would you like to meet again in order to help you address these things?' Similarly, with goals, each may be pursuing different and contradictory things. We will include them all in the message about the aims of therapy so that each member is supported in their priorities. An incompatibility here can be seen as a dilemma 'which we will work towards in trying to find a resolution'. In this way the arrows become aligned, as in the lower panel of Fig. 9.1, leaving the members feeling that they can all move forward together in a shared direction. It is important to note, though, that we will not necessarily refer back to the goals as part of the therapy. Neither we nor the family know at this point what the appropriate goals to aim for are, as they are being constructed from the 'problem-determined system' (Anderson, Goolishian, & Windermand, 1986). Change, as we shall see later, occurs spontaneously, in fresh directions which are impossible to predict at this stage.

In looking at the presenting problem, there is often a spokesperson who holds the power of being the most concerned and having the most to say about all the details. It is useful here to follow Haley's (1974) guideline and start by hearing from the least involved, or the lowest in the hierarchy, moving through to the spokesperson having their say.[4] In this way, all members are kept involved, a very important requirement in family interviewing. Failure to do this can lead to the spokesperson 'sewing it all up', leaving the others feeling that they have nothing to add, with their individual voices being ignored and not of interest. Following a principle that families should allow all the individuals to thrive and grow, this is a way of countering disempowerment. It does not mean that we cannot respectfully obtain the spokesperson's permission to proceed in this way. As stated in Table 9.2, we can counter conflict and over-strict hierarchy by facilitating the expression of each person's experiences and views.

As we begin to look at the presenting problem, or the one negotiated with the family to begin working on, in detail (Appendix A, Sec. 5), we shall be exploring its occurrence in time, place, and context, how often it occurs, when and where, how long it has been occurring, exceptions, when it is most and least noticeable. We can explore the onset of the problem in relation to a transition in the family life cycle (Chapter 6). We will all the time be considering the problem's relational context. With whom does it occur most? How are the relationships different when it is or isn't occurring? When it occurs what do different members *do* to deal with or respond to it? As we mentioned in Chapter 5, *attempted solutions* (AS's) or *corrective measures* are an essential part of problem maintenance (Procter & Walker, 1989; Watzlawick, Weakland, & Fisch, 1974). Questions looking at AS's are exemplified in Appendix A, Sec. 5. We can usefully obtain a picture of the whole family and professional system by asking what different people have suggested to remedy the issues. 'What does your father, your Granny, your friend, your doctor suggest you *do* when you are feeling like this?' We can think of the interaction between people in this in terms of the bow-tie diagram (see Figs. 7.1 and 5.2). What people suggest is governed by the way people *construe* the problem, by their *positions on the problem* (Fisch, Weakland, & Segal, 1982). These can also be asked for directly (Appendix A, Sec. 7). Understanding the range of different attempted solutions and positions on the problem (and on therapy—what therapeutic measures would be appropriate? Appendix A, Sec. 8) gives a vital picture of how the problem is functioning within the family construct system. Certain core family constructs and dimensions will emerge as being central in their construing. At a more practical level, finding out what has been tried (including any previous therapy they have experienced) clears the ground for developing fresh approaches and not suggesting something to which the response is 'we've tried that – it didn't help!'

As we work with the family and begin to understand their relational politics, we will become aware of what personal and family constructs are operating to govern their roles and positions. We learn to listen out for constructs as the family members talk. A little girl might say she likes 'Minecraft' so much because you can 'do what you like!' Or using the 'drawing and its opposite' technique (see Chapter 5), a boy might say the difference between the two pictures is 'being one of the family – being left out' (Ravenette, 1999b). What do we *do* with a construct? We can explore it in various different ways. We have four main alternatives, using the 'joystick' (see Fig. 9.2). This gives the interviewer four main directions to move forward in exploring construing. We can go down to subordinates and elaborate the construct, asking for examples. We will be given a story which, in turn, will contain more constructs, which we can explore. We can ask for the contrast pole—'When can't you do what you like?'—and seek examples of that, continuing with the pole which leads to the most fruitful material. We can 'ladder' it (see Chapter 5), moving up to superordinate values, asking 'Which would

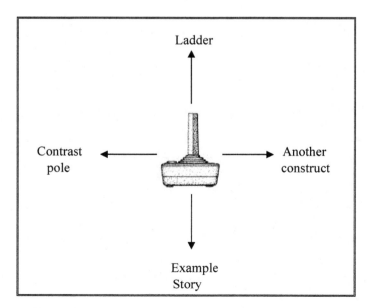

Fig. 9.2 What to do with a construct—the 'joystick'

you prefer to be?', 'Why?' Or we can ask, 'What's another way we could look at this?' and either elicit a new construct or provide one which seems useful. When we were interviewing a child diagnosed with autism in this way, his mother said, 'This is very interesting. You talk to him differently to me. It reveals the difficulties and misunderstandings he has with relationships' (Procter, 2000, p. 72).

When a construct is important to a person, a light seems to turn on and they will be eager to say more about it. We could say that constructs are a 'gateway' into a person's world. This applies too at the level of family construing. In the first interview of one of us (HP) with a family with a member, Peter, who had become completely mute and catatonic, the construct of 'talkative' seemed central in their system. I asked, 'Who in the family is the most talkative?' This question was met with guffaws of laughter as they pointed to Peter's father, who, they said, had difficulty in keeping his mouth shut. I heard that Peter's sister, Ruth, again with much laughter, was the most talkative of the three children. It seemed no coincidence that Peter was enacting the extreme contrast pole by becoming completely silent. When Peter started talking again, on the way home immediately after a significant session, he told me at the next meeting about all that he had been doing in tremendous detail (Procter, 1987). He seemed to have 'slot-rattled' (see Chapter 8) back into talking nineteen to the dozen.

We can use the 'joystick' to guide our interviewing in relation to family constructs, applying it to the way members are polarised along dimensions, taking two opposing positions, and who in the family identifies or agrees with a position, or takes a mediating role between them (Ugazio, 2013). These may arise from differences in construing deriving from the maternal and paternal families of origin, as we discussed in Chapter 7. This became a central theme in the therapy of a couple who had lost two children. The parents had very different beliefs about how to deal with grief and bereavement arising from their different cultural backgrounds (Procter, 2009b). The mother gave very graphic examples of how she would be greeted with tremendous sympathy in the village shop in her country of origin compared to her experiences in England, from where her husband originated. Here in the UK, she felt, after a few weeks, she was expected to 'get over it and get on with life'.

The apparent difference in superordinate construing and values between husband and wife in this had been leading to significant tension between them, considerably adding to their grief and leaving her feeling alienated.

Using the 'professional dyadic constructs' or 'meta-constructs' shown in Table 7.1 allows us to explore the relationships in more depth and to encourage another important move in the therapy listed in Table 9.2: moving from individual to relational construing. As we begin to use the discourse of relationships, the family will tend to start construing their situation in these terms and to move from relating to others on the basis of their characteristics and behaviour (monadic construing) to how they actually relate, and how they would wish to relate, in pairs and in threesomes. It is much easier to change relationships than to change individuals, although when the relationships shift, people do change accordingly. This involves a shift from 'You need to change' to 'How can I change to make things better?' A new level of responsibilities and possibilities opens up. As we mentioned in Chapter 5, the bow-tie diagram, drawn up with the family, can be useful in making this shift. We may enter into a discourse of 'full intersubjectivity' in which there is reciprocal sociality together with a mutual concern for the state of the relationships between members, as we described in Chapter 4.

Therapeutic Change in Family Intervention

All the methods of working with the family which we have discussed are designed to make the dialogue, or as Mair (2015c) prefers to call it, the *conversation,* as rich as possible. We agree with Rober (2017, p. 53) when he says, 'the focus is on having a rich dialogue with all the family members about their worries'. Just as individuals are, for Kelly, a 'form of motion', so are families, once freed from repetitious interactions and fruitless struggles. All families potentially have the resources and the creativity to move forward and resolve their difficulties. Every family situation and therapeutic path is unique, so it is impossible to have general answers to the question 'What do we *do* to solve a certain type of problem?' But we do not need to answer this question because the locus of change is *in the family*. This takes a burden off the therapist, who is often expected to 'have the answers' and to 'know what to do' to resolve human problems. This does not mean that we take no notice of research that indicates useful effective intervention with particular classes of problems. We should be free to use any ideas and resources arising from research and other therapeutic approaches which we can subsume within the PRCP framework. But we will be wary of approaches that provide general 'explanations' for problems. Indeed, for us, explanations about the historic causes and reasons for problems are often given too great an emphasis in everyday thinking and in many approaches to counselling and psychotherapy. This does not preclude going into the past, for example, hearing about traumatic experiences and how they are informing the family's views. The purpose here is to gain a better understanding of, and to work with, construing in the present, which may be perpetuating problems. Past events in themselves do not directly influence present and future events.[5]

This is suggested by the way change often occurs. A family will quite often return for the next session saying 'things have been a bit better'. A good family session no doubt has a role in enabling this spontaneous change to occur, but we do not want to take any credit for that. Rather, as we have presented in Appendix A, Sect. 10, we will ask, 'How did you manage it?', 'How do you think she managed it?'; and, a very useful question is, 'I know it's the last thing you would want to do, but how would you go about making things worse again?' (Fisch et al., 1982). We learned to call this the 'insight question' as it often reveals the very processes that we felt were perpetuating the problem, but discovered by the family in a spontaneous and natural way.

Change involves *reconstruction*, developing new ways of construing the situation, self, the others, and the relationships. As we have said, this mostly occurs spontaneously in the context of a therapeutic process that involves careful clarification and emotional understanding, which enables revision of the members' constructs. Sometimes, when the time is right, we may provide new ways of construing the situation in the form of metaphors and reframes. Earlier in their careers, the authors were influenced by Haley (1963, 1974) and the Milan Team (Selvini,

Boscolo, Cecchin, & Prata, 1978) in what has been labelled *paradoxical* interventions. Kelly (1955, p. 656) himself used this when he said to a girl who had developed a limp that she should 'not go too fast in getting rid of the limp...such things are hard to get rid of all at once.' But within the PRCP framework, such interventions are given with the genuine intention of supporting the members in their construing, not in any way designed to 'trick' the family into change, as this kind of intervention is sometimes construed. When all the members of the family are supported and validated, the frustration and 'expressed emotion', with its associated negative arousal, well known to encourage relapse and even to initiate 'schizophrenia' and other conditions (Vaughn & Leff, 1976), will be reduced. The most important thing here is to support each member in how they are construing and approaching things and not apply pressure for change (obviously making an exception to this in the case of abuse or violence[6]). In another case of helping a family with a catatonic member, Jonathan, who had been claiming he was Jesus, we said to his father:

> 'You are right to be angry with him, to assert your authority...continue to do this, but don't expect him to go along with you...The way you have been handling it is very good.' And to, Mark, the brother, 'You have been taking a joking, humorous stance' (said with approval). And to the mother, 'You have been thinking about the religious side of it...keep close to him, keep him under your wing'. (Procter, 1985a, p. 347)

Suggesting that they continue in their current approaches changes the *context* of the relational situation. The members see their habitual actions as now according with the therapist, rather than arising solely in response to the situation. Validation of construing allows a person to consider alternatives without threat, and to change and elaborate their position, freeing them to develop new ways of proceeding.

This intervention proved to mark a turning point in the therapy, with Jonathan appearing at the next family session without a trace of catatonic symptoms, nor any other signs of the serious psychotic state he had been in for several months (Procter, 1985a). The therapy took place in the traditional format of a family therapy clinic, using live supervision and a one-way mirror, the small clinic team having carefully planned the message during a break in the interview in the style of the Milan approach. It contained, in addition to the above supportive messages to the family members, the provision of a major new way of construing what Jonathan had been going through:

> Jonathan in doing what he's been doing has been keeping everyone involved. Jonathan, it's a natural response that you have. It's what he should be doing. Jonathan is going through a period of late adolescence where a great deal of work and learning has to be done concerning intimate relationships, about the implications of making close relationships both within and outside the family. Testing out what other relationships you have, working out the pecking order, the hierarchy particularly with regard to mother and father. In being close to your mother and challenging your father's authority. (Procter, 1985a, p. 346)

This constituted a new way of making sense of a number of features of his behaviour, which had involved him indiscriminately sleeping with several girls whilst on holiday, during which he had broken down and become preoccupied by sin, labelling black things and his family members as 'evil' and white things as 'good', and being preoccupied by the meanings of pop-song lyrics. The therapeutic breakthrough was achieved without recourse to any anti-psychotic medication. It was the most striking case in a series of interventions with people diagnosed with schizophrenia[7] using family therapy that we conducted during the 1980s, including the work with Peter, mentioned earlier (Procter 1987), many years before the important 'Open Dialogue' work of Seikkula and his colleagues (2006).

Later on, one of us (HP), having moved from working with adults to joining a child and adolescent mental health team (CAMHS), started using Andersen's (1987) 'reflecting team approach'. Rather than leaving the session and planning an intervention, the reflecting team method involved the observing team members coming into the room at the end of the session and having a conversation about the interview between themselves, whilst the family and therapist listened to them. The team, who do not talk together whilst observing the session in order to have a genuine dialogue, would share their thoughts about the situation, supporting all the family members, with different team members being able to identify with members according to their gender and stage of life, with children and adults. The therapist, using the questions in Appendix A, Sect. 11, would then ask the family for their responses to what they had heard. This method proved to be reliably acceptable to families, with such comments as, 'The team have got it right. That young lady on the right – she understood us completely!' The approach fits very well with Kelly's constructive alternativism. The team members' naturally unique construing arising from their own life experiences, different disciplines and therapeutic approaches typically covers a lot of ground in a rich way that does justice to the complexity of family situations. After that, the team members would remain in the room, concluding the session with a brief discussion involving everyone.

This raises interesting questions in relation to working alongside diagnosis in psychiatric and paediatric contexts. Our position towards diagnosis is not necessarily antithetical. As Kelly (1955, p. 10) said, in discussing psychological versus physiological constructions of situations, 'events on which facts are based hold no institutional loyalties'. We can construe them using either framework. Psychiatric diagnosis is used for establishing normative distinctions upon which decisions about the prescription of medication and other physical treatments are made. But working with the relational context is relevant and vital in either domain, whether the identified patient's condition is primarily organic as in neurological or developmental disorders or is primarily psychogenic. Family therapy is useful and applicable whatever the aetiology of the patient's condition. In working in Adult Mental Health, our practice was usually to de-emphasise and avoid diagnostic discourse, in that the constructs involved do not directly lead to useful life decisions. Our colleagues, Burbach and Stanbridge (1998), continued the tradition of early intervention in psychosis in Somerset, successfully integrating it with family management approaches in which a psycho-educational approach to psychosis was used.

We argue that family therapy is the treatment of choice where a person who is unwilling or unable to communicate is concerned, whether this is seen as catatonic, elective mutism, or due to learning disabilities or developmental disorders. Figure 9.3 is a metaphor for learning about Jonathan as a person by asking the people who know him, allowing him to be present as a person, despite his silence (Procter, 1985a). We must be

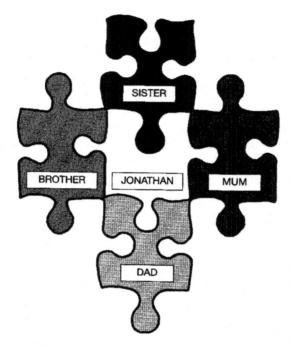

Fig. 9.3 Building up a picture of Jonathan's world by asking other family members about him (From Procter [2005])

careful, of course, not to be treating him as an 'object of interest' spoken of only in the third person as a 'he'. This was done by cross-checking with him continually, treating what the others say as only guesses, and asking, 'Is that right, Jonathan?', even though he was giving not the slightest response. It is notable that after he started talking again, he was able to remember in detail all the conversations we had had. At the time we had no idea whether he would ever emerge from his catatonic state. This requires the maintenance of hope and faith that he remains as a person with consciousness, feelings, and opinions.

Part of the work of one of us (HP) in child services included specialising in people diagnosed with autistic spectrum disorders (ASD) and other developmental disorders (Procter, 2000, 2001). Child services are more complex than those for adult mental health problems in that they tend to be situated in a network involving the school, social services, paediatrics, and the voluntary sector. Working with families of a child diagnosed with ASD included visiting the school and working closely with other professionals helping the child. Part of the work often involved being part of a multidisciplinary team set up to diagnose developmental disorders, consisting of HP in the role of clinical psychologist, a consultant paediatrician, a speech and language therapist, and an educational psychologist. We started using the reflecting team approach in that context too, discussing together, in front of the family, having made our assessments of the child. This proved to be very valuable and appreciated by families, as they could witness the complexities involved in making such a judgement. Making a diagnosis in the case of developmental disorders is an important process in ensuring that the right specialist support system, as well as appropriate financial help, is put in place to support the child in the family and in school. Working with the interface between parents and teachers is a crucial part of working with a child diagnosed with ASD. Issues developing between parents and the school, who are often mutually critical, is a common scenario; a polarisation more likely to develop because the child typically finds it difficult to communicate experiences between one environment and the other. Procter and Mason (2004) listed 22 concerns about children diagnosed with ASD in school, together with 22 associated ways forward and solutions, which proved useful in this context.

Further Applications

It is not possible to do justice to all the aspects of working with families using the PRCP framework in one chapter. We have emphasised here working with the most serious and challenging cases in the belief that less severe situations will be covered by some of the approaches described. More can be found in Procter (1985a, 2000, 2005), and approaches for working with families where the child is presented as needing help in Procter (2007a). Notable also is the work of Cunningham and Davis (1985) and McDonald and Mancuso (1987) on working with parents within the PCP framework. There is a useful literature on PCP work with couples (G. Neimeyer, 1985), marital violence (Doster, 1985), and working with sexual difficulties (Winter, 2005b). We shall now move on to working with the approach in conducting group psychotherapy.

Notes

1. Boszormenyi-Nagy (1987) called this *multilateral partiality*, getting 'every person to bring in his or her subjective accounts and their understandings of the others...as one person is heard and held accountable, it is easier for others to be heard...(this strengthens) the relationship between family members...(leading) to a more genuine dialogue between them' (Friedman, 1998, pp. 35–36).
2. Art materials and executive toys emphasise that the visual and kinaesthetic can be just as important as the aural and linguistic. For a discussions of toys and working with children, see Procter (2007a).
3. In the current climate, therapists can be constrained to stick with working with referred problems in a diagnosis-centred ethos. We must insist that collateral issues in the family are often of primary importance in problem formation and resolution and that working with them often allows effective brief intervention.
4. This may need careful negotiating, as the 'spokesperson' may be very powerful in a delicate convening process.
5. We may recall from Chapter 1 Kelly's statement that he does not 'believe a client or therapist has to lie down and let facts crawl all over him'. Clearly traumata that lead to life-changing injury affect us, but how we construe and react to them is central to their effects on our lives.
6. In such cases, we shall want to help the perpetrator find better ways of dealing with things, but it may be that the situation falls outside of therapy as the appropriate intervention, necessitating the involvement of police or children's safeguarding services.
7. It is important in this work to have a close relationship with the psychiatric admissions ward. In our work in Bridgwater, UK (Procter & Pieczora, 1993; Procter & Stephens, 1984), we were able to set up a family interview within two days of a person being admitted with psychotic presentations. A course of therapy with the family was negotiated which would continue whether the client was in the ward or back in the community. A member of the ward

staff would sit in on the sessions in the hospital. Criteria for early discharge were negotiated in the family session, which became the executive site for decision making. Thus, power and control were vested in the family rather than with the hospital team.

References

Andersen, T. (1987). The reflecting team. *Family Process, 26,* 416–428.

Anderson, H., Goolishian, H. A., & Windermand, L. (1986). Problem determined systems: Towards transformation in family therapy. *Journal of Strategic & Systemic Therapies, 5,* 1–13.

Boszormenyi-Nagy, I. (1987). *Foundations of Contextual Therapy: Collected Papers of Ivan Bosxormenyi-Nagy, M.D.* New York: Brunner/Mazel.

Burbach, F. R., & Stanbridge, R. I. (1998). A family intervention in psychosis service integrating the systemic and family management approaches. *Journal of Family Therapy, 20,* 311–325.

Burnham, S. (2008). *Let's Talk: Using Personal Construct Psychology to Support Children and Young People: Using Personal Construct Theory in School.* New York: Sage (Lucky Duck Books).

Butler, R. J., & Green, D. (2007). *The Child Within: Taking the Young Person's Perspective by Applying Personal Construct Theory* (2nd ed.). Chichester, UK: Wiley.

Cade, B. (1998). Honesty is still the best policy. *Journal of Family Therapy, 20,* 143–152.

Crane, D. R., & Payne, S. H. (2011). Individual versus family psychotherapy in managed care: Comparing the costs of treatment by the mental health professionals. *Journal of Marital and Family Therapy, 37,* 273–289.

Cunningham, C., & Davis, H. (1985). *Working with Parents: Frameworks for Collaboration.* Milton Keynes, UK: Open University Press.

Doster, J. A. (1985). A personal construct assessment of marital violence. In F. Epting & A. W. Landfield (Eds.), *Anticipating Personal Construct Psychology* (pp. 225–232). Lincoln: University of Nebraska Press.

Fisch, R., Weakland, J. H., & Segal, L. (1982). *The Tactics of Change: Doing Therapy Briefly.* San Francisco: Jossey-Bass.

Friedman, M. (1998). Buber's philosophy as the basis for dialogical psychotherapy and contextual therapy. *Journal of Humanist Psychology, 38*(1), 25–40.

Haley, J. (1963). *Strategies of Psychotherapy.* New York: Grune and Stratton.

Haley, J. (1974). *Problem Solving Therapy: New Strategies for Effective Family Therapy.* San Francisco: Jossey-Bass.

Kelly, G. A. (1955). *The Psychology of Personal Constructs. Vol. I, II.* New York: Norton (2nd printing: 1991, London and New York: Routledge).

Mair, J. M. M. (2015c). Psychotherapy, conversation and storytelling. In D. A. Winter & N. Reed (Eds.), *Toward a Radical Re-definition of Psychology: The Selected Works of Miller Mair* (pp. 131–146). London: Routledge.

McDonald, D. E., & Mancuso, J. C. (1987). A constructivist approach to parent training. In R. Neimeyer & G. Neimeyer (Eds.), *Personal Construct Therapy Casebook* (pp. 172–189). New York: Springer.

Moran, H. (2014). *Using Personal construct psychology (PCP) in practice with children and adolescents.* Online eBook: https://issuu.com/pcpinpractice/docs/using_personal_construct_psychology.

Neimeyer, G. J. (1985). Personal constructs in the counseling of couples. In F. R. Epting & A. W. Landfield (Eds.), *Anticipating Personal Construct Psychology* (pp. 201–215). Lincoln: University of Nebraska Press.

Pottle, S. (1984). Developing a network-oriented services for elderly people and their carers. In A. Treacher & J. Carpenter (Eds.), *Using Family Therapy* (pp. 149–165). Oxford, UK: Blackwell.

Procter, H. G. (1985a). A construct approach to family therapy and systems intervention. In E. Button (Ed.), *Personal Construct Theory and Mental Health* (pp. 327–350). Croom Helm: Beckenham, UK.

Procter, H. G. (1987). Change in the family construct system: Therapy of a mute and withdrawn schizophrenic patient. In R. Neimeyer & G. Neimeyer (Eds.), *Personal Construct Therapy Casebook* (pp. 153–171). New York: Springer.

Procter, H. G. (2000). Autism and family therapy: A personal construct approach. In S. Powell (Ed.), *Helping Children with Autism to Learn* (pp. 63–77). London: David Fulton.

Procter, H. G. (2001). Personal construct psychology and autism. *Journal of Constructivist Psychology, 14,* 105–124.

Procter, H. G. (2005). Techniques of personal construct family therapy. In D. A. Winter & L. L. Viney (Eds.), *Personal Construct Psychotherapy: Advances in Theory, Practice and Research* (pp. 94–108). London: Whurr.

Procter, H. G. (2007a). Construing within the family. In R. Butler & D. Green (Eds.), *The Child Within: Taking the Young Person's Perspective by Applying Personal Construct Theory* (2nd ed., pp. 190–206). Chichester, UK: Wiley.

Procter, H. G. (2009b). Reflexivity and reflective practice in personal and relational construct psychology. In J. Stedmon & R. Dallos (Eds.), *Reflective Practice in Psychotherapy and Counselling* (pp. 93–114). Milton Keynes, UK: Open University Press.

Procter, H. G., & Mason, R. (2004). *Autism in School: Concerns and Ways Forward*. Retrieved from: https://www.academia.edu/11648453/Autism_in_School_Concerns_and_Ways_Forward_by_Harry_Procter_and_Rachel_Mason_2004_.

Procter, H. G., & Pieczora, R. (1993). A family oriented community mental health centre. In A. Treacher & J. Carpenter (Eds.), *Using Family Therapy in the 90's* (pp. 131–144). Oxford, UK: Blackwell.

Procter, H. G., & Stephens, P. K. E. (1984). Developing family therapy in the day hospital. In A. Treacher & J. Carpenter (Eds.), *Using Family Therapy* (pp. 133–148). Oxford, UK: Blackwell.

Procter, H. G., & Walker, G. (1989). Brief therapy. In E. Street & W. Dryden (Eds.), *Family Therapy in Britain* (pp. 127–149). Milton Keynes, UK: Open University Press.

Ravenette, T. (Ed.). (1999a). *Personal Constructs in Educational Psychology: A Practitioner's View*. London: Whurr.

Ravenette, T. (1999b). A drawing and its opposite: An application of the notion of the 'construct' in the elicitation of children's drawings. In T. Ravenette (Ed.), *Personal Constructs in Educational Psychology: A Practitioner's View* (pp. 125–137). London: Whurr.

Rober, P. (2017). *In Therapy Together: Family Therapy as a Dialogue*. London: Palgrave.

Seikkula, J., Aaltonen, J., Alakare, B., Haarakangas, K., Keränen, J., & Lehtinen, K. (2006). Five-year experience of first-episode non-affective psychosis in open-dialogue approach: Treatment principles, follow-up outcomes, and two case studies. *Psychotherapy Research, 16*, 214–228.

Selvini, M. P., Boscolo, L., Cecchin, G., & Prata, G. (1978). *Paradox and Counterparadox: A New Model in the Therapy of the Family in Schizophrenic Transaction*. New York: Jason Aronson.

Stratton, P. (2010). *The Evidence Base of Systemic Family and Couples Therapy*. London: Association for Family Therapy.

Ugazio, V. (2013). *Semantic Polarities and Psychopathologies in the Family: Permitted and Forbidden Stories*. New York: Routledge.

Vaughn, C. E., & Leff, J. P. (1976). The measurement of expressed emotion in the families of psychiatric patients. *British Journal of Social and Clinical Psychology, 15,* 157–165.

Walker, G., & Procter, H. G. (1980). Brief therapeutic approaches: Their value in contemporary day care. *New Directions for Psychiatric Day Services* (pp. 34–41). London: NAMH.

Watzlawick, P., Weakland, J., & Fisch, R. (1974). *Change: Principles of Problem Formation and Problem Resolution.* New York: Norton.

Winter, D. A. (2005b). Towards a personal construct sex therapy. In D. A. Winter & L. L. Viney (Eds.), *Personal Construct Psychotherapy: Advances in Theory, Practice and Research* (pp. 287–295). London: Whurr.

10

Group Psychotherapy

As we have seen, a central component of personal and relational construct psychotherapy is experimentation. Since this experimentation is likely primarily to be in the interpersonal sphere, testing out new constructions of, and ways of behaving with, others, what better setting could be provided for it than the relatively protected environment of a psychotherapy group? For Kelly (1955, p. 1156), this was 'like having a well-equipped social laboratory with a variety of figures in it'. He considered that this variety allows the client to discover which of their constructs are relatively permeable, being applicable to a number of people, and which are impermeable. A further advantage, in Kelly's view, is that it facilitates the revision of the rigid construing that he described as preemptive or constellatory (see Chapter 3). If, for example, the client holds negative constellatory constructions of followers of a particular religion, he or she may find such constructions invalidated by interactions with such followers in a psychotherapy group. In general, a group will provide the client with a variety of validational evidence for his or her constructions, together with, as Kelly also pointed out, the opportunity

© The Author(s) 2020
H. Procter and D. A. Winter, *Personal and Relational Construct Psychotherapy*,
Palgrave Texts in Counselling and Psychotherapy,
https://doi.org/10.1007/978-3-030-52177-6_10

to disperse dependencies on particular group members. A final advantage of group psychotherapy noted by Kelly is that it is economical of therapist time.

Kelly's Model of Group Psychotherapy

Kelly (1955) presented a six-phase model of the development of a psychotherapy group. The first phase, *initiation of mutual support*, focuses on attempting to ensure that each group member feels that at least one other member is trying to construe matters in the same way as him or her. Kelly's preferred method of achieving this was by the use of a series of enactments (see Chapter 8), generally of hypothetical situations and usually each involving a pair of group members, followed by the other members giving feedback on whom they identified with in each enactment. The second phase, *initiation of primary role relationships*, is particularly concerned with group members construing each other's construing processes, which may be facilitated by considering how other members felt during the enactments or by conducting new enactments in which members portray each other. In the third phase, *initiation of mutual primary enterprises*, the focus shifts to the design and execution of experiments within the group based on members' construing of each other. The fourth phase, *exploration of personal problems*, involves discussion and enactment of situations from members' lives, while the fifth phase, *exploration of secondary roles*, mainly concerns members' roles in the outside world and their construing of the constructions of people in this world, including similarities and differences between these people and group members. Finally, in the sixth phase, *exploration of secondary enterprises*, group members experiment in the outside world and report the outcomes of their experiments to the group.

Kelly was not alone amongst group psychotherapists in proposing a stage model of group development. However, a problem with such models, just as with stage models of individual development, is that groups, like individuals, rarely conveniently operate in a neat, linear fashion, as Kelly (1955) himself acknowledged. In one group that attempted to follow Kelly's model, the therapists 'found that, despite their attempts to regulate the move from one phase to another, certain members of the group would jump the gun and initiate activities relevant to other phases' (Morris, 1977, p. 121). In another personal construct psychotherapy group, albeit incorporating some modifications to Kelly's original approach (such as asking group members to set homework assignments for others, who reported back to the group on the outcome of these experiments), the therapists reported that 'the group members were bringing such important material so quickly that we were having to devise the structure as we went along' (Dunnett & Llewelyn, 1988, p. 196). We would therefore not advocate any attempt to follow Kelly's model rigidly in running a psychotherapy group. Nevertheless, it is worth bearing in mind some general principles evident in his model. One is that, as in individual psychotherapy, care should be taken that a base of support and validation is provided before group members embark on potentially invalidating and threatening experimentation. Related to this is that experimentation should commence in the relatively safe confines of the group, perhaps facilitated by enactment, before extending to the real world outside the group. Finally, there should be a focus on seeing the world through the eyes of others, whether these be fellow group members or people in the outside world.

Variants of Personal and Relational Group Psychotherapy

Aids to Experimentation

Most of the techniques that we have described in previous chapters can be incorporated in a personal and relational construct psychotherapy group, primarily to facilitate experimentation. For example, Kelly (1955) himself used fixed-role therapy (see Chapter 8) in a group format, providing fixed roles to the group members, who were aware of each other's roles. In a variation to this procedure, Epting and Nazario (1987) asked group members, in pairs, to exchange self-characterisations and to add a paragraph to each other's characterisation to develop a new role for the other to enact. In another variation, the 'multiple role group', members are asked to enact roles concerning a particular theme, for example 'maleness' (Epting & Amerikaner, 1980). Further examples of the use of fixed roles in a group setting have been provided by Beail and Parker (1991) and Laming (2006).

Even if not used as a basis for developing fixed roles, sharing of group members' self-characterisations, or of more extensive autobiographical writing (Botella, 1991; Botella & Feixas, 1992–1993), may be a valuable exercise (Dunnett & Llewelyn, 1988; Jackson, 1992; Levy, 1987; Llewelyn & Dunnett, 1987; Stewart, 1995). Although not specifically designed for therapeutic use, a structured way in which this might be done, if the group is divided into pairs, is Mair's (1970) 'conversational approach'. Here, each person writes a 'public' character sketch of the self, which he or she is willing to disclose, and a 'private' sketch, as well as two corresponding sketches of the other. They then share their 'public' sketches of each other, note their reactions to how they are described, and ask the other for any necessary elaboration of the sketch. This is followed by discussion of the evidence on which the sketch is based and any further evidence that would be required for the other to be more certain of the conclusions portrayed in the sketch. Each partner is then asked to make inferences about the other on the basis of the sketch that he or she has written. A similar procedure may then be adopted in relation to the participants' 'public' sketches of themselves. These interactions may lead each participant to experiment with new constructions following the session, and in a further stage each may be asked to speculate about the other's experiments.

The self-characterisation is not the only personal and relational construct assessment technique that may be used to aid the group process. Others that have been employed by group therapists include laddering (Cummins, 2006; Laming, 2006; Llewelyn & Dunnett, 1987), the ABC model (Cummins, 2006; Laming, 2006; Selby, 2006), bow-tie diagrams (Cummins, 2006), and repertory grid technique (Batty & Hall, 1986; Kerrick-Mack, 1978; Stewart, 1995), including the completion of group grids (Llewelyn & Dunnett, 1987). Perceiver element grids could clearly also be adapted for use in group therapy.

Structured aids to playful experimentation may be of particular value in psychotherapy groups with children and adolescents, and some of these have been listed by Viney, Truneckova, Weekes, and Oades (1997). For example, Agnew (1985), whose group for children was presented as a 'Magic Garden', 'a changing place where the familiar and unfamiliar lived together' (p. 242), used props such as puppets. Similarly, in Jackson's (1992) groups for adolescents, there was the use of drawings, games, scripted plays, discussion of stories, and video recordings. The value of such methods is not limited to groups with children and adolescents, however, as evidenced by Foster and Viney's (2001, 2005) use of Ravenette's (1999b) technique of drawing a situation and its opposite in workshops with women experiencing menopause. The situation in this case was a choice being faced by the women, who were then invited to enact the 'opposite' choice. In groups with people diagnosed with posttraumatic stress disorder, Stewart (1995) has asked group members to draw sketches of memories, the self, group moments, and transitions, as well as graphs of their post-trauma lives.

Interpersonal Transaction Groups

The most well elaborated variant of personal construct group psychotherapy is the Interpersonal Transaction (IT) Group, devised by Landfield and Rivers (1975) as a means of facilitating the development of role relationships. In the original format of such groups, members, at the beginning and end of each session, write on slips of paper how they feel and do not feel, attach these 'mood tags' to their clothes, and circulate around the room. The remainder of the session is largely taken up with dyadic interactions, in which pairs of group members talk about a topic provided by the therapist before 'rotating' to a new dyad until each member has interacted with every other. Each interaction generally lasts for between six and eight minutes, and can be structured in such a way that one member talks about the topic and the other listens for half of the time before they reverse roles. Group members are instructed that in these interactions they should try to understand each other but not be critical. The rotating dyads are followed by 'plenary' group discussion

Table 10.1 R. Neimeyer's (1988, p. 187) bridging questions to facilitate the transition between the dyadic and plenary stage of an IT group

1. What sorts of things did you find out about other group members during your conversations?
2. Whose experience did you most identify with?
3. In what ways did you and other group members differ?
4. Did you hear anything that surprised you?
5. Did you find what you had to say changed or developed in any way over the course of the conversations?
6. How did the conversations influence the way you think about the topic?
7. Is there anything you would like to explore further?
8. What questions do you have at this point for other group members?
9. How did the things you discussed relate to the problem (e.g., depression, incest) that you brought in?

of the experience of the dyadic interactions, perhaps facilitated by the bridging questions suggested by R. Neimeyer (1988) (see Table 10.1). A new topic is provided for each group session, of which there are rarely more than twenty.

R. Neimeyer (1988) provides various other useful suggestions of variations in the IT Group procedure, including possible topics for the dyadic interactions. These topics are usually framed in terms of a contrast, and are generally selected for their therapeutic relevance, perhaps with an increasing focus on issues relevant to the group members' presenting problems. For example, in IT Groups for clients presenting with agoraphobia, the topics, derived from the research described in Chapter 7, were:

- situations leading to disagreement or conflict with other people, and how I feel in such situations; situations in which other people are in disagreement or conflict with me, and how they might feel in such situations....
- advantages for me of being better able to go out and more independent; disadvantages for me of being better able to go out and more independent....
- me as I would be without agoraphobia; me as I definitely would not be without agoraphobia' (Winter & Metcalfe, 2005, pp. 160–163).

Dependable Strengths Articulation Process

In Forster's (1991) dependable strengths articulation process, group participants are each asked to identify 16 of their experiences associated with joy, pride, and a sense of accomplishment; to identify, and talk about, dependable strengths that they have used in these experiences; to prioritise these strengths on the basis of their replication in at least three of the experiences and their anticipated utility in the person's areas of concern; and to provide evidence that the strengths are dependable, including the writing of self-descriptions in terms of the strengths.. Although this process was not initially developed for use in the clinical setting, it may be a valuable tool, at least in an adapted form (in which, for example, the number of good experiences to be identified is fewer than 16), for the group therapist who wishes to facilitate more positive self-construing.

Structural Features of Personal and Relational Psychotherapy Groups

Group Composition

As with other psychotherapy groups, a personal construct group will usually consist of about ten members, including one or two therapists. If conducted in an IT format, it is useful if there is an even number of clients, but if this is not possible one of the therapists can participate in the dyadic interactions. In selecting clients for therapy groups, the primary consideration, in Kelly's (1955) view, was that they should be ready to look at the world through the eyes of others. He also considered it desirable that they should have some permeable constructs that can be applied to a variety of people, and should have some constructs indicating dependency, but few concerning factual descriptions of others. Because of his theoretical position concerning guilt (see Chapter 3), he regarded clients who felt guilty as good candidates for group psychotherapy since this could enable them to feel less dislodged from their core roles. Contrary to some popular opinion, he also considered that 'group psychotherapy may be the treatment of choice for seriously disturbed clients' (Kelly, 1955, p. 1156). Similarly, in contrast to views that depression is an exclusion criterion for group psychotherapy, it has been argued that, because of the particular features of their construing, group psychotherapy may be the treatment of choice for clients who are depressed (R. Neimeyer, 1985c; Winter, 1985a, 1989).[1]

There are some advantages in the members of a group being fairly heterogeneous since this is likely to facilitate experimentation and the revision of preemptive and constellatory constructions. On the other hand, homogeneous groups may be conducive to clients feeling supported, and to what Yalom (1970) described as the group curative factor of 'universality', the '"welcome to the human race" experience' (p. 10) of feeling that one is no longer alone. Evidence of this process has been provided by repertory grid studies indicating that clients come to view themselves as more similar to other people over the course of group psychotherapy (Winter, 1997).

As we have seen, the IT Group format may be adapted to focus on areas relevant to particular presenting problems. Indeed, this type of group was first developed for use with problem drinkers, and has subsequently been used with various other groups of clients presenting with common problems: for example, those with eating disorders (Button, 1987); incest survivors (Alexander & Follette, 1987; Alexander, Neimeyer, Follette, Moore, & Harter, 1989); troubled adolescents (Truneckova & Viney, 2005); people with social anxiety (Beail & Parker, 1991); and clients diagnosed with borderline personality disorder (Gillman-Smith & Watson, 1985). However, the IT format is not an essential feature of personal construct psychotherapy for homogeneous groups of clients, and different formats have been used in personal construct therapy groups with people who stutter (Dalton, 1983; Evesham, 1987; Evesham & Fransella, 1985; Levy, 1987); people who abuse drugs (Dawes, 1985); people who are suicidal (Stefan & Von, 1985); people who have problems relating to anger (Cummins, 2006; Laming, 2006; Selby, 2006); people diagnosed with post-traumatic stress disorder (Stewart, 1995); people affected by HIV (Viney, Allwood, &

Stillson, 1991); women living with breast cancer (Lane & Viney, 2005a); and couples (G. Neimeyer, 1985; Procter & Pottle, 1980).

Group Structure

The early sessions of a course of personal construct group psychotherapy are often fairly structured, partly in order to counter anxiety and threat, and the later sessions less so. This gradual reduction in structure may even be the case in groups that commence with the use of an IT format since, as described by Winter and Metcalfe (2005) and Gillman-Smith and Watson (1985), this format may be dispensed with, or at least the time devoted to dyadic interactions reduced, after the initial sessions. The latter workers conceptualised their group in terms of the phases of the Circumspection-Preemption-Control Cycle (see Chapter 3), with the IT sessions being part of the Circumspection phase. Other personal construct psychotherapists have also based at least some of their group sessions on themes relating to aspects of construing. For example, in Lane and Viney's (2005a) groups for women with breast cancer, the eight sessions had the themes of commonality; individuality; self construction; self-disclosure; alternative meanings; alternative meanings about self and relationships; retelling of cancer stories; and choice. Other personal construct processes that have been explicitly focused on in personal construct psychotherapy groups, sometimes incorporating a psychoeducational element, include the Experience Cycle, sociality, aggression, hostility, and slot rattling (Cummins, 2006; Laming, 2006; Llewelyn & Dunnett, 1987; Stewart, 1995).

There is some research support for a progression from high to lower structure in therapy groups. This indicates that structured early sessions may foster self-disclosure, which in turn facilitates attempts to construe the construction processes of others, and subsequent group cohesion (G. Neimeyer & Merluzzi, 1982). Structured sessions, including those that are psychoeducational, may also be particularly appropriate for certain types of clients, for example those who construe tightly (Winter, 1997) and those at the younger (Viney et al., 1997) or older (Botella, 1991) ends of the age spectrum.

The Utility of a Personal Construct Approach to Group Psychotherapy

As we have seen, the process of group psychotherapy may usefully be viewed from a personal construct psychotherapy perspective. Thus, in the early sessions, perhaps facilitated by structured exercises, there is likely to be an emphasis on commonality and validation of construing, together with sociality. In the later sessions, the focus is likely to be on gradual experimentation within and then beyond the group, with group members acting as validating agents (Landfield, 1980) for each other's construing. The group process can also be usefully viewed in terms of cyclical patterns of construing such as Kelly's (1955) Experience, Creativity, and Circumspection-Preemption-Control Cycles (see Chapter 3). It has been suggested that this understanding of processes of construing in groups, whatever the orientation of the therapy concerned, is the primary contribution of personal construct theory, rather than personal construct group psychotherapy being an approach in its own right (Dunnett & Llewelyn, 1988; Koch, 1985). However, in our view, it is precisely its understanding of processes of individual, relational, and group construing that provides the basis for a distinctive personal and relational construct approach to group psychotherapy. While we have provided some examples of such forms of group therapy, we consider that there is rich potential for further developments in this field.

Note

1. Specifically, group psychotherapy may enable the depressed person's construing to become less constricted; may invalidate negative self-construing by demonstrating that he or she is valued by others; may promote less bleak construing of the future as the person, for example, witnesses the recovery of other group members; may enable the person to construe the self as less different from others; and may be likely to invalidate positive constructions of depression, as well as preemptive and constellatory constructions (Winter, 1985a).

References

Agnew, J. (1985). Childhood disorders or the venture of children. In E. Button (Ed.), *Personal Construct Theory and Mental Health* (pp. 224–245). London: Croom Helm.

Alexander, P. C., & Follette, V. M. (1987). Personal constructs in the group treatment of incest. In R. A. Neimeyer & G. J. Neimeyer (Eds.), *Personal construct therapy casebook* (pp. 211–229). New York: Springer.

Alexander, P. C., Neimeyer, R. A., Follette, V., Moore, M. K., & Harter, S. (1989). A comparison of group treatments of women sexually abused as children. *Journal of Consulting and Clinical Psychology, 57,* 479–483.

Batty, C., & Hall, E. (1986). Personal constructs of students with eating disorders: Implications for counselling. *British Journal of Guidance and Counselling, 14,* 306–313.

Beail, N., & Parker, S. (1991). Group fixed-role therapy: A clinical application. *International Journal of Personal Construct Psychology, 4,* 85–96.

Botella, L. (1991). Psychoeducational groups with older adults: An integrative personal construct rationale and some guidelines. *International Journal of Personal Construct Psychology, 4,* 397–408.

Botella, L., & Feixas, G. (1992–1993). The autobiographical group: A tool for the reconstruction of past life experience with the aged. *International Journal of Aging and Human Development, 36,* 303–319.

Button, E. (1987). Construing people or weight?: An eating disorders group. In R. A. Neimeyer & G. J. Neimeyer (Eds.), *Personal Construct Therapy Casebook* (pp. 230–244). New York: Springer.

Cummins, P. (2006). The Tuesday group. In P. Cummins (Ed.), *Working with Anger: A Constructivist Approach* (pp. 13–24). Chichester, UK: Wiley.

Dalton, P. (1983). Maintenance of change: Towards the integration of behavioural and psychological procedures. In P. Dalton (Ed.), *Approaches to the Treatment of Stuttering* (pp. 163–184). London: Croom Helm.

Dawes, A. (1985). Construing drug dependence. In E. Button (Ed.), *Personal Construct Theory and Mental Health* (pp. 182–194). London: Croom Helm.

Dunnett, G., & Llewelyn, S. (1988). Elaborating personal construct theory in a group setting. In G. Dunnett (Ed.), *Working with People: Clinical Uses of Personal Construct Psychology* (pp. 186–201). London: Routledge.

Epting, F. R., & Amerikaner, M. (1980). Optimal functioning: A personal construct approach. In A. Landfield & L. M. Leitner (Eds.), *Personal Construct Psychology: Psychotherapy and Personality* (pp. 55–73). New York: Wiley.

Epting, F. R., & Nazario, A., Jr. (1987). Designing a fixed role therapy: Issues, techniques, and modifications. In R. A. Neimeyer & G. J. Neimeyer (Eds.), *Personal Construct Therapy Casebook* (pp. 277–289). New York: Springer.

Evesham, M. (1987). Residential courses for stutterers: Combining technique and personal construct psychology. In C. Levy (Ed.), *Stuttering Therapies: Practical Approaches* (pp. 61–71). London: Croom Helm.

Evesham, M., & Fransella, F. (1985). Stuttering relapse: The effects of a combined speech and psychological reconstruction programme. *British Journal of Disorders of Communication, 20,* 237–248.

Forster, J. R. (1991). Facilitating positive changes in self-constructions. *International Journal of Personal Construct Psychology, 4,* 281–292.

Foster, H., & Viney, L. L. (2001). Meanings of menopause: Development of a PCP model. In J. M. Fisher & N. Cornelius (Eds.), *Challenging the Boundaries: PCP Perspectives for the New Millennium* (pp. 87–108). Farnborough, UK: EPCA Publications.

Foster, H., & Viney, L. L. (2005). Personal construct workshops for women experiencing menopause. In D. A. Winter & L. L. Viney (Eds.), *Personal Construct Psychotherapy: Advances in Theory, Practice and Research* (pp. 320–332). London: Croom Helm.

Gillman-Smith, I., & Watson, S. (1985). Personal construct group psychotherapy for borderline personality disorder. In D. A. Winter & L. L. Viney (Eds.), *Personal Construct Psychotherapy: Advances in Theory, Practice and Research* (pp. 189–197). London: Croom Helm.

Jackson, S. (1992). A PCT therapy group for adolescents. In P. Maitland & D. Brennan (Eds.), *Personal Construct Theory Deviancy and Social Work* (pp. 163–174). London: Inner London Probation Service/Centre for Personal Construct Psychology.

Kelly, G. A. (1955). *The Psychology of Personal Constructs. Vol. I, II.* New York: Norton (2nd printing: 1991, London and New York: Routledge).

Kerrick-Mack, J. (1978). The role construct repertory grid as a process for facilitating self-awareness and personal growth. In F. Fransella (Ed.), *Personal Construct Psychology 1977* (pp. 117–118). London: Academic Press.

Koch, H. (1985). Group psychotherapy. In E. Button (Ed.), *Personal Construct Theory and Mental Health* (pp. 302–326). London: Croom Helm.

Laming, C. J. (2006). Shedding violent expressions of anger constructively. In P. Cummins (Ed.), *Working with Anger: A Constructivist Approach* (pp. 25–43). Chichester, UK: Wiley.

Landfield, A. W. (1980). Personal construct psychotherapy: A personal construction. In A. W. Landfield & L. M. Leitner (Eds.), *Personal Construct Psychology: Psychotherapy and Personality* (pp. 122–140). New York: Wiley.

Landfield, A. W., & Rivers, P. C. (1975). An introduction to interpersonal transaction and rotating dyads. *Psychotherapy: Theory, Research and Practice, 12,* 365–373.

Lane, L. G., & Viney, L. L. (2005a). Group work with women living with breast cancer. In D. A. Winter & L. L. Viney (Eds.), *Personal Construct Psychotherapy: Advances in Theory, Practice and Research* (pp. 310–319). London: Croom Helm.

Levy, C. (1987). Interiorised stuttering: A group therapy approach. In C. Levy (Ed.), *Stuttering Therapies: Practical Approaches* (pp. 104–121). London: Croom Helm.

Llewelyn, S., & Dunnett, G. (1987). The use of personal construct theory in groups. In R. A. Neimeyer & G. J. Neimeyer (Eds.), *Personal Construct Therapy Casebook* (pp. 245–260). New York: Springer.

Mair, J. M. M. (1970). Experimenting with individuals. *British Journal of Medical Psychology, 43,* 245–256.

Morris, J. B. (1977). Appendix 1: The prediction and measurement of change in a psychotherapy group using the repertory grid. In F. Fransella & D. Bannister (Eds.), *A Manual for Repertory Grid Technique* (pp. 120–148). London: Academic Press.

Neimeyer, G. J. (1985). Personal constructs in the counseling of couples. In F. R. Epting & A. W. Landfield (Eds.), *Anticipating Personal Construct Psychology* (pp. 201–215). Lincoln, Nebraska: University of Nebraska Press.

Neimeyer, G. J., & Merluzzi, T. V. (1982). Group structure and group process: Personal construct therapy and group development. *Small Group Behavior, 13,* 150–164.

Neimeyer, R. A. (1985c). Group psychotherapies for depression: An overview. *International Journal of Mental Health, 13,* 3–7.

Neimeyer, R. A. (1988). Clinical guidelines for conducting Interpersonal Transaction Groups. *International Journal of Personal Construct Psychology, 1,* 181–190.

Procter, H. G., & Pottle, S. (1980). Experiences and guidelines in running an open couples' psychotherapy group. *Journal of Family Therapy, 2,* 233–242.

Ravenette, T. (1999b). A drawing and its opposite: An application of the notion of the 'construct' in the elicitation of children's drawings. In T. Ravenette (Ed.) *Personal Constructs in Educational Psychology: A Practitioner's View* (pp. 125–137). London: Whurr.

Selby, G. (2006). Time and tools?: Tools or time? In P. Cummins (Ed.), *Working with Anger: A Constructivist Approach* (pp. 45–64). Chichester, UK: Wiley.

Stefan, C., & Von, J. (1985). Suicide. In E. Button (Ed.), *Personal Construct Theory and Mental Health* (pp. 132–152). London: Croom Helm.

Stewart, J. (1995). Reconstruction of the self: Life-span-oriented group psychotherapy. *Journal of Constructivist Psychology, 8,* 129–148.

Truneckova, D., & Viney, L. L. (2005). Personal construct group work with troubled adolescents. In D. A. Winter & L. L. Viney (Eds.), *Personal Construct Psychotherapy: Advances in Theory, Practice and Research* (pp. 271–286). London: Croom Helm.

Viney, L. L., Allwood, K., & Stillson, L. (1991). Reconstructive group therapy with HIV-affected people. *Counselling Psychology Quarterly, 4,* 247–258.

Viney, L. L., Truneckova, D., Weekes, P., & Oades, L. (1997). Personal construct group work with school-based adolescents: Reduction of risk-taking. *Journal of Constructivist Psychology, 9,* 169–185.

Winter, D. A. (1985a). Group therapy with depressives: A personal construct theory perspective. *International Journal of Mental Health, 13,* 67–85.

Winter, D. A. (1989). Group therapy as a means of facilitating reconstruing in depressives. *Group Analysis, 22,* 39–48.

Winter, D. A. (1997). Personal construct theory perspectives on group psychotherapy. In P. Denicolo & M. Pope (Eds.), *Sharing Understanding and Practice* (pp. 210–221). Farnborough, UK: EPCA Publications.

Winter, D. A., & Metcalfe, C. (2005). From constriction to experimentation: Personal construct psychotherapy for agoraphobia. In D. A. Winter & L. L. Viney (Eds.), *Personal Construct Psychotherapy: Advances in Theory, Practice and Research* (pp. 148–157). London: Whurr.

Yalom, I. D. (1970). *The Theory and Practice of Group Psychotherapy.* New York: Basic Books.

11

Reflexivity, Reflective Practice, and Supervision

Reflexivity

Personal construct psychology prides itself in being the first approach to place *reflexivity* at the heart of both the theory and practice of how we should go about helping people in psychotherapy, and indeed of conducting all our activities including research, training, and consultation. But what *is* reflexivity? We shall spend some time looking at the meaning of this concept, which, since Kelly introduced it in the 1950s, has blossomed in various guises into an extensive literature covering several disciplines, including psychology, sociology, and philosophy. Thomas and Harri-Augstein (1988, p. 97) wrote that Kelly's notion of reflexivity 'remains for us one of the most revealing ideas about the nature of human beings'.

The ideas captured by the word reflexivity go back, of course, to ancient Greece and through philosophers such as Locke, Kant, and Hegel (Wiley, 1994). Mead (1934) used the term in describing how self-consciousness enables an individual to contemplate him or herself as a whole, as a subject-and-object combined. But with Kelly, we find reflexivity elaborated as a principle and an array of practices: it plays a

© The Author(s) 2020
H. Procter and D. A. Winter, *Personal and Relational Construct Psychotherapy*,
Palgrave Texts in Counselling and Psychotherapy,
https://doi.org/10.1007/978-3-030-52177-6_11

radical role with implications for the relationships between professionals and their clients, or researchers and their research participants, and how they should work together. At the core of this, for Kelly, we need to be able, in our theories and pronouncements, to have these apply just as much to ourselves as they do to our subjects or to the people we are helping: he says that any psychological theory must be 'reflexive; it must also *account for itself* as a product of psychological processes' (1955, pp. 38–39, our italics). He achieved reflexivity by claiming, as we saw in Chapter 2, that *all people are scientists*. Both client and therapist are continually 'struggling to make sense of life, or some aspect of it, to understand themselves and other people in their situations. Both are scientists, or more specifically *psychologists*, that operate in fundamentally the same way—making hypotheses, evaluating evidence and revising assumptions' (Procter, 2009b, p. 94). Bannister (1985b, p. 14) wrote:

> In developing personal construct theory, Kelly specifically set out to make it a reflexive theory at a number of levels. Reflexivity is evident because PCT is itself a form of construing and has the characteristics of construing delineated in the theory. Users of PCT…can comment on their own activity in using the theory in *the same terms* that they comment on the activities of their clients, students or subjects. (our italics)

A vital implication of reflexivity is that it reconstitutes the relationship between the therapist and client as one of collaboration between equals engaged in a process of inquiry. No longer does the therapist have the status of the expert whose interpretations are presented as the 'truth' (Burr, 2015), a hierarchical situation which can all too easily create an unhealthy dependency if it is taken seriously. Of course, therapists need to be as knowledgeable and skilful as possible but this does not exceed clients' authoritative access to their own situations, however confused or unconfident they may be. This is the basis for a strong sense of respect that professionals need to maintain towards those they help, together with an obligation to question continuously their own formulations and assumptions, a process we refer to as *reflective practice* (Stedmon & Dallos, 2009).

A number of features of PCP allow it to be reflexive at both theoretical and practical levels. The first is its claim that constructs, or meanings, are *bipolar* as we saw in the Dichotomy Corollary (Chapter 3). This in itself makes reflexivity possible. It gives us the capacity 'to turn back on the line of thought being taken and examine its assumptions, reaffirm its direction, or bring this direction into serious question—even negating it altogether' (Rychlak, 1994, p. 30). If somebody tries to summarise what our position is on something, we are always free to say, 'no, that's not quite right', even if we don't know why, or if we find it hard to put into words what is wrong with the statement. In this way, we are never complete slaves to the discourses and social constructions of the societies into which we are thrown.

Another important feature of PCP which enables reflexivity is the idea of the hierarchy of construct systems as outlined in the Organization Corollary (see Chapter 3). The idea here is that we are able to 'subsume' construct systems, either others' positions or approaches or our own subsystems (cf. Jones, 2020). The therapist tries to *subsume* the client's views of the world in the credulous approach, and the supervisor *subsumes* the way the therapist is formulating his or her case, including the construing involved in emotional reactions to the client, in helping to optimise therapeutic progress. Subsuming involves bringing a way of construing into our own framework of understanding, remaining as faithful as possible to the original meanings and, as the Sociality Corollary implies, 'stepping into the shoes' of this other view of the world with the minimum amount of contamination. PCP is a 'meta-theory', a 'theory of theories', as well as a theoretical and therapeutic approach in its own right. It enables us to bring into our work other therapeutic approaches and understandings of problems from theories and research, utilising them, but within a coherent overall framework (Procter, 2009b). In this way, we are well able, as supervisors, to work with therapists from different orientations, whilst sometimes, if necessary, not even sharing our Kellian formulations. PRCP in this way is very 'broad-minded' and able to use any approach, as long as it throws further light on the situation and how to make progress.

Reflexivity involves using a set of superordinate constructs which can subsume other ways of looking at things, but also have the power to extend, revise, and elaborate them: a superordinate construct has a governing or guiding role, helping a person, as Mair (2015, p. 115) says, 'to order his constructions in ways which will establish priorities in action.' 'The superordinate systems…are free to invoke new arrangements among the systems which are subordinate to them' (Kelly, 1955, p. 78), including the resolution of inconsistencies and contradictions that may arise in their application. It is important, though, not to think that in subsuming we are creating a *superior*, more satisfactory or 'accurate' view. With the egalitarian stance outlined above, our construing is just another way of looking at things, but hopefully one that will generate some new understandings and open up some new paths forward.

Personal and Relational Reflexivity

Reflexivity involves two levels—the subsuming, superordinate constructs and the particular construing being reflected upon.[1] Wiley, drawing on Mead, calls these the First and Second Orders of reflexivity. It is useful to separate these two 'orders' of construing even though in practice, as Wiley (1994, pp. 84–85) says, they illuminate and 'glide into each other imperceptibly'. Table 11.1 illustrates reflexivity operating in three domains—in the individual, in relationships, and in social construing. Again, these all intermingle but it is clarifying to separate them. At the individual, or personal, level, we apply reflexivity to ourselves, subsuming *our own* construing in an area of life, for example in reflecting on the constructs involved in our feelings of anger or irritation with someone. In this sense, reflexivity is the application of the Sociality Corollary to

Table 11.1 Orders of reflexivity in three different domains (adapted from Wiley, 1994)

	Personal	Relational	Social
Second Order 'meta'	Construing our own construing	Conversation about the conversation	Ideological inquiry Kellian critique
First Order	Construing	Joint action and conversation	Social and cultural constructs

ourselves. An example could be reflecting on our own construing in a difficult supervisory situation: How can I help this therapist with her dilemmas? Is the way I am construing her work helping to facilitate the therapy? We will tend to be thinking at this level in an ongoing manner throughout the work as we 'continuously apply our theory to our own psychological processes' (McWilliams, 1996, p. 60). The 'diagnostic constructs' that we described in Chapter 3 constitute a vital resource in examining the content and process of the constructs we find ourselves applying to self and other in therapy and supervision. For example, we might be supervising a therapist whose client increasingly fails to complete homework assignments. We might usefully draw upon Kelly's professional construct of hostility to reflect on whether he or she is setting assignments that the client finds difficult or meaningless in order to extort evidence for the therapist's construction of the client as 'resistant'.

With personal reflexivity, each partner in a relationship construes their own position (individual reflexivity) including reflecting on their construing of the other's position (Sociality Corollary) in an ongoing manner.[2] We can add to this each one's personal construing of the *relationship* between them—how much agreement, empathy, and understanding there is between them, the hierarchy and power aspects of the relationship, and so on, judging it on dimensions such as those in Table 7.1. Leitner (1990) insists that the therapist has an *obligation* to understand the quality of the relationship with the client by monitoring his or her own experience of it. Chiari and Nuzzo (1996) write:

It is not sufficient that therapists subsume their clients' construction processes…it is necessary as well that the therapist consider the relationship as a reality that cannot be reduced to what takes place independently within each of its members…When they observe the client's processes, they must be aware that those processes are such within the client's relationship with them; they must accept a reflexive attitude and regard themselves as an integrating and fundamental part of the relationship…therapists' skill lie in their facility in understanding the dimensions used by the client and the capacity to extricate themselves from these dimensions and present themselves to the client so as to interact orthogo-nally[3] with them and encourage the pursuit of alternative ways of relating (p. 42).

Leitner's (1985a) concept of the *optimal therapeutic distance* is useful here (see Chapter 8). Leitner (1990) writes that the relationship needs to be close enough for the therapist to experience the client's feelings but distant enough to recognise them as the other's feelings. Excessive close-ness may lead therapists to feel the problems as their own, endangering their ability to subsume clients' construing and to interact 'orthogonally', losing their reflexive stance. Leitner points out how demanding keeping the right balance here can be.

Each client or family member will construe the relationship, and how they feel it *should* be, differently, governed by their 'position on treat-ment' (Chapter 7). Ugazio (2013) argues that there is 'no single way of building a therapeutic relationship'. There are as many ways as the number of constructs used by the client or family to constitute it. It is important that the therapist is not 'boxed in' to a restrictive role, having their 'manoeuvrability' compromised (Fisch, Weakland, & Segal, 1982) and being drawn into dysfunctional cycles. Ugazio and Castelli (2015) give examples of the therapist being drawn into a competitive process, governed by the clients' construct of *winning* versus *losing* or judged according to the dimension of morally *good* versus *not good enough*, their dominant construing. Procter (2009b) describes a case where he had come to be seen as 'English', like her husband, and therefore 'not able to understand the depth of her loss', by a woman from another culture. This was resolved temporarily by bringing in a co-therapist from her culture for two sessions. The two women discussed the wife's experi-ences in detail, allowing her to feel fully understood and for the work to be continued thereafter.

In the second column of Table 11.1, we enter the realm of what Burnham called *relational reflexivity* (2005, p. 4). He defined this as:

The intention, desire, processes and practices through which therapists and clients explicitly engage one another in coordinating their resources so as to create a relationship with therapeutic potential, involving initiating, responding to and developing opportunities to consider, explore, experiment with and elaborate the ways in which they relate.

Here, therapist and client are able to share their ideas and negotiate how they should work together, engaging in a process of joint inquiry. They step out of their dyadic role relationship and take up 'an observer position...developing a conversation on the content and process of the consultation' (Kenny, 1988, p. 153). As we saw in Fig. 4.3, this requires a situation of *full intersubjectivity*, where each one is construing the relationship, the *joint action* ('Us'), but also each is able to share how both are construing, how 'We' are seeing things and hope to see things. It will involve comparing, agreeing, differing, and negotiating. Burnham's work chimes well with our approach with his discussion of 'social differences as a context for learning and learning as a context for differences' (Burnham, Alvis Palma, & Whitehouse, 2008, p. 529). The promotion of relationally reflexive working relationships in therapy and supervision transforms the work into a fully collaborative enterprise.

Social and Ideological Reflexivity

In the third column of Table 11.1, we begin to look at how we can become aware of and reflect on the very assumptions and presuppositions that arise from the society, culture, and language into which we as human beings are all thrown, including our discourses and practices, our theories and models, our biases and prejudices. We inevitably carry a tremendous number of background assumptions and ways of looking at things derived from our culture and the very language that we speak. As Ravenette (1977, p. 264) wrote, 'people are, by and large, ignorant of their constructs and construct systems, and in this sense their construct systems are part of that large aspect of living and experience which is taken for granted'.

In spite of initiating a paradigm shift by raising the question of reflexivity in the human sciences, PCP has been criticised for not being aware enough of its own origins and presuppositions, of not being radical enough in critiquing itself (Holland, 1981; Solas, 1992). Holland pre-emptively accused PCP of demonstrating 'weak reflexivity', restricting us to only examining our own personal constructions, being limited to the domain of psychotherapy, and 'avoiding nearly all the questions that arise when we seek to go beyond the therapeutic situation into society at large' (Holland, 1981, p. 25). Strong reflexivity is said to 'expose ideology; it gets to the levels of meaning imposed by social structures and which are held not to be accessible to normal reflection' (Warren, 1998, p. 139).

However, we do not see that PCP need be restricted in this way, and indeed we claim that it is just as radical a tool as the later develop-ments derived from social constructionism and the sociology of scientific knowledge. It has no axe to grind, it is a tool, a methodology for teasing out meanings, with 'no substance, no content' (Fransella, 1995, p. 125) to impose apart from a commitment to democracy and egalitarianism (Warren, 1998). Its users are free to make a sharp critique of society and the ideologies that it reveals. The power of the approach resides in its unit of analysis—bipolar constructs—which are utilised by cultures, societies, and ideologies just as much as by individuals (Procter, 2016b). Kelly (1996) himself described how different nations hold different sets of constructs, and institutions have their own 'corporate constructs' (Balnaves & Caputi, 1993). Ideologies are seen to perpetuate their power by privileging one pole over the other in 'binary oppositions' such as those making discriminations within gender, class, or ethnicity (Cixous, 2000; Derrida, 1976). These are identical to socially held constructs in Kelly's sense, and are well able to be elicited and critiqued using PCP methods. Social and ideological construing, for PCP, is incorpo-rated into personal construing via identification with *validating agents*, persons or groups 'to whom we listen, with whom we may debate and perhaps even automatically obey as we make our choices' (Landfield, 1988, p. 242). Descriptions of these groups and figures (which may be real, historical, or fictional), noting people's attitudes to their opin-ions and views and asking for real or imagined conversations with them, will reveal a plethora of social construing. As Solas (1992) remarks, constructs 'circulate in the world in specific forms of discourse, partic-ular ways of writing, thinking and talking' (p. 382). PCP is well aware of this level of construction (Scheer, 2008). As Mair (2014, p. 124) says,

'All tellings are political in the sense that they reflect the hidden structure of power and privilege in which the speaker and the audience are located'. In examining students' casual conversations, Kalekin-Fishman (2005) shows how 'power-laden construing is kept alive and sustains the ideologies that privilege certain groups and categories of people, for example western middle-class norms and conventions that define what is appropriate behaviour' (Procter 2016b, p. 147).

Twentieth-century theorists and philosophers have rightly argued for the importance of language itself in shaping our overall constructions and understandings of the world in which we live. To tease out presuppositions, we always need an external, superordinate frame of reference in order to do so. This may be provided by another discipline such as radical sociology or Vygotskyan theory, as in our early critique of PCP (Procter & Parry, 1978), but ultimately, the argument is that all these approaches are framed in *language*. But as we saw in earlier chapters, Kelly always insisted that construing and language, however intimately related they may be, are separate domains, with much construing being *preverbal* and not articulated in words. To say that only language is operating to structure us is to see individuals as passive recipients or even to deny the existence of persons and authors. The discourse analyst Harvey Sacks speaks of how *impervious* and robust normative cultural knowledge is to the dictates of personal experience (Sacks, 1992, cited in Edwards, 1997). But as Wiley (1994) points out:

> The fact that language can talk about or reflect on itself, whether in face-to-face groups, social organisations, or cultural texts, does not explain human beings. These supra-human forms are certainly valid and useful kinds of reflexivity, but they cannot replace the kind that defines the self. On the contrary, it is the self that explains them. (p. 97)

Frank (1989) argues that what we need is 'a theory of the individual subject that internalises structures in a nonidentical way and re-externalises them in altered form' (cited in Warren, 1998, p. 98). Cultures and language are continually evolving due to the actions and creativity of countless individuals.

It is interesting that some of the postmodern criticisms of PCP are delivered in a condescending tone of 'we know best' that risks a return to the asymmetric relationship that Kelly's breakthrough specifically wanted to avoid. Knafo (2016, p. 25) argues that many reflexive scholars largely overestimate their own subject position, assuming that they 'could be objective about the very thing they have the least reasons to be objective about: themselves'. Earlier, Gouldner (1970) had written, 'Sociologists are no more ready than other men [sic] to cast a cold eye on their own doings' (p. 488). 'They should cease acting as if they treat 'sociologists who study, and "laymen" who are studied, as distinct breeds of men. There is only one breed of man' (p. 490). A scientific approach, especially when being applied to human life, needs to maintain a tentative stance of humility and utilise Kelly's 'invitational mood' as we outlined in Chapter 2: 'Let's see if this way of looking at things takes us forward'. There is at any point in time obviously a limit to which anyone is bound in the process of reflexivity, determined by the available frameworks of understanding that have evolved so far.

PCP has a much wider application in terms of political critique and intervention than the practice of psychotherapy. Indeed, the feminist psychologist Wilkinson (1988, p. 498) asserts that a serious application of reflexivity, in Kelly's sense, is 'one of our most powerful tools in working for change' in challenging the inequalities of the dominant paradigm in disciplines and institutions. The central values implicit in PCP practice, respect, acceptance (without necessary agreement), and tolerance of people, imply that we actively promote anti-discriminatory practice and work to build systems that uphold these values. This was a governing principle in the work of one of us (HP) in building clinic teams to work with families, explicitly designed to replace the oppressive practice of the medical model in a psychiatric service (Procter & Pieczora, 1993; Procter & Stephens, 1984) and in a paediatric team for the diagnosis of autistic spectrum disorders (Procter, 2000). After hearing the medical construing of a case which emphasised almost exclusively a focus on symptoms, diagnoses, and medication, he found himself asking over and over again—What is going on in this client's situation? Who is involved and how do they all construe the difficulties? It proved possible to gradually help colleagues to broaden their range of convenience in this way and to begin to provide a radically different type of service in terms of how interventions were made. A democratisation of team functioning in which the voices of the most junior members were heard and valued, in line with the Kellian principle that anyone's unique experience and perspective can potentially contribute to the understanding of a clinical situation, was achieved. Unfortunately, this ethos may prove more difficult to maintain with the introduction of more top-down management styles in health and social services.

A useful method of reflecting on and addressing important areas of construing and prejudice in therapy, supervision, and training situations, known as the 'Social Graces', was introduced by Burnham (2008, 2012). He constructed a list of domains of social difference, using the acronym 'GGRRAAACCCEEESS' (see Table 11.2). Burnham, Alvis Palma, and Whitehouse (2008) describes these as continuously operational and influential in the contexts for therapy and learning.

It is useful to have this list and its associated acronym as a way of considering these topics, which can be emotive and make us uncomfortable. We may start by asking which of the areas seem most relevant or which seem most difficult to understand. The construing involved will vary from very high to low levels of cognitive awareness, or the topic's relevance may be denied or repudiated. Burnham classifies the Graces on dimensions of *visible* versus *invisible* and *voiced* versus *unvoiced*. In PCP terms, the constructs may be *core* or *peripheral*, depending on how much they are tied into a person's identity. Misunderstanding may arise in a relationship if a 'Grace' is core for one participant and peripheral for another, with the former maximising its importance in response to minimisation by the other. One person may think nationality or race is the key to another's identity, whereas the other asserts, for example, that

Table 11.2 The social graces

G	Gender, Geography
R	Race, Religion
A	Age, Ability, Appearance, Accent
C	Class, Culture, Caste
E	Education, Ethnicity, Economics
S	Spirituality, Sexuality

their religion, being a musician, and being loyal to their family are far more important (Du Preez, 1979).

PCP methods are ideally suited to eliciting and revising construing associated with the Graces. Simić, Jokić, and Vukelić, (2019) used PEGs to help trainee teachers to reflect on their construing of pupils. Some of them showed negative attitudes to 'today's youth', describing them as 'indolent, indifferent and offensive, believing that they should be "re-educated"' (p. 11). After discussing their grids, they realised that this was prejudice and were able to recognise that all students are different, with their own needs and circumstances. This would come under the category of *age* in the above list. Repertory grids were used in a study of anti-lesbian and gay prejudice in a multi-ethnic sample (Moradi, Berg van den, & Epting, 2006), and Fukuyama and Neimeyer (1985) studied cross-cultural construing using a specially designed repertory grid, the Cultural Attitudes Repertory Technique (CART). More generally, repertory grids have been used in many studies to investigate therapists' and other professionals' construing of the people in their care, looking at counter-transference (Ryle, 1975; Ryle & Lipshitz, 1974), psychiatrists' insight into their clients' inner worlds (Rowe & Slater, 1976), and nurses' construing of acute ward patients (Addison, 2016).

The effect of prejudice is particularly relevant in working across cultures and ethnicities in therapy. In an early study, the pioneering black American psychologist Horace Bond (1927, cited in Morawski, 2005) found that in IQ testing of black children, they received much higher scores if tested by a black versus a white experimenter. These results were systematically ignored by the establishment but clearly have implications for the therapy situation too. One hopes that the addressing of prejudice and the building of transcultural collaboration through reflective practice can counter such detrimental effects and allow good therapeutic alliances to be built between people of different cultural backgrounds. For Kelly (1996), people can extricate themselves from the 'grooves' marked out for them by society, but not by simply ignoring or fighting cultural constructs. One must 'construe one's way out' of them, approaching the matter from the standpoint of a superordinate set of overriding principles and values (Kelly, 1955; Procter, 2016b).

We have looked at reflexivity at length in this chapter because of its central importance in therapeutic practice and its multi-faceted complexity. We will conclude now by looking at some implications of our account for supervision and teamwork.

Reflective Practice and Supervision

Dunnett (1988) wrote that the reflexivity of PCP provides us with a mechanism to gain knowledge of oneself, of one's needs, limitations, frustrations, vulnerabilities, and of how we deal with events. Reflecting on our own construing paradoxically can help to make clients' needs clearer to us. It allows us to make more fruitful interventions, more innovative and sensitive approaches to therapy, and to signal when we need to take a case to formal supervision. It allows us to function as relatively autonomous practitioners, essential when we have a busy caseload and can only realistically discuss a small proportion of our cases with a supervisor or colleagues. Even when we are in supervision, a vital part of the process is listening to ourselves giving our account as we present it. In putting things into words and sharing our thoughts and feelings, new ideas and directions will spontaneously come into our minds: 'Ah, now I know what I could do!' A core function in clinical supervision is fostering the supervisee's reflexivity (R. Neimeyer, Woodward, Pickover, & Smigelsky, 2016).

Balzani, Del Rizzo, and Sandi, (2011), using Kelly's scientist metaphor, see supervision as a laboratory. Supervisor and therapist/s engage in continuous experimentation involving a series of co-constructed shared experiments, a playful approach in which new perspectives can be generated. An example of this could be Thomas' (2009) method: she draws on Mair's *community of selves* (see Chapters 2 and 8) and has the therapist imagine and enact his or her 'cast of characters'; what would each one say about the situation, how do they interact, how would they relate to the supervisor, and so on. This is an 'internal' version of Andersen's (1987) *reflecting team* which is so useful in working with couples and families (see Chapter 9).

Feixas (1992a) argues for a 'therapist-centred' approach to supervision. Supervisor and therapist have different types of expertise; the focus is on the therapist and on his or her complaints; alternative views about the problem are generated in a reflexive learning context. Kenny (1988) looks for selectivity in therapists' construing, identifying blind-spots and sometimes asking for experiences or constructions which they feel reluctant to discuss in the session. Viney and Epting (1997, p. 13) write: 'The supervisor should never tell the therapist what to do in the therapy hour…the supervisor must not start thinking that she knows what should be done. The initiative for actually conducting the therapy must always rest with the therapist'.

Whilst we agree with these sentiments, it is important to recognise the inherent complexity of supervision. This is illustrated in Table 11.3. Using the symbols S for supervisor, T for supervisee or therapist, and C for client/s, we can see that there are numerous layers of sociality, constructions of construing, to be borne in mind. In the top row, how is the client construing the therapist's view of the client? Next, how is the therapist seeing the client's construing of self, others, and of the therapist him- or herself? And then, how is the supervisor seeing how client and therapist see each other and how the therapist is construing herself? Finally, we have how the therapist thinks the supervisor is seeing the therapist. And the list could go on: here, we have only considered monadic construing and not yet how each sees the relationships. When seeing a family or group, all the relationships between the members and with the therapist need to be noted!

This may seem overwhelming, but in practice need not be so. The table functions as a useful check on dynamics that may not be being recognised. The important thing is to understand that the supervision relationship is *triadic*. As the supervisor hears the account, he or she will identify with the client/s and consider what it is like for them to be in

Table 11.3 The complexity of supervision

C → (T → C)
T → (C → C), T → (C → O), T → (C → T)
S → (C → T), S → (T → C), S → (T → T)
T → (S → T), etc.

this therapy. The relational process takes place between three protagonists even though the client is physically absent. As Feixas (1992a, p. 198) says, 'It is very difficult for a therapist to have a picture of both the client and him- or herself in the therapy process. Supervision offers a privileged context in which to reflect on that process'. The supervisor provides a safe setting and viewpoint which is facilitative, subsuming both the client's and therapist's realities and mediating between them.

Table 11.4 gives an example drawn from R. Neimeyer, Woodward, Pickover, and Smigelsky (2016). We have constructed a PEG from their

Table 11.4 PEG showing therapist Brian's construing in his therapy with Jeannie in supervision (our italics)

	Brian	Jeannie	The therapy	Reflections
Brian	I felt *frustrated* with myself...felt I was more of a 'buddy' than her therapist. I was hoping *to get to the bottom of what was going on.* I was nervous asking the questions. (T—T) Miffed at her playfulness. I believe she *genuinely didn't know* she was 'skating on the ice'. (T—C)	Not talking about anything important to her in the session: *superfluous* topics. She acknowledged she was 'rambling'. She might have felt a little *awkward.* She may have felt a little sense of me as a *scolding* therapist. Hesitant to talk about the 'big stuff' (history of abusive relationships). (T—C)	I would like her to take more of a 'take charge' kind of answer because I feel it relates to her goal of 'developing more confidence'. I do like her and didn't want to make her feel uncomfortable. My next line of questions was meant to *probe* what was going on with her 'rambling'	I would spend more time exploring her own *inability* to identify what accounted for her rambling. I may have tried too much to offer her possible *explanations.* Supervision brought forth *hidden layers* going on inside me—the *driving forces* that were motivating me as a therapist. (T—T)

description of using Guiffrida's (2015) supervision technique of 'Questioning the Questions'. The supervisor focuses on the questions that the therapist asks and how the client responds to these. It is a powerful way of identifying a therapist's construing of the client and the therapy, particularly when video is available to watch the minutiae of interaction. The PEG shows the therapist Brian's construing of himself, of his client Jeannie (who is in her mid-20's, consulting with a history of troubled and abusive relationships), of the therapy, and of his reflections in supervision after the twelfth session of therapy. This PEG, which can be supplemented with additional rows giving the views of the client and supervisor, is a powerful supervision tool in itself.

Brian's construing is focused more on himself than on her construing. His formulation and position on therapy involves 'getting to the bottom of what is going on', which is contrasted to his seeing her talk as 'superfluous' and 'skating on ice'. He assumes that *explanation* would be an important therapeutic ingredient. He feels he has knowledge which she lacks ('her inability'; 'she genuinely didn't know…') and that he needs to 'probe' into 'hidden layers', a metaphor he uses for himself, where there are 'driving forces'.

At a relational level, they seem to be caught in a loop, which could be captured in a bow-tie diagram (Chapters 4 and 5), with him wanting to probe and her feeling awkward and 'rambling', perhaps avoiding going into her history of abuse. Her responses validate what he sees as resistance and avoidance. As we said earlier, we are able as PCP supervisors to help people practise within other models of therapy. His psychoanalytic formulation, from a PCP point of view, remains 'objectivist', with his rather judgemental construing of her behaviour as 'superfluous'. But it is important to accept and utilise his construing credulously and help him make sense of things from his position.

We may then hope to extend and elaborate his views and supplement them, helping him to get more aware of her world and how she is construing herself and her relational situation by eliciting her constructs using PCP methods. It could be helpful to draw up the bow-tie in supervision, and possibly even to have him share it with Jeannie in the next session, encouraging relational reflexivity. Brian and Jeannie could draw up a PEG such as the one presented here, adding a second row detailing her construing and reflections. Or more simply he may ask what is *her* position on treatment: 'How do you feel I ought to be helping you at this stage of our therapy?' (Appendix 1, Section 9). If she feels she needs to talk about her past experiences, this could resolve the impasse, as they would then again be collaborating in a joint path. From a PCP point of view, we need to be careful not to commit what Viney and Epting (1997) call the 'historical fallacy', that events earlier in a person's history are the same events that determine what comes after them. In PCP, how events are construed *in the present* is given much more emphasis. Events in the past affect current situations through current construing, perhaps concerning issues of trust and safety or of current figures reminding her of the people who were abusive. It could be, though, that resolution has already been achieved, as the authors imply when they say it could be a 'mostly satisfying completion of a useful therapy' (Neimeyer, Woodward, Pickover, &Smigelsky, 2016, p. 108), with her rambling and being a 'buddy' as evidence of her having already begun to achieve the goal of self-confidence that she was hoping for.

To summarise, focussing on the therapists' needs and their construing of their clients is clearly a vital part of supervision, but it is also important for the supervisor to gain sufficient detail about the case in order to help co-construct a joint formulation with the therapist, as we described in Chapter 7. To do so, we would need to know considerably more about Jeannie's current relational experiences and construing associated with these. Figure 11.1 illustrates the main options for steering a supervision session: we can move between a focus on the therapist and their construing and one of getting more understanding of the case, and back again. This may lead the therapist to get further detail in the subsequent session. The horizontal choices remind us to keep a balance involving carefully listening to the therapist, remaining mainly non-directive but with judicious questions and suggestions where necessary.

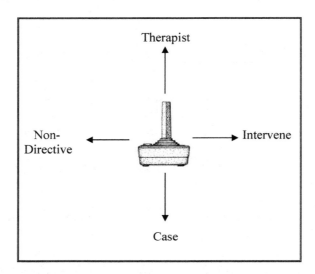

Fig. 11.1 The supervision joystick

The Formats and Context of Supervision, Reflective Practice, and Consultation

Supervision may take place one-to-one, in groups, or, as is common in family therapy, in live supervision with an observing team. The principles we have outlined can be applied in any of these formats. Viney and Truneckova (2008) and Truneckova, Viney, Maitland, and Seaborn (2010) describe models of personal construct peer consultation groups which may or may not have a designated lead supervisor, with different approaches described for each situation. They emphasise the importance for psychotherapists of having a supportive environment in carrying out this very stressful and responsible work. Unfortunately, in current health services and other such contexts, top-down and risk-averse management with prescribed and time-limited treatments, computer-based recording, and evaluation systems presents an enormous challenge to giving therapists the proper safe and confidential support or indeed any time to reflect. This situation, with its pervasive surveillance (Gilbert, 2001), and with therapist performance being judged by crude and superficial measures of outcome, contrasts starkly with the necessity to maintain a warm and supportive environment in which the vital process of growth and development of therapists is facilitated.

Nevertheless, if the culture of a health or care service does not appear to be conducive to therapeutic practice, personal and relational construct psychology approaches may have a role to play in influencing this culture through their use in consultation with clinical teams and service managers. Although it is beyond the scope of the present book to consider this in detail, there is a considerable literature on the application of personal construct interventions in consulting in organisations, including health services (Frances, 2016; Fransella, Jones, & Watson, 1988). This work has included the use of such methods as repertory grids, resistance to change grids, laddering, and pyramiding (see Chapter 6) to make managers and other staff more aware of the superordinate constructs that define their, and their organisations', values, with the ultimate aim of 'humanizing healthcare' (Brophy, 2016). Procter (2007b) used the 'gPEG', a specially designed perceiver element grid for working with a dysfunctional therapeutic team. The method involved eliciting goals for how each member would like to see themselves and the other members after some sessions of successful resolution of their difficulties. This formed a useful background to the consultation and discussion of their conflicts.

An example from a different cultural setting is that, working in the only psychiatric hospital in Sierra Leone, in which 75 per cent of the clients were kept in chains, Winter (2016a) used repertory grid technique and the ABC model (see Chapter 6) to explore why staff decided to shackle particular clients. It became apparent that those who were shackled were clients whom staff found difficult to construe, and who therefore provoked anxiety. This led to the encouragement of staff to adopt a more credulous approach, and interventions, including the use of music and dance, to enable staff to become more aware of the humanity of their clients (Winter, Brown, Goins, & Mason, 2016).

We shall now look at how our approach to psychotherapy compares and contrasts with other major approaches in current use.

Notes

1. Interestingly, Cronen, Johnson, and Lannamann (1982), who clearly draw on Kelly in both the form and the content of their theory, use the term reflexivity specifically to describe the reciprocal relationship between the two levels: 'Reflexivity exists whenever two elements in a hierarchy are so organized that each is simultaneously the context for and within the context of the other' (p. 4). They go on to describe 'strange loops', where there is a conflict between participants about which level is superordinate or subordinate. As Kelly (1955) says, people vary not only in the content of their construing but in the way the constructs are organised hierarchically. Ugazio (2013) relates this predicament to Feixas, Saúl, and Ávila-Espada's (2009) implicative dilemmas jointly faced by the participants. An example is given in Fig. 6.11, Chapter 6 with the couple negotiating the proverbial problem of how to squeeze a tube of toothpaste.
2. The recent development of the concept of *mentalisation* (Bateman & Fonagy, 2012) is similar and owes much to Kelly's work here.
3. Meaning subsuming with constructs that cut across the client's dimensions at right angles—see Chapters 1 and 7.

References

Addison, V. E. (2016). *The use of repertory grids to explore nursing staff's construal of adult service users admitted to a psychiatric inpatient ward.* Unpublished DClinPsy thesis, University of Manchester. Retrieved, May 2020, from: https://search.proquest.com/openview/22e14ef28f337f69da2fb db918102dc8/1?pq-origsite=gscholar&cbl=51922&diss=y.

Andersen, T. (1987). The reflecting team. *Family Process, 26,* 416–428.

Balnaves, M., & Caputi, P. (1993). Corporate constructs: To what extent are personal constructs personal? *International Journal of Personal Construct Psychology, 6,* 119–138.

Balzani, L., Del Rizzo, F., & Sandi, F. (2011). The journey as constructivist learner-teachers: How to become teachers of constructivist psychotherapy. In D. Stojnov, V. Džinović, J. Pavlović, & M. Frances (Eds.), *Personal*

Construct Psychology in an Accelerating World (pp. 169–179). Belgrade, Serbia: Serbian Constructivist Association.

Bannister, D. (1985b). The experience of self. In F. Epting & A. W. Landfield (Eds.), *Anticipating Personal Construct Psychology* (pp. 39–45). Lincoln: University of Nebraska Press.

Bateman, A. W., & Fonagy, P. (2012). *Handbook of Mentalizing in Mental Health Practice*. Washington, DC: American Psychiatric Publishing.

Bond, H. M. (1927). Some exceptional negro children. *The Crisis, 34*, 257–280.

Brophy, S. (2016). Humanizing healthcare: A personal construct psychology-based intervention. In D. A. Winter & N. Reed (Eds.), *The Wiley Handbook of Personal Construct Psychology* (pp. 293–305). Chichester, UK: Wiley-Blackwell.

Burnham, J. (2005). Relational reflexivity: A tool for socially constructing therapeutic relationships. In C. Flaskas, B. Mason, & A. Perlesz (Eds.), *The Space Between: Experience, Context, and Process in the Therapeutic Relationships* (pp. 1–180). London: Karnac.

Burnham, S. (2008). *Let's Talk: Using Personal Construct Psychology to Support Children and Young People: Using Personal Construct Theory in School*. New York: Sage (Lucky Duck Books).

Burnham, J. (2012). Developments in Social GRRAAACCEEESSS: Visible-invisible and voiced-unvoiced. In I. Krause (Ed.), *Culture and Reflexivity Systemic Psychotherapy* (pp. 139–162). London: Karnac.

Burnham, J., Alvis Palma, L., & Whitehouse, L. (2008). Learning as a context for differences and differences as a context for learning. *Journal of Family Therapy, 30*, 529–542.

Burr, V. (2015). *Introduction to Social Constructionism* (3rd ed.). London: Routledge.

Chiari, G., & Nuzzo, M. L. (1996). Psychological constructivisms: A metatheoretical differentiation. *Journal of Constructivist Psychology, 9*, 163–184.

Cixous, H. (2000). Sorties. In D. Lodge & N. Wood (Eds.), *Modern Criticism and Theory: A Reader* (3rd ed., pp. 358–365). London: Longman.

Cronen, V. E., Johnson, K. M., & Lannamann, J. W. (1982). Paradoxes, double binds, and reflexive loops: An alternative theoretical perspective. *Family Process, 21*, 91–112.

Derrida, J. (1976). *Of Grammatology*. Baltimore: John Hopkins University Press.

Du Preez, P. (1979). Politics and identity in South Africa. In P. Stringer & D. Bannister (Eds.), *Constructs of Sociality and Individuality* (pp. 341–364). London: Academic Press.

Dunnett, G., & Llewelyn, S. (1988). Elaborating personal construct theory in a group setting. In G. Dunnett (Ed.), *Working with People: Clinical Uses of Personal Construct Psychology* (pp. 186–201). London: Routledge.

Edwards, D. (1997). *Discourse and Cognition*. London: Sage.

Feixas, G. (1992a). A constructivist approach to supervision: Some preliminary thoughts. *Journal of Constructivist Psychology, 5*(2), 183–200.

Feixas, G., Saúl, L. A., & Ávila-Espada, A. (2009). Viewing cognitive conflicts as dilemmas: Implications for mental health. *Journal of Constructivist Psychology, 22,* 141–169.

Fisch, R., Weakland, J. H., & Segal, L. (1982). *The Tactics of Change: Doing Therapy Briefly*. San Francisco: Jossey-Bass.

Frances, M. (2016). Consulting in organizations. In D. A. Winter & N. Reed (Eds.), *The Wiley Handbook of Personal Construct Psychology* (pp. 282–292). Chichester, UK: Wiley-Blackwell.

Frank, M. (1989). *What Is Neostructuralism?* (S. Wilke & R. Gray, trans.). Minneapolis: University of Minnesota Press (Original work in German (1984)).

Fransella, F. (1995). *George Kelly*. London: Sage.

Fransella, F., Jones, H., & Watson, J. (1988). A range of applications of PCP within business and industry. In F. Fransella & L. Thomas (Eds.), *Experimenting with Personal Construct Psychology* (pp. 405–417). London: Routledge & Kegan Paul.

Fukuyama, M. A., & Neimeyer, G. J. (1985). Using the Cultural Attitudes Repertory Technique (CART) in a cross-cultural counseling workshop. *Journal of Counseling & Development, 63,* 304–305.

Gilbert, T. (2001). Reflective practice and clinical supervision: Meticulous rituals of the confessional. *Journal of Advanced Nursing, 36,* 199–205.

Gouldner, A. W. (1970). *The Coming Crisis of Western Sociology*. New York: Avon Books.

Guiffrida, D. (2015). A constructive approach to counseling and psychotherapy supervision. *Journal of Constructivist Psychology, 28,* 40–52.

Holland, R. (1981). From perspectives to reflexivity. In H. Bonarius, R. Holland, & S. Rosenberg (Eds.), *Personal Construct Theory: Recent Advances in Theory and Practice* (pp. 23–29). London: Macmillan.

Jones, R. A. (2020). The presence of self in the person: Reflexive positioning and personal constructs psychology. *Journal for the Theory of Social Behaviour, 27*(4), 453–471.

Kalekin-Fishman, D. (2005). 'Plain talk': Producing and reproducing alienation. In D. Kalekin-Fishman & L. Langman (Eds.), *The Evolution of Alienation: Trauma, Promise and the Millennium* (pp. 283–307). Lanham, MD: Rowman and Littlefield.

Kelly, G. A. (1955). *The Psychology of Personal Constructs. Vol. I, II.* New York: Norton (2nd printing: 1991, London and New York: Routledge).

Kelly, G. A. (1996). Europe's matrix of decision. In D. Kalekin-Fishman & B. Walker (Eds.), *The Structure of Group Realities: Culture, Society, and Personal Construct Theory* (pp. 27–64). Malabar, Florida: Krieger.

Kenny, V. (1988). Changing conversations: A constructivist model of training for psychologists. In G. Dunnett (Ed.), *Working with People: Clinical Uses of Personal Construct Psychology* (pp. 140–157). London: Routledge.

Knafo, S. (2016). Bourdieu and the dead end of reflexivity: On the impossible task of locating the subject. *Review of International Studies, 42,* 25–47.

Landfield, A. (1988). Personal science and the concept of validation. *International Journal of Personal Construct Psychology, 1,* 237–249.

Leitner, L. M. (1985a). The terrors of cognition: On the experiential validity of personal construct theory. In D. Bannister (Ed.), *Issues and Approaches in Personal Construct Theory* (pp. 83–103). London: Academic Press.

Leitner, L. (1990). Sharing the mystery: A therapist's experience of personal construct psychotherapy. In H. Jones & G. Dunnett (Eds.), *Selected Papers from the 2nd British Conference on Personal Construct Psychology.* York, UK.

Mair, J. M. M. (2014). *Another Way of Knowing: The Poetry of Psychological Inquiry.* London: Raven Books.

Mair, J. M. M. (2015). The community of self. In D. A. Winter & N. Reed (Eds.), *Toward a Radical Re-definition of Psychology: The Selected Works of Miller Mair* (pp. 102–112). London: Routledge.

McWilliams, S. (1996). Accepting the invitational. In B. Walker, J. Costigan, L. Viney, & B. Warren (Eds.), *Personal Construct Theory: A Psychology of the Future* (pp. 57–78). Sydney: Australian Psychological Society.

Mead, G. H. (1934/1962). *Mind, Self and Society.* Chicago: University of Chicago Press.

Moradi, B., van den Berg, J., & Epting, F. (2006). Intrapersonal and interpersonal manifestations of anti-lesbian and gay prejudice: An application of personal construct theory. *Journal of Counselling Psychology, 53*(1), 57–66.

Morawski, J. G. (2005). Reflexivity and the psychologist. *History of Human Sciences, 18,* 77–105.

Neimeyer, R. A., Woodward, M., Pickover, A., & Smigelsky, M. (2016). Questioning our questions: A constructivist technique for clinical supervision. *Journal of Constructivist Psychology, 29,* 100–111.

Procter, H. G. (2000). Autism and family therapy: A personal construct approach. In S. Powell (Ed.), *Helping Children with Autism to Learn* (pp. 63–77). London: David Fulton.

Procter, H. G. (2007b) Manual for Using the G-PEG (Goals Perceiver Element Grid) in Team Building and Consultation. Retrieved, April 2018, from: http://www.pcp-net.org/tools/G-PEG%20Manual%202015.pdf.

Procter, H. G. (2009b). Reflexivity and reflective practice in personal and relational construct psychology. In J. Stedmon & R. Dallos (Eds.), *Reflective Practice in Psychotherapy and Counselling* (pp. 93–114). Milton Keynes, UK: Open University Press.

Procter, H. G. (2016b). PCP, culture and society. In D. A. Winter & N. Reed (Eds.), *The Wiley Handbook of Personal Construct Psychology* (pp. 139–153). Chichester, UK: Wiley-Blackwell.

Procter, H. G., & Parry, G. (1978). Constraint and freedom: The social origin of personal constructs. In F. Fransella (Ed.), *Personal Construct Psychology 1977* (pp. 157–170). London: Academic Press.

Procter, H. G., & Pieczora, R. (1993). A family oriented community mental health centre. In A. Treacher & J. Carpenter (Eds.), *Using Family Therapy in the 90's* (pp. 131–144). Oxford, UK: Blackwell.

Procter, H. G., & Stephens, P. K. E. (1984). Developing family therapy in the day hospital. In A. Treacher & J. Carpenter (Eds.), *Using Family Therapy* (pp. 133–148). Oxford, UK: Blackwell.

Ravenette, T. (1977). Personal construct theory: An approach to the psychological investigation of children and young people. In D. Bannister (Ed.), *New Perspectives in Personal Construct Theory* (pp. 251–280). London: Academic Press.

Rowe, D., & Slater, P. (1976). Studies of the psychiatrist's insight into the patient's inner world. In P. Slater (Ed.), *The Measurement of Intrapersonal Space by Grid Technique* (Vol. 1, pp. 123–144)., *Explorations of Intrapersonal Space* London: Wiley.

Rychlak, J. F. (1994). *Logical Learning Theory.* Lincoln: University of Nebraska Press.

Ryle, A. (1975). *Frames and Cages: The Repertory Grid Approach to Human Understanding.* London: Sussex University Press.

Ryle, A., & Lipshitz, S. (1974). Towards an informed countertransference: The possible contribution of repertory grid techniques. *British Journal of Medical Psychology, 47,* 219–225.

Sacks, H. (1992). *Lectures on Conversation* (Vol. 1). Oxford, UK: Blackwell.

Scheer, J. W. (2008). Construing in the political realm—Reflections on the power of a theory. *Personal Construct Theory and Practice, 5,* 76–85.

Simić, N., Jokić, T., & Vukelić, M. (2019). Personal Construct Psychology in preservice teacher education: The path toward reflexivity. *Journalof Constructivist Psychology, 32*(1), 1–17.

Solas, J. (1992). Ideological dimensions implicit in Kelly's theory of personal constructs. *International Journal of Personal Construct Psychology, 5,* 377–391.

Stedmon, J., & Dallos, R. (Eds.). (2009). *Reflective Practice in Psychotherapy and Counselling.* Milton Keynes, UK: Open University Press.

Thomas, J. C. (2009). Personifying the cast of characters in experiential personal constructivist supervision. In L. M. Leitner & J. C. Thomas (Eds.), *Personal Constructivism: Theory and Applications* (pp. 253–278). New York: Pace University Press.

Thomas, L., & Harri-Augstein, S. (1988). Constructing environments that enable self-organised learning: The principles of intelligent support. In F. Fransella & L. Thomas (Eds.), *Experimenting with Personal Construct Psychology* (pp. 92–110). London: Routledge and Kegan Paul.

Truneckova, D., Viney, L., Maitland, H., & Seaborn, B. (2010). Personal construct peer consultation: Caring for the psychotherapists. *The Clinical Supervisor, 29,* 128–148.

Ugazio, V. (2013). *Semantic Polarities and Psychopathologies in the Family: Permitted and Forbidden Stories.* New York: Routledge.

Ugazio, V., & Castelli, D. (2015). The semantics grid of the dyadic therapeutic relationship (SG-DTR). *TPM—Testing Psychometrics, Methodology in Applied Psychology, 22,* 135–159.

Viney, L., & Epting, F. (1997) Toward a personal construct approach to supervision for counselling and psychotherapy. Paper presented at the XIIth. International Personal Construct Congress, Seattle, USA.

Viney, L. L., & Truneckova, D. (2008). Personal construct models of group supervision: Led and peer. *Personal Construct Theory & Practice, 5,* 131–138.

Warren, B. (1998). *Philosophical Dimensions of Personal Construct Psychology.* London: Routledge.

Wiley, N. (1994). *The Semiotic Self.* Chicago: University of Chicago Press.

Wilkinson, S. (1988). The role of reflexivity in feminist psychology. *Women's Studies International Forum, 11,* 493–502.

Winter, D. A. (2016a). Transcending war-ravaged biographies. In D. A. Winter & N. Reed (Eds.), *The Wiley Handbook of Personal Construct Psychology* (pp. 190–200). Chichester: Wiley-Blackwell.

Winter, D. A., Brown, R., Goins, S., & Mason, C. (2016). *Trauma, Survival and Resilience in War Zones: The Psychological Impact of War in Sierra Leone and Beyond*. Hove, UK: Routledge.

12

Relationships with Other Therapeutic Approaches

As we have seen, George Kelly originally presented his theory as a new psychology that was a radical alternative to what were the major existing approaches in the field, namely psychoanalysis and behaviourism. Over sixty years on, other therapeutic approaches have burgeoned to the extent that there is now a bewildering array of at least 500 different forms of psychological therapy (Karasu, 1986). It therefore seems timely to consider whether personal construct theory still offers a distinctive perspective on psychotherapy and counselling or whether its boundaries with at least some other types of therapy are now more blurred. We have touched on this question in earlier chapters but shall now consider it systematically in relation to each of the major, broad models of psychological therapy. Consistent with our theoretical approach, we shall outline both contrasts and similarities between each of these models and personal and relational construct psychotherapy, before going on to discuss philosophical compatibilities, and integrative possibilities, with contemporary developments of the models concerned.

© The Author(s) 2020   **249**
H. Procter and D. A. Winter, *Personal and Relational Construct Psychotherapy*,
Palgrave Texts in Counselling and Psychotherapy,
https://doi.org/10.1007/978-3-030-52177-6_12

Contrasts and Similarities with Alternative Models

Psychoanalysis

Contrasts

1. *Interpretations as Truths or Constructions*

Kelly (1969a, 1969b) was critical of the tendency of traditional psychoanalysts to provide their clients with interpretations as if these were absolute truths rather than, as in personal and relational construct psychotherapy, merely alternative constructions of the clients' predicaments.

2. *Testability of Theory*

Although such a view has not gone unchallenged (Fisher & Greenberg, 1978; Fonagy, 1982; Kline, 1981; Warren, 1983), Kelly (1969b) was not alone in regarding psychoanalysis as an unscientific theory and instead as consisting of 'rubber hypotheses' that were not amenable to experimental test.

3. *Dynamics*

Whereas psychodynamic approaches take a hydraulic view of the person, who is seen as being driven by libidinal forces, personal construct theory is 'completely nondynamic' (Kelly, 1969c, p. 217) in that it regards the person as a form of motion, not requiring propulsion by any 'forces'.

4. *The Person, and His/Her Emotions, as Essentially Bad*

Kelly did not accept the psychoanalytic tripartite concept of the individual as consisting of an ego, superego, and id, and the view of the person as essentially bad that this implied. Similarly, emotions such as hostility are not regarded in personal and relational construct psychotherapy as destructive forces, as tends to be the case in psycho-analysis (Kelly, 1969d).

5. *Temporal Focus*

Unlike psychoanalysis, personal and relational construct psychotherapy is not primarily concerned with the client's past, and indeed may be more concerned with the present and future. The client's history is also not viewed in terms of a fixed series of developmental stages. Nevertheless, personal and relational construct psychotherapy is likely not to be without consideration of the past, for example in order to understand the origins of the client's construing, and it has been suggested that an integration of personal construct theory and attachment theory may prove valuable in this process (Lorenzini & Sassaroli, 1995).

6. *Resistance*

As Kelly (1955, p. 1101) noted in regard to resistance, 'Since we do not employ a defensive theory of human motivation, the term does not have the important meaning it must necessarily assume for the psychoanalysts'. Rather, the client's resistance to therapy is viewed by the personal construct psychotherapist as a perfectly comprehensible attempt to preserve the integrity of his or her construct system (Fransella, 1993; Winter, 1992).

Similarities

1. *Concern with Meaning*

As Warren (1983) has described, both psychoanalysis and personal construct theory are essentially concerned with meaning and there-fore adopt a phenomenological and hermeneutic approach to therapy (essentially, one that is concerned, respectively, with experience and inter-pretation of meaning). In Warren's view, similarly to those of Ryle (1975) and Soldz (1988), such commonalities between the two approaches are particularly apparent in contemporary elaborations of psychoanalysis, in which the 'process of enquiry into meanings' is 'a mutual search rather than interpretations coming down from on high in the form of "stone tablets"' (Warren, 1983, p. 12).

2. *Levels of Awareness of Construing*

Although he did not use the concept of the unconscious, Kelly (1955), as we have seen, did acknowledge that some constructions may be at a low level of awareness. Personal and relational construct psychotherapy, just like psychoanalysis, may make the client more aware of such aspects of his or her construing.

3. *Defence Mechanisms*

Again, although they are not identical with such personal construct concepts as submergence and suspension, psychoanalytic defence mechanisms may be reframed in personal construct terms (Catina, Gitzinger, & Hoeckh, 1992; Ryle, 1975, 1978; Winter & Gournay, 1987), for example as strategies that allow the person to avoid testing out, and therefore risking invalidation of, particular constructions (Walker, 2002).

4. *Advantages of the Symptom*

Similarly to the concept of secondary gain in psychoanalysis, personal and relational construct psychotherapy considers that the client's symptoms may serve some purpose, or carry payoffs (Feixas, Saúl, & Ávila-Espada, 2009; Tschudi, 1977), for him or her. However, in contrast to psychoanalysis, they would not be regarded as providing compromise gratification of some *particular* desires or having some *particular* symbolic significance.

5. *Transference*

Transference was one of the few terms that Kelly (1955) borrowed from psychoanalysis, and indeed he saw it as the essence of all construing, since this always involves transferring one of the individual's constructs onto a new person or event (Soldz, 1993). Although the therapeutic relationship is therefore only one of many in which transference will be apparent, personal and relational construct psychotherapy, particularly in its experiential form (Leitner, Faidley, Dominici, Humphreys, Loeffler, Schlutsmeyer, & Thomas, 2005), is likely to focus at least some attention on this relationship.

6. *Loosening Techniques*

Several psychoanalytic techniques, such as free association and dream exploration, are likely to loosen the client's construing. The personal construct psychotherapist who wishes to achieve this end may use such techniques, although the reason for doing so will be very different from that of the psychoanalyst.

Cognitive-Behavioural Therapy

Contrasts

1. *Determinism*

Traditional cognitive-behavioural approaches, like traditional psychoanalysis, are deterministic, for example regarding the person as determined by his or her reinforcement history. As we have seen in Chapter 2, personal and relational construct psychotherapy does not privilege a deterministic view of the person.

2. *Reductionist versus Holistic Approach*

Rather than, as in cognitive-behavioural approaches, regarding learning and cognition as distinct psychological processes, the holistic view of the person adopted by Kelly and by personal and relational construct psychotherapy does not separate these processes from the rest of human functioning.

3. *Reflexivity*

Cognitive-behavioural approaches have been regarded, unlike personal construct theory, as not reflexive in that learning theory, on which such approaches were originally based, may 'account for all kinds of human behaviour *except* the formulation of learning theory' (Bannister & Fransella, 1986, p. 4). This is not to deny that contemporary cognitive-behavioural therapists have acknowledged the importance of reflective practice (Bennett-Levy, Thwaites, Chaddock, & Davis, 2009).

4. *Validity and Rationality*

Of the various forms of cognitive-behavioural therapy, 'rationalist' approaches stand in most marked contrast to personal and relational construct psychotherapy in that they are primarily concerned with the validity of the client's view of the world rather than its viability (Mahoney, 1988a, 1988b; Winter & Watson, 1999). Thus, they tend to dismiss the client's view as reflecting cognitive errors or distortions and irrational thinking.

5. *Manipulation and Directiveness*

Kelly (1969c, 1969e) viewed the traditional behavioural approach as manipulative in that, unlike personal construct psychotherapy, it attempts to modify behaviour without considering the constructions underlying it. Even when the client's constructions are considered, in rationalist cognitive approaches this may only be in order to direct the client away from these and towards a particular, supposedly more rational, set of beliefs.

6. *Content, Structure, and Process*

A contrast is also apparent between those cognitive-behavioural approaches that focus on the content of the client's cognitions and personal and relational construct psychotherapy, with its greater attention to the hierarchical structure of the construct system and the process of construing. In addition, the dichotomous nature of construing is generally not accepted by cognitive therapists. Indeed, this was the reason why Beck stopped using the term 'personal construct' (Weishaar, 1993), and while it has been suggested that the cognitive concept of schema is equivalent to the notion of a construct system or subsystem, some personal construct theorists have noted essential differences between these ideas (Epting, 1988).

7. *Levels of Awareness of Construing*

Traditional cognitive-behavioural therapies are also generally not particularly concerned with differences in the levels of accessibility of clients' cognitions (Sarason, 1978), unlike personal and relational construct psychotherapy.

8. *'Cognitive History'*

Although not greatly concerned with the past, personal and relational construct psychotherapy is likely to pay greater attention to the historical roots of clients' constructions than do many cognitive-behavioural approaches.

Similarities

1. *Concern with Clients' Constructions*

Most leading cognitive-behavioural therapists (Beck, Rush, Shaw, & Emery, 1979; Ellis, 1979; Goldfried, 1988; Guidano & Liotti, 1983; Mahoney & Arnkoff, 1978) have acknowledged a debt to Kelly in that his concern with the client's constructions was ahead of its time, predating and anticipating the 'cognitive revolution' in psychology and behaviour therapy.

2. *Facilitation of Experimentation*

Kelly (1970b) acknowledged that behaviour therapy is a way of encouraging experimentation, just as is often the case in personal and relational construct psychotherapy. To this end, both forms of therapy may employ both in-session and homework assignments (Neimeyer & Winter, 2007; Winter, 1992). In Kelly's view, the main difference between the two approaches is the identity of the principal investigator, this being the therapist in traditional behaviour therapy and the client in personal construct psychotherapy.

3. *Tightening Techniques*

Although this is not universally so (for example, relaxation exercises would not fall into this category), many cognitive-behavioural techniques (e.g. self-monitoring) are likely to tighten the client's construing, and may be used for this purpose by personal and relational construct psychotherapists. Some cognitive techniques are also not dissimilar to those developed by personal construct psychotherapists, as is the case with the downward arrow technique and laddering.

4. *Constructivist Trends*

Various contemporary and 'third wave' (Hayes, 2004) cognitive-behavioural approaches[1] can be regarded as closer to the 'constructivist' pole of the 'rationalist—constructivist' construct (essentially, the distinction between whether people are viewed as passively perceiving an independently existing real world or as actively creating their realities), and as such have more in common with personal and relational construct psychotherapy than the more traditional cognitive-behavioural therapies (Neimeyer & Raskin, 2001; Winter, 2018b). This includes a greater concern with cognitive structure and processes, with context, with the development of the client's cognitions, and with a collaborative approach to the therapeutic relationship.

Humanistic Therapies

Contrasts

1. *Givens of Existence*

The existential view that anxiety and other feelings result from confrontation with the 'givens of existence' (Yalom, 1980), or the human condition, contrasts with the personal and relational construct psychotherapy view of emotions as involving some awareness of likely changes in one's construing. Such changes may be precipitated by being confronted with particular aspects of the human condition but this is not necessarily so.

2. *True Self*

Personal and relational construct psychotherapy is more concerned with self-creation than self-discovery, unlike the focus in some humanistic approaches on the true self (Kelly, 1964).

3. *The Person as Naturally Good*

Kelly (1969f) made it clear that, although he did not view people as inherently evil, neither, unlike some humanistic approaches, did he see them as naturally good. What needed to be guarded against, in his view, was hostility, as he defined this term (see Chapter 3), since it may be destructive of others as well as the self and, at the very least, 'does not....contribute to human achievement' (p. 287).

4. *Acceptance*

Although Kelly's (1955) 'credulous approach', which is central to personal and relational construct psychotherapy, involves therapists taking what their clients say at face value and attempting to use their clients' constructs, it does not entail the uncritical acceptance suggested by person-centred therapy.

5. *Therapist Genuineness*

Another component of the therapeutic relationship emphasised by person-centred therapy, therapist genuineness, was not given so much weight by Kelly, who believed that the therapist could usefully choose various roles to play in relation to the client rather than simply being himself or herself.

6. *Structure and Process of Construing*

The personal and relational construct psychotherapist's concern with the structure and process of the client's construing tends not to be evident in traditional humanistic approaches although a focus on selfhood processes is apparent in some more recent approaches.

7. *Diagnosis*

Similarly, humanistic approaches, unlike personal and relational construct psychotherapy, tend not to be concerned with understanding the client's predicament, and formulating plans for therapy, in terms of a set of diagnostic constructs.

8. *Measurement and Rigour*

Kelly (1969g) considered that 'humanistic psychology needs a technology through which to express its humane intentions' (p. 135). He also criticised what he saw as its anti-intellectualism (just as Carl Rogers (1956) criticised personal construct psychotherapy for being too intellectual!) By contrast, with its theoretical structure and measurement techniques, personal construct psychology might be considered to provide what Rychlak (1977) has termed a 'rigorous humanism'.

Similarities

1. *Phenomenological Method*

The phenomenological method, which is central to some existential and humanistic approaches to therapy, is evident in the concern of personal and relational construct psychotherapy with the client's (and the therapist's) experience and with personal meaning (Armezzani & Chiari, 2014; Epting, 1984; Holland, 1970; Smail, 1978).

2. *Choice and Autonomy*

Humanistic approaches to psychology developed, like personal construct psychology, in opposition to the mechanism and reductionism of the dominant psychoanalytic and behavioural approaches. The 'basic postulates' and characteristics of this 'third force in psychology', such as the emphases on a holistic approach, on the person's capacity for choice, and on the relativism of all knowledge (Bugental, 1964), are entirely compatible with personal and relational construct psychotherapy.

3. *Commitment and Authenticity*

The emphasis in Kelly's (1970a) Experience Cycle on the optimally functioning person's committed encounter with their world has been regarded as similar to the existential notion of authenticity (Epting & Amerikaner, 1980).

4. *Rejection of Medical Model*

Both humanistic and personal and relational construct approaches reject a preemptive medical model view of psychological problems.

5. *Encouragement of Experimentation*

The encouragement of the client to act in new ways is as central to some humanistic approaches, such as Gestalt and process-experiential therapies, as it is to personal construct psychotherapy, although it contrasts with the non-directive stance of the traditional person-centred therapist.

6. *Importance of the Therapeutic Relationship*

Particularly in the experiential variant of personal construct psychotherapy (Leitner et al. 2005), there is a focus on the therapeutic relationship that is comparable to that in humanistic approaches and that contrasts with the encouragement of transference that characterises this relationship in psychoanalytic therapy. The therapeutic relationship tends to be a democratic one in both the personal construct and the humanistic approach, despite the fact that some humanistic practitioners have adopted a rather more directive, not to say authoritarian, style.

7. *Empathy*

The importance assigned to therapist empathy in person-centred therapy is comparable to the emphasis in personal and relational construct psychotherapy on therapist sociality, the construing of the client's construction processes.

8. *Group Therapy*

The considerable use of group approaches to therapy which, as we have seen in Chapter 10, has been made by personal construct psychotherapists is equivalent to that by humanistic therapists.

Systemic Therapy[2]

Contrasts

1. *Family Myths*

Although these have been largely superseded by more constructivist approaches, those traditional methods of family therapy that regard dysfunctional families as characterised by mythical or distorted beliefs are incompatible with personal and relational construct psychotherapy.

2. *Adversarial Approach*

Some systemic approaches have taken the view that to break through the family's homeostatic state, the therapist needs to adopt a prescriptive approach, which at times can appear manipulative and as viewing the therapist-family relationship as adversarial rather than, as in personal and relational construct psychotherapy, collaborative.

3. *Therapist as Expert*

The traditional approaches described above are generally ones in which the therapist is viewed as an expert and which adopt 'first-order cybernetic practice based on an artificial separation of the observer from the observed' as opposed to 'second-order cybernetic practice in which therapists are acutely aware of their own hand in the family's interactional matrix' (Fergus & Reid, 2002, p. 42). However, systemic approaches have developed considerably since their founding days and, as we shall see, the latter type of practice is evident in more contemporary systemic approaches as well as personal and relational construct psychotherapy.

4. *Exclusive Focus on the System*

Those systemic approaches that focus exclusively on the system at the expense of the individuals within it may be regarded as reductionist (Fergus & Reid, 2002) and contrast with our approach, with its joint focus at the personal and relational levels.

Similarities

1. *Family Construct Systems*

Although Kelly's focus was on the individual's personal construct system, personal and relational construct psychotherapy regards families and larger social groups as having shared construct systems (Feixas, 1992b, 1995; Procter, 1981, 1996, 2014; see Chapters 4, 7, and 9). This has commonalities with systemic concepts and with such notions as 'family paradigms' (Hoffman, 1981, 1988) and 'family belief systems' (Dallos, 1991). More recent trends have evidenced a growing convergence between systemic approaches and personal and relational construct psychotherapy (Procter & Ugazio, 2017), with Ugazio's concept of *semantic polarity* covering the same ground as the *family construct* (see Chapter 7).

2. *Concern with Process*

Systemic approaches and personal and relational construct psychotherapy share an emphasis on the process, rather than the content, of construing.

3. *Change through Action*

Both approaches also stress the importance of action in promoting change.

4. *Techniques*

As we have seen, several of the techniques employed by family therapists, such as reframing, circular questioning, the miracle question, and the use of metaphor and narrative, are consistent with a personal and relational construct approach and may be used by practitioners of this approach.

5. *Optimal Functioning*

The systemic view that ideally systems should maintain open but adequate boundaries has been regarded as compatible with the personal construct theory view of optimal functioning (Epting & Amerikaner, 1980).

6. Constructivist Foundations

Systemic and personal construct approaches can in general be considered to share constructivist epistemological foundations (Feixas, 1990, 1992b). However, as noted above, some methods of family therapy do not reflect constructivist assumptions, while others are more radically constructivist than personal construct theory in that they do not necessarily acknowledge the existence of a real world. Furthermore, many modern family therapy approaches, such as those that focus on the conversational co-construction of realities (Andersen, 1987), may more precisely be regarded as social constructionist (McNamee & Gergen, 1992) than constructivist in that they emphasise that constructions arise through social interaction and are mediated by language. The integration of PCP with family systemic approaches described in this book is designed to pull these various approaches into a coherent framework.

7. Person as Story-Teller

The 'narrative turn' in psychology (Bruner, 1991; Sarbin, 1986), with its focus on the stories that people tell, has been reflected in trends in systemic therapies, such as a focus on the multiple narrators in a family and the possible differences and incompatibilities in their stories. It also has considerable commonality with personal and relational construct psychotherapy and with a constructivist approach more generally (Botella, Corbella, Gómez, Herrero, & Pacheco, 2005; Musicki, 2017). Indeed, some post-Kellian personal construct psychotherapists have suggested the person as story-teller as an alternative to Kelly's metaphor of the person as scientist (Mair, 1988, 1989), and have developed narrative variants of personal construct psychotherapy (Botella & Herrero, 2000; Chiari & Nuzzo, 2010; Neimeyer, 2004). In addition, Fransella's (1970) view of the symptom as a 'way of life' (see Chapters 3 and 8) can be considered similar to the notion of a 'problem-saturated narrative' (White & Epston, 1990). Procter (2009a) sees narratives and constructs as complementing each other: a construct carries stories and a story communicates one or more constructs. Figures 5.1 and 9.2 show how we can productively move between these two levels in the interview.

Personal and Relational Construct Psychotherapy and Constructivism

In Chapter 2, we suggested that PRCP can be placed on a dimension half way between radical constructivism and social constructionism (see Fig. 2.1). Personal construct psychology may be regarded as the first constructivist psychological theory and personal construct psychotherapy the first thoroughgoing constructivist psychological therapy. Indeed, some psychotherapists from within the personal construct tradition have come to describe their approaches as constructivist psychotherapy (Chiari & Nuzzo, 2010; Neimeyer, 2009). Constructivism is a philosophical tradition that may be traced back to early Greeks, such as Gorgias and Epictetus, but which took root in the seventeenth and eighteenth centuries with the work of Vico, Kant, and Berkeley (Winter & Neimeyer, 2015). Its early psychological elaborations, in addition to Kelly's theory, included Piaget's developmental psychology and Bartlett's view of memory as an active process of reconstruction. As we have seen, constructivism essentially takes the view that people actively construct their worlds, but (as might be expected for a constructivist approach!) there are several variants of this view, differing, for example, in the extent to which the real world is regarded as accessible, or even to exist, beyond people's constructions of it, and in their emphasis on personal or social constructions. Thus, *trivial constructivism*, in which the person is seen as constructing representations of the real world (which, in *limited realism*, it is assumed can be accessed directly), has been contrasted with *radical* constructivism, in which (as exemplified in the writings of the cyberneticists von Glasersfeld and von Foerster and the biologists Maturana and Varela) the person is regarded as organising and adapting to their world (Mahoney, 1988a). Similarly, *epistemological constructivism*, which acknowledges the existence of a real world, albeit one that can only be known through one's constructions of it, has been contrasted with *hermeneutic constructivism*, which regards the world as depending upon people's 'languaging' of it (as originally proposed by the philosopher Bentham and later elaborated by the sociologists Berger and Luckmann) (Chiari & Nuzzo, 1996). Although there is debate as to where personal construct psychology should be positioned on such dimensions (Chiari

& Nuzzo, 1996, 2004, 2010; Paris & Epting, 2004; Raskin, 2002; Stevens, 1998; Warren, 1998), these nuances need not concern us here.

What is of greater relevance to the topic of this chapter is that, as will have been apparent above, constructivist trends in all of the major models of psychotherapy are producing therapeutic approaches that are more compatible with personal and relational construct psychotherapy than are the traditional applications of most of these models (Neimeyer & Mahoney, 1995; Neimeyer & Rood, 1997). Such constructivist therapies include, in the psychoanalytic tradition, Adlerian psychotherapy (Watts & Phillips, 2004) and Spence's (1984) approach that focuses upon narrative rather than historical truth; various therapies developed within the cognitive-behavioural tradition, such as process-oriented cognitive therapy (Guidano, 1991), Mahoney's (2003) constructive psychotherapy, and O'Connor's (2015) 'constructionist clinical psychology for cognitive behaviour therapy'[3]; within the humanistic tradition, some post-Rogerian variants of client-centred therapy (Wexler & Rice, 1974), process-experiential therapy (Elliott, Watson, Goldman, & Greenberg, 2004), and some existential approaches (Lincoln & Hoffman, 2019); and narrative (Musicki, 2017; White & Epston, 1990), radical constructivist (Anderson & Goolishian, 1988), and solution-focused (De Shazer, 1994) approaches developed within the systemic paradigm, as well as Hoffman's (1988) constructivist position for family therapy. Other therapies that may be considered to share at least some constructivist assumptions with personal and relational construct psychotherapy include developmental therapy (Ivey, 1986); meaning-making therapy (Carlsen, 1988); coherence therapy (formerly depth-oriented brief therapy) (Ecker & Hulley, 1996, 2008); therapeutic approaches derived from dialogical self theory (Hermans & DiMaggio, 2004); Buddhist-inspired psychotherapy (McWilliams, 2012); some integrative therapies, such as cognitive-analytic therapy (Ryle, 1990) and attachment narrative therapy (Dallos, 2006); and, although they are more technique-focussed, neuro-linguistic psychotherapy (O'Connor & Seymour, 2002) and some forms of hypnotherapy (Erickson & Rossi, 1979).

Personal and Relational Construct Psychotherapy and Therapeutic Integration

Personal and relational construct psychotherapy may be regarded as technically eclectic (Norcross, 1986) in that, as in our earlier examples concerning the facilitation of loosening and tightening, it borrows techniques from other models but coherently conceptualises the choice of these techniques and their mode of action in terms of personal and relational construct theory rather than the theories from which the techniques were derived. It has also been argued that personal construct theory, or constructivism more broadly (Feixas & Botella, 2004; Neimeyer & Feixas, 1990; Raskin, 2007), may provide a framework for the mutually enriching integration of other models with similar assumptions, or what Neimeyer (1988a) has termed 'theoretically progressive integrationism'. Neimeyer notes the differences between this view and the 'common language for the psychotherapies' proposed by Ryle (1978), whose subsequent development of cognitive-analytic therapy (Ryle, 1990) drew heavily upon personal construct theory and its techniques. At a more superordinate level, personal construct theory may also provide a model for the provision of a therapeutic service staffed by therapists of alternative therapeutic persuasions, to whom clients are allocated on the basis of considerations of the clients' 'personal styles' and the type of reconstruing that is sought in each case (Winter, 1985, 1990). George Kelly (1969c) was puzzled and amused by, and dismissive of, early labelling of his theory as merely a form of one of the major existing psychological models (e.g., as cognitive, behavioural, psychoanalytic, or existential). However, in an increasingly constructivist zeitgeist, personal and relational construct psychotherapy is more similar to some of the contemporary, postmodern variants of other therapeutic models than to the 'modernist' approaches that were being applied at the time that Kelly devised his theory. Furthermore, post-Kellian developments in personal and relational construct psychotherapy can be conveniently classified in terms of their similarities with particular other models (Winter, 2016b). Nevertheless, despite these similarities and the integrative potential of personal and relational construct psychotherapy, it remains a distinctive therapeutic approach (Winter, 2015a). Although the numerous inappropriate attempts to classify it as a cognitive therapy have tended to be replaced by those that portray it as merely another approach concerned with meaning-making, the rigour of its theoretical basis and techniques remains unparalleled amongst such approaches. We shall now consider how it fares, in comparison with other approaches, in terms of evidence of its effectiveness.

Notes

1. Such approaches may be considered to include schema therapy (Young, Klosko, & Weishaar, 2003); metacognitive therapy (Fisher & Wells, 2009); dialectical behaviour therapy (Linehan, 1993); mindfulness-based cognitive therapy (Segal, Williams, & Teasdale, 2002); acceptance and commitment therapy (Hayes & Lillis, 2012); compassion-focused therapy (Gilbert, 2010); and cognitive behavioural analysis system of psychotherapy (McCullough Jr., 2000).
2. We are grateful to Sigurd Reimers for his comments on this section.
3. This is presented as a constructionist and phenomenological approach to cognitive-behavioural therapy, with 'far-reaching implications' (O'Connor, 2015, p. 3) and draws upon constructivist methods such as repertory grid technique. However, it could have gone much further in exploiting the potential of such methods and in providing a truly radical alternative to cognitive-behavioural therapy rather than accepting the cognitive-behavioural label (Winter, 2015b).

References

Andersen, T. (1987). The reflecting team. *Family Process, 26,* 416–428.

Anderson, H., & Goolishian, H. (1988). Human systems as linguistic systems: Evolving ideas about the implications for theory and practice. *Family Process, 27,* 371–393.

Armezzani, M., & Chiari, G. (2014). Ideas for a phenomenological interpretation and elaboration of personal construct theory: Part 2. Husserl and Kelly: A case of commonality. *Costruttivismi, 1,* 168–185.

Bannister, D., & Fransella, F. (1986). *Inquiring Man*. London: Routledge (first published by Penguin (1971)).

Beck, A. T., Rush, A. J., Shaw, B. F., & Emery, G. (1979). *Cognitive Therapy of Depression*. New York, NY: Guilford.

Bennett-Levy, J., Thwaites, R., Chaddock, A., & Davis, M. (2009). Reflective practice in cognitive-behavioural therapy. In J. Stedmon & R. Dallos (Eds.), *Reflective Practice in Psychotherapy and Counselling* (pp. 136–155). Milton Keynes: Open University Press.

Botella, L., & Herrero, O. (2000). A relational constructivist approach to narrative therapy. *European Journal of Psychotherapy and Counselling, 3,* 407–418.

Botella, L., Corbella, S., Gómez, T., Herrero, O., & Pacheco, M. (2005). A personal construct approach to narrative and post-modern therapies. In D. A. Winter & L. L. Viney (Eds.), *Personal Construct Psychotherapy: Advances in Theory, Practice and Research* (pp. 69–80). London: Croom Helm.

Bruner, J. (1991). The narrative construction of reality. *Critical Inquiry, 18,* 1–21.

Bugental, J. (1964). The third force in psychology. *Journal of Humanistic Psychology, 4,* 19–26.

Carlsen, M. B. (1988). *Meaning-Making: Therapeutic Processes in Adult Development*. New York, NY: Norton.

Catina, A., Gitzinger, I., & Hoeckh, H. (1992). Defence mechanisms: An approach from the perspective of personal construct psychology. *International Journal of Personal Construct Psychology, 5,* 249–257.

Chiari, G., & Nuzzo, M. L. (1996). Psychological constructivisms: A metatheoretical differentiation. *Journal of Constructivist Psychology, 9,* 163–184.

Chiari, G., & Nuzzo, M. L. (2004). Steering personal construct theory towards hermeneutic constructivism. In J. D. Raskin & S. K. Bridges (Eds.), *Studies in Meaning 2: Bridging the Personal and Social in Constructivist Psychology* (pp. 51–65). New York, NY: Pace University Press.

Chiari, G., & Nuzzo, M. L. (2010). *Constructivist Psychotherapy: A Narrative Hermeneutic Approach*. London: Routledge.

Dallos, R. (1991). *Family Belief Systems, Therapy and Change: A Constructional Approach*. Maidenhead, UK: Open University Press.

Dallos, R. (2006). *Attachment Narrative Therapy*. Maidenhead, UK: Open University Press.

De Shazer, S. (1994). *Words Were Originally Magic*. New York, NY: Norton.

Ecker, B., & Hulley, L. (1996). *Depth Oriented Brief Therapy: How to Be Brief When You Were Trained to be Deep, and Vice Versa*. San Francisco: Jossey-Bass.

Ecker, B., & Hulley, L. (2008). Coherence therapy: Swift changes at the root of symptom production. In J. D. Raskin & S. K. Bridges (Eds.), *Studies in Meaning 3: Constructivist Psychotherapy in the Real World* (pp. 57–84). New York, NY: Pace University Press.

Elliott, R., Watson, J. C., Goldman, R. N., & Greenberg, L. S. (2004). *Learning Emotion-Focused Therapy: The Process-Experiential Approach to Change.* Washington, DC: American Psychological Association.

Ellis, A. (1979). The theory of rational-emotive therapy. In A. Ellis & J. M. Whiteley (Eds.), *Theoretical and Empirical Foundations of Rational-Emotive Therapy* (pp. 33–60). Monterey: Brooks/Cole.

Epting, F. R. (1984). *Personal Construct Counseling and Psychotherapy.* New York, NY: Wiley.

Epting, F. R. (1988). Journeying into the personal constructs of children. *International Journal of Personal Construct Psychology, 1,* 53–61.

Epting, F. R., & Amerikaner, M. (1980). Optimal functioning: A personal construct approach. In A. Landfield & L. M. Leitner (Eds.), *Personal Construct Psychology: Psychotherapy and Personality* (pp. 55–73). New York, NY: Wiley.

Erickson, M. H., & Rossi, E. L. (1979). *Hypnotherapy: An Exploratory Casebook.* Oxford: Irvington.

Feixas, G. (1990). Personal construct theory and the systemic therapies: Parallel or convergent trends? *Journal of Marital and Family Therapy, 16,* 1–20.

Feixas, G. (1992b). Personal construct approaches to family therapy. In G. J. Neimeyer & R. A. Neimeyer (Eds.), *Advances in Personal Construct Psychology* (Vol. 2, pp. 217–255). Greenwich, CT: JAI Press.

Feixas, G. (1995). Personal constructs in systemic practice. In R. A. Neimeyer & M. J. Mahoney (Eds.), *Constructivism in Psychotherapy* (pp. 305–337). Washington, DC: American Psychological Association.

Feixas, G., & Botella, L. (2004). Psychotherapy integration: Reflections and contributions from a constructivist epistemology. *Journal of Psychotherapy Integration, 14,* 192–222.

Feixas, G., Saúl, L. A., & Ávila-Espada, A. (2009). Viewing cognitive conflicts as dilemmas: Implications for mental health. *Journal of Constructivist Psychology, 22,* 141–169.

Fergus, K. D., & Reid, D. W. (2002). Integrating constructivist and systemic metatheory in family therapy. *Journal of Constructivist Psychology, 15,* 41–63.

Fisher, S., & Greenberg, R. P. (1978). *The Scientific Evaluation of Freud's Theories and Therapy.* New York, NY: Basic Books.

Fisher, P., & Wells, A. (2009). *Metacognitive Therapy: Distinctive Features.* Hove, UK: Routledge.

Fonagy, P. (1982). The integration of psychoanalysis and experimental science: A review. *International Review of Psychoanalysis, 9,* 125–145.

Fransella, F. (1970). Stuttering: Not a symptom but a way of life. *British Journal of Communication Disorders, 5,* 22–29.

Fransella, F. (1993). The construct of resistance in psychotherapy. In L. M. Leitner & N. G. M. Dunnett (Eds.), *Critical Issues in Personal Construct Psychotherapy* (pp. 117–134). Malabar: Krieger.

Gilbert, P. (2010). *Compassion Focused Therapy: Distinctive Features.* Hove, UK: Routledge.

Goldfried, M. R. (1988). Personal construct therapy and other theoretical orientations. *International Journal of Personal Construct Psychology, 1,* 317–327.

Guidano, V. F. (1991). *The Self in Process.* New York, NY: Guilford.

Guidano, V. F., & Liotti, G. (1983). *Cognitive Processes and Emotional Disorders: A Structural Approach to Psychotherapy.* New York: Guilford Press.

Hayes, S. C. (2004). Acceptance and commitment therapy, relational frame theory, and the third wave of behavioural and cognitive therapies. *Behaviour Therapy, 35,* 339–365.

Hayes, S. C., & Lillis, J. (2012). *Acceptance and Commitment Therapy.* Washington, DC: American Psychological Association.

Hermans, H. J. M., & DiMaggio, G. (2004). *The Dialogical Self in Psychotherapy.* New York, NY: Brunner-Routledge.

Hoffman, L. (1981). *Foundations of Family Therapy: A Conceptual Framework for Systems Change.* New York, NY: Basic Books.

Hoffman, L. (1988). A constructivist position for family therapy. *Irish Journal of Psychology, 9,* 110–129.

Holland, R. (1970). George Kelly: Constructive innocent and reluctant existentialist. In D. Bannister (Ed.), *Perspectives in Personal Construct Theory* (pp. 111–132). London: Academic Press.

Ivey, A. E. (1986). *Developmental Therapy.* San Francisco: Jossey-Bass.

Karasu, T. B. (1986). The psychotherapies: Benefits and limitations. *American Journal of Psychotherapy, 40,* 324–343.

Kelly, G. A. (1955). *The Psychology of Personal Constructs. Vol. I, II.* New York: Norton (2nd printing: 1991, London and New York, NY: Routledge).

Kelly, G. A. (1964). The language of hypothesis: Man's psychological instrument. *Journal of Individual Psychology, 20,* 137–152.

Kelly, G. A. (1969a). The autobiography of a theory. In B. Maher (Ed.), *Clinical Psychology and Personality: The Selected Papers of George Kelly* (pp. 46–65). New York, NY: Wiley.

Kelly, G. A. (1969b). Man's construction of his alternatives. In B. Maher (Ed.), *Clinical Psychology and Personality: The Selected Papers of George Kelly* (pp. 66–93). New York, NY: Wiley.

Kelly, G. A. (1969c). The psychotherapeutic relationship. In B. Maher (Ed.), *Clinical psychology and Personality: The Selected Papers of George Kelly* (pp. 216–223). New York, NY: Wiley.

Kelly, G. A. (1969d). Hostility. In B. Maher (Ed.), *Clinical Psychology and Personality: The Selected Papers of George Kelly* (pp. 267–280). New York, NY: Wiley.

Kelly, G. A. (1969e). In whom confide: On whom depend for what? In B. Maher (Ed.), *Clinical Psychology and Personality: The Selected Papers of George Kelly* (pp. 189–206). New York, NY: Wiley.

Kelly, G. A. (1969f). The threat of aggression. In B. Maher (Ed.), *Clinical Psychology and Personality: The Selected Papers of George Kelly* (pp. 281–288). New York, NY: Wiley.

Kelly, G. A. (1969g). Humanistic methodology in psychological research. In B. Maher (Ed.), *Clinical Psychology and Personality: The Selected Papers of George Kelly* (pp. 133–146). New York, NY: Wiley.

Kelly, G. A. (1970a). A brief introduction to personal construct theory. In D. Bannister (Ed.), *Perspectives in Personal Construct Theory* (pp. 3–20). London: Academic Press.

Kelly, G. A. (1970b). Behaviour is an experiment. In D. Bannister (Ed.), *Perspectives in Personal Construct Theory* (pp. 255–269). London: Academic Press.

Kline, P. (1981). *Fact and Fantasy in Freudian Theory*. London: Methuen.

Leitner, L. M., Faidley, A. J., Dominici, D., Humphreys, C., Loeffler, V., Schlutsmeyer, M., & Thomas, J. (2005). Encountering an other: Experiential personal construct psychotherapy. In D. A. Winter & L. L. Viney (Eds.), *Personal Construct Psychotherapy: Advances in Theory, Practice and Research* (pp. 54–68). London: Whurr.

Lincoln, J., & Hoffman, L. (2019). Toward an integration of constructivism and existential psychotherapy. *Journal of Constructivist Psychology, 32,* 108–125.

Linehan, M. M. (1993). *Cognitive-Behavioral Treatment of Borderline Personality Disorder*. New York, NY: Guilford.

Lorenzini, R., & Sassaroli, S. (1995). Attachment as an informative relationship. *International Journal of Personal Construct Psychology, 3,* 239–248.

Mahoney, M. J. (1988a). Constructive metatheory: I. Basic features and historical foundations. *International Journal of Personal Construct Psychology, 1,* 1–35.

Mahoney, M. J. (1988b). Constructive metatheory: II. Implications for psychotherapy. *International Journal of Personal Construct Psychology, 1,* 299–315.

Mahoney, M. J. (2003). *Constructive Psychotherapy: A Practical Guide.* New York, NY: Guilford.

Mahoney, M., & Arnkoff, D. (1978). Cognitive and self-control therapies. In S. Garfield & A. Bergin (Eds.), *Handbook of Psychotherapy and Behavior Change* (3rd ed., pp. 689–722). New York, NY: Wiley.

Mair, J. M. M. (1988). Psychology as storytelling. *International Journal of Personal Construct Psychology, 1,* 125–137.

Mair, J. M. M. (1989). Kelly, Bannister, and a story-telling psychology. *International Journal of Personal Construct Psychology, 2,* 1–15.

McCullough, J. P., Jr. (2000). *Treatment for Chronic Depression: Cognitive Behavioral Analysis System of Psychotherapy (CBASP).* New York, NY: Guilford.

McNamee, S., & Gergen, K. J. (Eds.). (1992). *Therapy as Social Construction.* London: Sage.

McWilliams, S. (2012). Mindfulness and extending constructivist psychotherapy integration. *Journal of Constructivist Psychology, 25,* 230–250.

Musicki, V. (2017). How might personal construct psychology benefit from narrative approaches? *Journal of Constructivist Psychology, 30,* 360–370.

Neimeyer, R. A. (1988a). Integrative directions in personal construct therapy. *International Journal of Personal Construct Psychology, 1,* 283–297.

Neimeyer, R. A. (2004). Fostering posttraumatic growth: A narrative contribution. *Psychological Inquiry, 15,* 53–59.

Neimeyer, R. A. (2009). *Constructivist Psychotherapy.* London: Routledge.

Neimeyer, R. A., & Feixas, G. (1990). Constructivist contributions to psychotherapy integration. *Journal of Integrative and Eclectic Psychotherapy, 9,* 4–20.

Neimeyer, R. A., & Mahoney, M. J. (Eds.). (1995). *Constructivism in Psychotherapy.* Washington, DC: American Psychological Association.

Neimeyer, R. A., & Raskin, J. D. (2001). Varieties of constructivism in psychotherapy. *Handbook of Cognitive-Behavioral Therapies* (Vol. 2, pp. 393–430). New York, NY: Guilford.

Neimeyer, G. J., & Rood, L. (1997). Contemporary expressions of constructivist psychotherapy. In G. J. Neimeyer & R. A. Neimeyer (Eds.), *Advances in Personal Construct Psychology* (Vol. 4, pp. 185–205). Greenwich, CT: JAI Press.

Neimeyer, R. A., & Winter, D. A. (2007). Personal construct therapy. In N. Kazantzis & L. L'Abate (Eds.), *Handbook of Homework Assignments in Psychotherapy: Research, Practice and Prevention* (pp. 151–171). New York, NY: Springer.

Norcross, J. C. (1986). Eclectic psychotherapy: An introduction and overview. In J. C. Norcross (Ed.), *Handbook of Eclectic psychotherapy* (pp. 3–24). New York, NY: Brunner/Mazel.

O'Connor, P. (2015). *A Constructionist Clinical Psychology for Cognitive Behaviour Therapy*. Hove, UK: Routledge.

O'Connor, J., & Seymour, S. (2002). *Introducing Neuro-Linguistic Programming: Psychological Skills for Understanding and Influencing People*. London: Element.

Paris, M. E., & Epting, F. (2004). Social and personal construction: Two sides of the same coin. In J. D. Raskin & S. K. Bridges (Eds.), *Studies in Meaning 2: Bridging the Personal and Social in Constructivist Psychology* (pp. 3–35). New York: Pace University Press.

Procter, H. G. (1981). Family construct psychology: An approach to understanding and treating families. In S. Walrond-Skinner (Ed.), *Developments in Family Therapy: Theories and Applications since 1948* (pp. 350–366). London: Routledge and Kegan Paul.

Procter, H. G. (1996). The family construct system. In D. Kalekin-Fishman & B. Walker (Eds.), *The Structure of Group Realities: Culture, Society, and Personal Construct Theory* (pp. 161–180). Malabar, FL: Krieger.

Procter, H. G. (2009a). The construct. In R. J. Butler (Ed.), *Reflections in Personal Construct Theory* (pp. 21–40). Chichester, UK: Wiley-Blackwell.

Procter, H. G. (2014). Qualitative grids, the relationality corollary and the levels of interpersonal construing. *Journal of Constructivist Psychology, 27,* 243–262.

Procter, H. G., & Ugazio, V. (2017). Family constructs and semantic polarities: A convergent perspective? In D. A. Winter, P. Cummins, H. G. Procter, & N. Reed (Eds.), *Personal Construct Psychology at 60: Papers from the 21st International Congress* (pp. 68–89). Newcastle upon Tyne, UK: Cambridge Scholars Publishing.

Raskin, J. D. (2002). Constructivism in psychology: Personal construct psychology, radical constructivism, and social constructionism. In J. D.

Raskin & S. K. Bridges (Eds.), *Studies in Meaning: Exploring Constructivist Psychology* (pp. 1–25). New York, NY: Pace University Press.

Raskin, J. D. (2007). Assimilative integration in constructivist psychotherapy. *Journal of Psychotherapy Integration, 17,* 50–69.

Rogers, C. R. (1956). Intellectual psychotherapy. *Contemporary Psychology, 1,* 357–358.

Rychlak, J. F. (1977). *The Psychology of Rigorous Humanism.* New York, NY: Wiley-Interscience.

Ryle, A. (1975). *Frames and Cages: The Repertory Grid Approach to Human Understanding.* London: Sussex University Press.

Ryle, A. (1978). A common language for the psychotherapies. *British Journal of Psychiatry, 113,* 585–594.

Ryle, A. (1990). *Cognitive-Analytic Therapy: Active Participation in Change: A new Integration in Brief Therapy.* Chichester, UK: Wiley.

Sarason, I. G. (1978). Three lacunae of cognitive therapy. *Cognitive Therapy and Research, 3,* 223–235.

Sarbin, T. R. (1986). The narrative as a root metaphor for psychology. In T. R. Sarbin (Ed.), *Narrative Psychology: The Storied Nature of Human Conduct* (pp. 3–21). New York, NY: Praeger.

Segal, Z. V., Williams, J. M. G., & Teasdale, J. D. (2002). *Mindfulness-Based Cognitive Therapy for Depression: A New Approach to Preventing Relapse.* New York. NY: Guilford.

Smail, D. J. (1978). *Psychotherapy: A Personal Approach.* London: Dent.

Soldz, S. (1988). Constructivist tendencies in recent psychoanalysis. *International Journal of Personal Construct Psychology, 1,* 329–347.

Soldz, S. (1993). Beyond interpretation: The elaboration of transference in personal construct therapy. In L. M. Leitner & N. G. M. Dunnett (Eds.), *Critical Issues in Personal Construct Psychotherapy* (pp. 173–192). Malabar, FL: Krieger.

Spence, D. P. (1984). *Narrative Truth and Historical Truth: Meaning and Interpretation in Psychoanalysis.* New York, NY: Norton.

Stevens, C. D. (1998). Realism and Kelly's pragmatic constructivism. *Journal of Constructivist Psychology, 11,* 283–308.

Tschudi, F. (1977). Loaded and honest questions: A construct theory view of symptoms and therapy. In D. Bannister (Ed.), *New Perspectives in Personal Construct Theory* (pp. 321–350). London: Academic Press.

Walker, B. M. (2002). Nonvalidation vs. (In)validation: Implications for theory and practice. In J. D. Raskin & S. K. Bridges (Eds.), *Studies in*

Meaning: Exploring Constructivist Psychology (pp. 49–61). New York, NY: Pace University Press.

Warren, W. G. (1983). *Personal construct theory and psychoanalysis: An exploration.* Paper presented at Vth. International Congress on Personal Construct Psychology, Boston.

Warren, B. (1998). *Philosophical Dimensions of Personal Construct Psychology.* London: Routledge.

Watts, R. E., & Phillips, K. A. (2004). Adlerian psychology and psychotherapy: A relational constructivist approach. In J. D. Raskin & S. K. Bridges (Eds.), *Studies in Meaning 2: Bridging the Personal and Social in Constructivist Psychology* (pp. 267–289). New York, NY: Pace University Press.

Weishaar, M. E. (1993). *Aaron T. Beck.* London: Sage.

Wexler, D. A., & Rice, L. N. (Eds.). (1974). *Innovations in Client-Centered Therapy.* New York, NY: Wiley.

White, M., & Epston, D. (1990). *Narrative Means to Therapeutic Ends.* Adelaide, Australia: Dulwich Centre Publications.

Winter, D. A. (1985). Personal styles, constructive alternativism and the provision of a therapeutic service. *British Journal of Medical Psychology, 58,* 129–136.

Winter, D. A. (1990). Therapeutic alternatives for psychological disorder: Personal construct psychology investigations in a health service setting. In G. J. Neimeyer & R. A. Neimeyer (Eds.), *Advances in Personal Construct Psychology* (Vol. 1, pp. 89–116). Greenwich, CT: Jai Press.

Winter, D. A. (1992). *Personal Construct Psychology in Clinical Practice: Theory, Research and Applications.* London: Routledge.

Winter, D. A. (2015a). What does the future hold for personal construct psychology? In J. D. Raskin & S. K. Bridges (Eds.), *Studies in Meaning 5: Perturbing the Status Quo in Constructivist Psychology* (pp. 28–63). New York, NY: Pace University Press.

Winter, D. A. (2015b). Towards a less mechanistic cognitive behaviour therapy. *PsycCRITIQUES, 60,* Article 3.

Winter, D. A. (2016b). The continuing clinical relevance of personal construct psychology: A review. In D. A. Winter & N. Reed (Eds.), *The Wiley Handbook of Personal Construct Psychology* (pp. 203–217). Chichester: Wiley-Blackwell.

Winter, D. A. (2018b). Cognitive behaviour therapy: From rationalism to constructivism? In D. Loewenthal & G. Proctor (Eds.), *Why Not CBT? Against and For CBT Revised* (pp. 219–229). PCCS Books: Monmouth, UK.

Winter, D. A., & Neimeyer, R. A. (2015). Constructivist therapy. In E. Neukrug (Ed.), *Encyclopedia of Theory in Counseling and Psychotherapy*. Los Angeles: Sage.

Winter, D. A., & Watson, S. (1999). Personal construct psychotherapy and the cognitive therapies: Different in theory but can they be differentiated in practice? *Journal of Constructivist Psychology, 12*, 1–22.

Yalom, I. D. (1980). *Existential Psychotherapy*. New York, NY: Basic Books.

Young, J. E., Klosko, J. S., & Weishaar, M. E. (2003). *Schema Therapy: A Practitioner's Guide*. New York, NY: Guilford.

Winter, D., & Gournay, K. (1987). Constriction and construction in agoraphobia. *British Journal of Medical Psychology, 60*, 233–244.

13

Evidence Base

Evidence-Based Practice

Since the 1990s, the dominant ethos in psychological therapy services has been one of the provision of what in the USA were originally termed empirically validated (Task Force on Promotion and Dissemination of Psychological Procedures, 1995), and later empirically supported, therapies, and what in the UK has been termed evidence-based practice (Department of Health, 1996). A stark message was provided (in this case in a review of strategic policy for psychological therapies in the English National Health Service) that 'It is unacceptable...to continue to provide therapies which decline to subject themselves to research evaluation. Practitioners and researchers alike must accept the challenge of evidence-based practice, one result of which is that treatments which are shown to be ineffective are discontinued' (Parry & Richardson, 1996, p. 43).

One of the results of this ethos has been the production of 'shopping lists' of what are deemed to be efficacious[1] therapies (Chambless & Hollon, 1998; Chambless et al., 1998; Roth & Fonagy, 2005). A glance at these lists will indicate that they are

H. Procter and D. A. Winter, *Personal and Relational Construct Psychotherapy*,
Palgrave Texts in Counselling and Psychotherapy,
https://doi.org/10.1007/978-3-030-52177-6_13

dominated by cognitive-behavioural therapies, as is also the case in the treatment guidelines produced by organisations such as, in the UK, the National Institute of Clinical and Health Excellence (NICE, 2014). This organisation's guidelines were implemented in the UK in the 'Improving Access to Psychological Therapies' programme, which was designed to '**give people with mental illness the choice of psychological therapy**' (Centre for Economic Performance, 2006, p. 14, bold in original), but which again largely limits this choice to variants of cognitive-behavioural therapy (Winter, 2007b).

With the sheer number of different types of psychological therapies on offer, anything that appears to simplify the decision processes of those who hold the therapeutic purse strings is likely to be seen as a welcome relief. However, the evidence-based/empirically supported therapies initiative has provoked considerable debate, Trinder (2000a) cautioning that 'there are worrying signs…that evidence-based practice is in danger of becoming a means by which managers can force a particular and narrow definition of effective practice upon researchers and practitioners' (p. 238), and Holmes, Murray, Perron, and Rail (2006) regarding it as 'a good example of microfascism' (p. 180). Furthermore, even the editor of the leading handbook on psychotherapy research, Michael Lambert, considers that:

> The current interest in generating lists of "empirically supported" therapies for specific disorders is controversial and misguided. To advocate empirically supported therapies as preferable or superior to other treatments would be premature. Not only is this endeavor impractical, but research support is lacking. Advocation at this level is not supported by past or current research evidence. (Lambert & Ogles, 2004, p. 180)

Detailed coverage of this debate is beyond the scope of the present book, but we shall outline some of the areas of relevance to personal and relational construct psychotherapy before going on to review the 'evidence base' for this form of therapy.

Philosophical Position

The evidence-based/empirically supported therapies movement is not philosophically or politically neutral, or indeed free of the demands of the marketplace. Rather, it has been regarded as consistent with a managerialist, risk-conscious, consumer-focused (Trinder, 2000b), and 'outcome-oriented' (Gold, 1995) society, in which there is 'sustained optimism' concerning reason and science (Giddens, 1991), an 'ideology of control' (Miles, Grey, Polychronis, & Melchiorri, 2002, p. 99), and an emphasis on the quick (and cheap) fix. Thus, it is no coincidence that the author of the report that led to the previously mentioned Improving Access to Psychological Therapies initiative, and an associated book on happiness (Layard, 2006), is an economist!

The philosophical position that underlies the evidence-based/empirically validated therapies movement is considered by Slife (2004) to be *naturalism*, which 'essentially postulates that natural laws and/or principles ultimately govern the events of nature, including our bodies, behaviors, and minds' (p. 45). It is very apparent that these philosophical assumptions are much more compatible with some therapeutic approaches than with others. To quote Slife (2004) again,

> Is it merely coincidental that the therapies that match the values of objectivist science are those that are the most scientifically supported?....Is it merely coincidental, in this light, that cognitive behavioral therapy has virtually the same epistemological assumption (values) as traditional science.... The positive empirical evaluations of this therapy may be the result of systematic bias rather than efficacy without such bias. (pp. 51–52)

By contrast, the therapies that are most likely to be 'empirically violated' or 'disenfranchised' in a naturalistic climate of empirical validation are constructivist, humanistic, and systemic approaches (Bohart, O'Hara, & Leitner, 1998; Botella, 2000; Messer, 2001).

Research Design

The randomised controlled trial, in which participants are randomly allocated to a treatment group or a control group, is generally regarded as the 'gold standard' in research evaluating the efficacy of psychological therapies. However, in privileging such a design, research using other designs, some of which have been argued to be more suitable for the study of therapies focusing upon such areas as meanings and relationships, has been marginalised. These include process-outcome studies, qualitative research, and case studies, although guidelines that have been produced for such approaches (Dixon-Woods, Shaw, Agarwal, & Smith, 2004; Edwards, Dattilio, & Bromley, 2004; Elliott, 2002; Elliott, Fischer, & Rennie, 1999; Spencer, Ritchie, & O'Connor, 2003) can ensure a degree of rigour no less than that of a randomised controlled trial. Randomised controlled trials are in any case not always ethically appropriate; are not well equipped to provide reliable evidence of harmful effects of treatment; often have questionable external validity,[2] the rather 'sanitised' conditions studied in many randomised controlled trials bearing little resemblance to normal clinical practice; and may even have dubious internal validity when applied to psychological therapies (Borkovec & Castonguay, 1998; Kazdin, 1994; Rawlins, 2008; Westen, Novotny, & Thompson-Brenner, 2004). The adequacy of some of the research on which treatment guidelines are based may therefore be called into question, and Mackay, Barkham, Rees, and Stiles (2003) estimated that only 11 per cent of the literature contributing to one such guideline met minimum quality standards.

The research designs favoured by the evidence-based practice movement essentially reflect a medical model approach using the 'drug metaphor' (Stiles & Shapiro, 1989), with criteria for empirically supported psychological therapies in the USA being based on those accepted for drug therapies by the United States Food and Drug Administration. Indeed, psychotherapy researchers have not just mimicked but have exceeded medical researchers in their use of randomised controlled trials (Howard, Orlinsky, & Lueger, 1995). One reflection of the medical model approach is that, in order to stand any chance of being included in the evidence base on which treatment guidelines are based, research on a psychological therapy needs to be conducted on specific client groups, normally defined in terms of psychiatric diagnostic categories. This is likely to be to the disadvantage of research on forms of therapy, such as personal and relational construct psychotherapy, which are critical of, and tend not to use, psychiatric nosology (Bohart et al., 1998). Since researchers are encouraged to recruit clients with relatively pure diagnoses rather than the comorbid presentations that are typical of everyday clinical practice, the external validity of such research is limited. Another limitation related to the focus on psychiatric diagnostic categories is that the favoured outcome measures tend to assess symptom severity rather than areas, such as personal meanings and interpersonal relationships, that may be more relevant to the focus of an approach such as personal and relational construct psychotherapy.

Another medical model-based requirement that arguably favours cognitive-behavioural therapies is that treatment approaches studied in psychotherapy research should be manualised. Although it has been argued that this is to the disadvantage of humanistic and constructivist therapies, where 'creative improvisation' is more evident (Bohart et al., 1998), personal and relational construct psychotherapy approaches are, as we have seen (Feixas & Compañ, 2016), quite capable of being manualised, albeit in a way that is not highly prescriptive and inflexible.

A further way in which the medical model is reflected in the evidence-based practice approach, and the research that it has generated, is the assumption that techniques specific to particular forms of therapy are their principal active ingredients. However, estimates of the variance in treatment outcome accounted for by such specific factors have indicated that this is very low, ranging from 8 (Wampold, 2001) to 15 (Lambert, 1992) per cent. Neither has support for the specificity of psychological therapies been obtained from studies that have focused on disentangling their ingredients, leading Wampold (2001) to conclude that 'the ingredients of the most conspicuous treatment on the landscape, cognitive-behavioral treatment, are apparently not responsible for the benefits of this treatment' (pp. 147–148). Instead, non-specific factors that have been found to have not inconsiderable effects on treatment outcomes in research studies are characteristics of the therapist, the therapist-client relationship, client expectancies, and the therapeutic allegiance of the researcher (Caine, Wijesinghe, & Winter, 1981; Lambert, 1992; Luborsky et al., 1999; Orlinsky, Ronnestad, & Willutzki, 2004). Indeed, evidence of the impact of the therapist-client relationship on treatment outcome has led Humphreys, Dutile, & Leitner (2001) to conclude that a therapy, such as experiential personal construct psychotherapy, which focuses on this relationship should for this reason alone be regarded as empirically validated!

An alternative, or at least a complement, to evidence-based practice and its associated research designs is 'practice-based evidence' (Margison et al., 2000), in which data are collected from routine clinical practice. Such an approach is generally reliant on 'practice research networks' (Audin et al., 2001), consisting of large numbers of collaborating clinicians, who may be able to generate very large datasets with high external validity. These datasets may then form the basis for the setting of standards, for example in regard to treatment outcome, against which therapeutic practice can be benchmarked (Barkham & Mellor-Clark, 2000; Barkham et al., 1998). They thus facilitate possibilities for the enhancement of outcome and 'maximising the benefits of psychotherapy' (Green & Latchford, 2012) by, for example, feeding back data on client progress to therapists (Lambert, Hansen, & Finch, 2001).

Evidence and Its Interpretation

The notion of evidence-based practice has been rejected by some constructivists as it has been seen to imply that one can access, and obtain objective knowledge of, a real world of evidence. However, Kelly's (1955) original metaphor of the person as scientist is fully consistent with the collection and consideration of evidence for one's constructions (in this case concerning the effectiveness of particular therapies). The personal and relational construct perspective, though, emphasises that there are several types of evidence, some more privileged than others, and that all of these are very subject to interpretation and alternative construction. The evidence-based/empirically validated therapies movement tends to take a hierarchical view of evidence (Eccles & Mason, 2001; Guyatt et al., 1995), with replicated randomised controlled trials (and the meta-analysis or systematic review of these) at the top of the hierarchy. However, such a hierarchy can be regarded to reflect a 'methodological imperialism' or 'paradigmatic hegemony' (Bohart, 2000) that, as we have seen, favours particular therapeutic approaches. Similarly, Miles et al. (2002) criticise the 'shocking arrogance' of those who claim to have 'unique access to scientific and clinical truth' (p. 88), and describe evidence-based medicine as a 'scientific fetishism' that exalts probability values and denigrates clinical expertise. Even Sir Michael Rawlins (2008), the Chair of the National Institute of Health and Clinical Excellence (NICE), an organisation that bases its guidelines on hierarchies of evidence, now takes the view that 'Hierarchies place RCTs on an undeserved pedestal' (p. 2), and that they 'replace judgement with an oversimplistic, pseudo-quantitative, assessment of the quality of the available evidence' (p. 34). The approach termed best evidence synthesis (Slavin, 1995) addresses this problem to some extent by, for example, employing a two-dimensional hierarchy of study utility considering both internal and external validity (Ogilvie, Egan, Hamilton, & Petticrew, 2005).

Even if it is agreed what constitutes appropriate evidence, the translation of this evidence into treatment guidelines does not necessarily, or even usually, involve a straightforward, scientific process of interpretation. Chambless and Ollendick (2001) admit that the American Psychological Association Task Force that produced its lists of empirically validated therapies did not use 'hard and fast decision rules', and did not provide evidence on its decision-making process or on the reliability of its decisions. Inconsistencies are also apparent between some of the NICE recommendations regarding psychological therapies and the reported evidence, leading to the question of whether these recommendations 'are based less on a balanced review of the evidence base than on the allegiances of members of the Guideline Development Group or political considerations' (Winter, 2010, p. 6). Similarly, Miles et al. (2002), referring to NICE, comment that 'inconsistent and varied use of evidence appraisal methodologies and biased interpretation of scientific data in order to arrive at conclusions of economic convenience, more often than not in the face of substantial objections by learned clinical societies and bodies of internationally recognized medical experts, is little short of scandalous and completely symptomatic of the cancer of politicization of health services' (p. 99).

Therefore, while treatment guidelines are generally accepted uncritically as the basis for decisions concerning psychological therapy service provision, it would be as well to bear in mind the comment of Trinder (2000a) on evidence-based practice that 'In some areas certainty is more founded, whilst in other areas, beyond the biological, the search for certainty poses considerable dangers in inherently complex and uncertain worlds. Whilst evidence is potentially helpful it is important not to be seduced into an unwarranted sense of security' (p. 237).

Evidence Base for Personal and Relational Construct Psychotherapy

Although questions have been raised about various aspects of evidence-based practice, it is clear that therapies whose practitioners refuse to engage in this process are likely to be threatened with extinction. The lack of mention of personal and relational construct psychotherapies in lists of evidence-based therapies such as Roth and Fonagy's (1996) *What Works for Whom?* might suggest that the future for such therapies is bleak. However, close scrutiny of the second edition of this influential book will reveal a footnote concerning the evidence base for personal construct therapy (PCT) in which the authors acknowledge that such factors as eschewing of psychiatric diagnosis and the use of 'measures that are designed to detect shifts in process and meaning, rather than shifts in symptomatic functioning' mean that 'what is available is philosophically at variance with a conventional review such as this one. This latter point could be used to argue that the absence of reports of evidence for PCT in this book reflects our selection bias rather than a real absence of evidence' (Roth & Fonagy, 2005, p. 492).

Given Roth and Fonagy's frank caveat, the question that should now be asked is what else works for whom, given a more balanced assessment of the available evidence. In answering this question, it will be apparent that there is, in fact, a not inconsiderable evidence base for personal construct psychotherapy, including studies not only of therapeutic outcome but also of the treatment process (Winter, 2003d).

Therapeutic Outcome

As well as being demonstrated in numerous case examples (e.g., R. Neimeyer & G. J. Neimeyer, 1987; Winter, 1992, 2003c; Winter & Viney, 2005), the outcome of personal construct psychotherapy has been investigated in a number of research studies. These have been conducted on individual, couple, and group treatment modalities and on a wide range of client and non-client groups, including heterogeneous adult referrals to psychotherapy services (Morris, 1977; Watson & Winter, 2005), people with speaking anxiety (Karst & Trexler, 1970), those who stutter (Evesham & Fransella, 1985), individuals with social anxiety (Beail & Parker, 1991; Nagae & Nedate, 2001), snake phobics (Lira, Nay, McCullough, & Etkin, 1975), people diagnosed with agoraphobia (Winter, Gournay, Metcalfe, & Rossotti, 2006), those diagnosed with schizophrenic thought disorder (Bannister, Adams-Webber, Penn, & Radley, 1975), problem drinkers (Landfield, 1979; Landfield & Rivers, 1975), depressed people (Feixas et al., 2016; Paz, Montesano, Winter, & Feixas, 2019; Sheehan, 1985), people with eating disorders (Button, 1987), individuals with anger problems (Pekkala & Dave, 2005), people who have self-harmed (Winter, Sireling et al., 2007), adults who were sexually abused as children (Alexander, Neimeyer, & Follette, 1991; Alexander, Neimeyer, Follette, Moore, & Harter, 1989), domestic abusers (Horley & Francoeur, 2003), troubled adolescents (Jackson, 1992; Truneckova & Viney, 2011), adolescent offenders (Sewell & Ovaert, 1997; Viney & Henry, 2002; Viney, Henry, & Campbell, 2001), older adults (Botella & Feixas, 1992–1993; Viney, Benjamin, & Preston, 1989), general hospital patients (Viney, Clarke, Bunn, & Benjamin, 1985a, 1985b, 1985c), people with chronic pain (Haugli, Steen, Laerum, Finset, & Nygaard, 2000, 2001), survivors of breast cancer (Lane & Viney, 2005b), women approaching the menopause (Foster & Viney, 2005), mothers of children with special needs (Lovenfosse & Viney, 1999), AIDS caregivers (Viney, Crooks,

& Walker, 1995), staff in homes for older people (Malins, Couchman, Viney, & Grenyer, 2004), and exercise programme participants (Annesi, 2002).

The findings of many of these outcome studies have been synthesised in three meta-analyses, the statistical technique in which a common metric, the effect size,[3] is calculated for every study. Effect sizes of 0.20, 0.50, and 0.80 are generally regarded as representing small, medium, and large effects respectively (Cohen, 1988). The results of the meta-analyses are summarised in Table 13.1. The first (Viney, Metcalfe, & Winter, 2005) revealed a medium post-treatment effect size (0.55) in favour of personal construct psychotherapy when compared with a non-active (e.g. waiting list) control condition, and a smaller, but still significant, post-treatment effect size (0.37) favouring personal construct psychotherapy in comparison with other active interventions (i.e., other forms of therapy). At follow-up, personal construct psychotherapy clients still showed greater improvement than those in non-active control conditions (effect size 0.48), but there was no significant difference between personal construct and other active interventions (effect size 0.06 in the direction of greater improvement in other interventions). The second meta-analysis by these authors (Metcalfe, Winter, & Viney, 2007) focused solely on those studies conducted in clinical settings, and revealed a similar pattern of results but with smaller effect sizes. Comparing personal construct psychotherapy with non-active controls, effect sizes favouring personal construct psychotherapy were 0.34 post-treatment and 0.30 at follow-up assessment. There was no significant difference in outcome between personal construct and other active interventions at either post-treatment (effect size 0.20) or follow-up (effect size 0.07) assessment. Finally, a comparison of pre-and post-therapy scores on outcome measures in personal construct psychotherapy clients indicated a medium effect size (0.68).

Another meta-analysis of personal construct psychotherapy outcome studies, by Holland, Neimeyer, Currier, and Berman (2007), used somewhat different criteria for inclusion of studies, for example excluding unpublished studies and those where personal construct psychotherapy seemed peripherally related to the treatment investigated, but not excluding those that did not fully report statistical results. Holland et al.

Table 13.1 Summary of meta-analyses of outcome of personal construct psychotherapy

Authors	N Studies	N Participants	Studies published	Population	ES Vs. alternative	ES Vs. no treatment
Viney et al. (2005)	18	1044	1975–2005	Heterogeneous	0.37 (−0.06 FU)	0.55 (0.48 FU)
Metcalfe et al. (2007)	23	1228	1985–2006	Heterogeneous	0.24 (0.07 FU) [0.36 non-clinical samples]	0.34 (0.30 FU) [1.04 non-clinical samples]
Holland et al. (2007)	22	1305	1975–2006	Heterogeneous	0.21 (0.13 FU)	0.38 (0.22 FU)

Notes N = number; ES = effect size; FU = follow-up

also considered all outcome measures used in each study rather than identifying the principal outcome measure. This meta-analysis revealed smaller effect sizes in favour of personal construct psychotherapy (0.38 and 0.22 for comparisons with non-active controls at post-treatment and follow-up respectively; and 0.21 and 0.13 for comparisons with active controls at post-treatment and follow-up respectively) than did Viney et al. (2005) and Metcalfe et al. (2007). For studies that included both post-treatment and follow-up assessments, treatment gains were maintained at the latter assessment. Interestingly, this meta-analysis also demonstrated that improvement was greater on symptom measures than on measures more focussed upon clients' construing. Holland and Neimeyer (2009) subsequently found that, although there was no significant difference in effect sizes between different categories of presenting problem, the largest effect size (0.85) was for problems involving anxiety and fear, and effect sizes were smaller when more severe problems were treated.

Since these meta-analyses, there have been a few more studies of the outcome of variants of personal and relational construct psychotherapy. Some of these concern dilemma-focussed intervention, adding to a growing body of research evidence concerning dilemmas and their resolution during psychotherapy. Comparing group cognitive-behavioural therapy plus an individual dilemma-focussed intervention with group plus individual cognitive-behavioural therapy in the treatment of depression, comparable and significant reduction in symptoms and psychological distress was found in both conditions, with large effect sizes (Feixas et al., 2016). There was also no difference between the two conditions in the number of participants who resolved their dilemmas, but dilemma resolution was associated with reduction of symptoms and psychological distress (Paz et al., 2019).

Two further studies have investigated the outcome of relational therapeutic approaches drawing upon personal construct psychotherapy. In the treatment of postpartum depression, Tavares Pinheiro et al. (2014) demonstrated significant reductions in depression during treatment, maintained at one-year follow-up, during both relational construct therapy (RCT) and cognitive-behavioural therapy, but reduction in anxiety during treatment only in the relational construct therapy condition. They conclude that 'RCT was more effective than CBT' (p. 65). Keshavarz-Afshar, Nosrati, Azad-Marzabadi, and Eslahi (2017) reported significant improvement on a range of outcome measures in couples receiving personal construct marital therapy but not in those in a waiting list control group.

There has been no research specifically looking at family therapy conducted from a personal and relational construct perspective. It is worth mentioning, though, that in a large scale mental health study, Crane and Payne (2011) asserted that 'family therapy proved to be substantially more cost-effective than individual or "mixed" psychotherapy'. Stratton (2010) concludes that family therapy has proven effectiveness for all those conditions for which it has been properly researched and that there is very substantial supportive evidence for its effectiveness from diverse research and clinical experience. Extensive clinical experience over many years would suggest that bringing personal and relational construct psychotherapy perspectives and methods into family work can only enhance its effectiveness (Procter, 2000, 2005, 2007).

The overall conclusion that can be drawn from all of the studies reviewed above is that personal construct psychotherapy is considerably more effective than non-active control conditions, and at least as effective as other, including cognitive-behavioural, therapies, at both post-treatment and follow-up assessments. Its effectiveness has now been recognised in two reviews of the psychotherapy research literature (Carr, 2009; Cooper, 2008), although in both of these it is classified as a cognitive-behavioural therapy!

Therapeutic Process

As we have seen, Carr (2009) and Cooper (2008) are not alone in classifying personal construct psychotherapy as a cognitive-behavioural approach. In view of this and other such classifications, as well as the equivalence in effectiveness of personal and relational construct and other psychotherapies, the question arises of whether this form of therapy does indeed constitute a distinctive approach. This question has been addressed in studies of the therapeutic process, what actually happens in therapy.

In one such study, Viney (1994) provided evidence of similarities between personal construct and person-centred therapy, and differences from rational-emotive therapy, in the way in which therapists responded to expressions by the client of 'distressed emotion'. Specifically, in personal construct and person-centred therapy, there was more acknowledgement by the therapist of the client's distress, and this tended to lead to further expressions of distress, whereas in rational-emotive therapy client distress tended to be regarded as a manifestation of irrationality. In a study comparing personal construct psychotherapy and rationalist cognitive therapy (Winter & Watson, 1999), analysis of session transcripts revealed that personal construct psychotherapists used less directive responses, but more interpretation, confrontation, and exploration, than did cognitive therapists. The transcripts also indicated that personal construct psychotherapists showed less negative attitudes towards their clients, and that their clients showed greater participation and more complex levels of 'processing' of their experiences. A more facilitative therapeutic process was apparent in the personal construct psychotherapy transcripts in those clients who construed less tightly, and who were more concerned with their inner worlds, while the reverse was the case in the cognitive therapy transcripts. This suggests a differential response of clients with different 'personal styles' of construing the world to these two types of therapy. On a questionnaire measure of facilitative therapeutic conditions, personal construct psychotherapists reported more positive feelings for their clients, and were less likely to assume that they understood their clients' views. Leading exponents of the two forms of therapy were also able blindly to differentiate between transcripts of the two types of therapy with a high degree of accuracy.

In addition to these studies of individual personal construct psychotherapy, there has been some research on the treatment process in personal construct group psychotherapy, most of it conducted on interpersonal transaction groups. Harter and Neimeyer (1995) demonstrated that incest survivors attending such groups viewed the group process as involving less conflict than did those attending 'process groups', focusing upon interactions within the group. A qualitative study of personal construct group psychotherapy for adolescents indicated that the major themes of the group sessions were trust, closeness to others, sexuality, and power (Viney, Truneckova, Weekes, & Oades, 1997). In another study of adolescents, who in this case were attending interpersonal transaction groups, Truneckova and Viney (2001) found that group members experienced increasing levels of belonging, understanding, and acceptance, together with greater self-understanding and acceptance. Their group leaders reported similar group processes, and that the adolescents increasingly questioned their construing, experimented with new behaviours, and developed self-validation and self-regard by understanding similarities and differences between group members. A small study of interpersonal transaction groups for clients diagnosed with borderline personality disorder indicated that they viewed their group sessions as characterised both by greater conflict and greater avoidance than did clients attending dialectical behaviour therapy groups (Winter, Watson, Gillman-Smith, Gilbert, & Acton, 2003). Although these findings differ somewhat from those of other studies of interpersonal transaction groups, the clients in these groups viewed their most important therapeutic events as episodes of self-disclosure, in contrast to dialectical behaviour therapy clients, whose most important events involved guidance. The authors characterise the interpersonal transaction groups as something of an 'interpersonal crucible' and the dialectical behaviour therapy groups as more akin to a classroom experience. A final study of interpersonal transaction groups focussed upon clients diagnosed with agoraphobia, finding that those who attended personal construct groups perceived the group as involving greater smoothness, less avoidance, and more experiences of self-understanding than did clients attending supportive groups conducted in the same format (Winter, Gournay, & Metcalfe, 1999; Winter & Metcalfe, 2005). Self-understanding was also identified as a therapeutic factor in personal construct psychotherapy groups for breast cancer survivors, as were identification with others, acceptance, instillation of hope, and self-disclosure (Lane & Viney, 2005b). An alternative approach to examining treatment process in personal construct group psychotherapy was adopted by Winter (1997), who asked therapists to indicate the interventions that they would make if confronted by particular group situations, presented in vignettes. It was found that, compared to those of group analysts, the anticipated interventions of personal construct psychotherapists made less reference to the therapists' views of the meaning of group events.

A further significant question concerning the process of personal and relational construct psychotherapy is whether this involves demonstrable reconstruction. Such reconstruction is evident in many case studies, several of which have used repertory grid technique to monitor the reconstruing process (Winter, 1992). Although in larger-scale outcome studies, as we have seen, Holland et al. (2007) found less change on measures of construing than on those of symptoms, significant reconstruction is still apparent in most of these studies. Furthermore, symptom reduction in dilemma-focused intervention has been found to be accompanied by self-narrative reconstruction and dilemma resolution (Fernandes, 2007; Montesano, Gonçalves, & Feixas 2016; Paz et al., 2019; Senra, 2010), and resolution of conflicts of construing during personal construct psychotherapy has also been observed by Winter and Bell (2020).

It can be concluded that the above studies provide evidence of the distinctiveness of personal and relational construct psychotherapy as well as revealing particular aspects of the therapeutic process in this form of therapy that, consistent with its theoretical basis, are related to positive treatment outcome.

Implications

Research

The resistance, at least initially, of many personal and relational construct psychotherapists to play what was seen as the evidence-based practice game may be regarded as a suicidal stance, at least as regards the survival of this form of therapy. Aspects of this stance, such as a resistance to using symptom-based outcome measures or quantitative research designs, also may display a profound lack of sociality not only with health service commissioners but also with clients, since both are likely to construe successful treatment in terms of degree of symptom reduction (Winter, 2015a). In any case, symptom-based measures can be complemented by measures of construing and personal meaning, and quantitative and qualitative approaches (arguably neither of which is more compatible with a constructivist position than the other, despite the contrary assertions of some constructivists) can be used in conjunction, a prime example of this being the repertory grid. This is evident in much of the research that we have reviewed, the results of which indicate that personal construct psychotherapy should now be able to join the ranks of evidence-based therapies.

While such research should continue, particularly on the more under-researched relational construct psychotherapy, this is not altogether easy in a climate in which funding both for clinical services and research is likely to be predominantly directed towards therapies that are already accepted as evidence-based. This is despite Roth and Fonagy's (2005) assertion that 'Where the appropriate research has not yet been done, the absence of evidence for efficacy is not evidence for ineffectiveness, and valuable approaches that offer appropriate and demonstrably clinically effective care should not perish for lack of funding' (p. 53). However, in the absence of research grants and of large numbers of clients receiving these therapies as financial support for them is cut, options are still available for personal and relational construct psychotherapists to add to the evidence base for their approach. These include adopting a practice-based evidence approach by forming practice research networks to pool outcome data on large numbers of clients; and using rigorous single case research designs, such as hermeneutic single-case efficacy design (Elliott, 2002), as demonstrated in Senra's (2010) research on dilemma-focused intervention.

Clinical Services and Guidelines

The process of inclusion of a therapy in treatment guidelines may not be entirely straightforward, involving as it does many influences, including group processes in guideline panels (Pagliari & Grimshaw, 2002). However, we are confident that personal and relational construct psychotherapy will eventually find its way into such guidelines, particularly if its practitioners overcome their aversion to carrying out research on client groups defined in terms of psychiatric diagnostic categories (which would simply involve speaking the language of health service commissioners rather than necessarily implying acceptance that these categories reflect real disease entities). They may also need to overcome their resistance to slick marketing, which arguably, rather than superior effectiveness, is the defining characteristic of those therapies that are favoured by guideline development panels.

Until such time, however, how can personal and relational construct psychotherapists survive when faced with directors or funders of clinical services who limit the approaches that they are prepared to support to therapies accepted as evidence-based? One solution would simply be to argue, on the basis of the research that we have presented, that this treatment approach *is* evidence-based. However, if only approaches that are included in official treatment guidelines, such as those of NICE, are regarded as acceptable, there are still solutions available to personal and relational construct psychotherapists. One is, at least as a temporary strategy, to swallow their pride and purism and to claim that their approach is a constructivist variant of some officially accepted form of therapy, such as cognitive or systemic therapy. Descriptions of personal construct psychotherapy by authors such as Cooper (2008) and Carr (2009) could even be used to justify such a construction! With their tendency to subsume any approach that is effective, even Buddhism, cognitive-behavioural therapists would be likely to welcome personal and relational construct psychotherapy to their ranks. After all, Beck is reported to have said that 'if it works, it's CBT' (Beutler, 2017). Another solution for personal and relational construct psychotherapists would be to use some of the techniques that we have described as part of a more accepted therapy. This is similar to the approach taken by O'Connor (2015) with his 'constructionist clinical psychology for cognitive behaviour therapy', although this fails to exploit fully the potential of the techniques concerned.

As well as the direct provision of therapy, a further way in which personal and relational construct psychotherapists could contribute to a clinical service, as we have seen in Chapter 12, is by fostering the integration of a range of other therapies as alternative approaches that could be matched to clients' construing.

Training

As a distinctive and evidence-based therapy, personal and relational construct psychotherapy can in its own right be a subject for training programmes. If this is consistent with a country's psychotherapy regulations (as has, for example, been the case in the UK and Italy), such programmes can provide a route to qualification as a registered psychotherapist. As indicated in Chapter 11, training in personal and relational construct psychotherapy is likely to have distinctive features, for example relating to a focus on reflexivity.

Personal and relational construct psychotherapy, or particular techniques derived from it, can also very appropriately be included in generic training programmes for a range of health professionals. For example, in the UK, clinical psychology training programmes are required to equip trainees with 'knowledge and practice in at least two evidence-based models of formal psychological interventions, of which one must be cognitive behaviour therapy' and for which 'skills must be evidenced against a competence framework' (British Psychological Society, 2019, pp. 17–18). If it is regarded as evidence-based, and if a competence framework is produced, there is no reason why personal and relational construct psychotherapy could not be one of the interventions concerned. A limiting factor, however, is one of various vicious cycles that stunt the growth of any therapies that are not favoured in treatment guidelines, making the therapeutic rich richer and the poor poorer. This is that few therapeutic services may allow provision of such therapies, thus reducing opportunities for supervised practice placements, consequently limiting the number of students who can be trained in the approaches concerned and therefore the number of programmes that will be willing to offer such training.

Even if a generic training programme does not offer a fully-fledged training in personal and relational construct psychotherapy, techniques derived from this approach may be usefully taught to its students. Analogously to the constructive alternativist approach to the organisation of a clinical service (Winter, 1985b), a whole generic training programme can also be organised in terms of the philosophy underlying personal and relational construct psychotherapy, as in the clinical psychology training programme described by Winter (1999).

Conclusions

In this book we have presented a therapeutic approach that is primarily based upon, but also extends, particularly in the relational sphere, George Kelly's personal construct psychotherapy. It therefore derives from a form of psychotherapy that offers a distinctive alternative to, and has been shown to be at least as effective as, other major therapeutic models. It is a very flexible approach, as attested by its successful application with a very wide range of client groups across the age spectrum in individual, group, couple, and family therapy settings as well as with wider social systems. Although our primary focus in this book has been with work in 'mental health' settings, the applicability of the approach is by no means limited to such settings but extends, for example, to work with clients in forensic settings (Horley, 2003), people with physical illnesses and disabilities (Viney, 1983), those with intellectual disabilities (Davis & Cunningham, 1985), people diagnosed with autistic spectrum disorders (Procter, 2000, 2001) and people experiencing dementia (Morris, 2000, 2004; Robbins, 2005).

At the beginning of the twenty-first century, we live in a world in which all too often it seems that the emphasis is on certain truths (albeit some of which may be 'faked'), simplistic approaches to the solution of problems, extreme views (including preemptive or constellatory negative construing of people who are different), and a failure to attempt to understand those with opposing views. In such a climate, which is as evident in services for people with psychological problems as in other domains, a therapeutic approach which does justice to the complexity of people's predicaments and social contexts and, above all, is profoundly credulous and respectful of the views of others is surely to be welcomed.

Notes

1. A distinction that should be noted here is that between efficacy, the outcome of a therapy in a research trial, and effectiveness, its outcome in routine clinical practice (Cochrane, 1972). As we shall see, the former does not necessarily imply the latter.
2. The internal validity of a study refers to its methodological adequacy, whereas its external validity concerns the applicability of its findings to the real world.
3. In studies that compare a group receiving an intervention with a control group, the effect size is usually calculated as the difference between the means of the two groups on an outcome measure divided by the standard deviation of the control group or the pooled standard deviation of the two groups. In studies that examine change over the course of treatment, the effect size is generally calculated as the difference between pre- and post-treatment means on an outcome measure divided by the pre-treatment standard deviation.

References

Alexander, P. C., Neimeyer, R. A., & Follette, V. M. (1991). Group therapy for women sexually abused as children: A controlled study and investigation of individual differences. *Journal of Interpersonal Violence, 6*, 218–231.

Alexander, P. C., Neimeyer, R. A., Follette, V., Moore, M. K., & Harter, S. (1989). A comparison of group treatments of women sexually abused as children. *Journal of Consulting and Clinical Psychology, 57*, 479–483.

Annesi, J. J. (2002). Goal-setting protocol in adherence to exercise by Italian adults. *Perceptual and Motor Skills, 94*, 453–458.

Audin, K., Mellor-Clark, J., Barkham, M., Margison, F., McGrath, G., Lewis, S., & Parry, G. (2001). Practice research networks for effective psychological therapies. *Journal of Mental Health, 10*, 241–251.

Bannister, D., Adams-Webber, J. R., Penn, W. I., & Radley, A. R. (1975). Reversing the process of thought disorder: A serial validation experiment. *British Journal of Social and Clinical Psychology, 14*, 169–180.

Barkham, M., Evans, C., Margison, F., McGrath, G., Mellor-Clark, J., Milne, D., & Connell, J. (1998). The rationale for developing and implementing core outcome batteries for routine use in service settings and psychotherapy outcome research. *Journal of Mental Health, 7,* 35–47.

Barkham, M., & Mellor-Clark, J. (2000). Rigour and relevance: The role of practice-based evidence in the psychological therapies. In N. Rowland & G. Goss (Eds.), *Evidence-Based Counselling and Psychological Therapies* (pp. 126–144). London: Routledge.

Beail, N., & Parker, S. (1991). Group fixed-role therapy: A clinical application. *International Journal of Personal Construct Psychology, 4,* 85–96.

Beutler, L. Psychotherapy researcher (Personal communication, 2017).

Bohart, A. C. (2000). Paradigm clash: Empirically supported treatments versus empirically supported psychotherapy practice. *Psychotherapy Research, 10,* 488–493.

Bohart, A. C., O'Hara, M., & Leitner, L. M. (1998). Empirically violated treatments: Disenfranchisement of humanistic and other therapies. *Psychotherapy Research, 8,* 141–157.

Borkovec, T. D., & Castonguay, L. G. (1998). What is the scientific meaning of empirically supported therapy? *Journal of Consulting and Clinical Psychology, 66,* 136–142.

Botella, L. (2000). Personal Construct Psychology, constructivism, and psychotherapy research. In J. W. Scheer (Ed.), *The Person in Society: Challenges to a Constructivist Theory* (pp. 362–372). Giessen, Germany: Psychosozial-Verlag.

Botella, L., & Feixas, G. (1992–1993). The autobiographical group: A tool for the reconstruction of past life experience with the aged. *International Journal of Aging and Human Development, 36,* 303–319.

British Psychological Society. (2019). *Standards for the Accreditation of Doctoral Programmes in Clinical Psychology.* Leicester, UK: British Psychological Society.

Button, E. (1987). Construing people or weight?: An eating disorders group. In R. A. Neimeyer & G. J. Neimeyer (Eds.), *Personal Construct Therapy Casebook* (pp. 230–244). New York: Springer.

Caine, T. M., Wijesinghe, O. B. A., & Winter, D. A. (1981). *Personal Styles in Neurosis: Implications for Small Group Psychotherapy and Behaviour Therapy.* London: Routledge and Kegan Paul.

Carr, A. (2009). *What Works with Children, Adolescents, and Adults? A Review of Research on the Effectiveness of Psychotherapy.* London: Routledge.

Centre for Economic Performance. (2006). *The Depression Report: A New Deal for Depression and Anxiety Disorders.* London: London School of Economics and Political Science.

Chambless, D. L., Baker, M. J., Baucom, D. H., Beutler, L. E., Calhoun, K. S., & Daiuto, A. (1998). Update on empirically validated therapies, II. *The Clinical Psychologist, 51,* 3–16.

Chambless, D. L., & Hollon, S. D. (1998). Defining empirically supported therapies. *Journal of Consulting and Clinical Psychology, 66,* 7–18.

Chambless, D. L., & Ollendick, T. H. (2001). Empirically supported psychological interventions: Controversies and evidence. *Annual Review of Psychology, 52,* 685–716.

Cochrane, A. (1972). *Effectiveness and Efficiency: Random Reflection on Health Services.* London: Nuffield Provincial Hospitals Trust.

Cohen, J. (1988). *Statistical Power Analyses for the Behavioral Sciences.* Hillsdale, NJ: Lawrence Erlbaum.

Cooper, M. (2008). *Essential Research Findings in Counselling and Psychotherapy: The Facts are Friendly.* London: Sage.

Crane, D. R., & Payne, S. H. (2011). Individual versus family psychotherapy in managed care: Comparing the costs of treatment by the mental health professionals. *Journal of Marital and Family Therapy, 37,* 273–289.

Davis, H., & Cunningham, C. (1985). Mental handicap: People in context. In E. Button (Ed.), *Personal Construct Theory and Mental Health* (pp. 246–261). London: Croom Helm.

Department of Health. (1996). *Research and Development: Towards an Evidence-Based Health Service.* London: HMSO.

Dixon-Woods, M., Shaw, R. L., Agarwal, S., & Smith, J. A. (2004). The problem of appraising qualitative research. *BMJ Quality and Safety, 13,* 223–225.

Eccles, M., & Mason, J. (2001). How to develop cost-conscious guidelines. *Health Technology Assessment, 5,* 1–69.

Edwards, D. G. A., Dattilio, F. M., & Bromley, D. B. (2004). Developing evidence-based practice: The role of case-based research. *Professional Psychology: Research and Practice, 35,* 589–597.

Elliott, R. (2002). Hermeneutic single-case efficacy design. *Psychotherapy Research, 12,* 1–21.

Elliott, R., Fischer, C. T., & Rennie, D. L. (1999). Evolving guidelines for publication of qualitative research studies in psychology and related fields. *British Journal of Clinical Psychology, 38,* 215–229.

Evesham, M., & Fransella, F. (1985). Stuttering relapse: The effects of a combined speech and psychological reconstruction programme. *British Journal of Disorders of Communication, 20,* 237–248.

Feixas, G., Bados, A., Garcia-Grau, E., Paz, C., Montesano, A., Compañ, V., & Lana, F. (2016). A dilemma-focused intervention for depression: A multi-center, randomized controlled trial with a 3-month follow-up. *Depression and Anxiety, 33,* 862–869.

Feixas, G., & Compañ, V. (2016). Dilemma-focused intervention for unipolar depression: A treatment manual. *BMC Psychiatry, 16,* 235.

Fernandes, E. M. (2007). When what I wish makes me worse…to make coherence flexible. *Psychology and Psychotherapy, 80,* 165–180.

Foster, H., & Viney, L. L. (2005). Personal construct workshops for women experiencing menopause. In D. A. Winter & L. L. Viney (Eds.), *Personal Construct Psychotherapy: Advances in Theory, Practice and Research* (pp. 320–332). London: Croom Helm.

Giddens, A. (1991). *Modernity and Self-Identity: Self and Society in the Late Modern Age.* Redwood City: Stanford University Press.

Gold, J. R. (1995). The place of process-oriented psychotherapies in an outcome-oriented psychology and society. *Applied and Preventive Psychology, 4,* 61–74.

Green, D., & Latchford, G. (2012). *Maximising the Benefits of Psychotherapy: A Practice-Based Evidence Approach.* Chichester, UK: Wiley.

Guyatt, G. H., Sackett, D. L., Sinclair, J. C., Hayward, R., Cook, D. J., Cook, R. J., … & Jaeschke, R. (1995). Users' guides to the medical literature: IX. A method for grading healthcare recommendations. *JAMA, 274,* 1800–1804.

Harter, S. L., & Neimeyer, R. A. (1995). Long term effects of child sexual abuse: Toward a constructivist theory of trauma and its treatment. In R. A. Neimyer & G. J. Neimeyer (Eds.), *Advances in Personal Construct Psychology* (Vol. 3, pp. 229–269). Greenwich, CT: JAI Press.

Haugli, L., Steen, E., Laerum, E., Finset, A., & Nygaard, R. (2000). Agency orientation and chronic musculoskeletal pain: Effects of a group learning program based on the personal construct theory. *Clinical Journal of Pain, 16,* 281–289.

Haugli, L., Steen, E., Laerum, E., Finset, A., & Nygaard, R. (2001). Learning to have less pain—Is it possible? A one-year follow-up study of the effects of a personal construct group learning programme on patients with chronic musculoskeletal pain. *Patient Education and Counseling, 45,* 111–118.

Holland, J. M., & Neimeyer, R. A. (2009). The efficacy of personal construct therapy as a function of the type and severity of the presenting problem. *Journal of Constructivist Psychology, 22,* 170–185.

Holland, J. M., Neimeyer, R. A., Currier, J. M., & Berman, J. S. (2007). The efficacy of personal construct therapy: A comprehensive review. *Journal of Clinical Psychology, 63,* 93–107.

Holmes, D., Murray, S. J., Perron, A., & Rail, G. (2006). Deconstructing the evidence-based discourse in health sciences: Truth, power and fascism. *International Journal of Evidence-Based Healthcare, 4,* 180–186.

Horley, J. (Ed.). (2003). *Personal Construct Perspectives on Forensic Psychology.* Hove, UK: Brunner-Routledge.

Horley, J., & Francoeur, A. (2003). *Domestic assault from a PCP perspective.* Paper presented at XVth. International Congress of Personal Construct Psychology, Huddersfield, UK.

Howard, K. I., Orlinsky, D. E., & Lueger, R. J. (1995). The design of clinically relevant outcome research: Some considerations and an example. In M. Aveline & D. A. Shapiro (Eds.), *Research Foundations of Psychotherapy Practice* (pp. 3–48). Chichester, UK: Wiley.

Humphreys, C. L., Dutile, R., & Leitner, L. (2001). *Empirical support for experiential personal construct therapy: A common 'factor analysis'.* Paper presented at XIVth. International Congress of Personal Construct Psychology, Wollongong, Australia.

Jackson, S. (1992). A PCT therapy group for adolescents. In P. Maitland & D. Brennan (Eds.), *Personal Construct Theory Deviancy and Social Work* (pp. 163–174). London: Inner London Probation Service/Centre for Personal Construct Psychology.

Karst, T. O., & Trexler, L. D. (1970). Initial study using fixed role and rational-emotive therapy in treating speaking anxiety. *Journal of Consulting and Clinical Psychology, 34,* 360–366.

Kazdin, A. E. (1994). Methodology, design, and evaluation in psychotherapy research. In A. E. Bergin & S. L. Garfield (Eds.), *Handbook of Psychotherapy and Behavior Change* (pp. 19–71). Oxford: Wiley.

Kelly, G. A. (1955). *The Psychology of Personal Constructs. Vol. I, II.* New York: Norton (2nd printing: 1991, London and New York: Routledge).

Keshavarz-Afshar, H., Nosrati, F., Azad-Marzabadi, E., & Eslahi, N. (2017). The effectiveness of personal construct therapy on marital satisfaction. *Iran Red Crescent Medical Journal, 19,* 1–7.

Lambert, M. J. (1992). Psychotherapy outcome research: Implications for integrative and eclectic therapists. In J. C. Norcross & M. R. Goldfried (Eds.), *Handbook of Psychotherapy Integration* (pp. 94–129). New York: Basic Books.

Lambert, M. J., Hansen, N. B., & Finch, A. E. (2001). Patient-focused research: Using patient outcome data to enhance treatment effects. *Journal of Consulting and Clinical Psychology, 69*, 159–172.

Lambert, M. J., & Ogles, B. M. (2004). The efficacy and effectiveness of psychotherapy. In M. J. Lambert (Ed.), *Bergin and Garfield's Handbook of Psychotherapy and Behavior Change* (pp. 139–193). New York: Wiley.

Landfield, A. W. (1979). Exploring socialization through the interpersonal transaction group. In P. Stringer & D. Bannister (Eds.), *Constructs of Sociality and Individuality* (pp. 133–152). London: Academic Press.

Landfield, A. W., & Rivers, P. C. (1975). An introduction to interpersonal transaction and rotating dyads. *Psychotherapy: Theory, Research and Practice, 12*, 365–373.

Lane, L. G., & Viney, L. L. (2005b). The effects of personal construct group therapy on breast cancer survivors. *Journal of Consulting and Clinical Psychology, 73*, 284–292.

Layard, R. (2006). *Happiness: Lessons from a New Science.* Harmondsworth, UK: Penguin.

Lira, F. T., Nay, R., McCullough, J. P., & Etkin, M. W. (1975). Relative effects of modeling and role playing in the treatment of avoidance behaviors. *Journal of Consulting and Clinical Psychology, 43*, 608–618.

Lovenfosse, M., & Viney, L. L. (1999). Understanding and helping mothers of children with 'special needs' using personal construct group work. *Community Mental Health Journal, 5*, 431–442.

Luborsky, L., Diguer, L., Seligman, D. A., Rosenthal, R., Krause, E. D., Johnson, S., … & Schweizer, E. (1999). The researcher's own therapy allegiances: A "wild card" in comparisons of treatment efficacy. *Clinical Psychology: Science and Practice, 6*(1), 95–106.

Mackay, H. C., Barkham, M., Rees, A., & Stiles, W. B. (2003). Appraisal of published reviews of research on psychotherapy and counselling with adults 1990–1998. *Journal of Consulting and Clinical Psychology, 71*, 652–656.

Malins, G. L., Couchman, L., Viney, L. L., & Grenyer, B. F. S. (2004). Time to talk: Evaluation of a staff-resident quality time intervention on the perception of staff in aged care. *Clinical Psychologist, 8*, 48–52.

Margison, F. R., Barkham, M., Evans, C., McGrath, G., Clark, J. M., Audin, K., & Connell, J. (2000). Measurement and psychotherapy: Evidence-based practice and practice-based evidence. *British Journal of Psychiatry, 177*(2), 123–130.

Messer, S. B. (2001). Empirically supported treatments: What's a nonbehaviorist to do? In B. D. Slife, R. N. Williams, & S. H. Barlow (Eds.), *Critical Issues in Psychotherapy: Translating New Ideas into Practice* (pp. 3–19). London: Sage.

Metcalfe, C., Winter, D., & Viney, L. (2007). The effectiveness of personal construct psychotherapy in clinical practice: A systematic review and meta-analysis. *Psychotherapy Research, 17*, 431–442.

Miles, A., Grey, J., Polychronis, A., & Melchiorri, C. (2002). Critical advances in the evaluation and development of clinical care. *Journal of Evaluation in Clinical Practice, 8*, 87–102.

Montesano, A., Gonçalves, M. M., & Feixas, G. (2016). Self-narrative reconstruction after dilemma-focused intervention for depression: A comparison of good and poor outcome cases. *Psychotherapy Research, 27*, 112–126.

Morris, J. B. (1977). Appendix 1: The prediction and measurement of change in a psychotherapy group using the repertory grid. In F. Fransella & D. Bannister (Eds.), *A Manual for Repertory Grid Technique* (pp. 120–148). London: Academic Press.

Morris, C. (2000). Working with people: Making sense of dementia. *Journal of Dementia Care, 8*(4), 23–25.

Morris, C. (2004). Personal construct psychology and person centred care. In G. M. M. Jones & B. M. L. Miesen (Eds.), *Care-Giving in Dementia: Researches and Applications* (Vol. 3, pp. 65–90). Hove and New York: Brunner-Routledge.

Nagae, N., & Nedate, K. (2001). Comparison of constructive cognitive and rational cognitive psychotherapies for students with social anxiety. *Constructivism in the Human Sciences, 6*, 41–49.

Neimeyer, R. A., & Neimeyer, G. J. (Eds.). (1987). *Personal Construct Therapy Casebook*. New York: Springer.

NICE. (2014). *The Guidelines Manual*. London: National Institute for Health and Clinical Excellence.

O'Connor, P. (2015). *A Constructionist Clinical Psychology for Cognitive Behaviour Therapy*. Hove, UK: Routledge.

Ogilvie, D., Egan, M., Hamilton, V., & Petticrew, M. (2005). Systematic reviews of health effects of social interventions: 2. Best available evidence: How low should you go? *Journal of Epidemiology and Community Health, 59*, 886–892.

Orlinsky, D. E., Rønnestad, M. H., & Willutzki, U. (2004). Fifty years of psychotherapy process-outcome research: Continuity and change. In M. J. Lambert (Ed.), *Bergin and Garfield's Handbook of Psychotherapy and Behavior Change* (pp. 307–389). New York: Wiley.

Pagliari, C., & Grimshaw, J. (2002). Impact of group structure and process on multidisciplinary evidence-based guideline development: An observational study. *Journal of Evaluation in Clinical Practice, 8,* 145–153.

Parry, G., & Richardson, A. (1996). *NHS Psychotherapy Services in England: Review of Strategic Policy.* London: NHS Executive.

Paz, C., Montesano, A., Winter, D., & Feixas, G. (2019). Cognitive conflict resolution during psychotherapy: Its impact on depressive symptoms and psychological distress. *Psychotherapy Research, 29,* 45–57.

Pekkala, D., & Dave, B. (2005). Evaluation. In P. Cummins (Ed.), *Working with Anger* (pp. 199–212). London: Wiley.

Pinheiro, R. T., Botella, L., de Avila Quevedo, L., Pinheiro, K. A. T., Jansen, K., Osório, C. M., … & da Silva, R. A. (2014). Maintenance of the effects of cognitive behavioral and relational constructivist psychotherapies in the treatment of women with postpartum depression: A randomized clinical trial. *Journal of Constructivist Psychology, 27,* 59–68.

Procter, H. G. (2000). Autism and family therapy: A personal construct approach. In S. Powell (Ed.), *Helping Children with Autism to Learn* (pp. 63–77). London: David Fulton.

Procter, H. G. (2001). Personal construct psychology and autism. *Journal of Constructivist Psychology, 14,* 105–124.

Procter, H. G. (2005). Techniques of personal construct family therapy. In D. A. Winter & L. L. Viney (Eds.), *Personal Construct Psychotherapy: Advances in Theory, Practice and Research* (pp. 94–108). London: Whurr.

Procter, H. G. (2007). Construing within the family. In R. Butler & D. Green (Eds.), *The Child Within: Taking the Young Person's Perspective by Applying Personal Construct Theory* (2nd ed., pp. 190–206). Chichester, UK: Wiley.

Rawlins, M. (2008). De Testimonio: On the evidence for decisions about the use of therapeutic interventions. *Clinical Medicine, 8,* 579–588.

Robbins, S. (2005). Looking forward towards the end—Working with older people. In D. A. Winter & L. L. Viney (Eds.), *Personal Construct Psychotherapy: Advances in Theory, Practice and Research* (pp. 296–309). London: Croom Helm.

Roth, A., & Fonagy, P. (1996). *What Works for Whom? A Critical Review of Psychotherapy Research.* New York: Guilford.

Roth, A., & Fonagy, P. (2005). *What Works for Whom? A Critical Review of Psychotherapy Research* (2nd ed.). New York: Guilford.

Senra, J. (2010). *Personal reconstruction processes in personal construct therapy for implicative dilemmas.* Unpublished doctoral thesis, University of Minho.

Sewell, K. W., & Ovaert, L. B. (1997). *Group treatment of post-traumatic stress in incarcerated adolescents: Structural and narrative impacts on the permeability of self-construction.* Paper presented at XII International Congress of Personal Construct Psychology, Seattle, WA.

Sheehan, M. J. (1985). A personal construct study of depression. *British Journal of Medical Psychology, 58,* 119–128.

Slavin, R. E. (1995). Best evidence synthesis: An intelligent alternative to meta-analysis. *Journal of Clinical Epidemiology, 48,* 9–18.

Slife, B. D. (2004). Theoretical challenges to therapy practice and research: The constraint of naturalism. In M. J. Lambert (Ed.), *Bergin and Garfield's Handbook of Psychotherapy and Behavior Change* (pp. 44–83). New York: Wiley.

Spencer, L., Ritchie, J., & O'Connor, W. (2003). Analysis: Practices, principles and processes. In J. Ritchie & J. Lewis (Eds.), *Qualitative Research Practice: A Guide for Social Science Students and Researchers* (pp. 199–218). London: Sage.

Stiles, W. B., & Shapiro, D. A. (1989). Abuse of the drug metaphor in psychotherapy process-outcome research. *Clinical Psychology Review, 9,* 521–543.

Stratton, P. (2010). *The Evidence Base of Systemic Family and Couples Therapy.* London: Association for Family Therapy.

Task Force on Promotion and Dissemination of Psychological Procedures. (1995). Training in and dissemination of empirically-validated psychological treatments. *The Clinical Psychologist, 48,* 3–23.

Trinder, L. (2000a). A critical appraisal of evidence-based practice. In L. Trinder & S. Reynolds (Eds.), *Evidence-Based Practice: A Critical Appraisal* (pp. 212–241). Oxford, UK: Blackwell Science.

Trinder, L. (2000b). Introduction: The context of evidence-based practice. In L. Trinder & S. Reynolds (Eds.), *Evidence-Based Practice: A Critical Appraisal* (pp. 1–16). Oxford, UK: Blackwell Science.

Truneckova, D., & Viney, L. L. (2001). Can personal construct group work be an effective intervention with troubled adolescents? *Australian Journal of Psychology, 53*(supplement), 106.

Truneckova, D., & Viney, L. L. (2011). Evaluating personal construct group work with troubled adolescents. *Journal of Counseling and Development, 85,* 450–460.

Viney, L. L. (1983). *Images of Illness.* Melbourne, Australia: Krieger.

Viney, L. L. (1994). Sequences of emotional distress expressed by clients and acknowledged by therapists: Are they associated more with some therapists than others? *British Journal of Clinical Psychology, 33,* 469–481.

Viney, L. L., Benjamin, Y. N., & Preston, C. A. (1989). An evaluation of personal construct therapy with the elderly. *British Journal of Medical Psychology, 62,* 35–41.

Viney, L. L., Clarke, A. M., Bunn, T. A., & Benjamin, Y. N. (1985a). An evaluation of three crisis intervention programs for general hospital patients. *British Journal of Medical Psychology, 58,* 75–86.

Viney, L. L., Clarke, A. M., Bunn, T. A., & Benjamin, Y. N. (1985b). The effect of a hospital-based counselling service on the physical recovery of surgical and medical patients. *General Hospital Psychiatry, 7,* 294–301.

Viney, L. L., Clarke, A. M., Bunn, T. A., & Benjamin, Y. N. (1985c). Crisis-intervention counselling: An evaluation of long- and short-term effects. *Journal of Counseling Psychology, 32,* 29–39.

Viney, L. L., Crooks, L., & Walker, B. M. (1995). Anxiety in community-based AIDS caregivers before and after personal construct counseling. *Journal of Clinical Psychology, 51,* 274–280.

Viney, L. L., & Henry, R. M. (2002). Evaluating personal construct and psychodynamic group work with adolescent offenders and non-offenders. In R. A. Neimeyer & G. J. Neimeyer (Eds.), *Advances in Personal Construct Psychology: New Directions and Perspectives* (pp. 259–294). Westport, CT: Praeger.

Viney, L. L., Henry, R. M., & Campbell, J. (2001). The impact of group work on offender adolescents. *Journal of Counseling and Development, 79,* 373–381.

Viney, L. L., Metcalfe, C., & Winter, D. A. (2005). The effectiveness of personal construct psychotherapy: A systematic review and meta-analysis. In D. A. Winter & L. L. Viney (Eds.), *Personal Construct Psychotherapy: Advances in Theory, Practice and Research* (pp. 347–364). London: Whurr.

Viney, L. L., Truneckova, D., Weekes, P., & Oades, L. (1997). Personal construct group work with school-based adolescents: Reduction of risk-taking. *Journal of Constructivist Psychology, 9,* 169–185.

Wampold, B. E. (2001). *The Great Psychotherapy Debate: Models, Methods, and Findings.* Mahwah, NJ: Lawrence Erlbaum.

Watson, S., & Winter, D. A. (2005). A process and outcome study of personal construct psychotherapy. In D. A. Winter & L. L. Viney (Eds.), *Personal Construct Psychotherapy: Advances in Theory, Practice and Research* (pp. 335–346). London: Whurr.

Westen, D., Novotny, C. M., & Thompson-Brenner, H. (2004). The empirical status of empirically supported psychotherapies. *Psychological Bulletin, 130,* 631–663.

Winter, D. A. (1985b). Personal styles, constructive alternativism and the provision of a therapeutic service. *British Journal of Medical Psychology, 58,* 129–136.

Winter, D. A. (1992). *Personal Construct Psychology in Clinical Practice: Theory, Research and Applications.* London: Routledge.

Winter, D. A. (1997). Personal construct theory perspectives on group psychotherapy. In P. Denicolo & M. Pope (Eds.), *Sharing Understanding and Practice* (pp. 210–221). Farnborough, UK: EPCA Publications.

Winter, D. A. (1999). Psychological problems: Alternative perspectives on their explanation and treatment. In D. Messer & F. Jones (Eds.), *Psychology and Social Care* (pp. 362–382). London: Jessica Kingsley.

Winter, D. A. (2003c). Repertory grid technique as a psychotherapy research measure. *Psychotherapy Research, 13,* 25–42.

Winter, D. A. (2003d). The evidence base for personal construct psychotherapy. In F. Fransella (Ed.), *International Handbook of Personal Construct Psychology* (pp. 265–272). Chichester, UK: Wiley.

Winter, D. A. (2007b). Improving access or denying choice? *Mental Health and Learning Disabilities Research and Practice, 4,* 73–82.

Winter, D. (2010). Allegiance revisited. *European Journal of Psychotherapy and Counselling, 12,* 3–9.

Winter, D. A. (2015a). What does the future hold for personal construct psychology? In J. D. Raskin & S. K. Bridges (Eds.), *Studies in Meaning 5: Perturbing the Status Quo in Constructivist Psychology* (pp. 28–63). New York: Pace University Press.

Winter, D. A., & Bell, R. C. (2020/in press). A method for measuring conflict in repertory grid data: A review of research. *Journal of Constructivist Psychology.* https://doi.org/10.1080/10720537.2020.1805073.

Winter, D. A., Gournay, K., & Metcalfe, C. (1999). A personal construct psychotherapy intervention for agoraphobia: Theoretical and empirical basis, treatment process and outcome. In J. M. Fisher & D. J. Savage (Eds.), *Beyond Experimentation into Meaning* (pp. 146–160). Lostock Hall, UK: EPCA Publications.

Winter, D. A., Gournay, K. J. M., Metcalfe, C., & Rossotti, N. (2006). Expanding agoraphobics' horizons: An investigation of the effectiveness of a personal construct psychotherapy intervention. *Journal of Constructivist Psychology, 19,* 1–29.

Winter, D. A., & Metcalfe, C. (2005). From constriction to experimentation: Personal construct psychotherapy for agoraphobia. In D. A. Winter & L. L. Viney (Eds.), *Personal Construct Psychotherapy: Advances in Theory, Practice and Research* (pp. 148–157). London: Whurr.

Winter, D., Sireling, L., Riley, T., Metcalfe, C., Quaite, A., & Bhandari, S. (2007). A controlled trial of personal construct psychotherapy for deliberate self-harm. *Psychology and Psychotherapy, 80,* 23–37.

Winter, D. A., & Viney, L. (Eds.). (2005). *Personal Construct Psychotherapy: Recent Advances in Theory, Practice and Research.* London: Whurr.

Winter, D. A., & Watson, S. (1999). Personal construct psychotherapy and the cognitive therapies: Different in theory but can they be differentiated in practice? *Journal of Constructivist Psychology, 12,* 1–22.

Winter, D. A., Watson, S., Gillman-Smith, I., Gilbert, N., & Acton, T. (2003). Border crossing: A personal construct therapy approach for clients with a diagnosis of borderline personality disorder. In G. Chiari & M. L. Nuzzo (Eds.), *Psychological Constructivism and the Social World* (pp. 342–352). Milan, Italy: FrancoAngeli.

Appendices

Appendix A: Useful Questions in Interviewing Families and Children

QUESTION	RATIONALE
1. Greeting	
Did you find the place all right?	Orients to time and context just before session
What would you have been doing otherwise?	
2. Members' lives and interests	
What do you like doing? How do you spend your time?	Interests, activities: what spontaneously motivates
Which school do you go to? Who is your teacher?	
How's your relationship with your teacher?	
What do you like best? What are you best at?	
What would you like to be doing in a couple of years' time?	
Who are your best friends? What do you like doing together?	

(continued)

H. Procter and D. A. Winter, *Personal and Relational Construct Psychotherapy*,
Palgrave Texts in Counselling and Psychotherapy,
https://doi.org/10.1007/978-3-030-52177-6

(continued)

QUESTION	RATIONALE
What does your Dad do for his work?	Knowledge of each other's interests, activities, and roles
Have you been to your Mum's place of work?	
What do they like doing in their spare time?	Encouraging interaction
How would you like to use this meeting?	
3. The Family	
Where are you from originally?	Background experience, culture, maternal and paternal families of origin (MFO, PFO)
Are your parents still living? Are they together?	
Of your grandparents, who's your favourite?	
Whose beliefs in the family do you respect most?	
Has your Mum any brothers and sisters?	Parents' childhood experiences
Where does she come (oldest, middle, youngest)?	
What do you call him?	Towards eliciting dyadic construing
What's the nicest thing about your Dad?	
How often do you see your Dad?	
What do you enjoy doing together?	
4.Solution Focus and Goals	
What's the happiest time you've had in the last two weeks?	Elaborate under 'Progress' (section 10) below
When have the difficulties been the least noticeable?	Kelly's 7th Question—see Table 5.1
Can you tell me about a time when things were okay?	
How many dry beds have you had since our last meeting?	
What will have to happen to indicate that the goal has been reached?	Procter (1985a, p. 339)
Suppose a miracle happened tonight while you were asleep and all the problems you have told me about were gone, what would you first notice that was different when you woke tomorrow?	De Shazer's (1988) 'Miracle Question'
How would you like Jim to be relating to the twins?	Relational goal

(continued)

(continued)

QUESTION	RATIONALE
If we were to work together for some sessions and it was a successful piece of work, what would things be like then?	Goal question, seeding idea of successful therapy
How would you know that a useful piece of work had been completed?	Projection into the future
If you were closer and happier, what would you want to do together?	Elaborating goal situation
What would be the first sign, the smallest step that would indicate that progress is being made?	MRI Brief Therapy Question 'Step'
How would you notice the difference if you were happier together?	Goal defined visually
When things are better, what would you want to put your time and energy into instead?	New opportunities on resolution of problems
5. The Problem	
Who's been worrying most in the family recently? Who next? Who the least?	Milan Circular Question: ranking family members on construct of 'worry'
Who have *you* been worrying about the most?	Difficulties of other family members
What will your Mum and Dad say they are worrying about? (To other:) Is she right?	

(continued)

(continued)

QUESTION	RATIONALE
What is bothering you mainly at the moment?	*Worry* and *bother* everyday normalising terms
Can you give an example?	
What happens? What does he do exactly?	
Can you give an example of that?	
Where does this occur most often? At home or at school?	
When is it most distressing—morning, afternoon, evening, weekends?	Defining the problem in time, place, context
How often has this been happening?	
Is it sometimes worse, sometimes better?	
How long does it go on for?	
Who was there?	
What other difficulties are there at the moment?	Towards *listing the difficulties* the family faces
How long do you have to go back to find a time when things were okay?	Onset of difficulties
Can you tell me a bit more about this?	Rober (2017): 'The most important questions a family therapist can ask!' (p. 128)
Can you help me to understand?	
Can you help me to understand why it is better to remain silent?	Rober (2017): dealing with hesitation (p. 141)
6. Attempted Solutions	MRI: A *problem* is a *difficulty* and its failing *attempted solution* maintaining each other
When the problem occurs what do you do to try and make things better?	Attempted solution
How well did that work?	
What else have you tried?	List all other attempted solutions
What do you think she should do when the two boys are fighting?	Milan Circular Question
What have other people suggested?	
Does your mother (husband, son, sister, doctor) know about this?	Survey all in the network via their attempted solutions and suggestions, defining them in a helping role
What does she say to you in the way of advice?	
When your mother tries to get Mark to eat and he refuses, what does your father do?	Milan Circular Questions: evoking triadic construing
And when he shouts at Mark what does your mother do?	

(continued)

(continued)

QUESTION	RATIONALE
What would he do if you did nothing?	
Have you ever seen anyone like me before?	Previous therapy—what did they suggest, was it helpful?
How helpful was this?	
7. PositionontheProblem	
How do you explain this behaviour occurring?	MRI Questions: 'position on problem': eliciting construing about the nature and cause of the problem
What do you make of this situation?	
What is your best guess as to why it is occurring?	
Have you got any theories about it?	
8.Family Constructs and Relationships	
How do you see your daughter as a person?	As a *person*: monadic construing
How did your family see you as a person? (give me three ways)	
Who does she take after more, her mother, granddad, or step-dad?	From Laing (1981, p. 18)
Who is she closer to? In what way are they different? Similar? As a parent, which of your parents do you think you are most similar to?	Identity: Similarities/differences Closeness (dyadic construing)
What do you think she was thinking: how does she see the situation?	Sociality
What was he cross about?	Exploring system re emotions, conflict, agreement/disagreement
Who gets most upset? Tom, James, or Sharon	
Who gets the next most?	
(To other) Do you agree with her?	
What difference would it make if it was your father looking after you most of the time and you saw your mother at weekends? How do you see the relationship between your sister and your mother? Of the six relationships between you, which pair argue the least?	Milan Circular Questions: Relationship and Difference: Elaborating Relational Construing
What was life like for you when you were nine?	From Adult Attachment Interview (Dallos, 2006)

(continued)

QUESTION	RATIONALE
How did people see you as a person at that time?	
What did you do when you were upset or hurt?	
Have you heard about your Dad's life when he was that age?	Identifying with parent's life as a child
Before you had this difficulty, how did you get on with your mother?	
What difference would it make if she was a boy, he was a girl?	Milan questions
Who had the most influence in your family?	
If you no longer had the problem, how would their relationship be different?	Milan Question: function and impact of the problem
Do you think you would be closer or not so close?	
Who in the family is still missing Nan the most? Who next?	Loss and bereavement
When you feel sad about that, who is the best person to talk to?	
9. Position ontherapy	
Who suggested you come and see me?	MRI Question: position on treatment
How come you came for help at this time rather than sooner or later?	
Who was the keenest that you come, you, your friend, or your doctor?	MRI 'Customers for change' in the system
Have you got any ideas about what we should do to sort things out?	Position on treatment
If you could sort this problem out without knowing why it occurred would that be okay?	Position on explanation
If you could get over this problem without knowing how you did it, would that be alright?	
If we could find a way of James settling in the family, would you be interested?	Towards contracting for therapy, where putting James into care instead has been voiced
Would you like to do some work with me to try to sort this out?	Towards commitment to a course of therapy
Do you want to do some work on this then?	Reflection on therapy

(continued)

(continued)

QUESTION	RATIONALE
What do you feel about how the session is going?	
10. Progress	(Give as much time, or more, to exploring improvements and change as you do to the problem!)
What makes you say that things are better?	Defining the improvement
Have you got any idea how you managed it?	Agency and perceived agency
How do you think she managed to sort this out?	
I know it's the last thing you would want to do, but how would you go about making things go back to how they were before this improvement occurred?	(Fisch et al., 1982). Addressing relapse: 'The Insight Question'—can reveal in retrospect what factors were causing problem according to the client
What would have to happen for things to get more difficult again?	
Would you like me to offer you another appointment?	Progress sufficient to discontinue therapy?
11.Reflecting Team	For when an observing team or co-therapists reflect on the session (usually in the 3rd person while the family listen) (Andersen, 1987)
Was there anything they said you particularly agreed with?	Questions to elicit family members' responses to the Reflecting Team Statement
Was there anything they shouldn't have said?	
How did it feel, what did you think, when they were talking?	
12. Follow-up	
Can you give me an idea of how things are now?	
When you first came, what were you concerned about mainly?	Evaluating change and therapy at follow-up
Is this now better, worse, or the same?	
Were there any other problems you were concerned about?	
Is that better, worse, or the same?	
Have you had any other treatment for any of these problems?	
Have any new problems cropped up since we saw you?	

Appendix B: Useful Questions in Interviewing Children

QUESTION	RATIONALE
Greeting	
Hello, are you Sam? My name's Harry, it's really nice to meet you!	In waiting room: taking an interest in children's activity
That looks really interesting. What's happening there?	Settling before moving through to the therapy room
What would you have been doing at school today?	
Interests	It is often useful to talk to the children first, with permission from parents if necessary
What do you like doing best? How do you spend your free time?	Finding topics to talk about and explore
What did you do last weekend?	Activities at school, with friends
Who is your teacher? Is she a nice person?	
What do you like best? What are you best at?	
Who are your best friends? What do you like doing together?	Other members of the family's activities
Have you been to your Mum's place of work?	
What does your Dad do for his work?	
Family	
Who lives in your home?	Who is in the situation and relationships with them
What's your sister's name? Do you two get on well together?	
What do you call your Mum's Mum? Does she live near you?	
Who's your favourite grandparent?	Position in family, in sibling order and hierarchy
Has your Mum any brothers and sisters?	
Where does she come—is she the oldest, middle, or youngest?	
What's it like to be the oldest?	
How often do you see your Dad?	Contact with separated parent
What do you enjoy doing together?	
Worries	
Who's been worrying most in your family recently? Who next? Who the least?	
Who have you been worrying about most often?	Worry and bother are nice words to explore difficulty—everyone feels these things
What will Mum say she's been worrying about? Is she right?	

(continued)

(continued)

QUESTION	RATIONALE
What is it that's bothering you at the moment? Can you give me an example? What happens? Where does this happen most, at home or at school? When is it worst—morning, afternoon, evening, or at weekends? Is it sometimes worse, sometimes better? How long does it go on for? Who was there? Why do you think it's happening?	Defining the problem
Is there anything else you're unhappy about?	Other problems: towards listing difficulties
Attempted solutions	MRI: a *problem* is a *difficulty* and its failing *attempted solution* maintaining each other
What do you do to try and make things better? Did that work? What else have you tried? What do you think Mum should do with two boys who are fighting? What does Dad say? Does your friend know about this? What does she say to you? When he shouts at Mark, what does Mum do?	Exploring various people's suggestions and advice
What would happen if he did nothing?	Doing nothing as an option
Constructs	
Who are you? Tell me three things that best describe you	'Who Are You' technique—Ravenette (1999a)
What sort of person are you?	
What sort of person do other people say you are?	Identity
Of your friends, who likes you the most? Why?	View of self by positive figures
How are you and your brother similar? How are you different?	Similarities and differences in the family
Who are you more like, your Mum, or your Dad? In what way?	
How would I know that somebody was happy, lonely, angry?	Signs of different emotions
Who calls you lazy?	Deconstructing negative attribution
What would a person be doing to be lazy?	
Relationships	
Tell me three nice things about your Dad	'Three things'—Ravenette (1999c)
What was he cross about?	
Who gets the most upset? Tom, James, or Sharon?	Tracking situations and sequences

(continued)

(continued)

QUESTION	RATIONALE
Do you agree with her?	
Would it be different if you lived with your Dad and you saw your Mum on a Saturday?	Two separated parents: Contact
How do your sister and your Mum get on?	Relationships and conflict in the family
Which two people argue the least?	
What was life like when you were five?	Earlier developmental pictures
Have you heard about your Dad's life when *he* was twelve?	
If this wasn't happening, would you be closer?	
Who in the family is still missing Nan the most? Who else is?	Loss and bereavement, sadness
When you are sad, who is the best person to talk to about it?	
Goals	
When have you been happiest in the last week?	Using this material to define a goal
Tell me about a time when things were okay.	
If you had three wishes, what would you wish for?	Constructing and defining goals
If things changed a teeny-weeny bit, what would be different?	
When things are better, what will you want to do instead?	
If we could find a way to make life more like that, would you be interested?	Linking goals to the therapy
Therapy	
Who wanted you to come and see me?	Others' positions on what to do
Who was the keenest that you come, you or your Mum?	
Have you seen anyone like me before?	
How can we make things happier?	Position on therapy
Would you like to come and talk again with me?	Negotiating therapy with the child, not just the parents
How do you feel this meeting's going?	Reflection on meeting
Progress	
How's it been better?	Defining improvement
Do you know how you managed it?	Agency
What would make it worse again?	Relapse
What would have to happen to make it worse again?	Factors in relapse
Evaluation	
When you first came, what were you worried about?	Evaluating therapy and change
Is it better now, worse, or the same?	

Bibliography

Addison, V. E. (2016). *The use of repertory grids to explore nursing staff's construal of adult service users admitted to a psychiatric inpatient ward.* Unpublished DClinPsy thesis, University of Manchester. Retrieved, May 2020, from: https://search.proquest.com/openview/22e14ef28f337f69da2fb db918102dc8/1?pq-origsite=gscholar&cbl=51922&diss=y.

Agnew, J. (1985). Childhood disorders or the venture of children. In E. Button (Ed.), *Personal Construct Theory and Mental Health* (pp. 224–245). London: Croom Helm.

Aldridge, D. (1998). *Suicide: The Tragedy of Hopelessness.* London: Jessica Kingsley.

Alexander, P. C., & Follette, V. M. (1987). Personal constructs in the group treatment of incest. In R. A. Neimeyer & G. J. Neimeyer (Eds.), *Personal construct therapy casebook* (pp. 211–229). New York: Springer.

Alexander, P. C., Neimeyer, R. A., & Follette, V. M. (1991). Group therapy for women sexually abused as children: A controlled study and investigation of individual differences. *Journal of Interpersonal Violence, 6,* 218–231.

Alexander, P. C., Neimeyer, R. A., Follette, V., Moore, M. K., & Harter, S. (1989). A comparison of group treatments of women sexually abused as children. *Journal of Consulting and Clinical Psychology, 57,* 479–483.

Andersen, T. (1987). The reflecting team. *Family Process, 26,* 416–428.

Anderson, E. (2014). Dewey's moral philosophy. In E. N. Zalta (Ed.), *The Stanford Encyclopedia of Philosophy* (Spring 2014 ed.). https://plato.stanford. edu/archives/spr2014/entries/dewey-moral. Accessed 25 January 2018.

Anderson, H., & Goolishian, H. (1988). Human systems as linguistic systems: Evolving ideas about the implications for theory and practice. *Family Process, 27,* 371–393.

Anderson, H., Goolishian, H. A., & Windermand, L. (1986). Problem determined systems: Towards transformation in family therapy. *Journal of Strategic & Systemic Therapies, 5,* 1–13.

Annesi, J. J. (2002). Goal-setting protocol in adherence to exercise by Italian adults. *Perceptual and Motor Skills, 94,* 453–458.

Anscombe, G. E. M., & Wright, G. H. V. (Eds.). (1981). *Ludwig Wittgenstein: Zettel.* Oxford, UK: Blackwell.

Armezzani, M., & Chiari, G. (2014). Ideas for a phenomenological interpretation and elaboration of personal construct theory: Part 2. Husserl and Kelly: A case of commonality. *Costruttivismi, 1,* 168–185.

Audin, K., Mellor-Clark, J., Barkham, M., Margison, F., McGrath, G., Lewis, S., & Parry, G. (2001). Practice research networks for effective psychological therapies. *Journal of Mental Health, 10,* 241–251.

Balnaves, M., & Caputi, P. (1993). Corporate constructs: To what extent are personal constructs personal? *International Journal of Personal Construct Psychology, 6,* 119–138.

Balzani, L., Del Rizzo, F., & Sandi, F. (2011). The journey as constructivist learner-teachers: How to become teachers of constructivist psychotherapy. In D. Stojnov, V. Džinović, J. Pavlović, & M. Frances (Eds.), *Personal Construct Psychology in an Accelerating World* (pp. 169–179). Belgrade, Serbia: Serbian Constructivist Association.

Bannister, D. (1960). Conceptual structure in thought-disordered schizophrenics. *Journal of Mental Science, 106,* 1230–1249.

Bannister, D. (1962). The nature and measurement of schizophrenic thought disorder. *Journal of Mental Science, 108,* 825–842.

Bannister, D. (1963). The genesis of schizophrenic thought disorder: A serial invalidation hypothesis. *British Journal of Psychiatry, 109,* 680–686.

Bannister, D. (1965). The genesis of schizophrenic thought disorder: Re-test of the serial invalidation hypothesis. *British Journal of Psychiatry, 111,* 377–382.

Bannister, D. (1968). The logical requirements of research into schizophrenia. *British Journal of Psychiatry, 114*(507), 181–188.

Bannister, D. (1985a). The psychotic disguise. In W. Dryden (Ed.), *Therapists' Dilemmas* (pp. 39–45). London: Harper and Row.

Bannister, D. (1985b). The experience of self. In F. Epting & A. W. Landfield (Eds.), *Anticipating Personal Construct Psychology* (pp. 39–45). Lincoln: University of Nebraska Press.

Bannister, D., Adams-Webber, J. R., Penn, W. I., & Radley, A. R. (1975). Reversing the process of thought disorder: A serial validation experiment. *British Journal of Social and Clinical Psychology, 14,* 169–180.

Bannister, D., & Bott, M. (1973). Evaluating the person. In P. Klein (Ed.), *New Approaches to Psychological Medicine* (pp. 157–177). Chichester, UK: Wiley.

Bannister, D., & Fransella, F. (1966). A grid test of schizophrenic thought disorder. *British Journal of Social & Clinical Psychology, 5*(2), 95–102.

Bannister, D., & Fransella, F. (1986). *Inquiring Man*. London: Routledge (first published by Penguin (1971)).

Bannister, D., & Mair, J. M. M. (1968). *The Evaluation of Personal Constructs*. London: Academic Press.

Bannister, D., & Salmon, P. (1966). Schizophrenic thought disorder, specific or diffuse? *British Journal of Medical Psychology, 39,* 215–219.

Barbour, P. J., & Bourne, D. (2020/in press). Developing sociality in a post-conflict Northern Ireland: An application of the Perceiver Element Grid. *Journal of Constructivist Psychology.*

Barkham, M., Evans, C., Margison, F., McGrath, G., Mellor-Clark, J., Milne, D., & Connell, J. (1998). The rationale for developing and implementing core outcome batteries for routine use in service settings and psychotherapy outcome research. *Journal of Mental Health, 7*(1), 35–47.

Barkham, M., & Mellor-Clark, J. (2000). Rigour and relevance: The role of practice-based evidence in the psychological therapies. In N. Rowland & G. Goss (Eds.), *Evidence-Based Counselling and Psychological Therapies* (pp. 126–144). London: Routledge.

Baron-Cohen, S. (1997). *Mindblindness: An Essay on Autism and Theory of Mind*. London: MIT Press.

Bateman, A. W., & Fonagy, P. (2012). *Handbook of Mentalizing in Mental Health Practice*. Washington, DC: American Psychiatric Publishing.

Bateson, G. (1972a). *Steps to an Ecology of Mind*. Chicago: University of Chicago Press.

Bateson, G. (1972b). A theory of play and fantasy. Reprinted in Bateson, G. (Ed.). *Steps to an Ecology of Mind* (pp. 177–193). Chicago: University of Chicago Press.

Bateson, G. (1979). *Mind and Nature: A Necessary Unity.* London: Fontana/Collins.

Bateson, G., Jackson, D. D., Haley, J., & Weakland, J. (1956). Toward a theory of schizophrenia. *Behavioral Science, 1,* 251–264.

Batty, C., & Hall, E. (1986). Personal constructs of students with eating disorders: Implications for counselling. *British Journal of Guidance and Counselling, 14,* 306–313.

Beail, N., & Parker, S. (1991). Group fixed-role therapy: A clinical application. *International Journal of Personal Construct Psychology, 4,* 85–96.

Beck, A. T., Rush, A. J., Shaw, B. F., & Emery, G. (1979). *Cognitive Therapy of Depression.* New York: Guilford.

Bell, R. C. (2009). *GRIDSTAT, Version 5: A Program for Analyzing the Data of a Repertory Grid* (computer software). Department of Psychology, University of Melbourne.

Bell, R. C. (2014). Did Hinkle prove laddered constructs are superordinate? A re-examination of his data suggests not. *Personal Construct Theory and Practice, 11,* 1–4.

Bell, R. C. (2016). Methodologies of assessment. In D. A. Winter & N. Reed (Eds.), *The Wiley Handbook of Personal Construct Psychology* (pp. 71–87). Chichester, UK: Wiley-Blackwell.

Bendinelli, G., & Lui, C. (2014). Play as a way of knowing, learning and changing. In H. Moran (Ed.), *Using Personal Construct Psychology (PCP) in Practice with Children and Adolescents* (pp. 88–98). https://issuu.com/pcp inpractice/docs/using_personal_construct_psychology.

Bennett-Levy, J., Thwaites, R., Chaddock, A., & Davis, M. (2009). Reflective practice in cognitive-behavioural therapy. In J. Stedmon & R. Dallos (Eds.), *Reflective Practice in Psychotherapy and Counselling* (pp. 136–155). Milton Keynes: Open University Press.

Beutler, L. Psychotherapy researcher (Personal communication, 2017).

Bhandari, S., Winter, D. A., Messer, D., & Metcalfe, C. (2011). Family characteristics and long-term effects of childhood sexual abuse. *British Journal of Clinical Psychology, 50,* 435–451.

Blumer, H. (1966). Sociological implications of the thought of George Herbert Mead. *American Journal of Sociology, 71,* 535–544.

Bohart, A. C. (2000). Paradigm clash: Empirically supported treatments versus empirically supported psychotherapy practice. *Psychotherapy Research, 10,* 488–493.

Bohart, A. C., O'Hara, M., & Leitner, L. M. (1998). Empirically violated treatments: Disenfranchisement of humanistic and other therapies. *Psychotherapy Research, 8,* 141–157.

Bond, H. M. (1927). Some exceptional negro children. *The Crisis, 34,* 257–280.

Borkovec, T. D., & Castonguay, L. G. (1998). What is the scientific meaning of empirically supported therapy? *Journal of Consulting and Clinical Psychology, 66,* 136–142.

Boszormenyi-Nagy, I. (1987). *Foundations of Contextual Therapy: Collected Papers of Ivan Bosxormenyi-Nagy, M.D.* New York: Brunner/Mazel.

Botella, L. (1991). Psychoeducational groups with older adults: An integrative personal construct rationale and some guidelines. *International Journal of Personal Construct Psychology, 4,* 397–408.

Botella, L. (2000). Personal Construct Psychology, constructivism, and psychotherapy research. In J. W. Scheer (Ed.), *The Person in Society: Challenges to a Constructivist Theory* (pp. 362–372). Giessen, Germany: Psychosozial-Verlag.

Botella, L., Corbella, S., Gómez, T., Herrero, O., & Pacheco, M. (2005). A personal construct approach to narrative and post-modern therapies. In D. A. Winter & L. L. Viney (Eds.), *Personal Construct Psychotherapy: Advances in Theory, Practice and Research* (pp. 69–80). London: Croom Helm.

Botella, L., & Feixas, G. (1992–1993). The autobiographical group: A tool for the reconstruction of past life experience with the aged. *International Journal of Aging and Human Development, 36,* 303–319.

Botella, L., & Herrero, O. (2000). A relational constructivist approach to narrative therapy. *European Journal of Psychotherapy and Counselling, 3,* 407–418.

Brentano, F. (1995). *Psychology from an Empirical Standpoint.* London: Routledge.

British Psychological Society. (2019). *Standards for the Accreditation of Doctoral Programmes in Clinical Psychology.* Leicester, UK: British Psychological Society.

Brophy, S. (2016). Humanizing healthcare: A personal construct psychology-based intervention. In D. A. Winter & N. Reed (Eds.), *The Wiley Handbook of Personal Construct Psychology* (pp. 293–305). Chichester, UK: Wiley-Blackwell.

Bruch, M. (1998). The development of case formulation approaches. In M. Bruch & F. W. Bond (Eds.), *Beyond Diagnosis: Case Formulation Approaches in Cognitive-Behavioural Therapy* (pp. 1–23). Chichester, UK: Wiley.

Bruner, J. (1991). The narrative construction of reality. *Critical Inquiry, 18,* 1–21.

Bugental, J. (1964). The third force in psychology. *Journal of Humanistic Psychology, 4,* 19–26.

Burbach, F. R., & Stanbridge, R. I. (1998). A family intervention in psychosis service integrating the systemic and family management approaches. *Journal of Family Therapy, 20,* 311–325.

Burnham, J. (2005). Relational reflexivity: A tool for socially constructing therapeutic relationships. In C. Flaskas, B. Mason, & A. Perlesz (Eds.), *The Space Between: Experience, Context, and Process in the Therapeutic Relationships* (pp. 1–180). London: Karnac.

Burnham, J. (2012). Developments in Social GRRAAACCEEESSS: Visible-invisible and voiced-unvoiced. In I. Krause (Ed.), *Culture and Reflexivity Systemic Psychotherapy* (pp. 139–162). London: Karnac.

Burnham, J., Alvis Palma, L., & Whitehouse, L. (2008). Learning as a context for differences and differences as a context for learning. *Journal of Family Therapy, 30,* 529–542.

Burnham, S. (2008). *Let's Talk: Using Personal Construct Psychology to Support Children and Young People: Using Personal Construct Theory in School.* New York: Sage (Lucky Duck Books).

Burr, V. (2015). *Introduction to Social Constructionism* (3rd ed.). London: Routledge.

Burr, V., Giliberto, M., & Butt, T. (2014). Construing the cultural other and the self: A personal construct analysis of English and Italian perceptions of national character. *International Journal of Intercultural Relations, 39,* 53–65.

Butler, R. J. (2001). *The Self Image Profiles for Children and Adolescents.* London: The Psychological Corporation.

Butler, R. J. (Ed.). (2009). *Reflections in Personal Construct Theory.* Chichester, UK: Wiley-Blackwell.

Butler, R. J., & Green, D. (2007). *The Child Within: Taking the Young Person's Perspective by Applying Personal Construct Theory* (2nd ed.). Chichester, UK: Wiley.

Butt, T. (1995). Ordinal relationships between constructs. *Journal of Constructivist Psychology, 8,* 227–236.

Butt, T. (2000). Pragmatism, constructivism and ethics. *Journal of Constructivist Psychology, 13,* 85–101.

Butt, T. (2004). Understanding, explanation, and personal constructs. *Personal Construct Theory and Practice, 1*, 21–27.

Butt, T. (2013). Toward a pragmatic psychology. *Journal of Constructivist Psychology, 26*, 218–224.

Button, E. (Ed.). (1985). *Personal Construct Theory and Mental Health*. Beckenham, UK: Croom Helm.

Button, E. (1987). Construing people or weight?: An eating disorders group. In R. A. Neimeyer & G. J. Neimeyer (Eds.), *Personal Construct Therapy Casebook* (pp. 230–244). New York: Springer.

Button, E. J. (1993). *Eating Disorders: Personal Construct Therapy and Change*. Chichester, UK: Wiley.

Cade, B. (1998). Honesty is still the best policy. *Journal of Family Therapy, 20*, 143–152.

Caine, T. M., Foulds, G. A., & Hope, D. (1967). *Manual of the Hostility and Direction of Hostility Questionnaire*. London: University of London Press.

Caine, T. M., Wijesinghe, O. B. A., & Winter, D. A. (1981). *Personal Styles in Neurosis: Implications for Small Group Psychotherapy and Behaviour Therapy*. London: Routledge and Kegan Paul.

Caputi, P., Breiger, R., & Pattison, P. (1990). Analyzing implications grids using hierarchical models. *International Journal of Personal Construct Psychology, 3*, 77–90.

Caputi, P., Viney, L. L., Walker, B. M., & Crittenden, N. (Eds.). (2011). *Personal Construct Methodology*. Chichester, UK: Wiley-Blackwell.

Carlsen, M. B. (1988). *Meaning-Making: Therapeutic Processes in Adult Development*. New York: Norton.

Carr, A. (2009). *What Works with Children, Adolescents, and Adults? A Review of Research on the Effectiveness of Psychotherapy*. London: Routledge.

Castiglioni, M., Faccio, E., Veronese, G., & Bell, R. C. (2013). The semantics of power among people with eating disorders. *Journal of Constructivist Psychology, 26*, 62–76.

Catina, A., Gitzinger, I., & Hoeckh, H. (1992). Defence mechanisms: An approach from the perspective of personal construct psychology. *International Journal of Personal Construct Psychology, 5*, 249–257.

Centre for Economic Performance. (2006). *The Depression Report: A New Deal for Depression and Anxiety Disorders*. London: London School of Economics and Political Science.

Chambless, D. L., Baker, M. J., Baucom, D. H., Beutler, L. E., Calhoun, K. S., & Daiuto, A. (1998). Update on empirically validated therapies, II. *The Clinical Psychologist, 51*, 3–16.

Chambless, D. L., & Hollon, S. D. (1998). Defining empirically supported therapies. *Journal of Consulting and Clinical Psychology, 66,* 7–18.

Chambless, D. L., & Ollendick, T. H. (2001). Empirically supported psychological interventions: Controversies and evidence. *Annual Review of Psychology, 52,* 685–716.

Chiari, G. (2017a). *George A. Kelly and His Personal Construct Theory.* https://drive.google.com/file/d/0BwZ5ZCZCN9j-MGZ3bFlpT1hDQVU/view. Accessed 25 January 2018.

Chiari, G. (2017b). Highlighting intersubjectivity and recognition in Kelly's sketchy view of personal identity. In D. Winter, P. Cummins, H. G. Procter, & N. Reed (Eds.), *Personal Construct Psychology at 60: Papers from the 21st International Congress* (pp. 54–67). Newcastle upon Tyne, UK: Cambridge Scholars Publishing.

Chiari, G., & Nuzzo, M. L. (1996). Psychological constructivisms: A metatheoretical differentiation. *Journal of Constructivist Psychology, 9,* 163–184.

Chiari, G., & Nuzzo, M. L. (2004). Steering personal construct theory towards hermeneutic constructivism. In J. D. Raskin & S. K. Bridges (Eds.), *Studies in Meaning 2: Bridging the Personal and Social in Constructivist Psychology* (pp. 51–65). New York: Pace University Press.

Chiari, G., & Nuzzo, M. L. (2010). *Constructivist Psychotherapy: A Narrative Hermeneutic Approach.* London: Routledge.

Chiari, G., Nuzzo, M. L., Alfano, V., Brogna, P., D'Andrea, T., Di Battista, G., … & Stiffan, E. (1994). Personal paths of dependency. *Journal of Constructivist Psychology, 7,* 17–34.

Cipolletta, S., Mascolo, M., & Procter, H. G. (2020/in press), Intersubjectivity, joint action and sociality. *Journal of Constructivist Psychology.*

Cipolletta, S., & Racerro, G. (2003). Testing the serial invalidation hypothesis in the genesis of schizophrenic thought disorder: A research with repertory grids. In G. Chiari & M. L. Nuzzo (Eds.), *Psychological Constructivism and the Social World* (pp. 353–368). Milan, Italy: Franco Angeli.

Cixous, H. (2000). Sorties. In D. Lodge & N. Wood (Eds.), *Modern Criticism and Theory: A Reader* (3rd ed., pp. 358–365). London: Longman.

Cochrane, A. (1972). *Effectiveness and Efficiency: Random Reflection on Health Services.* London: Nuffield Provincial Hospitals Trust.

Cohen, J. (1988). *Statistical Power Analyses for the Behavioral Sciences.* Hillsdale, NJ: Lawrence Erlbaum.

Cooper, E. (2011). *Exploring the personal constructs of looked after children and their foster carers: A qualitative study.* Unpublished DClinPsy thesis, University of Hertfordshire.

Cooper, M. (2008). *Essential Research Findings in Counselling and Psychotherapy: The Facts are Friendly*. London: Sage.

Coppock, C., Winter, D., Ferguson, S., & Green, A. (2017). Using the Perceiver Element Grid (PEG) to elicit intrafamily construal following parental Acquired Brain Injury. *Personal Construct Theory and Practice, 14*, 25–39.

Crane, D. R., & Payne, S. H. (2011). Individual versus family psychotherapy in managed care: Comparing the costs of treatment by the mental health professionals. *Journal of Marital and Family Therapy, 37*, 273–289.

Cromwell, R. (2016). Foreword. In D. A. Winter & R. Reed (Eds.), *The Wiley Handbook of Personal Construct Psychology* (pp. xx–xxvii). Chichester, UK: Wiley.

Cronen, V. E., Johnson, K. M., & Lannamann, J. W. (1982). Paradoxes, double binds, and reflexive loops: An alternative theoretical perspective. *Family Process, 21*, 91–112.

Cummins, P. (2005). The experience of anger. In D. A. Winter & L. L. Viney (Eds.), *Personal Construct Psychotherapy: Advances in Theory, Practice and Research* (pp. 239–255). London: Whurr.

Cummins, P. (2006). The Tuesday group. In P. Cummins (Ed.), *Working with Anger: A Constructivist Approach* (pp. 13–24). Chichester, UK: Wiley.

Cunningham, C., & Davis, H. (1985). *Working with Parents: Frameworks for Collaboration*. Milton Keynes, UK: Open University Press.

Dallos, R. (1991). *Family Belief Systems, Therapy and Change: A Constructional Approach*. Maidenhead, UK: Open University Press.

Dallos, R. (2006). *Attachment Narrative Therapy*. Maidenhead, UK: Open University Press.

Dallos, R., & Procter, H. G. (1984). *Family Processes: An Interactional View*. D307 Social Psychology Course, Open University, Milton Keynes.

Dalton, P. (1983). Maintenance of change: Towards the integration of behavioural and psychological procedures. In P. Dalton (Ed.), *Approaches to the Treatment of Stuttering* (pp. 163–184). London: Croom Helm.

Davis, C. (2012). *Women's narratives of dementia: An exploration of the impact of male dementia on families*. Unpublished DClinPsych thesis, University of Surrey.

Davis, H., & Cunningham, C. (1985). Mental handicap: People in context. In E. Button (Ed.), *Personal Construct Theory and Mental Health* (pp. 246–261). London: Croom Helm.

Davis, H., Stroud, A., & Green, L. (1989). Child characterization sketch. *International Journal of Personal Construct Psychology, 2*, 323–337.

Dawes, A. (1985). Construing drug dependence. In E. Button (Ed.), *Personal Construct Theory and Mental Health* (pp. 182–194). London: Croom Helm.

De Boeck, P., & Rosenberg, S. (1988). Hierarchical classes: Model and data analysis. *Psychometrika, 53,* 361–381.

De Saussure, F. (1959). *Course in General Linguistics.* New York: The Philosophical Library.

De Shazer, S. (1988). *Clues: Investigating Solutions in Brief Therapy.* New York: Norton.

De Shazer, S. (1994). *Words Were Originally Magic.* New York: Norton.

Department of Health. (1996). *Research and Development: Towards an Evidence-Based Health Service.* London: HMSO.

Derrida, J. (1976). *Of Grammatology.* Baltimore: John Hopkins University Press.

Dewey, J. (1932). *Ethics. The Later Works, 1925–1953* (Vol. 7). Carbondale: Southern Illinois University Press.

DiLollo, A., Manning, W. H., & Neimeyer, R. A. (2005). Cognitive complexity as a function of speaker role for adult persons who stutter. *Journal of Constructivist Psychology, 18,* 215–236.

Division of Clinical Psychology. (2011). *Good Practice Guidelines on the Use of Psychological Formulation.* Leicester, UK: British Psychological Society.

Dixon-Woods, M., Shaw, R. L., Agarwal, S., & Smith, J. A. (2004). The problem of appraising qualitative research. *BMJ Quality and Safety, 13,* 223–225.

Doster, J. A. (1985). A personal construct assessment of marital violence. In F. Epting & A. W. Landfield (Eds.), *Anticipating Personal Construct Psychology* (pp. 225–232). Lincoln: University of Nebraska Press.

Dougherty, C. J. (1980). The common root of Husserl's and Peirce's phenomenologies. *The New Scholasticism, 54,* 305–325.

Du Preez, P. (1979). Politics and identity in South Africa. In P. Stringer & D. Bannister (Eds.), *Constructs of Sociality and Individuality* (pp. 341–364). London: Academic Press.

Duck, S. (1973). *Personal Relationships and Personal Constructs: A Study of Friendship Formation.* London: Wiley.

Dunn, J., & Plomin, R. (1991). Why are siblings so different? The significance of differences in sibling experiences within the family. *Family Process, 30*(3), 271–283.

Dunnett, G., & Llewelyn, S. (1988). Elaborating personal construct theory in a group setting. In G. Dunnett (Ed.), *Working with People: Clinical Uses of Personal Construct Psychology* (pp. 186–201). London: Routledge.

Dzamonja-Ignjatovic, T. (1997). Suicide and depression from the personal construct perspective. In P. Denicolo & M. Pope (Eds.), *Sharing Understanding and Practice* (pp. 222–234). Farnborough, UK: EPCA Publications.

Eccles, M., & Mason, J. (2001). How to develop cost-conscious guidelines. *Health Technology Assessment, 5,* 1–69.

Ecker, B., & Hulley, L. (1996). *Depth Oriented Brief Therapy: How to Be Brief When You Were Trained to be Deep, and Vice Versa.* San Francisco: Jossey-Bass.

Ecker, B., & Hulley, L. (2008). Coherence therapy: Swift changes at the root of symptom production. In J. D. Raskin & S. K. Bridges (Eds.), *Studies in Meaning 3: Constructivist Psychotherapy in the Real World* (pp. 57–84). New York: Pace University Press.

Edwards, D. (1997). *Discourse and Cognition.* London: Sage.

Edwards, D. G. A., Dattilio, F. M., & Bromley, D. B. (2004). Developing evidence-based practice: The role of case-based research. *Professional Psychology: Research and Practice, 35,* 589–597.

Eells, T. D. (2006). History and current status of psychotherapy case formulation. In T. D. Eells (Ed.), *Handbook of Psychotherapy Case Formulation* (2nd ed., pp. 3–32). New York: Guilford.

Elliott, R. (2002). Hermeneutic single-case efficacy design. *Psychotherapy Research, 12,* 1–21.

Elliott, R., Fischer, C. T., & Rennie, D. L. (1999). Evolving guidelines for publication of qualitative research studies in psychology and related fields. *British Journal of Clinical Psychology, 38,* 215–229.

Elliott, R., Watson, J. C., Goldman, R. N., & Greenberg, L. S. (2004). *Learning Emotion-Focused Therapy: The Process-Experiential Approach to Change.* Washington, DC: American Psychological Association.

Ellis, A. (1979). The theory of rational-emotive therapy. In A. Ellis & J. M. Whiteley (Eds.), *Theoretical and Empirical Foundations of Rational-Emotive Therapy* (pp. 33–60). Monterey: Brooks/Cole.

Epting, F. R. (1984). *Personal Construct Counseling and Psychotherapy.* New York: Wiley.

Epting, F. R. (1988). Journeying into the personal constructs of children. *International Journal of Personal Construct Psychology, 1,* 53–61.

Epting, F. R., & Amerikaner, M. (1980). Optimal functioning: A personal construct approach. In A. Landfield & L. M. Leitner (Eds.), *Personal Construct Psychology: Psychotherapy and Personality* (pp. 55–73). New York: Wiley.

Epting, F. R., & Nazario, A., Jr. (1987). Designing a fixed role therapy: Issues, techniques, and modifications. In R. A. Neimeyer & G. J. Neimeyer (Eds.), *Personal Construct Therapy Casebook* (pp. 277–289). New York: Springer.

Epting, F. R., Suchman, D. L., & Nickeson, C. J. (1971). An evaluation of elicitation procedures for personal constructs. *British Journal of Psychology, 62,* 513–517.

Erbes, C. R., & Harter, S. L. (2002). Constructions of abuse: Understanding the effects of childhood sexual abuse. In J. D. Raskin & S. K. Bridges (Eds.), *Studies in Meaning: Exploring Constructivist Psychology* (pp. 27–48). New York: Pace University Press.

Erickson, M. H., & Rossi, E. L. (1979). *Hypnotherapy: An Exploratory Casebook.* Oxford: Irvington.

Eron, J. B., & Lund, T. W. (1993). How problems evolve and dissolve. Integrating narrative and strategic concepts. *Family Process, 32,* 291–309.

Español, S., Martínez, M., Bordoni, M., Camarasa, R., & Carretero, S. (2014). Forms of vitality play in infancy. *Integrative Psychological and Behavioral Science, 48,* 479–502.

Esterson, A. (1970). *The Leaves of Spring.* Harmondsworth, UK: Penguin.

Evesham, M. (1987). Residential courses for stutterers: Combining technique and personal construct psychology. In C. Levy (Ed.), *Stuttering Therapies: Practical Approaches* (pp. 61–71). London: Croom Helm.

Evesham, M., & Fransella, F. (1985). Stuttering relapse: The effects of a combined speech and psychological reconstruction programme. *British Journal of Disorders of Communication, 20,* 237–248.

Feixas, G. (1990). Personal construct theory and the systemic therapies: Parallel or convergent trends? *Journal of Marital and Family Therapy, 16,* 1–20.

Feixas, G. (1992a). A constructivist approach to supervision: Some preliminary thoughts. *Journal of Constructivist Psychology, 5*(2), 183–200.

Feixas, G. (1992b). Personal construct approaches to family therapy. In G. J. Neimeyer & R. A. Neimeyer (Eds.), *Advances in Personal Construct Psychology* (Vol. 2, pp. 217–255). Greenwich, CT: JAI Press.

Feixas, G. (1995). Personal constructs in systemic practice. In R. A. Neimeyer & M. J. Mahoney (Eds.), *Constructivism in Psychotherapy* (pp. 305–337). Washington, DC: American Psychological Association.

Feixas, G., Bados, A., Garcia-Grau, E., Paz, C., Montesano, A., Compañ, V., & Lana, F. (2016). A dilemma-focused intervention for depression: A multi-center, randomized controlled trial with a 3-month follow-up. *Depression and Anxiety, 33,* 862–869.

Feixas, G., & Botella, L. (2004). Psychotherapy integration: Reflections and contributions from a constructivist epistemology. *Journal of Psychotherapy Integration, 14,* 192–222.

Feixas, G., & Compañ, V. (2016). Dilemma-focused intervention for unipolar depression: A treatment manual. *BMC Psychiatry, 16,* 235.

Feixas, G., Erazo-Caicedo, M. I., Harter, S. L., & Bach, L. (2008). Construction of self and others in unipolar depressive disorders: A study using repertory grid technique. *Cognitive Therapy and Research, 32,* 386–400.

Feixas, G., Geldschläger, H., & Neimeyer, R. A. (2002). Content analysis of personal constructs. *Journal of Constructivist Psychology, 15,* 1–20.

Feixas, G., Montebruno, C., Dada, G., Del Castillo, M., & Compañ, V. (2010). Self construction, cognitive conflicts and polarization in bulimia nervosa. *International Journal of Clinical and Health Psychology, 10,* 445–457.

Feixas, G., Montesano, A., Compan, V., Salla, M., Dada, G., Pucurull, O., & Guardia, J. (2014a). Cognitive conflicts in major depression: Between desired change and personal coherence. *British Journal of Clinical Psychology, 53*(4), 369–385.

Feixas, G., Montesano, A., Erazo-Caicedo, M. I., Compañ, V., & Pucurull, O. (2014b). Implicative dilemmas and symptom severity in depression: A preliminary and content analysis study. *Journal of Constructivist Psychology, 27,* 31–40.

Feixas, G., Procter, H. G., & Neimeyer, G. (1992). Convergent lines of assessment: Systemic and constructivist contributions. In G. Neimeyer (Ed.), *Constructivist Assessment: A Casebook* (pp. 143–178). New York: Sage.

Feixas, G., & Saúl, L. A. (2004). The Multi-Center Dilemma Project: An investigation on the role of cognitive conflicts in health. *Spanish Journal of Psychology, 7,* 69–78.

Feixas, G., Saúl, L. A., & Ávila-Espada, A. (2009). Viewing cognitive conflicts as dilemmas: Implications for mental health. *Journal of Constructivist Psychology, 22,* 141–169.

Feixas, G., & Villegas, M. (1991). Personal construct analysis of autobiographical text: A method presentation and case illustration. *International Journal of Personal Construct Psychology, 4,* 51–83.

Feldman, M. M. (1975). The body image and object relations: Exploration of a method utilizing repertory grid technique. *British Journal of Medical Psychology, 48,* 317–332.

Fergus, K. D., & Reid, D. W. (2002). Integrating constructivist and systemic metatheory in family therapy. *Journal of Constructivist Psychology, 15,* 41–63.

Fernandes, E. M. (2007). When what I wish makes me worse...to make coherence flexible. *Psychology and Psychotherapy, 80,* 165–180.

Fisch, R., Weakland, J. H., & Segal, L. (1982). *The Tactics of Change: Doing Therapy Briefly.* San Francisco: Jossey-Bass.

Fisher, P., & Wells, A. (2009). *Metacognitive Therapy: Distinctive Features.* Hove, UK: Routledge.

Fisher, S., & Greenberg, R. P. (1978). *The Scientific Evaluation of Freud's Theories and Therapy.* New York: Basic Books.

Fivaz-Depeursinge, E., & Corboz-Warnery, J. (1999). *The Primary Triangle.* New York: Basic Books.

Fonagy, P. (1982). The integration of psychoanalysis and experimental science: A review. *International Review of Psychoanalysis, 9,* 125–145.

Forster, J. R. (1991). Facilitating positive changes in self-constructions. *International Journal of Personal Construct Psychology, 4,* 281–292.

Foster, H., & Viney, L. L. (2001). Meanings of menopause: Development of a PCP model. In J. M. Fisher & N. Cornelius (Eds.), *Challenging the Boundaries: PCP Perspectives for the New Millennium* (pp. 87–108). Farnborough, UK: EPCA Publications.

Foster, H., & Viney, L. L. (2005). Personal construct workshops for women experiencing menopause. In D. A. Winter & L. L. Viney (Eds.), *Personal Construct Psychotherapy: Advances in Theory, Practice and Research* (pp. 320–332). London: Croom Helm.

Frances, M. (2016). Consulting in organizations. In D. A. Winter & N. Reed (Eds.), *The Wiley Handbook of Personal Construct Psychology* (pp. 282–292). Chichester, UK: Wiley-Blackwell.

Frank, M. (1989). *What Is Neostructuralism?* (S. Wilke & R. Gray, trans.). Minneapolis: University of Minessota Press (Original work in German (1984)).

Fransella, F. (1970). Stuttering: Not a symptom but a way of life. *British Journal of Communication Disorders, 5,* 22–29.

Fransella, F. (1972). *Personal Change and Reconstruction: Research on a Treatment of Stuttering.* London: Academic Press.

Fransella, F. (1985). Individual psychotherapy. In E. Button (Ed.), *Personal Construct Theory and Mental Health* (pp. 277–301). London: Croom Helm.

Fransella, F. (1993). The construct of resistance in psychotherapy. In L. M. Leitner & N. G. M. Dunnett (Eds.), *Critical Issues in Personal Construct Psychotherapy* (pp. 117–134). Malabar: Krieger.

Fransella, F. (1995). *George Kelly.* London: Sage.

Fransella, F. (2001). The making of a psychologist: A late developer. In G. C. Bunn, A. D. Lovie, & G. C. Richards (Eds.), *Psychology in Britain: Historical Essays and Personal Reflections* (pp. 372–380). London: BPS Books and Science Museum.

Fransella, F., Bell, R., & Bannister, D. (2004). *A Manual for Repertory Grid Technique*. Chichester, UK: Wiley.

Fransella, F., Jones, H., & Watson, J. (1988). A range of applications of PCP within business and industry. In F. Fransella & L. Thomas (Eds.), *Experimenting with Personal Construct Psychology* (pp. 405–417). London: Routledge & Kegan Paul.

Friedman, M. (1998). Buber's philosophy as the basis for dialogical psychotherapy and contextual therapy. *Journal of Humanist Psychology, 38*(1), 25–40.

Fromm, M., & Bacher, A. (2014). *GridSuite 4* (Windows and Mac Ed.). Stuttgart: University of Stuttgart.

Fukuyama, M. A., & Neimeyer, G. J. (1985). Using the Cultural Attitudes Repertory Technique (CART) in a cross-cultural counseling workshop. *Journal of Counseling & Development, 63*, 304–305.

Gadamer, H.G. (1989). *Truth and Method* (J. Weinsheimer & D. G. Marshall, Trans., 2nd ed.). New York: Seabury Press.

Gaines, B. R., & Shaw, M. L. G. (1997). Knowledge acquisition, modelling and inference through the World Wide Web. *International Journal of Human-Computer Studies, 6*, 729–759.

Galbusera, L., & Fellin, L. (2014). The intersubjective endeavour of psychopathology research: Methodological reflections on a second-person perspective approach. *Frontiers in Psychology, 5*, 1–14.

Gara, M. A., Rosenberg, S., & Mueller, D. R. (1989). Perception of self and others in schizophrenia. *International Journal of Personal Construct Psychology, 2*, 253–270.

Garcia-Gutierrez, A., & Feixas, G. (2018). *GRIDCOR: A Repertory Grid Analysis Tool* (Version 6.0) [Web application]. Retrieved from http://www.repertorygrid.net/en.

García-Mieres, H., Niño-Robles, N., Ochoa, S., & Feixas, G. (2019). Exploring identity and personal meanings in psychosis using the repertory grid technique: A systematic review. *Clinical Psychology & Psychotherapy, 26*, 717–733.

Gergen, K. (1994). *Realities and Relationships: Soundings in Social Construction*. Cambridge: Harvard University Press.

Giddens, A. (1991). *Modernity and Self-Identity: Self and Society in the Late Modern Age*. Redwood City: Stanford University Press.

Gilbert, P. (2010). *Compassion Focused Therapy: Distinctive Features*. Hove, UK: Routledge.

Gilbert, T. (2001). Reflective practice and clinical supervision: Meticulous rituals of the confessional. *Journal of Advanced Nursing, 36*, 199–205.

Gillman-Smith, I., & Watson, S. (1985). Personal construct group psychotherapy for borderline personality disorder. In D. A. Winter & L. L. Viney (Eds.), *Personal Construct Psychotherapy: Advances in Theory, Practice and Research* (pp. 189–197). London: Croom Helm.

Gold, J. R. (1995). The place of process-oriented psychotherapies in an outcome-oriented psychology and society. *Applied and Preventive Psychology, 4*, 61–74.

Goldfried, M. R. (1988). Personal construct therapy and other theoretical orientations. *International Journal of Personal Construct Psychology, 1*, 317–327.

Gouldner, A. W. (1970). *The Coming Crisis of Western Sociology*. New York: Avon Books.

Green, D. (2005). Kids' stuff. In D. A. Winter & L. L. Viney (Eds.), *Personal Construct Psychotherapy: Advances in Theory, Practice and Research* (pp. 256–270). London: Whurr.

Green, D., & Latchford, G. (2012). *Maximising the Benefits of Psychotherapy: A Practice-Based Evidence Approach*. Chichester, UK: Wiley.

Grice, J. W. (2002). IDIOGRID: Software for the management and analysis of repertory grids. *Behavior, Research Methods, Instruments, and Computer, 34*, 338–341.

Guidano, V. F. (1991). *The Self in Process*. New York: Guilford.

Guidano, V. F., & Liotti, G. (1983). *Cognitive Processes and Emotional Disorders: A Structural Approach to Psychotherapy*. New York: Guilford Press.

Guiffrida, D. (2015). A constructive approach to counseling and psychotherapy supervision. *Journal of Constructivist Psychology, 28*, 40–52.

Guyatt, G. H., Sackett, D. L., Sinclair, J. C., Hayward, R., Cook, D. J., Cook, R. J., ... & Jaeschke, R. (1995). Users' guides to the medical literature: IX. A method for grading healthcare recommendations. *JAMA, 274*, 1800–1804.

Haley, J. (1963). *Strategies of Psychotherapy*. New York: Grune and Stratton.

Haley, J. (1967). Toward a theory of pathological systems. In J. Zuk & I. Nagy (Eds.), *Family Therapy and Disturbed Families* (pp. 11–27). Palo Alto, CA: Science and Behavior Books.

Haley, J. (1973). *Uncommon Therapy: The Psychiatric Techniques of Milton H. Erickson*. New York: W. W. Norton.

Haley, J. (1974). *Problem Solving Therapy: New Strategies for Effective Family Therapy*. San Francisco: Jossey-Bass.

Harré, R., & van Langenhove, L. (1999). *Positioning Theory*. Oxford, UK: Blackwell.

Harter, S. L., & Neimeyer, R. A. (1995). Long term effects of child sexual abuse: Toward a constructivist theory of trauma and its treatment. In R. A. Neimyer & G. J. Neimeyer (Eds.), *Advances in Personal Construct Psychology* (Vol. 3, pp. 229–269). Greenwich, CT: JAI Press.

Haugli, L., Steen, E., Laerum, E., Finset, A., & Nygaard, R. (2000). Agency orientation and chronic musculoskeletal pain: Effects of a group learning program based on the personal construct theory. *Clinical Journal of Pain, 16*, 281–289.

Haugli, L., Steen, E., Laerum, E., Finset, A., & Nygaard, R. (2001). Learning to have less pain—Is it possible? A one-year follow-up study of the effects of a personal construct group learning programme on patients with chronic musculoskeletal pain. *Patient Education and Counseling, 45*, 111–118.

Hayes, S. C. (2004). Acceptance and commitment therapy, relational frame theory, and the third wave of behavioural and cognitive therapies. *Behaviour Therapy, 35*, 339–365.

Hayes, S. C., & Lillis, J. (2012). *Acceptance and Commitment Therapy*. Washington, DC: American Psychological Association.

Heckmann, M. (2014). *The OpenRepGrid project—Software tools for the analysis and administration of repertory grid data*. Workshop held at the 12th. Biennial Conference of the European Personal Construct Association (EPCA), Brno, Czech Republic.

Heckmann, M., Pries, J. C., Engelhardt, T.-C., Meixner, J., Saúl, L. A., Perea-Luque, J. R., & López-González, M. A. (2019). On the relation between order of elicitation and subjective construct importance. *Journal of Constructivist Psychology, 32*, 18–32.

Hermans, H. J. M., & DiMaggio, G. (2004). *The Dialogical Self in Psychotherapy*. New York: Brunner-Routledge.

Hinkle, D. N. (1965). *The change of personal constructs from the viewpoint of a theory of construct implications*. Unpublished PhD thesis, Ohio State University.

Hinkle, D. N. (1970). The game of personal constructs. In D. Bannister (Ed.), *Perspectives in Personal Construct Theory* (pp. 91–110). London: Academic Press.

Hobart, R. E. (1934). Free will as involving determination and inconceivable without it. *Mind, 43*(169), 1–27.

Hoffman, L. (1981). *Foundations of Family Therapy: A Conceptual Framework for Systems Change*. New York: Basic Books.

Hoffman, L. (1988). A constructivist position for family therapy. *Irish Journal of Psychology, 9,* 110–129.

Holder, E. (2018). *Mothers' and professionals' construal of the role of mother in health care settings*. Unpublished DClinPsy. thesis, University of Hertfordshire.

Holland, R. (1970). George Kelly: Constructive innocent and reluctant existentialist. In D. Bannister (Ed.), *Perspectives in Personal Construct Theory* (pp. 111–132). London: Academic Press.

Holland, R. (1981). From perspectives to reflexivity. In H. Bonarius, R. Holland, & S. Rosenberg (Eds.), *Personal Construct Theory: Recent Advances in Theory and Practice* (pp. 23–29). London: MacMillan.

Holland, J. M., & Neimeyer, R. A. (2009). The efficacy of personal construct therapy as a function of the type and severity of the presenting problem. *Journal of Constructivist Psychology, 22,* 170–185.

Holland, J. M., Neimeyer, R. A., Currier, J. M., & Berman, J. S. (2007). The efficacy of personal construct therapy: A comprehensive review. *Journal of Clinical Psychology, 63,* 93–107.

Holmes, D., Murray, S. J., Perron, A., & Rail, G. (2006). Deconstructing the evidence-based discourse in health sciences: Truth, power and fascism. *International Journal of Evidence-Based Healthcare, 4,* 180–186.

Hookway, C. (2012). *The Pragmatic Maxim: Essays on Peirce and Pragmatism*. Oxford, UK: Oxford University Press.

Hopkins, N. J. (2012). Is there a typical agoraphobic core structure? *Personal Construct Theory and Practice, 9,* 19–27.

Horley, J. (Ed.). (2003). *Personal Construct Perspectives on Forensic Psychology*. Hove, UK: Brunner-Routledge.

Horley, J., & Francoeur, A. (2003). *Domestic assault from a PCP perspective*. Paper presented at XVth. International Congress of Personal Construct Psychology, Huddersfield, UK.

Howard, K. I., Orlinsky, D. E., & Lueger, R. J. (1995). The design of clinically relevant outcome research: Some considerations and an example. In M. Aveline & D. A. Shapiro (Eds.), *Research Foundations of Psychotherapy Practice* (pp. 3–48). Chichester, UK: Wiley.

Howells, K. (1983). Social construing and violent behaviour in mentally abnormal offenders. In J. W. Hinton (Ed.), *Dangerousness: Problems of Assessment and Prediction* (pp. 114–129). London: Allen and Unwin.

Hughes, S. L., & Neimeyer, R. A. (1990). A cognitive model of suicidal behavior. In D. Lester (Ed.), *Understanding Suicide: The State of the Art* (pp. 1–28). New York: Charles Press.

Hughes, S. L., & Neimeyer, R. A. (1993). Cognitive predictors of suicide risk among hospitalized psychiatric patients: A prospective study. *Death Studies, 17*, 103–124.

Humphreys, C. L., Dutile, R., & Leitner, L. (2001). *Empirical support for experiential personal construct therapy: A common 'factor analysis'.* Paper presented at XIVth. International Congress of Personal Construct Psychology, Wollongong, Australia.

Husserl, E. (1929). *Cartesian Meditations.* Dordrecht: Kluwer.

Ivey, A. E. (1986). *Developmental Therapy.* San Francisco: Jossey-Bass.

Jackson, S. (1992). A PCT therapy group for adolescents. In P. Maitland & D. Brennan (Eds.), *Personal Construct Theory Deviancy and Social Work* (pp. 163–174). London: Inner London Probation Service/Centre for Personal Construct Psychology.

Jackson, S. R., & Bannister, D. (1985). Growing into self. In D. Bannister (Ed.), *Issues and Approaches in Personal Construct Theory* (pp. 67–82). London: Academic Press.

James, W. (2003). Does consciousness exist? Reprinted in *Essays in Radical Empiricism* (pp. 1–20). New York: Dover.

Jenkin, A. C., Ellis-Caird, H., & Winter, D. A. (2020/in press). Moral judgments and ethical constructs in clinical psychology doctoral students. *Ethics and Behavior.*

Jenkin, A. C., & Winter, D. A. (2020/in press). Exploration of ethical construing in clinical psychology doctoral students: An adaptation of repertory grid technique. *Journal of Constructivist Psychology.*

Johnstone, L. (2014). Controversies and debates about formulation. In L. Johnstone & R. Dallos (Eds.), *Formulation in Psychology and Psychotherapy* (2nd ed., pp. 260–289). London: Routledge.

Jones, R. A. (2020). The presence of self in the person: Reflexive positioning and personal constructs psychology. *Journal for the Theory of Social Behaviour, 27*(4), 453–471.

Kalekin-Fishman, D. (2005). 'Plain talk': Producing and reproducing alienation. In D. Kalekin-Fishman & L. Langman (Eds.), *The Evolution of*

Alienation: Trauma, Promise and the Millennium (pp. 283–307). Lanham, MD: Rowman and Littlefield.

Karasu, T. B. (1986). The psychotherapies: Benefits and limitations. *American Journal of Psychotherapy, 40,* 324–343.

Karst, T. O. (1980). The relationship between personal construct theory and psychotherapeutic techniques. In A. W. Landfield & L. M. Leitner (Eds.), *Personal Construct Psychology: Psychotherapy and Personality* (pp. 166–184). New York: Wiley.

Karst, T. O., & Trexler, L. D. (1970). Initial study using fixed role and rational-emotive therapy in treating speaking anxiety. *Journal of Consulting and Clinical Psychology, 34,* 360–366.

Kazdin, A. E. (1994). Methodology, design, and evaluation in psychotherapy research. In A. E. Bergin & S. L. Garfield (Eds.), *Handbook of Psychotherapy and Behavior Change* (pp. 19–71). Oxford: Wiley.

Kelly, G. A. (1955). *The Psychology of Personal Constructs. Vol. I, II.* New York: Norton (2nd printing: 1991, London and New York: Routledge).

Kelly, G. A. (1959). *Values, knowledge and social control.* Centre for PCP document, Fransella/Mair Collection, University of Hertfordshire.

Kelly, G. A. (1961). Theory and therapy in suicide: The personal construct point of view. In M. Farberow & E. Shneidman (Eds.), *The Cry for Help* (pp. 255–280). New York: McGraw-Hill.

Kelly, G. A. (1964). The language of hypothesis: Man's psychological instrument. *Journal of Individual Psychology, 20,* 137–152.

Kelly, G. A. (1969a). Sin and psychotherapy. In B. Maher (Ed.), *Clinical Psychology and Personality: The Selected Papers of George Kelly* (pp. 165–188). New York: Wiley.

Kelly, G. A. (1969b). Personal construct theory and the psychotherapeutic interview. In B. Maher (Ed.), *Clinical Psychology and Personality: The Selected Papers of George Kelly* (pp. 224–264). New York: Wiley.

Kelly, G. A. (1969c). The autobiography of a theory. In B. Maher (Ed.), *Clinical Psychology and Personality: The Selected Papers of George Kelly* (pp. 46–65). New York: Wiley.

Kelly, G. A. (1969d). Man's construction of his alternatives. In B. Maher (Ed.), *Clinical Psychology and Personality: The Selected Papers of George Kelly* (pp. 66–93). New York: Wiley.

Kelly, G. A. (1969e). The psychotherapeutic relationship. In B. Maher (Ed.), *Clinical psychology and Personality: The Selected Papers of George Kelly* (pp. 216–223). New York: Wiley.

Kelly, G. A. (1969f). Hostility. In B. Maher (Ed.), *Clinical Psychology and Personality: The Selected Papers of George Kelly* (pp. 267–280). New York: Wiley.

Kelly, G. A. (1969g). In whom confide: On whom depend for what? In B. Maher (Ed.), *Clinical Psychology and Personality: The Selected Papers of George Kelly* (pp. 189–206). New York: Wiley.

Kelly, G. A. (1969h). The threat of aggression. In B. Maher (Ed.), *Clinical Psychology and Personality: The Selected Papers of George Kelly* (pp. 281–288). New York: Wiley.

Kelly, G. A. (1969i). Humanistic methodology in psychological research. In B. Maher (Ed.), *Clinical Psychology and Personality: The Selected Papers of George Kelly* (pp. 133–146). New York: Wiley.

Kelly, G. A. (1970a). A brief introduction to personal construct theory. In D. Bannister (Ed.), *Perspectives in Personal Construct Theory* (pp. 3–20). London: Academic Press.

Kelly, G. A. (1970b). Behaviour is an experiment. In D. Bannister (Ed.), *Perspectives in Personal Construct Theory* (pp. 255–269). London: Academic Press.

Kelly, G. A. (1980). A psychology of the optimal man. In A. W. Landfield & L. M. Leitner (Eds.), *Personal Construct Psychology: Psychotherapy and Personality* (pp. 18–35). New York: Wiley.

Kelly, G. A. (1996). Europe's matrix of decision. In D. Kalekin-Fishman & B. Walker (Eds.), *The Structure of Group Realities: Culture, Society, and Personal Construct Theory* (pp. 27–64). Malabar, Florida: Krieger.

Kenny, V. (1988). Changing conversations: A constructivist model of training for psychologists. In G. Dunnett (Ed.), *Working with People: Clinical Uses of Personal Construct Psychology* (pp. 140–157). London: Routledge.

Kerrick-Mack, J. (1978). The role construct repertory grid as a process for facilitating self-awareness and personal growth. In F. Fransella (Ed.), *Personal Construct Psychology 1977* (pp. 117–118). London: Academic Press.

Keshavarz-Afshar, H., Nosrati, F., Azad-Marzabadi, E., & Eslahi, N. (2017). The effectiveness of personal construct therapy on marital satisfaction. *Iran Red Crescent Medical Journal, 19,* 1–7.

Kline, P. (1981). *Fact and Fantasy in Freudian Theory*. London: Methuen.

Klion, R. E. (1993). Chemical dependency: A personal construct theory approach. In A. W. Landfield & L. M. Leitner (Eds.), *Critical Issues in Personal Construct Psychotherapy* (pp. 279–301). Melbourne, FL: Krieger.

Knafo, S. (2016). Bourdieu and the dead end of reflexivity: On the impossible task of locating the subject. *Review of International Studies, 42,* 25–47.

Koch, H. (1985). Group psychotherapy. In E. Button (Ed.), *Personal Construct Theory and Mental Health* (pp. 302–326). London: Croom Helm.

Kremsdorf, R. (1985). An extension of fixed-role therapy with a couple. In F. Epting & A. W. Landfield (Eds.), *Anticipating Personal Construct Psychology* (pp. 216–224). Lincoln: University of Nebraska Press.

Laing, R. D. (1971). The family and the 'family'. In R. D. Laing (Ed.), *The Politics of the Family and Other Essays* (pp. 3–18). Harmondsworth, UK: Penguin.

Laing, R. D. (1981). Intervention in social situations. In S. Walrond-Skinner (Ed.), *Developments in Family Therapy: Theories and Applications Since 1948* (pp. 16–29). London: Routledge and Kegan Paul.

Lambert, M. J. (1992). Psychotherapy outcome research: Implications for integrative and eclectic therapists. In J. C. Norcross & M. R. Goldfried (Eds.), *Handbook of Psychotherapy Integration* (pp. 94–129). New York: Basic Books.

Lambert, M. J., Hansen, N. B., & Finch, A. E. (2001). Patient-focused research: Using patient outcome data to enhance treatment effects. *Journal of Consulting and Clinical Psychology, 69,* 159–172.

Lambert, M. J., & Ogles, B. M. (2004). The efficacy and effectiveness of psychotherapy. In M. J. Lambert (Ed.), *Bergin and Garfield's Handbook of Psychotherapy and Behavior Change* (pp. 139–193). New York: Wiley.

Laming, C. J. (2006). Shedding violent expressions of anger constructively. In P. Cummins (Ed.), *Working with Anger: A Constructivist Approach* (pp. 25–43). Chichester, UK: Wiley.

Landfield, A. (1971). *Personal Construct Systems in Psychotherapy.* Chicago: Rand McNally.

Landfield, A. (1976). A personal construct approach to suicidal behaviour. In P. Slater (Ed.), *The Measurement of Intrapersonal Space by Grid Technique: Vol. 1. Explorations of Intrapersonal Space* (pp. 93–107). Wiley: London.

Landfield, A. W. (1979). Exploring socialization through the interpersonal transaction group. In P. Stringer & D. Bannister (Eds.), *Constructs of Sociality and Individuality* (pp. 133–152). London: Academic Press.

Landfield, A. W. (1980). Personal construct psychotherapy: A personal construction. In A. W. Landfield & L. M. Leitner (Eds.), *Personal Construct Psychology: Psychotherapy and Personality* (pp. 122–140). New York: Wiley.

Landfield, A. (1988). Personal science and the concept of validation. *International Journal of Personal Construct Psychology, 1,* 237–249.

Landfield, A. W., & Rivers, P. C. (1975). An introduction to interpersonal transaction and rotating dyads. *Psychotherapy: Theory, Research and Practice, 12,* 365–373.

Lane, L. G., & Viney, L. L. (2005a). Group work with women living with breast cancer. In D. A. Winter & L. L. Viney (Eds.), *Personal Construct Psychotherapy: Advances in Theory, Practice and Research* (pp. 310–319). London: Croom Helm.

Lane, L. G., & Viney, L. L. (2005b). The effects of personal construct group therapy on breast cancer survivors. *Journal of Consulting and Clinical Psychology, 73*, 284–292.

Layard, R. (2006). *Happiness: Lessons from a New Science*. Harmondsworth, UK: Penguin.

Leitner, L. M. (1985a). The terrors of cognition: On the experiential validity of personal construct theory. In D. Bannister (Ed.), *Issues and Approaches in Personal Construct Theory* (pp. 83–103). London: Academic Press.

Leitner, L. M. (1985b). Interview methodologies for construct elicitation: Searching for the core. In F. Epting & A. W. Landfield (Eds.), *Anticipating Personal Construct Psychology* (pp. 292–305). Lincoln: University of Nebraska Press.

Leitner, L. (1990). Sharing the mystery: A therapist's experience of personal construct psychotherapy. In H. Jones & G. Dunnett (Eds.), *Selected Papers from the 2nd British Conference on Personal Construct Psychology*. York, UK.

Leitner, L., & Cummins, P. (Eds.), (2019). *Experiential Personal Construct Psychotherapy: Selected Papers*. E-book available from: https://read.amazon.co.uk/?asin=B07SX92BSC.

Leitner, L. M., & Faidley, A. J. (1999). Creativity in experiential personal construct psychotherapy. *Journal of Constructivist Psychology, 12*, 273–286.

Leitner, L. M., Faidley, A. J., & Celentana, M. A. (2000). Diagnosing human meaning-making: An experiential constructivist approach. In R. A. Neimeyer & J. D. Raskin (Eds.), *Construction of Disorders: Meaning Making Frameworks for Psychotherapy* (pp. 175–203). Washington, DC: American Psychological Association.

Leitner, L. M., Faidley, A. J., Dominici, D., Humphreys, C., Loeffler, V., Schlutsmeyer, M., & Thomas, J. (2005). Encountering an other: Experiential personal construct psychotherapy. In D. A. Winter & L. L. Viney (Eds.), *Personal Construct Psychotherapy: Advances in Theory, Practice and Research* (pp. 54–68). London: Whurr.

Leitner, L. M., & Pfenninger, D. T. (1994). Sociality and optimal functioning. *Journal of Constructivist Psychology, 7*, 119–135.

Levi-Strauss, C. (1962). *Totemism*. Harmondsworth, UK: Penguin.

Levy, C. (1987). Interiorised stuttering: A group therapy approach. In C. Levy (Ed.), *Stuttering Therapies: Practical Approaches* (pp. 104–121). London: Croom Helm.

Lincoln, J., & Hoffman, L. (2019). Toward an integration of constructivism and existential psychotherapy. *Journal of Constructivist Psychology, 32,* 108–125.

Linehan, M. M. (1993). *Cognitive-Behavioral Treatment of Borderline Personality Disorder.* New York: Guilford.

Lira, F. T., Nay, R., McCullough, J. P., & Etkin, M. W. (1975). Relative effects of modeling and role playing in the treatment of avoidance behaviors. *Journal of Consulting and Clinical Psychology, 43,* 608–618.

Llewelyn, S., & Dunnett, G. (1987). The use of personal construct theory in groups. In R. A. Neimeyer & G. J. Neimeyer (Eds.), *Personal Construct Therapy Casebook* (pp. 245–260). New York: Springer.

Lorenzini, R., & Sassaroli, S. (1995). Attachment as an informative relationship. *International Journal of Personal Construct Psychology, 3,* 239–248.

Lovell, M. S. (2011). *The Churchills: A Family at the Heart of History—From the Duke of Marlborough to Winston Churchill.* London: Little, Brown.

Lovenfosse, M., & Viney, L. L. (1999). Understanding and helping mothers of children with 'special needs' using personal construct group work. *Community Mental Health Journal, 5,* 431–442.

Luborsky, L., Diguer, L., Seligman, D. A., Rosenthal, R., Krause, E. D., Johnson, S., ... & Schweizer, E. (1999). The researcher's own therapy allegiances: A "wild card" in comparisons of treatment efficacy. *Clinical Psychology: Science and Practice, 6*(1), 95–106.

Mackay, H. C., Barkham, M., Rees, A., & Stiles, W. B. (2003). Appraisal of published reviews of research on psychotherapy and counselling with adults 1990–1998. *Journal of Consulting and Clinical Psychology, 71,* 652–656.

MacMurray, J. (1961). *Persons in Relation.* London: Faber and Faber.

Mahoney, M. J. (1988a). Constructive metatheory: I. Basic features and historical foundations. *International Journal of Personal Construct Psychology, 1,* 1–35.

Mahoney, M. J. (1988b). Constructive metatheory: II. Implications for psychotherapy. *International Journal of Personal Construct Psychology, 1,* 299–315.

Mahoney, M. J. (2003). *Constructive Psychotherapy: A Practical Guide.* New York: Guilford.

Mahoney, M., & Arnkoff, D. (1978). Cognitive and self-control therapies. In S. Garfield & A. Bergin (Eds.), *Handbook of Psychotherapy and Behavior Change* (3rd ed., pp. 689–722). New York: Wiley.

Mair, J. M. M. (1970). Experimenting with individuals. *British Journal of Medical Psychology, 43,* 245–256.

Mair, J. M. M. (1988). Psychology as storytelling. *International Journal of Personal Construct Psychology, 1,* 125–137.

Mair, J. M. M. (1989). Kelly, Bannister, and a story-telling psychology. *International Journal of Personal Construct Psychology, 2,* 1–15.

Mair, J. M. M. (2014). *Another Way of Knowing: The Poetry of Psychological Inquiry.* London: Raven Books.

Mair, J. M. M. (2015a). The community of self. In D. A. Winter & N. Reed (Eds.), *Toward a Radical Re-definition of Psychology: The Selected Works of Miller Mair* (pp. 102–112). London: Routledge.

Mair, J. M. M. (2015b). Metaphors for living. In D. A. Winter & N. Reed (Eds.), *Toward a Radical Re-definition of Psychology: The Selected Works of Miller Mair* (pp. 73–101). London: Routledge.

Mair, J. M. M. (2015c). Psychotherapy, conversation and storytelling. In D. A. Winter & N. Reed (Eds.), *Toward a Radical Re-definition of Psychology: The Selected Works of Miller Mair* (pp. 131–146). London: Routledge.

Malins, G. L., Couchman, L., Viney, L. L., & Grenyer, B. F. S. (2004). Time to talk: Evaluation of a staff-resident quality time intervention on the perception of staff in aged care. *Clinical Psychologist, 8,* 48–52.

Malloch, S., & Trevarthen, C. (2018). The human nature of music. *Frontiers in Psychology, 9,* 1680.

Mancuso, J. C. (1976). Current motivational models in the elaboration of personal construct theory. *Nebraska Symposium on Motivation, 24,* 43–97.

Mancuso, J. C., & Adams-Webber, J. R. (1982). Anticipation as a constructive process: The fundamental postulate. In J. C. Mancuso & J. R. Adams-Webber (Eds.), *The Construing Person* (pp. 8–32). New York: Praeger.

Margison, F. R., Barkham, M., Evans, C., McGrath, G., Clark, J. M., Audin, K., & Connell, J. (2000). Measurement and psychotherapy: Evidence-based practice and practice-based evidence. *British Journal of Psychiatry, 177* (2), 123–130.

Mascolo, M. F., & Kallio, E. (2020). The phenomenology of between: An intersubjective epistemology for psychological science. *Journal of Constructivist Psychology, 33,* 1–28.

Mascolo, M. F., & Mancuso, J. C. (1990). Functioning of epigenetically involved emotion systems: A constructive analysis. *International Journal of Personal Construct Psychology, 3,* 205–222.

Mattila, A. (2001). *'Seeing Things in a New Light'—Reframing in Therapeutic Conversation.* Helsinki, Finland: Rehabilitation Foundation, Research Reports.

Maturana, H. R., & Varela, F. J. (1987). *The Tree of Knowledge: The Biological Roots of Human Understanding.* Boston: Shambhala.

McCoy, M. M. (1981). Positive and negative emotion: A personal construct theory interpretation. In H. Bonarius, R. Holland, & S. Rosenberg (Eds.), *Personal Construct Psychology: Recent Advances in Theory and Practice* (pp. 95–104). London: MacMillan.

McCullough, J. P., Jr. (2000). *Treatment for Chronic Depression: Cognitive Behavioral Analysis System of Psychotherapy (CBASP).* New York: Guilford.

McDonagh, D., & Adams-Webber, J. (1987). The implication potential of personal constructs in relation to their subjective importance and order of elicitation. *Social Behavior and Personality, 15,* 81–86.

McDonald, D. E., & Mancuso, J. C. (1987). A constructivist approach to parent training. In R. Neimeyer & G. Neimeyer (Eds.), *Personal Construct Therapy Casebook* (pp. 172–189). New York: Springer.

McNamee, S., & Gergen, K. J. (Eds.). (1992). *Therapy as Social Construction.* London: Sage.

McWilliams, S. (1996). Accepting the invitational. In B. Walker, J. Costigan, L. Viney, & B. Warren (Eds.), *Personal Construct Theory: A Psychology of the Future* (pp. 57–78). Sydney: Australian Psychological Society.

McWilliams, S. (2012). Mindfulness and extending constructivist psychotherapy integration. *Journal of Constructivist Psychology, 25,* 230–250.

Mead, G. H. (1934/1962). *Mind, Self and Society.* Chicago: University of Chicago Press.

Merleau-Ponty, M. (1962). *The Phenomenology of Perception.* London: Routledge.

Messer, S. B. (2001). Empirically supported treatments: What's a nonbehaviorist to do? In B. D. Slife, R. N. Williams, & S. H. Barlow (Eds.), *Critical Issues in Psychotherapy: Translating New Ideas into Practice* (pp. 3–19). London: Sage.

Metcalfe, C., Winter, D., & Viney, L. (2007). The effectiveness of personal construct psychotherapy in clinical practice: A systematic review and meta-analysis. *Psychotherapy Research, 17,* 431–442.

Miles, A., Grey, J., Polychronis, A., & Melchiorri, C. (2002). Critical advances in the evaluation and development of clinical care. *Journal of Evaluation in Clinical Practice, 8*, 87–102.

Minuchin, S. (1974). *Families and Family Therapy*. London: Tavistock.

Misak, C. (2011). Presidential address: American pragmatism and indispensability arguments. *Transactions of the Charles S. Peirce Society, 47*, 261–273.

Montesano, A., Feixas, G., Erazo-Caicedo, M. I., Saúl, L. A., Dada, G., & Winter, D. (2014). Cognitive conflicts and symptom severity in Dysthymia: "I'd rather be good than happy". *Salud Mental, 37*, 41–48.

Montesano, A., Gonçalves, M. M., & Feixas, G. (2016). Self-narrative reconstruction after dilemma-focused intervention for depression: A comparison of good and poor outcome cases. *Psychotherapy Research, 27*, 112–126.

Montesano, A., López-González, M. A., Saúl, L. Á., & Feixas, G. (2015). A review of cognitive conflicts research: A meta-analytic study of prevalence and relation to symptoms. *Neuropsychiatric Disease and Treatment, 12*, 2997–3006.

Moradi, B., van den Berg, J., & Epting, F. (2006). Intrapersonal and interpersonal manifestations of anti-lesbian and gay prejudice: An application of personal construct theory. *Journal of Counselling Psychology, 53*(1), 57–66.

Moran, D. (2000). *Introduction to Phenomenology*. London: Routledge.

Moran, H. (2014). *Using Personal construct psychology (PCP) in practice with children and adolescents*. Online eBook: https://issuu.com/pcpinpractice/docs/using_personal_construct_psychology.

Morawski, J. G. (2005). Reflexivity and the psychologist. *History of Human Sciences, 18*, 77–105.

Morris, J. B. (1977). Appendix 1: The prediction and measurement of change in a psychotherapy group using the repertory grid. In F. Fransella & D. Bannister (Eds.), *A Manual for Repertory Grid Technique* (pp. 120–148). London: Academic Press.

Morris, C. (2000). Working with people: Making sense of dementia. *Journal of Dementia Care, 8*(4), 23–25.

Morris, C. (2004). Personal Construct Psychology and person-centred care. In G. M. M. Jones & B. M. L. Miesen (Eds.), *Care-Giving in Dementia: Researches and Applications* (Vol. 3, pp. 65–90). Hove and New York: Brunner Routledge.

Morgan, C. D., & Murray, H. A. (1935). A method for investigating fantasies: The thematic apperception test. *Archives of Neurology & Psychiatry, 34*, 289–306.

Musicki, V. (2017). How might personal construct psychology benefit from narrative approaches? *Journal of Constructivist Psychology, 30,* 360–370.

Naffi, N., & Davidson, A.-L. (2017). Engaging host society youth in exploring how they construe the influence of social media on the resettlement of Syrian refugees. *Personal Construct Theory and Practice, 14,* 116–128.

Nagae, N., & Nedate, K. (2001). Comparison of constructive cognitive and rational cognitive psychotherapies for students with social anxiety. *Constructivism in the Human Sciences, 6,* 41–49.

Neimeyer, G. J. (Ed.). (1993). *Constructivist Assessment: A Casebook.* Newbury Park, CA: Sage.

Neimeyer, G. J. (1985). Personal constructs in the counseling of couples. In F. R. Epting & A. W. Landfield (Eds.), *Anticipating Personal Construct Psychology* (pp. 201–215). Lincoln: University of Nebraska Press.

Neimeyer, G. J., & Merluzzi, T. V. (1982). Group structure and group process: Personal construct therapy and group development. *Small Group Behavior, 13,* 150–164.

Neimeyer, G. J., & Rood, L. (1997). Contemporary expressions of constructivist psychotherapy. In G. J. Neimeyer & R. A. Neimeyer (Eds.), *Advances in Personal Construct Psychology* (Vol. 4, pp. 185–205). Greenwich, CT: JAI Press.

Neimeyer, R. A. (1985a). *The Development of Personal Construct Psychology.* Lincoln: University of Nebraska Press.

Neimeyer, R. A. (1985b). Personal constructs in clinical practice. In P. C. Kendall (Ed.), *Advances in Cognitive-Behavioural Research and Therapy* (Vol. 4, pp. 275–339). New York: Academic Press.

Neimeyer, R. A. (1985c). Group psychotherapies for depression: An overview. *International Journal of Mental Health, 13,* 3–7.

Neimeyer, R. A. (1987). An orientation to personal construct therapy. In R. A. Neimeyer & G. J. Neimeyer (Eds.), *Personal Construct Therapy Casebook* (pp. 3–19). New York: Springer.

Neimeyer, R. A. (1988a). Integrative directions in personal construct therapy. *International Journal of Personal Construct Psychology, 1,* 283–297.

Neimeyer, R. A. (1988b). Clinical guidelines for conducting Interpersonal Transaction Groups. *International Journal of Personal Construct Psychology, 1,* 181–190.

Neimeyer, R. A. (1993). Constructivist approaches to the measurement of meaning. In G. J. Neimeyer (Ed.), *Constructivist Assessment: A Casebook* (pp. 58–103). Newbury Park, CA: Sage.

Neimeyer, R. A. (1999). Narrative strategies in grief therapy. *Journal of Constructivist Psychology, 12,* 65–85.

Neimeyer, R. A. (2000). Narrative disruptions in the construction of self. In R. A. Neimeyer & J. A. Raskin (Eds.), *Constructions of Disorder: Meaning Making Frameworks for Psychotherapy* (pp. 207–241). Washington, DC: American Psychological Association.

Neimeyer, R. A. (2004). Fostering posttraumatic growth: A narrative contribution. *Psychological Inquiry, 15,* 53–59.

Neimeyer, R. A. (2005). Growing through grief: Constructing coherence in narratives of loss. In D. A. Winter & L. L. Viney (Eds.), *Personal Construct Psychotherapy: Advances in Theory, Practice and Research* (pp. 111–126). London: Whurr.

Neimeyer, R. A. (2009). *Constructivist Psychotherapy.* London: Routledge.

Neimeyer, R. A. (2016). Reconstructing meaning in bereavement. In D. A. Winter & N. Reed (Eds.), *The Wiley Handbook of Personal Construct Psychology* (pp. 254–264). Chichester, UK: Wiley.

Neimeyer, R. A., & Feixas, G. (1990). Constructivist contributions to psychotherapy integration. *Journal of Integrative and Eclectic Psychotherapy, 9,* 4–20.

Neimeyer, R. A., Klein, M. H., Gurman, A. S., & Greist, J. H. (1983). Cognitive structure and depressive symptomatology. *British Journal of Cognitive Psychotherapy, 1,* 65–73.

Neimeyer, R. A., & Mahoney, M. J. (Eds.). (1995). *Constructivism in Psychotherapy.* Washington, DC: American Psychological Association.

Neimeyer, R. A., & Neimeyer, G. J. (Eds.). (1987). *Personal Construct Therapy Casebook.* New York: Springer.

Neimeyer, R. A., & Raskin, J. D. (2001). Varieties of constructivism in psychotherapy. *Handbook of Cognitive-Behavioral Therapies* (Vol. 2, pp. 393–430). New York: Guilford.

Neimeyer, R. A., & Winter, D. A. (2006). To be or not to be: Personal constructions of the suicidal choice. In T. Ellis (Ed.), *Cognition and Suicide: Theory, Research and Practice* (pp. 149–169). Washington, DC: American Psychological Association.

Neimeyer, R. A., & Winter, D. A. (2007). Personal construct therapy. In N. Kazantzis & L. L'Abate (Eds.), *Handbook of Homework Assignments in Psychotherapy: Research, Practice and Prevention* (pp. 151–171). New York: Springer.

Neimeyer, R. A., Woodward, M., Pickover, A., & Smigelsky, M. (2016). Questioning our questions: A constructivist technique for clinical supervision. *Journal of Constructivist Psychology, 29,* 100–111.

NICE. (2014). *The Guidelines Manual*. London: National Institute for Health and Clinical Excellence.

Norcross, J. C. (1986). Eclectic psychotherapy: An introduction and overview. In J. C. Norcross (Ed.), *Handbook of Eclectic psychotherapy* (pp. 3–24). New York: Brunner/Mazel.

Oades, L. G., & Patterson, F. (2016). Experience cycle methodology: A qualitative method to understand the process of revising personal constructs. In D. A. Winter & N. Reed (Eds.), *The Wiley Handbook of Personal Construct Psychology* (pp. 125–136). Chichester, UK: Wiley-Blackwell.

Oades, L. G., & Viney, L. L. (2000). Experience cycle methodology: A new method for personal construct psychologists? In J. W. Scheer (Ed.), *The Person in Society: Challenges to a Constructivist Theory* (pp. 160–173). Giessen, Germany: Psychosozial Verlag.

Oades, L. G., & Viney, L. L. (2012). Experience cycle methodology: Understanding the construct revision pathway. In P. Caputi, L. L. Viney, B. M. Walker, & N. Crittenden (Eds.), *Personal Construct Methodology* (pp. 129–146). Chichester, UK: Wiley-Blackwell.

O'Connor, J., & Seymour, S. (2002). *Introducing Neuro-Linguistic Programming: Psychological Skills for Understanding and Influencing People*. London: Element.

O'Connor, P. (2015). *A Constructionist Clinical Psychology for Cognitive Behaviour Therapy*. Hove, UK: Routledge.

Ogilvie, D., Egan, M., Hamilton, V., & Petticrew, M. (2005). Systematic reviews of health effects of social interventions: 2. Best available evidence: How low should you go? *Journal of Epidemiology and Community Health, 59,* 886–892.

Orlinsky, D. E., Rønnestad, M. H., & Willutzki, U. (2004). Fifty years of psychotherapy process-outcome research: Continuity and change. In M. J. Lambert (Ed.), *Bergin and Garfield's Handbook of Psychotherapy and Behavior Change* (pp. 307–389). New York: Wiley.

Pagliari, C., & Grimshaw, J. (2002). Impact of group structure and process on multidisciplinary evidence-based guideline development: An observational study. *Journal of Evaluation in Clinical Practice, 8,* 145–153.

Paris, M. E., & Epting, F. (2004). Social and personal construction: Two sides of the same coin. In J. D. Raskin & S. K. Bridges (Eds.), *Studies in Meaning*

2: Bridging the Personal and Social in Constructivist Psychology (pp. 3–35). New York: Pace University Press.

Parry, G., & Richardson, A. (1996). *NHS Psychotherapy Services in England: Review of Strategic Policy*. London: NHS Executive.

Pavlović, J. (2011). Personal construct psychology and social constructionism are not incompatible: Implications of a reframing. *Theory and Psychology, 21,* 396–411.

Paz, C., Montesano, A., Winter, D., & Feixas, G. (2019). Cognitive conflict resolution during psychotherapy: Its impact on depressive symptoms and psychological distress. *Psychotherapy Research, 29,* 45–57.

Peirce, C. S. (1998a). Some consequences of four incapacities. In E. C. Moore (Ed.), *Charles S. Peirce: The Essential Writings* (pp. 85–118). New York: Prometheus Books.

Peirce, C. S. (1998b). Review of the works of George Berkeley. In E. C. Moore (Ed.), *Charles S. Peirce: The Essential Writings* (pp. 51–63). New York: Prometheus Books.

Peirce, C. S. (1998c). How to make your ideas clear. In E. C. Moore (Ed.), *Charles S. Peirce: The Essential Writings* (pp. 137–157). New York: Prometheus Books.

Peirce, C. S. (1998d). What pragmatism is. In E. C. Moore (Ed.), *Charles S. Peirce: The Essential Writings* (pp. 262–280). New York: Prometheus Books.

Pekkala, D., & Dave, B. (2005). Evaluation. In P. Cummins (Ed.), *Working with Anger* (pp. 199–212). London: Wiley.

Pinheiro, R. T., Botella, L., de Avila Quevedo, L., Pinheiro, K. A. T., Jansen, K., Osório, C. M., ... & da Silva, R. A. (2014). Maintenance of the effects of cognitive behavioral and relational constructivist psychotherapies in the treatment of women with postpartum depression: A randomized clinical trial. *Journal of Constructivist Psychology, 27,* 59–68.

Polkinghorne, D. E. (1995). Piaget's and Derrida's contributions to a constructivist psychotherapy. *Journal of Constructivist Psychology, 8,* 269–282.

Pottle, S. (1984). Developing a network-oriented services for elderly people and their carers. In A. Treacher & J. Carpenter (Eds.), *Using Family Therapy* (pp. 149–165). Oxford, UK: Blackwell.

Procter, H. G. (1978). *Personal construct theory and the family: A theoretical and methodological Study*. Unpublished PhD thesis, University of Bristol.

Procter, H. G. (1981). Family construct psychology: An approach to understanding and treating families. In S. Walrond-Skinner (Ed.), *Developments in Family Therapy: Theories and Applications since 1948* (pp. 350–366). London: Routledge and Kegan Paul.

Procter, H. G. (1985a). A construct approach to family therapy and systems intervention. In E. Button (Ed.), *Personal Construct Theory and Mental Health* (pp. 327–350). Beckenham, UK: Croom Helm.

Procter, H. G. (1985b). Repertory grid techniques in family therapy and research. In N. Beail (Ed.), *Repertory Grid Technique: Application in Clinical and Educational Settings* (pp. 218–242). Croom Helm: Beckenham, UK.

Procter, H. G. (1987). Change in the family construct system: Therapy of a mute and withdrawn schizophrenic patient. In R. Neimeyer & G. Neimeyer (Eds.), *Personal Construct Therapy Casebook* (pp. 153–171). New York: Springer.

Procter, H. G. (1996). The family construct system. In D. Kalekin-Fishman & B. Walker (Eds.), *The Structure of Group Realities: Culture, Society, and Personal Construct Theory* (pp. 161–180). Malabar, FL: Krieger.

Procter, H. G. (2000). Autism and family therapy: A personal construct approach. In S. Powell (Ed.), *Helping Children with Autism to Learn* (pp. 63–77). London: David Fulton.

Procter, H. G. (2001). Personal construct psychology and autism. *Journal of Constructivist Psychology, 14,* 105–124.

Procter, H. G. (2002). Constructs of individuals and relationships. *Context, 59,* 11–12.

Procter, H. G. (2005). Techniques of personal construct family therapy. In D. A. Winter & L. L. Viney (Eds.), *Personal Construct Psychotherapy: Advances in Theory, Practice and Research* (pp. 94–108). London: Whurr.

Procter, H. G. (2007a). Construing within the family. In R. Butler & D. Green (Eds.), *The Child Within: Taking the Young Person's Perspective by Applying Personal Construct Theory* (2nd ed., pp. 190–206). Chichester, UK: Wiley.

Procter, H. G. (2007b). Manual for Using the G-PEG (Goals Perceiver Element Grid) in Team Building and Consultation. Retrieved, April 2018, from: http://www.pcp-net.org/tools/G-PEG%20Manual%202015.pdf.

Procter, H. G. (2009a). The construct. In R. J. Butler (Ed.), *Reflections in Personal Construct Theory* (pp. 21–40). Chichester, UK: Wiley-Blackwell.

Procter, H. G. (2009b). Reflexivity and reflective practice in personal and relational construct psychology. In J. Stedmon & R. Dallos (Eds.), *Reflective Practice in Psychotherapy and Counselling* (pp. 93–114). Milton Keynes, UK: Open University Press.

Procter, H. G. (2014a). Peirce's contributions to constructivism and personal construct psychology: I. Philosophical aspects. *Personal Construct Theory & Practice, 11,* 6–33.

Procter, H. G. (2014b). Qualitative grids, the relationality corollary and the levels of interpersonal construing. *Journal of Constructivist Psychology, 27,* 243–262.

Procter, H. G. (2016a). Peirce's contributions to constructivism and personal construct psychology: II. Science, logic and Inquiry. *Personal Construct Theory & Practice, 13,* 210–265.

Procter, H. G. (2016b). PCP, culture and society. In D. A. Winter & N. Reed (Eds.), *The Wiley Handbook of Personal Construct Psychology* (pp. 139–153). Chichester, UK: Wiley-Blackwell.

Procter, H. G. (2016c). Useful questions in interviewing families and children. *Rivista Italiana di Costrutivismo, 4,* 124–134.

Procter, H. G. (2017). Comparing PCP with other approaches: Systemic theory, phenomenology and semiotics. *Personal Construct Theory & Practice, 14,* 137–139.

Procter, H. G., & Cummins, P. (2014). *Personal Construct Psychology and Qualitative Grids: A series of 5 videos introducing the methods.* Retrieved October 2019, from: https://www.youtube.com/watch?v=z3uS7UA0P9M&feature=youtu.be&list=PLQwfkFsf7l9dg5Q2afwWkWfIfbQGYCVwX.

Procter, H. G., & Mason, R. (2004). *Autism in School: Concerns and Ways Forward.* Retrieved from: https://www.academia.edu/11648453/Autism_in_School_Concerns_and_Ways_Forward_by_Harry_Procter_and_Rachel_Mason_2004_.

Procter, H. G., & Parry, G. (1978). Constraint and freedom: The social origin of personal constructs. In F. Fransella (Ed.), *Personal Construct Psychology 1977* (pp. 157–170). London: Academic Press.

Procter, H. G., & Pieczora, R. (1993). A family oriented community mental health centre. In A. Treacher & J. Carpenter (Eds.), *Using Family Therapy in the 90's* (pp. 131–144). Oxford, UK: Blackwell.

Procter, H. G., & Pottle, S. (1980). Experiences and guidelines in running an open couples' psychotherapy group. *Journal of Family Therapy, 2,* 233–242.

Procter, H. G., & Procter, M. J. (2008). The use of qualitative grids to examine the development of the construct of good and evil in Byron's play 'Cain: A mystery'. *Journal of Constructivist Psychology, 21,* 343–354.

Procter, H. G., & Stephens, P. K. E. (1984). Developing family therapy in the day hospital. In A. Treacher & J. Carpenter (Eds.), *Using Family Therapy* (pp. 133–148). Oxford, UK: Blackwell.

Procter, H. G., & Ugazio, V. (2017). Family constructs and semantic polarities: A convergent perspective? In D. A. Winter, P. Cummins, H. G. Procter, & N. Reed (Eds.), *Personal Construct Psychology at 60: Papers from the 21st*

International Congress (pp. 68–89). Newcastle upon Tyne, UK: Cambridge Scholars Publishing.

Procter, H. G., & Walker, G. (1989). Brief therapy. In E. Street & W. Dryden (Eds.), *Family Therapy in Britain* (pp. 127–149). Milton Keynes, UK: Open University Press.

Radley, A. (1979). Construing as praxis. In P. Stringer & D. Bannister (Eds.), *Constructs of Sociality and Individuality* (pp. 73–90). London: Academic Press.

Raskin, J. D. (2002). Constructivism in psychology: Personal construct psychology, radical constructivism, and social constructionism. In J. D. Raskin & S. K. Bridges (Eds.), *Studies in Meaning: Exploring Constructivist Psychology* (pp. 1–25). New York: Pace University Press.

Raskin, J. D. (2007). Assimilative integration in constructivist psychotherapy. *Journal of Psychotherapy Integration, 17,* 50–69.

Raskin, J. D., & Debany, A. E. (2018). The inescapability of ethics and the impossibility of 'anything goes': A constructivist model of ethical meaning making. *Journal of Constructivist Psychology, 31,* 343–360.

Ravenette, T. (1977). Personal construct theory: An approach to the psychological investigation of children and young people. In D. Bannister (Ed.), *New Perspectives in Personal Construct Theory* (pp. 251–280). London: Academic Press.

Ravenette, T. (1980). The exploration of consciousness: Personal construct intervention with children. In A. W. Landfield & L. M. Leitner (Eds.), *Personal Construct Psychology: Psychotherapy and Personality* (pp. 36–52). New York: Wiley.

Ravenette, T. (Ed.). (1999a). *Personal Constructs in Educational Psychology: A Practitioner's View.* London: Whurr.

Ravenette, T. (1999b). A drawing and its opposite: An application of the notion of the 'construct' in the elicitation of children's drawings. In T. Ravenette (Ed.), *Personal Constructs in Educational Psychology: A Practitioner's View* (pp. 125–137). London: Whurr.

Ravenette, T. (1999c). Personal construct psychology and the assessment of young people: The one-off interview. In T. Ravenette (Ed.), *Personal Constructs in Educational Psychology: A Practitioner's View* (pp. 195–206). London: Whurr.

Rawlins, M. (2008). De Testimonio: On the evidence for decisions about the use of therapeutic interventions. *Clinical Medicine, 8,* 579–588.

Reed, N., Winter, D., Schulz, J., Aslan, E., Soldevilla, J. M., & Kuzu, D. (2014). An exemplary life? A personal construct analysis of the autobiography of Rudolf Hoess, commandant of Auschwitz. *Journal of Constructivist Psychology, 27,* 274–288.

Rober, P. (2017). *In Therapy Together: Family Therapy as a Dialogue.* London: Palgrave.

Robbins, S. (2005). Looking forward towards the end—Working with older people. In D. A. Winter & L. L. Viney (Eds.), *Personal Construct Psychotherapy: Advances in Theory, Practice and Research* (pp. 296–309). London: Croom Helm.

Rogers, C. R. (1951). *Client-Centered Therapy: Its Current Practice, Implications, and Theory.* Boston: Houghton Mifflin.

Rogers, C. R. (1956). Intellectual psychotherapy. *Contemporary Psychology, 1,* 357–358.

Rorty, R. (1999). *Philosophy and Social Hope.* London: Penguin Books.

Rosenbaum, R. (1996). Form, formlessness and formulation. *Journal of Psychotherapy Integration, 6,* 107–117.

Roth, A., & Fonagy, P. (1996). *What Works for Whom? A Critical Review of Psychotherapy Research.* New York: Guilford.

Roth, A., & Fonagy, P. (2005). *What Works for Whom? A Critical Review of Psychotherapy Research* (2nd ed.). New York: Guilford.

Rowe, D. (2007). *My Dearest Enemy, My Dangerous Friend: Making and Breaking Sibling Bonds.* London: Routledge.

Rowe, D., & Slater, P. (1976). Studies of the psychiatrist's insight into the patient's inner world. In P. Slater (Ed.), *The Measurement of Intrapersonal Space by Grid Technique* (Vol. 1, pp. 123–144)., *Explorations of Intrapersonal Space* London: Wiley.

Rychlak, J. F. (1977). *The Psychology of Rigorous Humanism.* New York: Wiley-Interscience.

Rychlak, J. F. (1994). *Logical Learning Theory.* Lincoln: University of Nebraska Press.

Ryle, A. (1975). *Frames and Cages: The Repertory Grid Approach to Human Understanding.* London: Sussex University Press.

Ryle, A. (1978). A common language for the psychotherapies. *British Journal of Psychiatry, 113,* 585–594.

Ryle, A. (1990). *Cognitive-Analytic Therapy: Active Participation in Change: A new Integration in Brief Therapy.* Chichester, UK: Wiley.

Ryle, A., & Breen, D. (1972a). A comparison of adjusted and maladjusted couples using the double dyad grid. *British Journal of Medical Psychology, 45*, 375–382.

Ryle, A., & Breen, D. (1972b). Some differences in the personal constructs of neurotic and normal subjects. *British Journal of Psychiatry, 120*, 483–489.

Ryle, A., & Lipshitz, S. (1974). Towards an informed countertransference: The possible contribution of repertory grid techniques. *British Journal of Medical Psychology, 47*, 219–225.

Ryle, A., & Lipshitz, S. (1975). Recording change in marital therapy with the reconstruction grid. *British Journal of Medical Psychology, 49*, 281–285.

Ryle, A., & Lunghi, M. (1970). The dyad grid—A modification of repertory grid technique. *British Journal of Psychiatry, 117*, 323–327.

Ryle, G. (1963). *The Concept of Mind*. Harmondsworth, UK: Penguin Books.

Sacks, H. (1992). *Lectures on Conversation* (Vol. 1). Oxford, UK: Blackwell.

Sarason, I. G. (1978). Three lacunae of cognitive therapy. *Cognitive Therapy and Research, 3*, 223–235.

Sarbin, T. R. (1986). The narrative as a root metaphor for psychology. In T. R. Sarbin (Ed.), *Narrative Psychology: The Storied Nature of Human Conduct* (pp. 3–21). New York: Praeger.

Scheer, J. W. (2008). Construing in the political realm—Reflections on the power of a theory. *Personal Construct Theory and Practice, 5*, 76–85.

Scheler, M. (2009). *The Nature of Sympathy*. New Brunswick: Transaction Publishers (Original work, 1913).

Schütz, A. (1971). *Collected Papers Vol I: The Problem of Social Reality*. The Hague: Martinus Nijhoff.

Scott, R. D., & Ashworth, P. L. (1973). The shadow of the ancestor: A historical factor in the transmission of schizophrenia. *British Journal of Medical Psychology, 42*, 13–32.

Sedumedi, P. (2018). *I killed my child(ren): A qualitative study exploring the phenomenon of paternal filicide in the South African context*. Unpublished PhD thesis, University of Hertfordshire.

Sedumedi, T. P., & Winter, D. A. (2020/in press). I killed my children: Construing pathways to filicide. *Journal of Constructivist Psychology*.

Segal, Z. V., Williams, J. M. G., & Teasdale, J. D. (2002). *Mindfulness-Based Cognitive Therapy for Depression: A New Approach to Preventing Relapse*. New York: Guilford.

Seikkula, J., Aaltonen, J., Alakare, B., Haarakangas, K., Keränen, J., & Lehtinen, K. (2006). Five-year experience of first-episode non-affective psychosis in open-dialogue approach: Treatment principles, follow-up outcomes, and two case studies. *Psychotherapy Research, 16,* 214–228.

Selby, G. (2006). Time and tools?: Tools or time? In P. Cummins (Ed.), *Working with Anger: A Constructivist Approach* (pp. 45–64). Chichester, UK: Wiley.

Selvini, M. P., Boscolo, L., Cecchin, G., & Prata, G. (1978). *Paradox and Counterparadox: A New Model in the Therapy of the Family in Schizophrenic Transaction.* New York: Jason Aronson.

Selvini, M. P., Boscolo, L., Cecchin, G., & Prata, G. (1980). Hypothesizing–circularity–neutrality: Three guidelines for the conductor of the session. *Family Process, 19,* 3–12.

Senra, J. (2010). *Personal reconstruction processes in personal construct therapy for implicative dilemmas.* Unpublished doctoral thesis, University of Minho.

Sermpezis, C., & Winter, D. A. (2009). Is trauma the product of over or under-elaboration? A critique of the personal construct model of post-traumatic stress disorder. *Journal of Constructivist Psychology, 22,* 306–327.

Sewell, K. W. (1997). Posttraumatic stress: Towards a constructivist model of psychotherapy. In G. J. Neimeyer & R. A. Neimeyer (Eds.), *Advances in Personal Construct Psychology* (pp. 207–235). Greenwich, CT: JAI Press.

Sewell, K. W., Cromwell, R. L., Farrell-Higgins, J., Palmer, R., Ohlde, C., & Patterson, T. W. (1996). Hierarchical elaboration in the conceptual structure of Vietnam veterans. *Journal of Constructivist Psychology, 9,* 79–96.

Sewell, K. W., & Ovaert, L. B. (1997). *Group treatment of post-traumatic stress in incarcerated adolescents: Structural and narrative impacts on the permeability of self-construction.* Paper presented at XII International Congress of Personal Construct Psychology, Seattle, WA.

Sheehan, M. J. (1985). A personal construct study of depression. *British Journal of Medical Psychology, 58,* 119–128.

Sherover, C. M. (1987). Royce's pragmatic idealism and existential phenomenology. In R. S. Corrington, C. Hausman, & T. M. Seebohm (Eds.), *Pragmatism Considers Phenomenology* (pp. 143–165). Lanham, MD: The Center for Advanced Research in Phenomenology.

Shotter, J. (2011, March 5–9). *Language, joint action, and the ethical domain: The importance of the relations between our living bodies and their surroundings.* Paper presented at IIIrd Congreso de Psicologia y Responsabilidad Social. Bogota, Colombia.

Shotter, J. (2015). On being dialogical: An ethics of 'attunement'. *Context, 137,* 8–11.

Simić, N., Jokić, T., & Vukelić, M. (2019). Personal Construct Psychology in preservice teacher education: The path toward reflexivity. *Journal of Constructivist Psychology, 32*(1), 1–17.

Slater, P. (1970). Personal questionnaire data treated as a form of repertory grid. *British Journal of Social and Clinical Psychology, 9,* 357–370.

Slater, P. (1977). *The Measurement of Intrapersonal Space by Grid Technique. Vol. 2. Dimensions of Intrapersonal Space.* London: Wiley.

Slavin, R. E. (1995). Best evidence synthesis: An intelligent alternative to meta-analysis. *Journal of Clinical Epidemiology, 48,* 9–18.

Slife, B. D. (2004). Theoretical challenges to therapy practice and research: The constraint of naturalism. In M. J. Lambert (Ed.), *Bergin and Garfield's Handbook of Psychotherapy and Behavior Change* (pp. 44–83). New York: Wiley.

Smail, D. J. (1978). *Psychotherapy: A Personal Approach.* London: Dent.

Smail, D. (1996). *How to Survive Without Psychotherapy.* London: Constable.

Solas, J. (1992). Ideological dimensions implicit in Kelly's theory of personal constructs. *International Journal of Personal Construct Psychology, 5,* 377–391.

Soldz, S. (1988). Constructivist tendencies in recent psychoanalysis. *International Journal of Personal Construct Psychology, 1,* 329–347.

Soldz, S. (1993). Beyond interpretation: The elaboration of transference in personal construct therapy. In L. M. Leitner & N. G. M. Dunnett (Eds.), *Critical Issues in Personal Construct Psychotherapy* (pp. 173–192). Malabar, FL: Krieger.

Spence, D. P. (1984). *Narrative Truth and Historical Truth: Meaning and Interpretation in Psychoanalysis.* New York: Norton.

Spencer, L., Ritchie, J., & O'Connor, W. (2003). Analysis: Practices, principles and processes. In J. Ritchie & J. Lewis (Eds.), *Qualitative Research Practice: A Guide for Social Science Students and Researchers* (pp. 199–218). London: Sage.

Spiegelberg, H. (1976). *The Phenomenological Movement: A Historical Introduction* (Vol. 2). The Hague, Netherlands: Martinus Nijhoff.

Stam, H. J. (1998). Personal construct theory and social constructionism: Difference and dialogue. *Journal of Constructivist Psychology, 11,* 187–203.

Stedmon, J., & Dallos, R. (Eds.). (2009). *Reflective Practice in Psychotherapy and Counselling.* Milton Keynes, UK: Open University Press.

Stefan, C., & Von, J. (1985). Suicide. In E. Button (Ed.), *Personal Construct Theory and Mental Health* (pp. 132–152). London: Croom Helm.

Stein, M. (2007). Non-verbal techniques in personal construct psychotherapy. *Journal of Constructivist Psychology, 20,* 103–124.

Stern, D. (2010). *Forms of Vitality: Exploring Dynamic Experience in Psychology, the Arts, Psychotherapy, and Development*. Oxford, UK: Oxford University Press.

Stevens, C. D. (1998). Realism and Kelly's pragmatic constructivism. *Journal of Constructivist Psychology, 11*, 283–308.

Stewart, J. (1995). Reconstruction of the self: Life-span-oriented group psychotherapy. *Journal of Constructivist Psychology, 8*, 129–148.

Stewart, S., Procter, H. G., & Dallos, R. (2011). Fathers, sons and ADHD: A qualitative personal construct study. In D. Stojnov, V. Džinović, J. Pavlović, & M. Frances (Eds.), *Personal Construct Psychology in an Accelerating World* (pp. 109–126). Belgrade, Serbia: Serbian Constructivist Association, EPCA.

Stiles, W. B., & Shapiro, D. A. (1989). Abuse of the drug metaphor in psychotherapy process-outcome research. *Clinical Psychology Review, 9*, 521–543.

Stojnov, D. (1996). Kelly's theory of ethics: Hidden, mislaid or misleading? *Journal of Constructivist Psychology, 9*, 185–199.

Stojnov, D., Miletić, V., & Džinović, V. (2017). Subjectivity: Kelly's discourse and Foucault's constructs. *Personal Construct Theory & Practice, 14*, 146–157.

Stojnov, D., & Procter, H. G. (2012). Spying on the self: Reflective elaborations in personal and relational construct psychology. In M. Giliberto, F. Velacogna, & C. Dell'Aversano (Eds.), *PCP and Constructivism: Ways of Working, Learning and Living*. Firenze, Italy: Libri Liberi.

Stratton, P. (2010). *The Evidence Base of Systemic Family and Couples Therapy*. London: Association for Family Therapy.

Task Force on Promotion and Dissemination of Psychological Procedures. (1995). Training in and dissemination of empirically-validated psychological treatments. *The Clinical Psychologist, 48*, 3–23.

Thomas, J. C. (2009). Personifying the cast of characters in experiential personal constructivist supervision. In L. M. Leitner & J. C. Thomas (Eds.), *Personal Constructivism: Theory and Applications* (pp. 253–278). New York: Pace University Press.

Thomas, L., & Harri-Augstein, S. (1988). Constructing environments that enable self-organised learning: The principles of intelligent support. In F. Fransella & L. Thomas (Eds.), *Experimenting with Personal Construct Psychology* (pp. 92–110). London: Routledge and Kegan Paul.

Trevarthen, C. B. (1979). Communication and cooperation in early infancy: A description of primary intersubjectivity. In B. Bullowa (Ed.), *Before Speech*. Cambridge, UK: Cambridge University Press.

Trevarthen, C., & Aitken, K. J. (2001). Infant intersubjectivity: Research, theory, and clinical applications. *Journal of Child Psychology and Psychiatry, 42*, 3–48.

Trevarthen, C. B., & Delafield-Butt, J. (2017). Intersubjectivity in the imagination and feelings of the infant: Implications for education in the early years. In E. Jayne White & C. Dalli (Eds.), *Under-Three Year Olds in Policy and Practice* (pp. 17–39). Singapore: Springer.

Trevarthen, C., & Hubley, P. (1978). Secondary intersubjectivity: Confidence, confiding and acts of meaning in the first year. In A. Lock (Ed.), *Action, Gesture and Symbol*. London: Academic Press.

Trinder, L. (2000a). A critical appraisal of evidence-based practice. In L. Trinder & S. Reynolds (Eds.), *Evidence-Based Practice: A Critical Appraisal* (pp. 212–241). Oxford, UK: Blackwell Science.

Trinder, L. (2000b). Introduction: The context of evidence-based practice. In L. Trinder & S. Reynolds (Eds.), *Evidence-Based Practice: A Critical Appraisal* (pp. 1–16). Oxford, UK: Blackwell Science.

Truneckova, D., & Viney, L. L. (2001). Can personal construct group work be an effective intervention with troubled adolescents? *Australian Journal of Psychology, 53*(supplement), 106.

Truneckova, D., & Viney, L. L. (2005). Personal construct group work with troubled adolescents. In D. A. Winter & L. L. Viney (Eds.), *Personal Construct Psychotherapy: Advances in Theory, Practice and Research* (pp. 271–286). London: Croom Helm.

Truneckova, D., & Viney, L. L. (2011). Evaluating personal construct group work with troubled adolescents. *Journal of Counseling and Development, 85*, 450–460.

Truneckova, D., Viney, L., Maitland, H., & Seaborn, B. (2010). Personal construct peer consultation: Caring for the psychotherapists. *The Clinical Supervisor, 29*, 128–148.

Tschudi, F. (1977). Loaded and honest questions: A construct theory view of symptoms and therapy. In D. Bannister (Ed.), *New Perspectives in Personal Construct Theory* (pp. 321–350). London: Academic Press.

Tschudi, F. (1993). *Manual FLEXIGRID 5.21*. Oslo: Tschudi System Sales.

Tschudi, F., & Winter, D. (2011). The ABC model revisited. In P. Caputi, L. L. Viney, B. M. Walker, & N. Crittenden (Eds.), *Personal Construct Methodology* (pp. 89–108). Chichester, UK: Wiley-Blackwell.

Ugazio, V. (2013). *Semantic Polarities and Psychopathologies in the Family: Permitted and Forbidden Stories*. New York: Routledge.

Ugazio, V., & Castelli, D. (2015). The semantics grid of the dyadic therapeutic relationship (SG-DTR). *TPM—Testing Psychometrics, Methodology in Applied Psychology, 22*, 135–159.

Ugazio, V., & Guanieri, S. (2017). The family semantics grid II: Narrated polarities in couples. *Testing, Psychometrics, Methodology in Applied Psychology, 24*, 1–39.

Ugazio, V., Negri, A., & Fellin, L. (2015). Freedom, goodness, power, and belonging: The semantics of phobic, obsessive-compulsive, eating, and mood disorders. *Journal of Constructivist Psychology, 28*, 293–315.

Vaughn, C. E., & Leff, J. P. (1976). The measurement of expressed emotion in the families of psychiatric patients. *British Journal of Social and Clinical Psychology, 15*, 157–165.

Viney, L. L. (1983). *Images of Illness*. Melbourne, Australia: Krieger.

Viney, L. L. (1994). Sequences of emotional distress expressed by clients and acknowledged by therapists: Are they associated more with some therapists than others? *British Journal of Clinical Psychology, 33*, 469–481.

Viney, L. L., Allwood, K., & Stillson, L. (1991). Reconstructive group therapy with HIV-affected people. *Counselling Psychology Quarterly, 4*, 247–258.

Viney, L. L., Benjamin, Y. N., & Preston, C. A. (1989). An evaluation of personal construct therapy with the elderly. *British Journal of Medical Psychology, 62*, 35–41.

Viney, L. L., Clarke, A. M., Bunn, T. A., & Benjamin, Y. N. (1985a). An evaluation of three crisis intervention programs for general hospital patients. *British Journal of Medical Psychology, 58*, 75–86.

Viney, L. L., Clarke, A. M., Bunn, T. A., & Benjamin, Y. N. (1985b). The effect of a hospital-based counselling service on the physical recovery of surgical and medical patients. *General Hospital Psychiatry, 7*, 294–301.

Viney, L. L., Clarke, A. M., Bunn, T. A., & Benjamin, Y. N. (1985c). Crisis-intervention counselling: An evaluation of long- and short-term effects. *Journal of Counseling Psychology, 32*, 29–39.

Viney, L. L., Crooks, L., & Walker, B. M. (1995). Anxiety in community-based AIDS caregivers before and after personal construct counseling. *Journal of Clinical Psychology, 51*, 274–280.

Viney, L., & Epting, F. (1997). Toward a personal construct approach to supervision for counselling and psychotherapy. Paper presented at the XIIth International Personal Construct Congress, Seattle, USA.

Viney, L. L., & Henry, R. M. (2002). Evaluating personal construct and psychodynamic group work with adolescent offenders and non-offenders. In R. A. Neimeyer & G. J. Neimeyer (Eds.), *Advances in Personal Construct*

Psychology: New Directions and Perspectives (pp. 259–294). Westport, CT: Praeger.

Viney, L. L., Henry, R. M., & Campbell, J. (2001). The impact of group work on offender adolescents. *Journal of Counseling and Development, 79*, 373–381.

Viney, L. L., Metcalfe, C., & Winter, D. A. (2005). The effectiveness of personal construct psychotherapy: A systematic review and meta-analysis. In D. A. Winter & L. L. Viney (Eds.), *Personal Construct Psychotherapy: Advances in Theory, Practice and Research* (pp. 347–364). London: Whurr.

Viney, L. L., & Truneckova, D. (2008). Personal construct models of group supervision: Led and peer. *Personal Construct Theory & Practice, 5*, 131–138.

Viney, L. L., Truneckova, D., Weekes, P., & Oades, L. (1997). Personal construct group work with school-based adolescents: Reduction of risk-taking. *Journal of Constructivist Psychology, 9*, 169–185.

Viney, L. L., & Westbrook, M. T. (1981). Measuring patients' experienced quality of life: The application of content analysis scales in health care. *Community Health Studies, 5*, 45–52.

Von Glasersfeld, E. (1984). An Introduction to radical constructivism. In P. Watzlawick (Ed.), *The Invented Reality* (pp. 17–40). New York: Norton.

Von Glasersfeld, E. (1995). *Radical Constructivism: A Way of Knowing and Learning*. London: Falmer Press.

Vygotsky, L. S. (1978). *Mind in Society: The Development of Higher Psychological Processes*. Cambridge, MA: Harvard University Press.

Walker, B. M. (1992). Values and Kelly's theory: Becoming a good scientist. *International Journal of Personal Construct Psychology, 5*, 259–269.

Walker, B. M. (2002). Nonvalidation vs. (In)validation: Implications for theory and practice. In J. D. Raskin & S. K. Bridges (Eds.), *Studies in Meaning: Exploring Constructivist Psychology* (pp. 49–61). New York: Pace University Press.

Walker, B. M., Ramsay, F. L., & Bell, R. C. (1988). Dispersed and undispersed dependency. *International Journal of Personal Construct Psychology, 1*, 63–80.

Walker, B. M., & Winter, D. A. (2007). The elaboration of personal construct psychology. *Annual Review of Psychology, 58*, 453–477.

Walker, G., & Procter, H. G. (1980). Brief therapeutic approaches: Their value in contemporary day care. *New Directions for Psychiatric Day Services* (pp. 34–41). London: NAMH.

Wampold, B. E. (2001). *The Great Psychotherapy Debate: Models, Methods, and Findings*. Mahwah, NJ: Lawrence Erlbaum.

Warren, W. G. (1983). *Personal construct theory and psychoanalysis: An exploration.* Paper presented at Vth. International Congress on Personal Construct Psychology, Boston.

Warren, W. G. (1985). Personal construct psychology and contemporary philosophy: Examination of alignments. In D. Bannister (Ed.), *Issues and Approaches in Personal Construct Theory* (pp. 253–262). London: Academic Press.

Warren, B. (1998). *Philosophical Dimensions of Personal Construct Psychology.* London: Routledge.

Watson, S., & Winter, D. A. (2005). A process and outcome study of personal construct psychotherapy. In D. A. Winter & L. L. Viney (Eds.), *Personal Construct Psychotherapy: Advances in Theory, Practice and Research* (pp. 335–346). London: Whurr.

Watts, R. E., & Phillips, K. A. (2004). Adlerian psychology and psychotherapy: A relational constructivist approach. In J. D. Raskin & S. K. Bridges (Eds.), *Studies in Meaning 2: Bridging the Personal and Social in Constructivist Psychology* (pp. 267–289). New York: Pace University Press.

Watzlawick, P., Beavin, J., & Jackson, D. D. (1968). *Pragmatics of Human Communication.* New York: Norton.

Watzlawick, P., Weakland, J., & Fisch, R. (1974). *Change: Principles of Problem Formation and Problem Resolution.* New York: Norton.

Weinreich, P., & Saunderson, W. (2003). *Analysing Identity: Cross-Cultural, Societal and Clinical Contexts.* London: Taylor and Francis.

Weishaar, M. E. (1993). *Aaron T. Beck.* London: Sage.

Westen, D., Novotny, C. M., & Thompson-Brenner, H. (2004). The empirical status of empirically supported psychotherapies. *Psychological Bulletin, 130,* 631–663.

Wexler, D. A., & Rice, L. N. (Eds.). (1974). *Innovations in Client-Centered Therapy.* New York: Wiley.

White, M., & Epston, D. (1990). *Narrative Means to Therapeutic Ends.* Adelaide, Australia: Dulwich Centre Publications.

Wiley, N. (1994). *The Semiotic Self.* Chicago: University of Chicago Press.

Wilkinson, S. (1988). The role of reflexivity in feminist psychology. *Women's Studies International Forum, 11,* 493–502.

Winter, D. A. (1975). Some characteristics of schizophrenics and their parents. *British Journal of Social and Clinical Psychology, 14,* 279–290.

Winter, D. A. (1983). Logical inconsistency in construct relationships: Conflict or complexity? *British Journal of Medical Psychology, 56,* 79–88.

Winter, D. A. (1985a). Group therapy with depressives: A personal construct theory perspective. *International Journal of Mental Health, 13,* 67–85.

Winter, D. A. (1985b). Personal styles, constructive alternativism and the provision of a therapeutic service. *British Journal of Medical Psychology, 58,* 129–136.

Winter, D. A. (1987). Personal construct psychotherapy as a radical alternative to social skills training. In R. A. Neimeyer & G. J. Neimeyer (Eds.), *Personal Construct Therapy Casebook* (pp. 107–123). New York: Springer.

Winter, D. A. (1988). Reconstructing an erection and elaborating ejaculation. *International Journal of Personal Construct Psychology, 1,* 81–100.

Winter, D. A. (1989). Group therapy as a means of facilitating reconstruing in depressives. *Group Analysis, 22,* 39–48.

Winter, D. A. (1990). Therapeutic alternatives for psychological disorder: Personal construct psychology investigations in a health service setting. In G. J. Neimeyer & R. A. Neimeyer (Eds.), *Advances in Personal Construct Psychology* (Vol. 1, pp. 89–116). Greenwich, CT: Jai Press.

Winter, D. A. (1992). *Personal Construct Psychology in Clinical Practice: Theory, Research and Applications.* London: Routledge.

Winter, D. A. (1996). Psychotherapy's contrast pole. In J. W. Scheer & A. Catina (Eds.), *Empirical Constructivism in Europe: The Personal Construct Approach* (pp. 149–159). Giessen, Germany: Psychosozial Verlag.

Winter, D. A. (1997). Personal construct theory perspectives on group psychotherapy. In P. Denicolo & M. Pope (Eds.), *Sharing Understanding and Practice* (pp. 210–221). Farnborough, UK: EPCA Publications.

Winter, D. A. (1999). Psychological problems: Alternative perspectives on their explanation and treatment. In D. Messer & F. Jones (Eds.), *Psychology and Social Care* (pp. 362–382). London: Jessica Kingsley.

Winter, D. A. (2003a). Psychological disorder as imbalance. In F. Fransella (Ed.), *International Handbook of Personal Construct Psychology* (pp. 201–209). Chichester, UK: Wiley.

Winter, D. A. (2003b). Stress in police officers: Personal construct theory perspectives. In J. Horley (Ed.), *Personal Construct Perspectives on Forensic Psychology* (pp. 121–142). London: Routledge.

Winter, D. A. (2003c). Repertory grid technique as a psychotherapy research measure. *Psychotherapy Research, 13,* 25–42.

Winter, D. A. (2003d). The evidence base for personal construct psychotherapy. In F. Fransella (Ed.), *International Handbook of Personal Construct Psychology* (pp. 265–272). Chichester, UK: Wiley.

Winter, D. A. (2005a). Self harm and reconstruction. In D. A. Winter & L. L. Viney (Eds.), *Personal Construct Psychotherapy: Advances in Theory, Practice and Research* (pp. 127–135). London: Whurr.

Winter, D. A. (2005b). Towards a personal construct sex therapy. In D. A. Winter & L. L. Viney (Eds.), *Personal Construct Psychotherapy: Advances in Theory, Practice and Research* (pp. 287–295). London: Whurr.

Winter, D. A. (2007a). Construing the construction processes of serial killers and violent offenders: 2. The limits of credulity. *Journal of Constructivist Psychology, 20,* 247–275.

Winter, D. A. (2007b). Improving access or denying choice? *Mental Health and Learning Disabilities Research and Practice, 4,* 73–82.

Winter, D. A. (2008). Personal construct psychotherapy in a national health service setting: Does survival mean selling out? In J. D. Raskin & S. K. Bridges (Eds.), *Studies in Meaning: 3. Constructivist Therapy in the 'Real' World* (pp. 229–252). New York: Pace University Press.

Winter, D. A. (2009). The personal construct psychology view of psychological disorder: Did Kelly get it wrong? In L. M. Leitner & J. C. Thomas (Eds.), *Personal Constructivism: Theory and Applications* (pp. 279–295). New York: Pace University Press.

Winter, D. (2010). Allegiance revisited. *European Journal of Psychotherapy and Counselling, 12,* 3–9.

Winter, D. (2012). Still radical after all these years: George Kelly's 'The psychology of personal constructs'. *Clinical Child Psychology and Psychiatry, 18,* 276–283.

Winter, D. A. (2015a). What does the future hold for personal construct psychology? In J. D. Raskin & S. K. Bridges (Eds.), *Studies in Meaning 5: Perturbing the Status Quo in Constructivist Psychology* (pp. 28–63). New York: Pace University Press.

Winter, D. A. (2015b). Towards a less mechanistic cognitive behaviour therapy. *PsycCRITIQUES, 60,* Article 3.

Winter, D.A. (2016a). Transcending war-ravaged biographies. In D. A. Winter & N. Reed (Eds.), *The Wiley Handbook of Personal Construct Psychology* (pp. 190–200). Chichester: Wiley-Blackwell.

Winter, D. A. (2016b). The continuing clinical relevance of personal construct psychology: A review. In D. A. Winter & N. Reed (Eds.), *The Wiley Handbook of Personal Construct Psychology* (pp. 203–217). Chichester: Wiley-Blackwell.

Winter, D. A. (2018a). Self-harm and reconstruction: A personal construct theory perspective. *Journal of Psychotherapy and Counselling Psychology Reflections, 3,* 9–14.

Winter, D. A. (2018b). Cognitive behaviour therapy: From rationalism to constructivism? In D. Loewenthal & G. Proctor (Eds.), *Why Not CBT? Against and For CBT Revised* (pp. 219–229). PCCS Books: Monmouth, UK.

Winter, D. A. (2020/in press). Sociality and hostility: A pernicious mix. *Journal of Constructivist Psychology.* Published online, 11 Aug, 2020, from: https://doi.org/10.1080/10720537.2020.1805062.

Winter, D. A., & Bell, R. C. (2020/in press). A method for measuring conflict in repertory grid data: A review of research. *Journal of Constructivist Psychology.* https://doi.org/10.1080/10720537.2020.1805073.

Winter, D. A., Bell, R. C., & Watson, S. (2010). Midpoint ratings on personal constructs: Constriction or the middle way? *Journal of Constructivist Psychology, 23,* 337–356.

Winter, D., Bhandari, S., Lutwyche, G., Metcalfe, C., Riley, T., Sireling, L., & Watson, S. (2000). Deliberate and undeliberated self harm: Theoretical basis and evaluation of a personal construct psychotherapy intervention. In J. W. Scheer (Ed.), *The Person in Society: Challenges to a Constructivist Theory* (pp. 351–360). Giessen, Germany: Psychosozial-Verlag.

Winter, D. A., Brown, R., Goins, S., & Mason, C. (2016). *Trauma, Survival and Resilience in War Zones: The Psychological Impact of War in Sierra Leone and Beyond.* Hove, UK: Routledge.

Winter, D., Cummins, P., Procter, H. G., & Reed, N. (2017). *Personal Construct Psychology at 60: Papers from the 21st International Congress.* Newcastle upon Tyne, UK: Cambridge Scholars Publishing.

Winter, D. A., Feixas, G., Dalton, R., Jarque-llanazares, L., Laso, E., & Mallindine, C., Patient, S. (2007). Construing the construction processes of serial killers and violent offenders: 1. The analysis of narratives. *Journal of Constructivist Psychology, 20,* 1–22.

Winter, D. A., Goggins, S., Baker, M., & Metcalfe, C. (1996). Into the community or back to the ward? Clients' construing as a predictor of the outcome of psychiatric rehabilitation. In B. M. Walker, J. Costigan, L. L. Viney, & B. Warren (Eds.), *Personal Construct Theory: A Psychology for the Future* (pp. 253–276). Sydney: Australian Psychological Society.

Winter, D., & Gournay, K. (1987). Constriction and construction in agoraphobia. *British Journal of Medical Psychology, 60,* 233–244.

Winter, D. A., Gournay, K., & Metcalfe, C. (1999). A personal construct psychotherapy intervention for agoraphobia: Theoretical and empirical basis, treatment process and outcome. In J. M. Fisher & D. J. Savage (Eds.), *Beyond Experimentation into Meaning* (pp. 146–160). Lostock Hall, UK: EPCA Publications.

Winter, D. A., Gournay, K. J. M., Metcalfe, C., & Rossotti, N. (2006). Expanding agoraphobics' horizons: An investigation of the effectiveness of a personal construct psychotherapy intervention. *Journal of Constructivist Psychology, 19*, 1–29.

Winter, D. A., & Metcalfe, C. (2005). From constriction to experimentation: Personal construct psychotherapy for agoraphobia. In D. A. Winter & L. L. Viney (Eds.), *Personal Construct Psychotherapy: Advances in Theory, Practice and Research* (pp. 148–157). London: Whurr.

Winter, D. A., & Muhanna-Matar, A. (2020). Cycles of construing in radicalization and deradicalization: A study of Salafist Muslims. *Journal of Constructivist Psychology, 33*, 58–88.

Winter, D. A., & Neimeyer, R. A. (2015). Constructivist therapy. In E. Neukrug (Ed.), *Encyclopedia of Theory in Counseling and Psychotherapy*. Los Angeles: Sage.

Winter, D., & Procter, H. G. (2014). Formulation in personal and relational construct psychology: Seeing the world through clients' eyes. In L. Johnstone & R. Dallos (Eds.), *Formulation in Psychology and Psychotherapy* (2nd ed., pp. 145–172). London: Routledge.

Winter, D. A., & Reed, N. (Eds.). (2016). *The Wiley Handbook of Personal Construct Psychology*. Chichester, UK: Wiley-Blackwell.

Winter, D., Sireling, L., Riley, T., Metcalfe, C., Quaite, A., & Bhandari, S. (2007). A controlled trial of personal construct psychotherapy for deliberate self-harm. *Psychology and Psychotherapy, 80*, 23–37.

Winter, D. A., & Trippett, C. J. (1977). Serial change in group psychotherapy. *British Journal of Medical Psychology, 50*, 341–348.

Winter, D. A., & Viney, L. (Eds.). (2005). *Personal Construct Psychotherapy: Recent Advances in Theory, Practice and Research*. London: Whurr.

Winter, D. A., & Watson, S. (1999). Personal construct psychotherapy and the cognitive therapies: Different in theory but can they be differentiated in practice? *Journal of Constructivist Psychology, 12*, 1–22.

Winter, D. A., Watson, S., Gillman-Smith, I., Gilbert, N., & Acton, T. (2003). Border crossing: A personal construct therapy approach for clients with a diagnosis of borderline personality disorder. In G. Chiari & M. L. Nuzzo

(Eds.), *Psychological Constructivism and the Social World* (pp. 342–352). Milan, Italy: FrancoAngeli.

Wittgenstein, L. (1969). *On Certainty*. New York: Harper and Row.

Wright, K. J. T. (1970). Exploring the uniqueness of common complaints. *British Journal of Medical Psychology, 43,* 221–232.

Yalom, I. D. (1970). *The Theory and Practice of Group Psychotherapy*. New York: Basic Books.

Yalom, I. D. (1980). *Existential Psychotherapy*. New York: Basic Books.

Young, J. E., Klosko, J. S., & Weishaar, M. E. (2003). *Schema Therapy: A Practitioner's Guide*. New York: Guilford.

Zahavi, D. (2015). You, me, and we: The sharing of emotional experiences. *Journal of Consciousness Studies, 22,* 1–2.

Index

Printed by Printforce, United Kingdom